'This book is remarkable as it combines three books in one: an insightful explanation of the current status of insolvency law and practice in the four independent jurisdictions of the region (the Mainland, Hong Kong, Macao and Taiwan) from a Chinese perspective; a comparative analysis of the EU Insolvency Regulation and the Model Law; and a thoughtful and well-balanced proposal for an interregional cross-border insolvency regime that reflects the status of mutual trust between the regions. A perceptive study which will surely make a difference.'

Prof. Dr. Stephan Madaus, *The Martin Luther University of Halle-Wittenberg, Germany*

'If you would like to know about China's cross-border insolvency and interregional legal cooperation, this is a book I will recommend.'

Judge Zhu Rui, *People's Republic of China*

'This work is a much needed treatise on cross-border insolvency in the Greater China region. Dr Gong deserves to be firmly congratulated for producing this important work which repays careful study and contributes significantly to cross-border insolvency learning in the region.'

Look Chan Ho, *Head of Asia Restructuring and Insolvency, Freshfields Bruckhaus Deringer, Hong Kong*

T0371784

China's Insolvency Law and Interregional Cooperation

As a result of resumption of sovereignty over Hong Kong and Macao as well as the uncertain relationship between the Mainland and Taiwan, China has become a country composed of peculiar political compounds, resulting in four independent jurisdictions. This makes interregional legal cooperation a complicated yet compelling topic. Divided into five parts, this book considers possible solutions to problems in China's interregional cross-border insolvency cooperation. These solutions are developed on the basis of two groups of comparative studies, including comparison among the cross-border insolvency systems of the four independent jurisdictions in China and comparison between EU Insolvency Regulation and the UNCITRAL Model Law. The author discusses the advantages and disadvantages of the two systems and presents original recommendations for the way forward. The book will be a valuable resource for academics and policy makers in insolvency law, Asian law and comparative law.

Dr. Xinyi Gong was sponsored by China Scholarship Council to conduct her PhD research at Leiden University. Her research topic concerned China's interregional legal cooperation and comparative studies of cross-border insolvency, covering the Greater China Region (the Mainland China, Hong Kong, Macao and Taiwan), the EU Insolvency Regulation and UNCITRAL Model Law.

The Rule of Law in China and Comparative Perspectives
Series Editors:
Yuwen Li, Erasmus University Rotterdam, The Netherlands and
Fu Hualing, University of Hong Kong, Hong Kong

www.routledge.com/The-Rule-of-Law-in-China-and-Comparative-Perspectives/
book-series/CHINARULEOFLAW

There is no doctrine more effective than the rule of law in portraying the complex transformation of Chinese society from the rule of men towards the rule of law – a process inaugurated in post-Mao China which is continuing to advance legal reforms to the present day. In other parts of the world, striving for the rule of law is also evident: countries in transition face a similar mission, while the developed democratic countries are forced to tackle new challenges in retaining the high benchmark of the rule of law that has been established.

Research on the legal system in China and in comparison with other countries in the framework of the rule of law covers broad topics of public and private law, substantive law and procedural law, citizens' rights and law enforcement by courts. Based on this broad understanding of the rule of law, the series presents international scholarly work on modern Chinese law including: comparative perspectives, interdisciplinary, and empirical studies.

Other titles in this series

The Legal and Political Significance of the Sunflower and Umbrella Movements
Edited by Brian Christopher Jones

Legal Reforms and Deprivation of Liberty in Contemporary China
Edited by Elisa Nesossi, Sarah Biddulph, Flora Sapio and Susan Trevaskes

Conservation and Recreation in Protected Areas
Yun Ma

Administrative Litigation Systems in Greater China and Europe
Edited by Yuwen Li

The Judicial System and Reform in Post-Mao China
Yuwen Li

China's Insolvency Law and Interregional Cooperation

Comparative Perspectives from China and the EU

Xinyi Gong

LONDON AND NEW YORK

First published 2018
by Routledge

2 Park Square, Milton Park, Abingdon, Oxfordshire OX14 4RN
52 Vanderbilt Avenue, New York, NY 10017

Routledge is an imprint of the Taylor & Francis Group, an informa business

First issued in paperback 2020

British Library Cataloguing-in-Publication Data
A catalogue record for this book is available from the British Library

Library of Congress Cataloguing-in-Publication Data
Names: Gong, Xinyi, author.
Title: China's insolvency law and interregional cooperation : comparative
   perspectives from China and the EU / Xinyi Gong.
Description: New York, NY : Routledge, 2017. | Series: The rule of
   law in China and comparative perspectives | Includes bibliographical
   references and index.
Identifiers: LCCN 2017031672 | ISBN 9781138048584 (hardback)
Subjects: LCSH: Bankruptcy—China. | Bankruptcy—European Union
   countries. | Comparative law.
Classification: LCC K1370 .G66 2017 | DDC 346.5107/8—dc23
LC record available at https://lccn.loc.gov/2017031672

ISBN: 978-1-138-04858-4 (hbk)
ISBN: 978-0-367-59399-5 (pbk)

Typeset in Galliard
by Apex CoVantage, LLC

To my parents

Contents

Preface

While completing my doctoral dissertation, reforms to insolvency legislation were taking place in both east and west. In 2014, the problems of cross-border insolvency, especially involving Mainland-related companies, were brought to the attention of the Legislative Council of the Hong Kong SAR and it was suggested to adopt proper measures to address the issue. In 2015, the Judicial Yuan of Taiwan published the draft bankruptcy law (the Debt Clearance Act) that has been forwarded to the legislative procedure, in which a new chapter concerning recognition of foreign insolvency proceedings is included and the insolvency proceedings opened in the Mainland, the Hong Kong Special Administrative Region (SAR) and the Macao SAR also fall within the ambit of application. In the EU, the recast EU Insolvency Regulation entered into force in June 2015 and became effective on 26 June 2017.

It was also the very moment when trust issues arose within one country as well as a Union in the process of integration. In March and April 2014, the debating chamber of the Legislative Yuan in Taiwan was occupied by protesters against an agreement on opening up services trade between the Mainland and Taiwan. In September and October 2014, roads in the city center of the Hong Kong SAR were blocked by thousands of protesters due to disagreement with the Central Government on the method for the Chief Executive election. In June 2015, the reform on the method for the Chief Executive election proposed by the government was vetoed by the Legislative Council of the Hong Kong SAR.

And on 23 June, 2016, a referendum was held to decide whether the UK should leave or remain in the European Union. Leave won by 52% to 48%. In accordance with Article 50 of the Treaty on European Union (TEU), the two-year process of leaving the EU was triggered on 29 March, 2017. Following the UK's retreat, the interplay between interregional legal cooperation and the operation of primary and secondary EU law, in particular the recast EU Insolvency Regulation, which came into effect in June 2017, becomes an open question.

In the midst of uncertainty and reforms, I, who happened to be one of the witnesses to all those historical events, decided to write my dissertation all over again in order to record those events and tentatively sketch a balanced way, including 10 original recommendations, accompanied with comments, which are entitled "China's Inter-Regional Cross-border Insolvency Arrangement" ("CICIA"). A balanced way that can be tailored to China's regional cooperation arrangements could be achieved based on China's regional political, economic and legal cooperation reality, by exploring the current cross-border insolvency systems in individual regions of China, and through the comparative study between China and the EU on the main aspects of the regional regime, i.e. the EU Insolvency Regulation, as well as the UNICTRAL Model Law, which serves as the international standard for cross-border insolvency cooperation for more comprehensive reference. The book attempts to discover the most relevant elements of cross-border insolvency cooperation on the regional level in China and it is hoped that it could provide some "road signs" for future study and research on this topic.

I owe a debt of gratitude to my supervisor, Prof. Bob Wessels, for his kind help so far and the opportunity to conduct independent research as a PhD candidate in Leiden University. A special appreciation also goes to the China Scholarship Council, which financially supports me to conduct my research in an independent way. Last, but not the least, my sincere thanks go to those who rendered their voluntary assistance to the realization of this work.

Xinyi Gong
Shanghai, 31 March, 2017

Abbreviations

ALI	American Law Institute
ARATS	Association for Relations across the Taiwan Straits
Cap 32	Companies (Winding-up and Miscellaneous Provisions) Ordinance
Cap 622	New Companies Ordinance
CEPA	Closer Economic Partnership Agreements
CICIA	China's Inter-Regional Cross-border Insolvency Arrangement
COMI	center of main interests
CO	Companies Ordinance
CPCM	Civil Procedure Code of Macao
EBL	Enterprise Bankruptcy Law
ECFA	Economic Cooperation Framework Agreement
EC Regulation	EC Regulation on insolvency proceedings [Council Regulation (EC) 1346/2000
EU Regulation (recast)	Regulation (EU) of the European Parliament and of the Council on insolvency proceedings (recast) 2012/0340 (COD)
GDP	gross development product
Guide and Interpretation	Guide to Enactment and Interpretation of the UNCITRAL Model Law on Cross-Border Insolvency
HCCH	Hague Conference on Private International Law
HK	Hong Kong
HK and Macao Act	Act Governing Relations with Hong Kong and Macao
III	International Law Institute
Model Law	UNCITRAL Model Law on Cross-border Insolvency
Mainland Act	Act Governing Relations between Peoples of the Taiwan Area and the Mainland Area
Mainland–Hong Kong Arrangement	Arrangement on Reciprocal Recognition and Enforcement of Judgments in Civil and Commercial Matters by the Courts of the Mainland and of the Hong Kong Special Administrative Region Pursuant to Choice of Court Agreements between Parties Concerned

xiv *Abbreviations*

Mainland–Macao Arrangement	Arrangement Between the Mainland and the Macao Special Administrative Region on the Mutual Recognition and Enforcement of Civil and Commercial Judgments
PRC	People's Republic of China
Regulation*	EC Regulation and EU Regulation (recast)
UNCITRAL	United Nations Commission on International Trade Law
Virgós/Schmit Report	Virgós/Schmit Report on the Convention on Insolvency Proceedings, Brussels, 1996
SAR	Special Administrative Region
SEF	Straits Exchange Foundation
SOE	State Owned Enterprise
TBA	Taiwan Bankruptcy Act

Note

* The EC Regulation and the EU Regulation (recast) altogether will be referred to as the Regulation in this book in order to utilize the simplified expression to conduct comparison with the UNCITRAL Model Law.

Cases

Statutes

1 Introduction

This book is about seeking solutions to China's interregional cross-border insolvency cooperation. Those solutions are developed mainly on the basis of two groups of comparative studies, including comparison among the cross-border insolvency systems of the four independent jurisdictions in China and comparison between the EU Insolvency Regulation and the UNCITRAL Model Law. In the end, it tentatively provides 10 original recommendations, accompanied with comments, which are entitled "China's Inter-Regional Cross-border Insolvency Arrangement" ("CICIA").

Possibility of cooperation on a regional level

Integration encourages people to move increasingly across borders:

> They studied, worked, got married, had children, purchased property, divorced and died in a region other than the one they were from. Businesses started to offer their products and services across borders on a regular basis. They set up factories and subsidiaries in other regions and acquired companies there.[1]

As a result, the legal systems of individual jurisdiction become too integral a part to remain isolated. The entire European Union is "a form of cooperation between its Member States" (Weller, 2015), which is supervised and governed by its regional legal order. Meanwhile, China's integration was partly crystalized by the "one country, two systems" principle. Four independent jurisdictions (the Mainland,[2] Hong Kong, Macao and Taiwan) operate simultaneously and equally effectively within one country. That also gave rise to an interregional legal order, which involves the rules regulating the intersection between the Mainland and the three regions. The first intersection concerns interpretation of the constitutional document, i.e. the Basic Law, which is binding on the Mainland and the two SARs. The second intersection relates to the bilateral legal cooperation arrangements. (See Annex I for more detailed information.) The third intersection happens in the courtrooms of each region. For each decision involving interregional factors rendered, the courts make a contribution to the establishment of the interregional legal order.

What is essential to a regional legal order? Based on the EU's experience, it is loyalty and mutual trust. According to the *Oxford English Dictionary*, loyalty means faithful adherence to the sovereign or lawful government. In the EU, the principle of loyalty is embedded in the duty of sincere cooperation, which is now stipulated under Article 4(3) TEU (ex Article 10 EC, ex Article 5 EEC). It is a principle "central to the development of Union law since the 1960s and that it still shapes its structure today" (Klamert, 2014). The EU Commission indicated, "the whole EU legal system . . . is based on mutual trust."[3] However, it is noteworthy that the origin of such cooperation was initiated by an agreement between five European states (including, Belgium, Netherlands, Luxembourg, Italy and France) and Germany, while the bitter memory left by World War II was still fresh. In fact, the first agreement to cooperate was founded upon distrust. At that time, France feared emerging German industry compounded by Germany's increasing share of European steel production and then proposed the Schuman Plan (Diebold, 1959). The solidarity in coal and steel production could make any war between France and Germany "not merely unthinkable, but materially impossible".[4] The integration of the European Union, including judicial cooperation, was not achieved through a single plan. Nevertheless, it demonstrated that cooperation was also possible if the parties concerned were not in a faithful relationship but fully aware that an individual party was incapable of realizing certain goals alone. That probably explains why there are bilateral legal cooperation arrangements concluded between the Mainland and the three regions before a sense of rooted attachment to their country is fostered and trust in each other is completely built. To deal with a series of contemporary problems and realize a set of goals in the process of integration, it is in the common interest to cooperate and an individual region cannot manage alone. In China, regional legal cooperation is growing mainly through bilateral arrangements. Trust is most likely to evolve in contexts in which the parties find themselves in ongoing relationships (Cook et al., 2005).

The possibility of interregional insolvency cooperation is also connected with the nature of cross-border insolvency. Insolvency proceedings touch upon one of the most longstanding and dynamic relations, which is the debtor–creditor relation. As a predominant metaphor, the limited assets of a debtor are usually described as fishes in a common pool and the creditors as self-interested fishermen (Jackson, 2001; Jackson & Scott, 1989; Baird, Jackson, Alder, 1990; Block-Lieb, 1993). The resources in the common pool would be diminished if they could not be prevented from overuse by the individual creditors. The common pool problems are often viewed as a multi-player Prisoner's Dilemma game (Block-Lieb, 1997). In the two-person game that is played only once, both players must cooperate in order to maximize their joint welfare; (Baird, Gertner, Picker, 1998) in the n-person one-shot game, welfare maximization occurs only if all n players cooperate (Schelling, 1978; Molander, 1992). Accordingly, in order to ensure equal treatment of creditors and maximize value of the debtor's assets, insolvency proceedings are designed as a collective debt-collection mechanism. Although the analogy of the assets of an insolvent debtor to a common pool used to be hotly debated among bankruptcy scholars (Friedman, 1971; Countryman, 1985; Carlson, 1987; Roe, 1989; Roe, 1989; Korobkin, 1993; Block-Lieb, 1993), the conclusion that a need exists for the "collective remedy of bankruptcy" is hardly controversial on national level (Block-Lieb, 1993). As for cross-border insolvency, both the Model Law and the Regulation require that the proceedings must be collective.[5] More importantly, given its nature, cross-border insolvency can possibly bring higher degree of cooperation than ordinary civil and commercial matters. For instance, Taiwan adopted differentiated attitudes towards the civil and commercial judgments rendered in the Mainland, Hong Kong and Macao (which will be explained in Part II), which have been changed in the approved draft of the Debt Clearance Act (the 2015 Draft) issued by the Judicial Yuan of Taiwan in June 2015 and passed by the Executive Yuan of Taiwan in April 2016. It is stipulated under the 2015 Draft that Taiwan intends to apply uniform rules in matters of recognition of cross-border insolvency proceedings regardless of its place of origins among China, Hong Kong, Macao and other foreign countries for equal treatment of creditors.[6]

Lack of a regional cross-border insolvency framework

Cooperation is accompanied with uncertainty over the future. Insolvency could be a conflict trigger. Insolvency law on the whole is a response to credit, which is "the disposition of one man to trust another" (Posner, 2010). "The essence of credit system is people and firms that can be called debtors borrowing money" (Jackson, 2001). Insolvency law copes with the risk that a debtor fails to observe the obligation to repay. If the risk of debtor's default cannot be handled properly, that will incur distrust between creditors and debtors. Therefore, insolvency law basically helps to establish an enduring cooperative relationship between debtors and creditors. Cross-border insolvency adds complexity to the scenario because it involves creditors from the different jurisdictions and debtors' fragmented assets governed by different rules. Under that circumstance, what kind of rules should apply? No individual jurisdictions intend to regulate every action or event that occurs anywhere and the law implemented in each of them has its boundaries, which are shaped through the recognition of claims of other jurisdictions (Ten Wolde, 2013). Hence, coordination of rules on a regional and international level is necessary in order to provide proper reference for cross-border insolvency cooperation for the benefit of long-term and reliable cross-border debtor–creditor relations. Moreover, in order to maintain an enduring regional cooperative relationship, it is of significance to make arrangements for such conflict to be resolved in a smooth manner.

Unfortunately, coordination of rules on interregional insolvency proceedings cannot be found either in any local law of the respective jurisdictions or in any bilateral arrangements in China. In 2011, upon a request for recognition of the winding-up proceeding concerning *Norstar Automotive*, the High Court of Beijing referred a question to the Supreme People's Court in order to make clear whether or not the winding-up order rendered by the High Court of Hong Kong can be recognized in the Mainland China. The Supreme People's Court replied:

> In accordance with the Article 1 of Arrangement of the Supreme People's Court between the Mainland and the Hong Kong SAR on Reciprocal Recognition and Enforcement of the Decisions of Civil and Commercial Cases Pursuant to Choice of Court Agreements between Parties Concerned, the winding-up order in dispute does not fall within the ambit of the enforceable final judgment under the Arrangement and thus the Arrangement is irrelevant to this case. The Article 265 of the Civil Procedure Law and the Article 5 of the Enterprise Bankruptcy Law, which provide rules on recognition and enforcement of judgments rendered by the **foreign** courts [emphasis added by the author], cannot be applied to this case, either. The decision of your court that in accordance with the aforementioned legislation, recognition of the winding-up order in dispute can be granted is groundless.[7]

It is noteworthy that the High Court of Beijing tended to recognize the Hong Kong winding-up order based on those rules applicable to foreign judgments. In fact, the Supreme People's Court used to consider a court of SAR as a foreign factor as well.[8] In practice, the lower courts have followed this approach.[9] It is beyond doubt that no judges of the Mainland want to jeopardize the sovereignty of their motherland. Why then do they keep considering SARs as foreign-related in adjudicating the SAR-related cases? What is the real meaning of "foreign-related"? The current confusion in essence reflects a continuing dilemma regarding the status of the SARs in matters of cross-border civil and commercial judicial interaction in China. Although Hong Kong has politically returned to PRC, a comprehensive legislative and judicial approach is still lacking. In the aforementioned Reply of the Supreme People's Court, recognition of the civil and commercial judgments rendered in Hong Kong is limited to some particular legal relationship as stated in a bilateral arrangement, which refers to a civil or commercial contract between the parties concerned, excluding a contract of employment or a contract to which a natural person is involved as a party for purposes of personal consumption, family affairs or other non-commercial purposes (the Mainland–Hong Kong Arrangement).[10] The insolvency proceedings are still not included. Therefore, there is the lack of legal basis for the courts to make a decision (Gong, 2011). Those foreign-related rules were thus borrowed as alternatives to solve the problems. However, the Reply of the Supreme People's Court in 2011 seems to set the tone that they can no longer be deemed as an effective legal basis in dealing with recognition of cross-border insolvency proceedings between the two regions from the perspective of the Mainland.

The scope of the arrangement concerning the mutual recognition and enforcement of judgments between the Mainland and Macao is much wider. It covers civil and commercial cases, including labor disputes.[11] Although insolvency proceedings are not literally excluded, the Arrangement between the Mainland and the Macao Special Administrative Region on the Mutual Recognition and Enforcement of Civil and Commercial Judgments (the Mainland–Macao Arrangement) provides no specialized rules in dealing with the recognition of cross-border insolvency proceedings, which will cause problems, because in accordance with Article 20 of the Civil Procedure Code of Macao, the Macao courts shall have exclusive jurisdiction over lawsuits concerning the bankruptcy or insolvency of legal persons, whose domicile is within Macao. In accordance with Article 11 of the Mainland–Macao Arrangement, if the matter verified in the judgment according to the laws of the requested region shall be subject to the exclusive jurisdiction of the requested court, the requested court should refuse to recognize it.[12] Therefore, insolvency proceedings are in fact excluded from the bilateral recognition arrangement regime between the Mainland and Macao SAR.

Taiwan is a politically disputed territory. On the scenario of cross-strait legal cooperation, each side stipulated specialized rules in matters of recognition and enforcement of civil and commercial cases, which are parallel to the rules applicable to foreign cases. In the Mainland, the judicial interpretations[13] issued by the Supreme People's Court serve as the legal basis of recognition of Taiwan civil and commercial judgments. In Taiwan, the Mainland civil and commercial judgments are recognized based on the Act Governing Relations between the People of the Taiwan Area and the Mainland Area.[14] In 2009, the Mainland and Taiwan entered into the Agreement between Both Sides of the Taiwan Strait on Jointly Fighting against Crimes and Mutual Judicial Assistance. It is a general legal cooperation agreement that covers mutual judicial assistance in matters of criminal cases, service of documents, taking evidence as well as recognition and enforcement of civil cases and arbitral awards, in which rules concerning recognition of cross-strait insolvency proceedings have not been specified.

Structure of the book

In pursuit of the solutions to China's interregional insolvency cooperation, the book is mainly composed of five chapters. After resumption of its sovereignty over Hong Kong and Macao as well as the uncertain cross-strait relationship between the Mainland and Taiwan,

China becomes a country composed of peculiar political compounds, which results in four independent jurisdictions. That makes interregional legal cooperation a complicated but also a necessary topic. Chapter 1 introduces the lack of rules regulating interregional cross-border insolvency and the possibility of cooperation is sketched out.

Chapter 2 illustrates the birth and development of the "one country, two systems" principle and provides a general overview of the peculiar "four Chinas" composition from political and economic perspectives as well as its influences on interregional legal cooperation in China. In particular, it demonstrates the current arrangements for legal cooperation in matters of recognition and enforcement of civil and commercial judgments among the four regions, from which insolvency is excluded. As settled consensus, their contents and development furnish indispensable references for further discussion on interregional cross-border insolvency cooperation in China.

Chapter 3 provides an overview of the cross-border insolvency system in the four regions. For each region, it will start with a brief introduction to the local insolvency system in general. Further, it is followed by a more detailed introduction of the individual cross-border insolvency systems, which is mainly combined with case studies and analysis. In the end, the individual features of the cross-border insolvency systems among the four regions will be compared and summarized.

Chapter 4 conducts a comparative research between the Regulation and the UNICTRAL Model Law by laying emphasis on the key aspects, including jurisdiction (especially COMI), recognition and reliefs, enterprise groups as well as cooperation and communication. After having been operating over ten years, both the EC Regulation and the UNICTRAL Model Law are undergoing changes. In particular, the EC Regulation has been repealed through new substantive amendments, which brings in a recast EU Regulation. Meanwhile, the UNICTRAL Model Law has also been gradually developed by guides. Especially in 2013, the Guide to Enactment of the Model Law has been revised and retitled as Guide to Enactment and Interpretation. Therefore, the comparative research of the two international regimes will be conducted by way of abundant literature review and case analyses so that their similarities and differences in development can be explored in detail.

By referring to the current practice in China, Chapter 5 will attempt to find a balanced way between the Regulation and the Model Law and then tailor them into China's context, which is composed of ten recommendations attached with comments. Based on the result of the first round of comparison between the Regulation and the Model Law, the author will conduct the second round of comparison in this part in order to further examine compatibility of the results with the Mainland and the SARs to check out which one better fits into China's situation or whether China should establish something new for its own regional regime. The range of the regional arrangement covers the guiding principle, the overriding objective, form and scope, recognition and reliefs, public policy, cooperation and communication (single debtor and enterprise groups), cross-border insolvency agreements, functional dispute settlement mechanism, interregional case register and a separate arrangement for cross-strait insolvency cooperation (between the Mainland and Taiwan), which is independent intermediaries.

Notes

1 Reding, Viviane, From Maastricht to Lisbon: building a European area of Justice in small steps and great bounds, available at: http://europa.eu/rapid/press-release_SPEECH-13-960_nl.htm (last accessed on 31 March, 2017).

2 Throughout this book, the Mainland (China) purely serves as a geographic term to describe the geopolitical area under the jurisdiction of the People's Republic of China (PRC), generally excluding the PRC Special Administrative Regions of Hong Kong and Macao.
3 European Commission, Building Trust in Justice Systems in Europe "Assises de la Justice" Forum to Shape the Future of EU Justice Policy (Press Release), 21 November, 2013, available at: http://europa.eu/rapid/press-release_IP-13-1117_en.htm (last accessed on 31 March, 2017).
4 European Parliament, Selection of Texts concerning Institutional Matters of the Community for 1950–1982, Luxembourg: European Parliament, 1982, p. 47.
5 The Model Law, Article 2(a); EC Regulation, recital (10), Article 1(1); EU Regulation (recast), recital (12), (14), Article 1(1).
6 The 2015 Draft, Article 319. Clarification to the 2015 Draft, Chapter VI, Article 319.
7 [2011] Supreme People's Court Civil Others No. 19.
8 In the case of *Bank of China (Hong Kong) Limited v Shantou Hongye (Group) Co., Ltd*, [2002] Supreme People's Court Final Civil Division IV No. 6, the Supreme People's Court stated as the HKSAR and the Mainland of China belong to different jurisdictions, according to Several Opinions of the Supreme People's Court on the Implementation of the General Rules of the Civil Code of People's Republic of China, Article 194, when the **foreign-related** [emphasis added by the author] party to the contract makes a choice of the application law, the mandatory or prohibitory laws and regulations of PRC. cannot be circumvented".
9 *Gu Laiyun and others v Nardu Company Limited* [2006] Guangzhou Intermediate People's Court Civil Division IV First Instance No. 44, see also *Yong Zhe Express Service v Hong Kong Woolworths Group (Asia) Ltd.* [2009] Shanghai No. 1 Intermediate People's Court Civil Division V (Commercial) First Instance No. 32.
10 2006 Arrangement on Reciprocal Recognition and Enforcement of Judgments in Civil and Commercial Matters by the Courts of the Mainland and of the Hong Kong Special Administrative Region Pursuant to Choice of Court Agreements between Parties Concerned, Article 3.
11 Arrangement Between the Mainland and the Macao Special Administrative Region on the Mutual Recognition and Enforcement of Civil and Commercial Judgments, Article 1.
12 Ibid., Article 11(1).
13 1998 The Provisions of the Supreme People's Court on the People's Court's Recognition of the Verdicts on Civil Cases Made by Courts of Taiwan Province ([1998] Supreme People's Court Interpretation No. 11); 2009 Supplementary Provisions of the Supreme People's Court on the People's Courts' Recognition of Civil Judgments of the Relevant Courts of the Taiwan Region ([2009] Supreme People's Court Interpretation No. 4).
14 The Mainland Act, Article 74.

Reference list

Baird, Douglas G., Jackson, Thomas H., Adler, Barry E., *Cases, Problems and Materials on Bankruptcy* (2nd ed.), Little, Brown and Company, 1990, pp. 20–30
Baird, Douglas G., Gertner, Robert H., Picker, Randal C., *Game Theory and the Law*, Harvard University Press, 1998, pp. 31–35
Block-Lieb, Susan, *Fishing in Muddy Waters: Clarifying the Common Pool Analogy as Applied to the Standard for Commencement of a Bankruptcy Case*, 42 Am. U. L. Rev. 337, 1993, pp. 343, 346, 412–432
Block-Lieb, Susan, "Congress's Temptation to Defect: A Political and Economic Theory of Legislative Resolutions to Financial Common Pool Problems", 39 Ariz. L. Rev. 801, 1997, p. 811
Carlson, David Gray, Philosophy in Bankruptcy, 85 Mich. L. Rev. 1341, 1987
Cook, Karen S., Hardin, Russell, Levi, Margaret, *Cooperation without Trust?* Volume IX in the Russell Sage Foundation Series on Trust, 2005, p. 4
Countryman, Vern, "The Concept of a Voidable Preference in Bankruptcy", 38 Vand. L. Rev. 713, 1985, pp. 823–825
Diebold, William, *The Schuman Plan: A Study in Economic Cooperation, 1950–1959*, Frederick A. Praeger for the Council on Foreign Relation, 1959, p. 10

Friedman, Alan E., "The Economics of the Common Pool: Property Rights in Exhaustible Resources", 18 UCLA L. Rev. 855, 1971, p. 856

Gong, Xinyi, "When Hong Kong Becomes SAR, Is the Mainland Ready? – Problems of Judgments Recognition in Cross-border Insolvency Matters", *International Insolvency Review*, Vol. 20, Issue 1, 2011, p. 59

Jackson, Thomas, *The Logic and Limits of Bankruptcy Law*, 2001, Beard Books, pp. 7, 12–13

Jackson, Thomash, Scott, Robert, "On the Nature of Bankruptcy: An Essay on Bankruptcy Sharing and the Creditors' Bargain", 75 Va. L. Rev. 155, 1989, p. 178

Klamert, Marcus, *The Principle of Loyalty in EU*, Oxford University Press, 2014, p. 1

Korobkin, Donald R., "Contractarianism and the Normative Foundations of Bankruptcy Law", 71 Tex. L. Rev. 541, 1993, pp. 553–559

Molander, Per, "The Prevalence of Free Riding", 36 J. Conflict Resol 756, 1992, p. 759

Posner, Kenneth A., *Stalking the Black Swan: Research and Decision Making in a World of Extreme Volatility*, Columbia Business School Publishing, 2010, p. 17

Roe, Mark J., "Commentary on 'On the Nature of Bankruptcy': Bankruptcy", Priority, and Economics, 75 Va. L. Rev.,1989, pp. 219–220

Schelling, Thomas C., *Micromotives and Macrobehavior*, W. W. Norton & Company, 1978, p. 218

Ten Wolde, Mathijs, *The Relativity of Legal positions in Cross-Border Situations: The Foundations of Private Interregional Law, Private Intra-Community Law and Private International Law, in: A commitment to Private International Law: Liber Amicorum* Hans van Loon, Secretary-General Hague Conference. Cambridge: Intersentia, International Law Series, 2013, p. 575

Weller, Matthias, "Mutual Trust: In Search of the Future of European Union Private International Law", *Journal of Private International Law*, Vol. 11, No. 1, 64–102, 2015, p. 73

2 China's special political regime and current regional cross-border legal cooperation

Introduction

This chapter is mainly composed of three sections. What is China's "One Country, Two Systems" principle? The first section answers this question mainly from its political origin and development (legal foundation). The second section focuses on economic cooperation arrangements, including the dispute settlement mechanisms, between the Mainland and the two SARs as well as the cross-strait economic relation. The discussion in the final section is about the characteristics of the individual legal system in China and their influences on the current method of cross-border legal cooperation in matters of civil and commercial cases among the four regions.

Political integration

"One country, two systems" regime

To resume the exercise of sovereignty over Hong Kong[1] and Macao[2] after their colonial relationships fell due (Ghai, 1999),[3] the Mainland[4] has adopted the "one country, two systems" principle as the basic formula, which was written into the Sino-British Joint Declaration and Sino-Portuguese Joint Declaration. Generally speaking, that principle reflects the art of compromise. China used to be a unitary state, in which the central government is supreme and any administrative divisions exercise powers that the central government chooses to delegate. The idea was proposed by Deng Xiaoping, the former Leader of the People's Republic of China (PRC). The principle has created a special political regime. First of all, "one country" is the prerequisite for "two systems". Deng pointed out, "The systems can be different, but only the People's Republic of China can represent China in international affairs" (Wen, 2009). Secondly, the degree of autonomy enjoyed by the SARs is even higher than the states under a federal model, like the United States. Attention should be paid to the word "independent" that only occurs in front of the judicial power under both Basic Laws.[5] The independency of the courts in SARs is mainly reflected in the establishment of the Court of Final Appeal in both SARs, which is vested with the power of final adjudication in the SARs.[6] Besides, the courts of the SAR may also interpret other provisions of the Basic Law in adjudicating cases, except for the affairs that are the responsibility of the Central People's Government, or concerning the relationship between the Central Authorities and the Region.[7] Thirdly, the Mainland and the SARs are mutually restrained by the Basic Law, the constitutional document, which can only be enforced within the SARs, whereas not every article of the Constitution of PRC has effect in the SARs. In fact, the effect of the constitution of PRC in the SARs was in debate when drafting the Hong Kong SAR Basic law and is still controversial after reunification (Wang, 1997; Jiao, 1999; Wang, 2000; Xiao, 2003).

It can be differentiated from the European Union model because it is not composed of sovereign member states. There is only one sovereign state, i.e. China. Regarded as the mechanisms of achieving regional integration, however, these two systems share something in common. First of all, the idea of "one country, two systems" is realized through the Basic Law, which fosters the legal foundation of the reunification, like the Treaties. Secondly, on the economic scenario, although different economic systems are applied in the four regions and even the currencies used are all different, economic cooperation is still driven by the interdependent markets within the Greater China area, which is a special term referring to Mainland China, Hong Kong SAR, Macao SAR and Taiwan and a non-official phrase used in commercial activities to avoid any political connotation by businessmen. For instance, the Closer Economic Partnership Arrangements (CEPA) has been signed between the Mainland and the SARs in 2003. Taiwan, which is absent from the political integration, signed the agreement of economic cooperation with the Mainland in 2010, which is the Economic Cooperation Framework Agreement (ECFA). Those economic cooperative arrangements seem to be the sprouting of a common market. Thirdly, in EU the harmonization of legal conflicts, consisting of one of the most important parts of its integration, encourages and enhances the development of EU laws. The legal diversity and independent jurisdictions of different regions has been to the largest extent maintained in China. Consequently, the frequent interregional legal interaction requires a solution for coordinating legal conflicts. For example, according to the Annual Work Report of the Supreme People's Court of PRC, from 1993 to 1997, the people's courts all over the Mainland have heard 17,368 cases relating to Hong Kong and Macao. In 2016 alone, there were about 19,000 cases relating to Hong Kong and Macao, which were heard by the people's courts all over the Mainland.

Legal foundation: the basic law

The principle of "one country, two systems" is well defined by the Basic Law, which functions as an agreement signed between the central government and the SARs as a result of political integration. Both SARs (Hong Kong and Macao) have their own Basic Law, which are generally the same in structure and contents. The main line of the Basic Law is to keep everything unchanged as much as possible after the reunification and the high degree of autonomy has been maintained by the Basic Law in a comprehensive way. First of all, although China still has its unitary political system, China's central government cannot interfere with the affairs in those two regions except for foreign and defense affairs as well as other matters outside the limits of the autonomy of SARs. Secondly, the laws in force in the SARs will basically remain the same and most of the laws in the Mainland will not be enforced in the SARs.[8] Thirdly, the SARs shall be vested with executive power, legislative power and independent judicial power, including that of final adjudication.[9] Fourthly, the social and economic systems in the Mainland and the SARs operate in the same way respectively as they used to be. For example, the SARs have their own independent finances. The Central People's Government shall not levy taxes from the SAR. Furthermore, the SARs shall use their financial revenues exclusively for their own purposes. The SARs are still allowed to issue their own currencies, the Hong Kong dollar or Macao Pataca. The Hong Kong SAR retains the status of a free port and a separate customs territory. As for Macao, gambling and tourism are both the pillar industries of the Macao SAR. Therefore, special provisions, have been made to keep the promise that the previous way of life will remain unchanged in Macao SAR. In addition, the unique consultative coordination organizations composed of representatives from the government, the employers' organizations and the employees' organizations, which were set up in 1987, have been maintained in the Macao SAR. These kinds of organizations aim at reducing friction, improving mutual understanding and finally reaching agreement through reconciliation between the employers and the employees. They also help to promote the substantial improvement of the labor legislation and the economy in Macao. Fourthly, the SARs may on their own, using the name "Hong Kong, China" or "Macao, China", conclude and implement agreements with foreign states and regions and relevant international organizations in the appropriate fields, including the economic, trade, financial and monetary, shipping, communications, tourism, cultural and sports fields.[10]

The Basic Law is different from the treaties establishing the European Union. First of all, as the EU was not built upon a single plan but through concrete and continuous development, the treaties that contributed to its construction have experienced far-reaching reforms,[11] whereas the Basic Law is a preliminary attempt between the Mainland and the SARs, which is tentatively conducted for 50 years.[12] Secondly, the treaties gradually set up a political union in competition with the nation-state (Chalmers, Davies, Giorgio, 2010), which requires the latter to limit its sovereign rights for the benefit of the Union. The Basic Law set the tone for "one country" as its primary goal,[13] according to which the Mainland as Central Authority has to restrain its sovereign rights from interfering in the high degree autonomy enjoyed by the SARs. Thirdly, the treaties set up an institutional framework to carry out the practical work of the EU. It includes the Court of Justice of the European Union (CJEU), which plays a decisive role as guardian of "a new legal order of international law"[14] by examining "the spirit, the general scheme and the wording"[15] of the treaties. In China, there is no such institutional arrangement because the individual jurisdictions of the SARs are guaranteed to remain independent.[16] Fourthly, through coherent interpretation of the CJEU, the effects of the treaties extend not only to the Member States but also to the peoples of Europe.[17] The Basic Law is only applicable within the SARs.[18] As for the regional legal order that addresses the issues arising from the interplay between the Mainland and the SARs, it is mainly established on the basis of bilateral arrangements, which is to be discussed later in this chapter.

Economic integration

Closer Economic Partnership Arrangement (CEPA)

As the Basic Laws try to keep the socialist Mainland and the capitalist SARs from being mixed with each other,[19] the purpose of CEPA is to bring them closer. Due to the recession of Hong Kong's economy after the economic crisis in 1997, Tung Chee-hwa, the former Chief Executive of Hong Kong SAR, firstly proposed this arrangement. In order to help Hong Kong with its stable economic development and seek economic cooperation, both sides decided to open up their own markets to each other. In 2003, the Mainland and the Macao SAR signed CEPA, as well. Each CEPA contains a main text, six annexes, and annually signed supplementary agreements. The supplementary agreements of CEPA are signed annually by the Mainland with each SAR. Cooperation covers trade in goods, trade in services and trade and investment facilitation. The most substantial part of the cooperation in trade in goods is that by 1 January, 2006, the Mainland shall apply a zero tariff to all imports from Hong Kong SAR and Macao SAR. With regard to trade in services, according to Article 11 of each arrangement, the Mainland has promised to gradually ease and ultimately eliminate restrictions on the services provided by Hong Kong SAR and Macao SAR businessmen. Upon the request of either side, the Mainland and the SARs may, through consultation, pursue further liberalization of trade in services between them. These services, around 38 in total, include law, accounting, insurance, banking, securities, construction and real estate, medical and dental, advertising, trade mark agents, patent agents, employment agencies, personnel intermediary and tourism etc. Besides, the Mainland, Hong Kong SAR, and Macao SAR have agreed to further promote their investment facilitation in various areas, such as trade and investment promotion, especially including transparency in laws and regulations.

CEPA has also strengthened the possibility of trans-regional legal practice. Firstly, the Mainland legal services market has been widely opened to Hong Kong SAR and Macao SAR. For example, various liberalization measures to facilitate the freedom of the legal service have been adopted gradually in the annually concluded supplementary agreements of CEPA. Under Supplement I of CEPA, lawyers from Hong Kong SAR and Macao SAR providing professional assistance at the request of Mainland law firms on the basis of individual cases will not be required to apply for a Hong Kong or Macao legal consultant permit. Under Supplement III, Hong Kong and Macao residents who have acquired Mainland lawyer qualifications or legal professional qualifications and hold a Mainland lawyer's practice certificate are allowed to engage in activities as agents in matrimonial and succession cases relating to Hong Kong and Macao in the capacity of Mainland lawyers. Hong Kong and Macao barristers are allowed to act as agents in civil litigation cases in the Mainland in the capacity of citizens. Under Supplement VI, Hong Kong and Macao legal practitioners can apply to practice as lawyers in the Mainland. Under Supplement IX, the SAR law firms (offices) that have set up representative offices in the Mainland are allowed to operate in association with one to three Mainland law firms.

Cross-Strait Economic Cooperation Framework Agreement (ECFA)

Regardless of the divergent opinions on sovereign issues, an active tie between the Mainland and Taiwan, which is the cross-strait economic interaction, has been growing and blooming. Ever since 1978, the Mainland adopted a more moderate gesture towards Taiwan (the policy of PRC shifted from "Liberation of Taiwan" to "One County, Two Systems"). At the same time, PRC began to enforce its reform and opening-up policy. The PRC authorities especially indicated that investments by Taiwan residents were welcome and would receive preferential treatment. For instance, in 1994, Law of the People's Republic of China on the Protection of Taiwan Compatriot's Investment, of which Article 1 directly stated that the reason for making this law is to protect and encourage the investment by Taiwan compatriots and promote cross-strait economic development, was enacted by Mainland China. Pursuant to that law, the preferential treatment includes the promise of opening the Mainland's market to Taiwan investors, the preferential tax treatment and the protection of their legal property rights etc. Though direct trade and investment were still officially banned, the Taiwan government had basically turned a blind eye to the Taiwan investors' flocking to the Mainland (Silk, 1990). As an island region, Taiwan lacks the low cost of labor, raw materials, huge market volume plus the preferential treatment that the mainland can provide, while the Mainland needs the capital and investment from Taiwan. The supply and demand led to the indirect cross-strait economy to flourish.

The influence of economic activity could hardly be underestimated. The economic interaction has gradually lifted the ban on cross-strait contact. In 1988, Taiwan first approved indirect commercial dealings with the PRC, permitting indirect import of the commodities

(Tang, 2006). Since this tentative initial step, Taiwan authorities have abandoned or altered a number of previous laws restricting commerce and relations across the Strait. In 2001, Taiwan allowed limited postal, transportation, and trade links between the Fujian province cities of Xiamen, Mawei and Quanzhou of PRC, and the islands of Kinmen and Matsu, which are administered by Taiwan (known as the three mini-links).[20] Even though that kind of link was tortuous, routed through intermediate destinations, such as Hong Kong, Macao and South Korea, from 1988 to 2007, the Mainland attracted direct investment of US$45.76 billion from Taiwan. The trade volume between the mainland and Taiwan is up 15.4% year on year and the Chinese Mainland remains Taiwan's largest export market in 2007.[21] In December 2008, the Chinese Mainland and Taiwan, due to the economic benefits and the actual needs of their peoples, agreed to enforce the "three direct links", including the opening up of direct flights, direct shipping and direct post to each other. The relationship between the Mainland and Taiwan is driven by the economy instead. Silk once said "Today, there's no question that Taiwan has returned – but the troops aren't military and the motivation isn't political. The soldiers of propaganda have been replaced with businessmen – armed not with guns, but with cash" (Silk, 1990). He said so in 1990. In 2009, the former president of Taiwan Mr. Ma Ying-jeou said in his New Year's speech:

> [W]e should seize this opportunity to enhance Taiwan's economic standing in the world, but as economic relations between Taiwan and the Mainland become increasingly interdependent, we must also preserve the sovereignty and dignity of the Republic of China on Taiwan.[22]

In 2010, the conclusion of the Cross-strait Economic Cooperation Framework Agreement (ECFA) embarked on a new era of economic interaction between the two sides. That agreement is a preferential trade agreement between the governments of the Mainland China and Taiwan that aims to reduce tariffs and commercial barriers between the two sides. The "early harvest" list of tariff concessions covers 539 Taiwanese products and 267 Mainland Chinese goods. From 1 January 2012, tariffs on 90% of Early Harvest List goods of Taiwan have been reduced to zero.[23] The advantage to Taiwan would amount to US$13.8 billion, while Mainland China would receive benefits estimated at US$2.86 billion. The Taiwan items have a total export amount of about US$14 billion, or 4.8 times more than trade covered by the Mainland's early harvest list.[24] Besides, Mainland China will also open markets in 11 service sectors such as banking, securities, insurance, hospitals and accounting, while Taiwan agreed to offer wider access in seven areas, including banking and movies. With accession to the ECFA, it can be noticed that more investment flows across the strait from each side. (Please refer to Table 2.1 at the end of Chapter 2.) Unfortunately, the cross-strait economic relationship is not developed without controversy. It is reported that dozens of activists, mostly students, broke in the debating chamber of the Legislative Yuan, Taiwan's parliament, in Taipei on 18 March 2014 in order to resist an agreement on opening up services trade with the Mainland. The students continued to occupy the chamber till 10 April 2014 (Banyan, 2014), which overshadowed the development of cross-strait economic cooperation.

Dispute settlement mechanisms under the economic arrangements

Without a uniform interregional legal framework, cross-border business is subject to diverse rules and regulations in the individual jurisdictions, which can probably result in conflicts. For instance, like the legal services, liberalization of the accounting services of the Mainland's market for the SARs is gradually achieved.[25] Nonetheless, on 27 August 2012, the Securities and Futures Commission of Hong Kong SAR (HKSFC) commenced proceedings in the Court of First Instance against Ernst & Young Hong Kong (Ernst & Young) for failing to produce to the SFC specified accounting records. Ernst & Young claimed that it did not have the relevant records, which were held by its joint venture partner in the Mainland, Ernst & Young Hua Ming (EY Hua Ming), whose staff were the ones involved in the engagement. On following up the non-compliance, Ernst & Young then claimed the documents could not be produced because of restrictions under PRC law. As a result of a joint statement issued by PRC authorities on 20 October 2009, accounting records, including audit working papers, may be the subject of claims of state secrecy under PRC law and all Hong Kong accountants are required to obtain the consent of the relevant Mainland authorities before handing over any accounting records to regulators like the SFC even if the records are kept in Hong Kong. On the other hand, the SFC is entitled to require the disclosure of the accounting records pursuant to the Securities and Futures Ordinance and can invoke section 185 of the Securities and Futures Ordinance, which empowers the Court of First Instance to inquire into the circumstances of Ernst & Young's non-compliance with the SFC's request for these records. The court can order Ernst & Young to comply with the SFC's request if it is satisfied that Ernst & Young does not have any reasonable excuse for not complying.[26] In this case, the state secrecy restriction under the Mainland law and the disclosure of relevant accounting information under the Hong Kong statute led an accounting company that is doing cross-border business to a dilemma.

CEPA

In order to solve the possible legal conflicts generated from the CEPA framework, a dispute settlement mechanism, the Joint Steering Committee, has been set up. This committee aims to settle disputes arising from the interpretation or implementation of the CEPA.[27] This committee will comprise senior representatives or officials designated by the Mainland and SAR. Liaison offices are to be set up under the Steering Committee. Besides, working groups may be set up as the need arises. The way the Committee will work to solve conflicts is consultation in the spirit of friendship and cooperation.[28] The Steering Committee should make its decisions by consensus. CEPA is an experiment in developing China's regional economic cooperation. Its legal status is still under debate (Wang, 2004). The existing dispute settlement mechanism of CEPA is merely intergovernmental. However, it is a growing-up arrangement, which can be traced from its annually refreshed supplementary agreements to solve new problems out of the practice of the cross-border trade contact. It is possible that CEPA may give birth to a dispute settlement mechanism for cross-border commercial conflicts.

ECFA

In accordance with the Article 10 of the ECFA, an appropriate dispute settlement mechanism, the Cross-strait Economic Cooperation Committee, shall be set up, which serves as the organ to deal with disputes through consultancy and negotiation. The duty of the Committee also includes promotion of continuous economic cooperation between the two sides on the basis of ECFA.[29] Pursuant to ECFA, the Committee will convene a regular meeting on a semi-annual basis.[30] Up to April 2012, three regular meetings have been held, in which negotiation with respect to trade of goods, services and dispute settlement was carried out.

After the third regular meeting, the economic and trade organizations from each side are allowed to set up offices across the Taiwan Strait.[31]

Current legal cooperation within the four regions

Complicated legal composition

After reunification, the civil law system (the Mainland China and Macao) and the common law system (Hong Kong SAR) coexist within the scope of one political territory. The growth of Chinese Mainland's legal system alone is no less complicated. Generally speaking, it is mainly fashioned in a civil law style with China's own characteristics. After 1949, when the PRC was established, the new government employed the Soviet Union model as a reference to set up the new legal system. In the early 1980s, the idea of building a socialist law with Chinese characteristics was proposed by the Legislative Committee of the National People's Congress (NPC), which is the legislature of PRC. When the Communist Party decided to establish a "socialist market economy" and enforce an "opening-up policy" in 1992, it became imperative for China to assimilate its law with international practice, regardless of its socialist or capitalist nature, the Anglo-American or the European continental legal system. Therefore, the development of China's legal system nowadays, to a large extent, is promoted by legal transplantation (Chen, 2008). Taking the 2006 Enterprise Bankruptcy Law for example, the system of reorganization has been introduced into China by basically referring to Chapter 11 of the United States Bankruptcy Code (Han, 2004).

Having been deeply rooted in Hong Kong for over 150 years, the common law system has developed into the cornerstone of the entire legal and judicial system there. As Ghai once pointed out,

> one of the principal concerns of the Hong Kong people as China resumed sovereignty over Hong Kong was the future of the common law (an expression meaning not only judge-made law, but the entire legal and judicial system, including what were perceived to be the values and procedures of the common law). (Ghai, 2007)

Given that fact, the Basic Law does not cut off the links between common law and Hong Kong but wisely allows its continuity.[32] Nevertheless, following the reunification, the foundation of the laws applicable has been inevitably changed (Xie, 1988), which are empowered to be effective in Hong Kong in accordance with the Basic Law of Hong Kong SAR, instead of their former colonial basis. The judicial system previously practiced in Hong Kong has also been to the most extent maintained. For instance, the courts of the Hong Kong SAR may refer to precedents of other common law jurisdictions in the adjudication of cases.[33] Judges and other members of the judiciary of the Hong Kong SAR may be recruited from other common law jurisdictions.[34] Some reforms have been carried out as well. Firstly, the Court of Final Appeal of the Hong Kong SAR, which is vested with the power of final adjudication of the Hong Kong SAR, has been established. The colony Hong Kong did not have the power of final adjudication but belonged to the Privy Council of the UK. Secondly, the courts of the Hong Kong SAR are authorized by the Standing Committee of the National People's Congress (SCNPC, the legislature of PRC) to interpret on their own, in adjudicating cases, the provisions of the Basic Law, which are within the limits of the autonomy of the SAR.[35] Nonetheless, the "limits of the autonomy of the SAR" have not been clearly specified. As a result, conflicts over the scope of the independent power of interpretation of the Basic Law occurred in 1999 when the Hong Kong Court of Final Appeal adjudicated a number of cases regarding the right of Mainland-born children to stay in Hong Kong SAR.[36] Thirdly, the courts of the Hong Kong SAR may also interpret other provisions of this Law in adjudicating cases. However, if the interpretation of other provisions concerning affairs that are the responsibility of the Central People's Government, or concerning the relationship between the Central Authorities and the SAR and if such interpretation will affect the judgments on the cases, the courts should, before making their final judgments that are not appealable, seek an interpretation of the relevant provisions from the Standing Committee of the National People's Congress (SCNPC) through the Court of Final Appeal of the SAR.[37]

Macao used to have a dual civil law system in the style of civil law. Early from the transition period of the reunification till now, the Macao SAR has been carrying out the reforms of the local legal system with two aims. One is to make the local legal system separate from the former Portuguese legal system. Prior to 1976, Macao, as a colony, enjoyed little autonomy and the power of the local legislature was strictly limited. Portuguese laws directly dominated the local legal system. In fact, in addition to some local legislation, almost all important laws enforced in Macao came from Portugal (Mi, 1996). After 1976, due to the reform of the constitution of Portugal, Macao was authorized to independently make more laws according to its local situations. It is also noteworthy that all the laws were made and promulgated exclusively in the Portuguese language. However, Portugal had neglected to educate the local people in Portuguese; most of the local people are only able to speak Cantonese (a kind of dialect, the same in Hong Kong) and write Chinese.[38] As a result, the language gap greatly weakened the genuine effects of the laws among the local people and kept most of the local residents away from the courts. In particular, during the colonial period, a local resident who was not able to speak Portuguese had to hire an interpreter if engaged in a lawsuit because the judges and prosecutors only spoke Portuguese in courts. And the local residents had to go to Lisbon to appeal, because there were only courts of first instance in Macao before 1993 (Jian, 1994; Xian, 1997). At that time, a number of disputes, especially the civil disputes were solved or mediated by the local civic organizations in Macao (Gu, 2005; Liu, 2010). It was not until 1986 that the former Macao Government issued a decree to determine that the documents issued by the government, which closely related to the public, should be promulgated both in Portuguese and Chinese.[39] In 1988, Macao established the Office of Legal Interpretation (Wu, 1995), which promoted work on the Chinese versions of most of the laws, decrees and regulations. After the reunification, Chinese, together with Portuguese, has become the official language in Macao. Besides, the Macao SAR has reorganized its judicial system in accordance with the Basic Law. Firstly, it formally established a three-tier court system, including courts of first instance, intermediate courts and one Court of Final Appeal.[40] Nevertheless, owing to the late independency of the local judicial system and the monopoly of the Portuguese in the judicial system, the efficiency of the judicial system in Macao has been complained about for a long time and Macao is short of local legal professions. For instance, right after the reunification, there were 24 judges in the courts of first instance, five in the intermediate courts, and three in the Court of Final Appeal in accordance with the Annex attached to the former Macao Judicial Organic Law, while piles of cases were waiting for those judges to make decisions.[41]

The local legal system of Taiwan was inherited from the legal system established by the former Republic of China during China's Civil War (during the 1930s). The main components of the current Taiwan legal system include the basic codes of laws, bylaws, legal precedents and the interpretation of the Judicial Yuan, which is the supreme judiciary in Taiwan.[42] The codes of laws, following the former legal framework of the Republic of China (they are known as "the Complete Literatures on Six Laws" or "Six Codes"), which are the constitution law, the civil law, the criminal law, the civil procedure law, the criminal procedure law,[43] serve as the basic legal framework in Taiwan. Under those codes of laws, the related bylaws are made in the form of regulations, orders etc., to supplement their respective codes of laws. As the unique parts of the current local legal system in Taiwan, the legal precedents made by the Supreme Court of Taiwan through due process and interpretation made by the Council of Grand Justices of the Judicial Yuan also have a great impact. In accordance with the constitution law, the Court Organization Act and the law of the Council of Grand Justice etc., the precedents of the Supreme Court could be recognized as the ground of the decision after being certified by the Judicial Yuan. In accordance with the Court Organization Act (Article 57), the Supreme Court of Taiwan has made the Main Points of the Selection and Modification of the Legal Precedents, which later helped to foster the legal precedent system in Taiwan. The current Taiwanese laws continue to apply the traditional Chinese way of writing and expression, although the contents have been more or less modified or amended with the changing situation of Taiwan. First of all, most of the laws have been updated to supplement the outmoded part of the former legal system. Besides, driven by the Supreme Court of Taiwan, the development of local law has flourished greatly through interpretation. For example, under Article 1 of the Taiwan Civil Code, it is provided that if there is no applicable act for a civil case, the case shall be decided according to custom. If there is no such custom, the case shall be decided according to jurisprudence. In addition, the Supreme Court also declared that comparative law could be regarded as jurisprudence to interpret a provision (Wang, 2006). That declaration enables the courts to introduce modern theory from around the world into Taiwan's legal system and help to improve the local law by testing theory in the process of making judicial decisions. The judicial system of Taiwan is composed of the Judicial Yuan with its internal agencies and the agencies subject to it. The Judicial Yuan is a rare phenomenon and also an inheritance. (In 1928, the former government of the Republic of China established five governmental departments, including the Executive Yuan, the Legislative Yuan, the Judicial Yuan, the Examination Yuan, the Control Yuan, also known as "Five Yuans" structure. Taiwan keeps the former governmental organizations till now.) The status of the Judicial Yuan, whether it is a court or a judicial executive organ, is still under debate. In accordance with the Constitution Code (Article 77), the Judicial Yuan is the supreme judiciary, in charge of the civil, criminal and administrative trials and the civil service disciplinary. Nevertheless, it is stipulated under the Organization Law of the Judicial Yuan that there is no direct access for the Judicial Yuan to those trials. In 1999, the Council of Grand Justice passed the Interpretation of the Judicial Yuan No. 530, which proposed a court-oriented reform of the Judicial Yuan. In 2008, the Judicial Yuan Assembly passed the draft of the amendment of the Organization Law of the Judicial Yuan to promote the reform. But till now, the Judicial Yuan still does not interfere with civil or criminal trials of courts at different levels. The internal agencies are mainly composed of the Council of Grand Justices, which has the power of judicial interpretation and the establishment of the constitutional tribunal to commit the constitutional examination.

Legal cooperation between the Mainland and SARs

Bilateral arrangements

After reunification, the Mainland and SARs have entered into a set of legal cooperation arrangements in matters of service of documents, recognition and enforcement of arbitral awards as well as recognition and enforcements of judgments in civil and commercial matters. In this section, I will discuss the arrangements concerning recognition and enforcements of judgments in civil and commercial matters in detail. I will get back to the rest of the arrangements later in Recommendation 6 of Chapter 5.

In 2006, the Mainland and Hong Kong SAR entered into the Arrangement on Reciprocal Recognition and Enforcement of Judgments in Civil and Commercial Matters by the Courts of the Mainland and of the Hong Kong Special Administrative Region Pursuant to Choice of Court Agreements between Parties Concerned (hereinafter, the Mainland–Hong Kong Arrangement). The Mainland–Hong Kong Arrangement is incorporated into the Mainland legal system in the form of judicial interpretation, which is the Interpretation by the Supreme People's Court on the Arrangement on Reciprocal Recognition and Enforcement of Judgments in Civil and Commercial Matters by the Courts of the Mainland and of the Hong Kong Special Administrative Region Pursuant to the Choice of Court Agreements between Parties Concerned. Meanwhile, the Mainland–Hong Kong Arrangement is adopted by Hong Kong SAR through the Mainland Judgments (Reciprocal Enforcement) Ordinance of Hong Kong (the Mainland Judgments Ordinance). In line with the Mainland–Hong Kong Arrangement, it applies to an enforceable final judgment requiring payment of money in a civil and commercial case pursuant to a choice of court agreement in writing.[44] The payment of money requirement entails that the Mainland–Hong Kong Arrangement only governs a particular legal relationship for commercial purposes. That means, employment contracts and contracts to which a natural person acting for personal consumption, family or other non-commercial purposes is a party will be excluded.[45] Besides, there must be a contract in the written form, in which the parties concerned expressly agree that the court in the Mainland or the court in Hong Kong SAR has the exclusive jurisdiction over the disputes.[46] In addition, the judgment seeks that recognition and enforcement should be final and conclusive. It is noteworthy that the court of Hong Kong SAR holds quite different criteria of finality from the Mainland court. It is stipulated under the Civil Procedure Law of PRC[47] that all judgments and written orders of the Supreme People's Court, as well as judgments and written orders that may not be appealed against according to the law or that have not been appealed against within the prescribed time limit, shall be legally effective.[48] The procedure of trial supervision is also stipulated in the Civil Procedure Law, which allowing the original judgment with the legal effect to be reheard all over again under certain circumstances.[49] Accordingly, a Mainland judgment may not be considered final because of the procedure of trial supervision.[50] Nevertheless, that holding was overturned later in *Lee Yau Wing v Lee Shui Kwan*.[51]

In *Lee Yau Wing v Lee Shui Kwan*, the defendant failed at first instance and on appeal to a people's court in the Mainland, and the plaintiff sought summary judgment against the defendant before the Hong Kong court based on the Mainland appeal judgment. The defendant argued that the Mainland judgment was not final and conclusive due to the existence of the Mainland "trial supervision" system and therefore not enforceable in Hong Kong. After having consulted the opinions of legal experts, the Court of Appeal held that a Mainland judgment cannot be deemed as inconclusive and not final simply because of the existence of the "trial supervision" system under PRC law *per se*.[52] Later in *Shenzhen City Liangzi Jingshun Investment Management Co., Ltd. v Huang Binghuang and Another*, the plaintiff was a Mainland company, which filed the petition against Huang and Hong Kong Zhongxing (a Hong Kong company) to resolve contract disputes. Meanwhile, there were also parallel proceedings between the plaintiff and the defendants in the Mainland and the plaintiff petitioned to the High People's Court of Guangdong Province for re-trial of the

Mainland appeal, and thus claimed that the Mainland judgment was not final and conclusive and therefore not enforceable in Hong Kong. Her Honour Judge Marlene NG referred to the judgment in *Lee Yau Wing v Lee Shui Kwan*, holding:

> [I]n my view, the legal effect of the PRC Judgment is not a simple matter and should not be dealt with in summary way. Given (a) PRC law is a matter of fact to be proved by PRC legal experts, (b) there is fundamental conflict between the PRC expert opinion adduced by the Plaintiff and that by HK Zhongxing as to the effect of re-trial on the PRC Judgment and on the assignment of the HK Zhongxing Debt, (c) the guidance in the above authorities that such issue should be resolved at trial, (d) the dissenting judgment of Chung J in *Lee Yau Wing* to the effect that the trial supervision or re-trial system under PRC law did not undermine the final and conclusive nature of any PRC appeal judgment under the two-tier court system, I am convinced that HK Zhongxing's assertion of there being a valid and effective assignment of the HK Zhongxing Debt in its favour to buttress the defence of set-off has real prospect of success and should be left to trial.[53]

It seems that from the judicial points of view in Hong Kong, the "trial supervision" system under the Mainland law *per se* should not render a Mainland judgment inconclusive and not final. Furthermore, given the fact that the discrepancy of the concept of finality between the two sides is crucial to the system of recognition of cross-border judgments, a compromise has been made in signing the Mainland–Hong Kong Arrangement, in which the term "final and conclusive" is avoided; instead the concept of "final judgment with enforceability" is used. In the Mainland Judgments Ordinance, instead of applying the term "final judgment with enforceability", being final and conclusive is still set out as a compulsory condition for enforcing Mainland judgments. Although some scholars cast some doubts (Smart, 2005; Zhang, 2009) Ms. Tsang of the Department of Justice took the view that "under the Ordinance a Mainland judgment is final and conclusive if it falls into the enumerated list where no appeal is allowed or the time limit for appeal has expired or it is the decision of the second instance" (Tsang, 2008). Accordingly, as for civil and commercial disputes covered by the Mainland–Hong Kong Arrangement, the existence of the trial supervisory system will not prevent Mainland judgments from being recognized and enforced in Hong Kong, although they may not strictly fit the common law concept of finality. As for the judgments stay out of the regime, uncertainty is still awaiting because they depend on fluid judicial decisions in the respective jurisdictions instead of solid mutual arrangements.

In 2006, the Mainland and Macao SAR also entered into the Arrangement Between the Mainland and the Macao Special Administrative Region on the Mutual Recognition and Enforcement of Civil and Commercial Judgments (hereinafter, the Mainland–Macao Arrangement). Compared to the Mainland–Hong Kong Arrangement, the Mainland–Macao Arrangement improves cooperation of mutual recognition and enforcement of civil and commercial judgments in a more advanced way. First of all, the scope of the mutual recognition and enforcement between the Macao SAR and the Mainland is much wider, which is not limited to commercial purposes, including labor disputes and the compensation judgments or verdicts of criminal cases.[54] Secondly, there is no choice of court agreement requirement. The courts of Macao SAR and the Mainland with competent jurisdictions can recognize and enforce the judgments in civil and commercial matters of each other upon the request of the applicant.[55] As for the trial supervision system in the Mainland, it did not cause any problem with respect to the finality requirement under the Mainland–Macao

Arrangement. Moreover, in a case handed down by the Court of Final Appeal of Macao SAR, a Mainland judgment was granted recognition although it was being subject to the supervision trial procedure in the Mainland.[56]

Recognition in accordance with the local rules

Given the limited scope of the bilateral legal cooperation arrangements, each region simultaneously applies its own local rules to recognition and enforcement of interregional civil and commercial judgments. In the Mainland, the problems are mainly solved by the Supreme People's Court through its judicial interpretations. In 2008, the Supreme People's Court released a judicial interpretation, Notice of the Supreme People's Court on Issuing the Minutes of the Symposium on the Trial of Commercial Cases involving Hong Kong or Macao by Courts Nationwide.[57] In accordance with that judicial interpretation, acceptance of commercial cases involving Hong Kong SAR and Macao SAR should refer to the Civil Procedure Law of the PRC, which deals with special rules on foreign-related civil proceedings, and Provisions of the Supreme People's Court Concerning the Jurisdiction Problems of Foreign-related Civil and Commercial Cases.[58] Nevertheless, after reunification, it is somewhat ironic to continue to apply foreign-related rules to SARs, which reflects a continuing dilemma regarding the status of SARs in the area of cross-border civil and commercial judicial interaction in China. Despite political and economic integration, a corresponding legislative and judicial approach remains to be filled.

There are two main venues for a foreign civil and commercial judgment to be enforced in Hong Kong, i.e. statute and common law. Judgments from the courts of most countries will be enforced on the basis of common law. The exception is where a country has been designated under the Foreign Judgments (Reciprocal Enforcement) Ordinance (Cap 319) (the FJREO). The FJREO implemented in Hong Kong what was primarily an intra-Commonwealth scheme for reciprocal enforcement of judgments (Smart, 2005). Under the FJREO, a foreign judgment creditor may apply to the Court of First Instance to register a foreign judgment in Hong Kong. A registered foreign judgment has the same force and effect as a judgment issued by the registering court. After registration, the foreign judgment can be enforced as a Hong Kong judgment (Huang, 2010). The foreign countries listed on the schedule of the FJREO are somehow limited. Pursuant to the Preamble of Cap 319 s 2 FJREO, those countries are Commonwealth countries as are specified in the First Schedule of FJRECO, including Australia and Australian external territories, Bermuda, Brunei, India, Malaysia, New Zealand, Singapore and Sri Lanka (see Cap 319A, Sch. 1). The provisions of FJREO shall also extend to judgments given in the superior courts of any of the countries specified in the Second Schedule. They are Belgium, France, Germany, Italy, Austria, the Netherlands and Israel (see Cap 319A, Sch. 2). The Mainland, Macao SAR and Taiwan remain out of the scope of the statute and the judgments from those regions are generally recognized and enforced in accordance with common law, which means a judgment can be enforced pursuant to common law by bringing an action in the Hong Kong courts as a "foreign" judgment. The situation was partly improved after the Mainland–Hong Kong Arrangement was passed by the Legislative Council of Hong Kong SAR. The aforementioned Mainland Judgments Ordinance (Cap 597) came into effect in August 2008. From then on, Mainland judgments that fall within the ambit of the Mainland–Hong Kong Arrangement can be registered in Hong Kong provided that they meet certain conditions.[59] Once registered, they shall be of the same effect as if they had been a judgment originally given in the Court of First Instance of Hong Kong SAR and entered on the day of registration.[60]

In practice, it has been observed by one scholar that Macao courts usually do not refuse to recognize the judgments rendered in the Mainland but usually not on the basis of the Mainland–Macao Arrangement (Tu, 2013). According to Tu, "the Mainland–Macao Arrangement has been totally ignored by some judges and largely not applied by Macao courts as a whole" (Tu, 2013). Recognition of civil judgments is regularly governed by Article 1200-I of Civil Procedure Code of Macao (CPCM). Among the challenges that a foreign judgment could meet when seeking recognition in Macao SAR is the possibility of substantial review of the judgment, which involves review of the merits of a foreign judgment. The substantial review shall be initiated by a proper objection if new critical evidence refers to something that was unknown to the parties or has not been used in the judgment-rendering proceeding but can change the existing judgment into one more favorable to the losing party.[61] However, it rarely happens in practice. This is probably because the respondent has to respond to a judgment recognition and enforcement application within 15 days,[62] and might not have sufficient time to find some critical new evidence. The other possibility to cause substantial review is when a judgment is against a Macao resident, according to Macao conflict of laws, Macao substantive law should have been applied to solve the dispute, and the application of Macao substantive law leads to a judgment more favorable to the Macao resident compared to the foreign judgment.[63] This article reflects Macao's protectionism towards its residents. The underlying policy is that the Macao resident, who is the losing party, should receive the same treatment in the judgment-rendering court as he or she would receive in the Macao court if the action took place in Macao. In terms of formal review, the courts of Macao SAR shall ex officio just examine whether items a) and f) of Article 1200-I CPCM have been satisfied and the rest of the criteria shall be presumed to have been satisfied in the absence of evidence provided by the respondent to prove the contrary. That kind of judicial opinion was also held by the Court of Final Appeal of Macao SAR in the case No. TUI-S-43-2009-VC (in Chinese).[64] However, after checking the files or exercising its duties, if the courts can find out and verify the lack of items b), c), d) and e), the courts shall also ex officio refuse to render recognition.[65]

Legal cooperation between the Mainland and Taiwan

Bilateral arrangement

In 2009, the Mainland and Taiwan entered into the Agreement between Both Sides of the Taiwan Strait on Jointly Fighting against Crimes and Mutual Judicial Assistance (the Mainland–Taiwan Agreement). The Mainland–Taiwan Agreement contains 24 articles and lays more emphasis on cooperation related to criminal cases. It merely provides one article (Article 10) with respect to recognition and enforcement of civil judgments and arbitral awards, which shall be granted based on the principle of reciprocity without violating public order or good morals.

Recognition in accordance with the local rules

In 2009, the Supreme People's Court promulgated the Supplementary Provisions of the Supreme People's Court on the People's Courts' Recognition of Civil Judgments of the Relevant Courts of the Taiwan Region (hereinafter the Supplementary Provisions). The Supplementary Provisions firstly state that the civil judgments rendered in Taiwan that have been recognized by the people's courts have the same effect as those made by the people's courts.

If the execution applicant petitions for the enforcement of the recognized civil judgment, the people's court should accept the application, which means, from then on, the civil judgments made by the courts of Taiwan can be enforced in the Mainland. On 29 June 2015, the Supreme People's Court issued a more extensive judicial interpretation concerning recognition and enforcement of civil judgments rendered by Taiwan courts.[66] That judicial interpretation replaced the former four related judicial interpretation in matters of cross-strait legal cooperation.[67] The current judicial interpretation has extensive scope concerning the judgments that can request for recognition before the Mainland court, including the effective judgments, verdicts, mediation agreements and orders to pay as well as the judgments and the verdicts relating to civil damages compensation involved in criminal cases.[68] To facilitate the applicant to file a petition, the current judicial interpretation also allows more competent Mainland courts to seize the request, including the intermediate courts or specialized courts either at the domicile or habitual residence of the respondent or at the place where the asset is located.[69] The civil judgments that request for recognition should be verified as genuine and effective. The current judicial interpretation provides two means of verification. The applicant can request the Mainland court to verify the Taiwan judgment through the channel of cross-strait mutual judicial assistance in terms of serving legal documents, investigation and evidence collection. The Mainland court can ex officio verify the Taiwan judgment through the same channel.[70] If recognition of civil judgments will violate the fundamental principles of national laws, including the one country principle, or be detrimental to socio-public interests, the people's courts shall refuse to grant recognition.[71] Against the aforementioned complicated historical, political and economic background, diverse legal arrangements were established to recognize the civil judgments of different origins. The Mainland judgments shall be recognized pursuant to the Act Governing Relations between Peoples of the Taiwan Area and the Mainland Area (the Mainland Act), whereas the judgments of Hong Kong SAR and Macao SAR shall be recognized in accordance with the Act Governing Relations with Hong Kong and Macao (the Hong Kong and Macao Act).

Pursuant to the Article 74 of the Mainland Act, an application must be filed to a Taiwan court for a ruling to recognize the Mainland judgment. Meanwhile, two principles shall be applied for recognition, one is the preservation of public order or good morals (Article 74–1) and the other is the principle of reciprocity (Article 74–3). Public order or good morals is a vague concept. Some fear that its flexibility and the uncertain relationship between the Mainland and Taiwan will probably bring unpredictability to the recognition and enforcement of court judgments from the Mainland (Chen, 2002; Liu, 2009; Yu, 2010). In practice, however, the preservation of the public order or good morals seems to have been rarely applied (Huang, 2009). Many recognition application submitted to Taiwan's courts are related to the divorce judgments. The courts tend to recognize a divorce judgment although the parties concerned filed against Mainland decisions based on "fraud marriage", "not in accordance with Taiwan's Civil Code", "protectionism of the Mainland courts" etc. On the contrary, if the parties concerned have not been given the opportunity to take part in the proceeding and failed in the Mainland cases, the court will probably refuse to recognize the divorce judgments. For example, the party concerned was in prison and not able to attend the hearing in the Mainland court or the address of the party concerned was not absolutely clear, therefore the Mainland court could not inform him via service of notice by publication.[72] It can be concluded from the aforementioned cases that in general the Taiwan's courts follow the formal examination on the Mainland judgment recognition. The courts in Taiwan incline to utilize the preservation of public order or good morals as the shield to safeguard due process rather than interfering with substantial controversies.

The principle of reciprocity (Article 74–3) was amended in Article 74 of the Mainland Act on 14 May, 1997 and implemented from 1 July, 1997 by the Order of the Executive Yuan. In the Supreme Court judgment No. 2644 (1997), the Taiwan Supreme Court partly reversed the original judgment and remanded the case back to the original court, holding that besides the check of public order or good morals, before giving recognition to a mainland civil judgment, the lower court shall also take into necessary consideration whether the judgment made by a court in Taiwan may be recognized by the Mainland court in accordance with Article 74–3 of the Mainland Act. This is a typical "you scratch my back and I scratch yours" approach, which has been criticized even by local scholars for a long time (Chen, 1996; Chen, 2001). However, it is not hard to understand, because in 1997 cross-strait judicial interaction was still in its infancy. The reason for the amendment was written in the amendment order, stating it was unfair that an irrevocable civil ruling or judgment, or an arbitral award rendered in the Taiwan Area, still failed to receive recognition from the Mainland courts on the basis of mutual benefit. Therefore, Article 74–3 was amended in the Mainland Act in order to make the Chinese Authority aware of the issues of cross-strait judicial assistance, find solutions in good faith and protect the legal systems from both sides in favor of the individuals' interests. Nevertheless, cross-strait judicial cooperation has to develop hand in hand with cross-strait relations. For instance, thanks to the three-direct links implemented in 2008, the Supreme People's Court issued its judicial interpretation in the same year, in which judicial documents can for the first time be served directly to Taiwan by mail if the litigant has a definite address in Taiwan.[73]

With efforts made by both sides, cross-strait judicial assistance gradually moved forward. In the case of Taiwan Taipei District Court Application No. 2507 (2005), the court held that the judgment made by the High People's Court of Beijing Municipal did not violate public order or good morals and irrevocable civil ruling or judgment, or that arbitral awards rendered in the Taiwan Area were already able to be applied for the recognition to the Mainland courts. Therefore, the court finally recognized the judgment. Later the same parties concerned in the case got involved in the rehearing procedure of the former case in Beijing. After the High People's Court of Beijing Municipal reheard the case, the litigant came back to the Taipei District Court again and applied for the judgment recognition. The court recognized the judgment for the same reason.[74] The case was appealed to the Taiwan High Court. The High Court agreed with the lower court and turned down the appeal.[75] Nevertheless, Article 74 of the Mainland Act does not clarify what kind of effect will be generated after an irrevocable judgment rendered in the Mainland Area has been recognized in Taiwan, which resulted in controversies in theory in Taiwan. Someone argued that res judicata was not stimulated in the People's Civil Procedural Law promulgated on 9 April, 1991 in the Mainland. Therefore, it was questionable whether the courts of Taiwan should recognize the res judicata of the Mainland judgment (Chen, 2001). Some held the positive opinion, which is, if the parties concerned have been given a complete procedural guarantee in the Mainland Area, the related judgment shall have the legitimacy to be recognized as res judicata (Jiang, 2009). In practice, the point was made clear in 2007 when the Taiwan Supreme Court made decisions regarding this issue in the case between Zhejiang Textiles Import & Export Group Co., Ltd. (Zhejiang Textiles) and Evergreen International Storage and Transport Corp. (Evergreen). Zhejiang Textiles filed a petition against Uniglory Marine Corporation (which was later merged into Evergreen) in Shanghai. Zhejiang Textiles won after the second instance and received the irrevocable judgments in Shanghai and came to Taiwan for recognition. There were a series of judgments regarding the same dispute between the same parties concerned made by the Taiwan courts.[76] It is noteworthy that the Supreme Court clearly held that

> In accordance with the article 74 of the Mainland Act, where an irrevocable civil ruling or judgment rendered in the Mainland Area recognized by a court's ruling requires performance, it may merely serve as a writ of execution, *whereas it is not specified in the article that the irrevocable civil ruling or judgment rendered in the Mainland Area shall be considered the same validity as irrevocable civil ruling or judgment rendered in Taiwan* . . . However, the irrevocable civil ruling or judgment rendered in the Mainland Area shall only be recognized by the way of the ruling of Taiwan courts and shall only have the effect of execution instead of the same validity as irrevocable civil ruling or judgment rendered in Taiwan.[77]
>
> (emphasis added by the author)

After this Supreme Court decision, this case was turned all over again. Without the validity of the Mainland judgments, the Mainland party concerned failed to receive the recognition in Taiwan after having experienced six tortuous rounds of civil actions. The judgment of the Taiwan Supreme Court No. 2531 (2007) is indeed a turning point of cross-strait legal cooperation. The res judicata is the fundamental element of the judgment recognition. If the res judicata of the judgment is denied, that judgment could hardly be considered as recognized. The non-recognition of res judicata of the Mainland judgment in Taiwan could probably leave the effect of the Mainland judgment in uncertainty and its side effect on cross-strait legal cooperation can be anticipated (see Chapter 3). In 2009, the Mainland and Taiwan entered into Agreement between Both Sides of the Taiwan Strait on Jointly Fighting against Crimes and Mutual Judicial Assistance (the Mainland–Taiwan Agreement). The Mainland–Taiwan Agreement contains 24 articles and lays more emphasis on cooperation related to criminal cases. Article 10 of the Mainland–Taiwan Agreement provides that recognition and enforcement of civil judgments and arbitral awards shall be granted based on the principle of reciprocity without violating public order or good morals, which is identical to Article 74 of the Mainland Act. So far, no relevant decision has been rendered on the basis of the Mainland–Taiwan Agreement.

Parallel to the Mainland civil and commercial judgment recognition system provided for in the Mainland Act, it is stated in Article 42 of the Hong Kong and Macao Act that

> In determining the conditions for the *validity*, jurisdiction, and enforceability of civil judgments made in Hong Kong or Macao, Article 402 of the Code of Civil Procedure and Article 4–1 of the Compulsory Execution Law shall apply *mutatis mutandis*.
>
> (emphasis added by the author)

Article 56 of the Hong Kong Act also states that: "Mutual judicial assistance between the Taiwan Area and Hong Kong or Macao shall be conducted on a reciprocal basis." Article 402 of the Taiwan Code of Civil Procedure stipulates the recognition of the final and binding judgment rendered by a foreign court and Article 4–1 of the Compulsory Execution Law deals with the application for the writ of execution to enforce the foreign judgment or ruling. Therefore, it is obvious that the rules applied to the recognition of the civil decisions made by the Hong Kong courts are almost the same as those employed in foreign civil judgments in Taiwan. Different rules of the parallel judgments recognition result in different procedures. A preliminary proceeding shall be initiated for the recognition of Mainland civil judgments, whereas irrevocable civil judgments rendered in SARs enjoy the same automatic recognition procedure as foreign civil decisions (Chen, 2001; Jiang, 2009). It is also clearly stated that judgments rendered in the SARs shall be considered as the same validity in Taiwan. In an aforementioned judgment, the Taiwan Supreme Court decided that:

> Pursuant to article 402 of the Code of Civil Procedure, an irrevocable civil ruling or judgment rendered in foreign countries or in Hong Kong, Macao shall follow the mode of automatic recognition, i.e. once meeting the requirement of recognition, the validity of the irrevocable civil ruling or judgment shall be automatically recognized without the recognition ruling. However, the irrevocable civil ruling or judgment rendered in the Mainland Area shall only be recognized by the way of the ruling of Taiwan courts and shall only have the effect of execution instead of the same validity as irrevocable civil ruling or judgment rendered in Taiwan.[78]

Taiwan's parallel judgment recognition system and its non-recognition of res judicata of the Mainland judgment cause the uneven treatment towards the Mainland, Hong Kong SAR and Macao SAR, which now belong to one sovereignty. This kind of differentiated legal arrangement may increase the difficulty of cross-border legal cooperation.

Conclusion

The "one country, two systems" principle enabled China to resume its sovereignty over Hong Kong and Macao. Meanwhile, the two regions are also vested with a high degree of autonomy, which means the SARs, in accordance with the Basic Law, shall be vested with executive power, legislative power and independent judicial power, including that of final adjudication. Due to the implementation of CEPA, a regional common market in China is also emerging. In addition, there is a politically disputed region, Taiwan, which has its own executive power, legislative power and judicial power but has close economic contacts with Mainland China. After reunification, China becomes a country with mixed jurisdictions, including both civil law and common law, and its diverse legal characteristics are guaranteed by the Basic Law. A cross-border legal cooperation framework in matters of civil and commercial disputes

Table 2.1 Table of Outflow and Inflow between Taiwan and the Mainland

Statistics on Approved Taiwan Investment in the Mainland			*Statistics on Approved Mainland Investment in Taiwan*	
Year	*Case*	*Amount (unit: $1000)*	*Case*	*Amount (unit: $1000)*
2009	249	6,058,497	23	37,486
2010	518	12,230,146	79	94,345
2011	575	13,100,871	102	43,736
2012	454	10,924,406	138	328,067
2013	440	8,684,904	141	360,884
2014	388	9,829,805	136	334,631
2015	321	10,398,224	170	244,067

(Data collected from www.moeaic.gov.tw)

came into existence. However, compared to the active economic interaction among the four regions, the legal cooperation system is relatively insufficient. It lacks comprehensive rules concerning recognition and enforcement of civil and commercial cases throughout the whole regions. Instead, cooperation is conducted in the form of bilateral arrangements. Moreover, those arrangements merely provide cooperation in some selected areas, such as service of documents, recognition and enforcement of arbitral awards as well as civil and commercial judgments. With respect to recognition and enforcement of judgments, those bilateral arrangements are not open to all kinds of civil and commercial cases and the local rules apply for those left uncovered, which result in uncertainty in the course of cooperation. In particular, in Taiwan, the local rules provide different treatment of civil and commercial judgments rendered in different places. The implication for lack of comprehensive regional cross-border legal cooperation is that the cross-border economic participants among the four regions have to conduct their business seemingly in a jungle. Cross-border insolvency proceedings raise more such concern because they, according to the IMF, shall be responsible for the allocation of risk among participants in a market economy on a predictable, equitable, and transparent manner, whereas the absence of regional arrangements on cross-border insolvency proceedings could jeopardize long-term economic stability and cooperative relationship.[79]

Notes

1 Hong Kong SAR, in south-eastern China, covers 1,104 square kilometers, including Hong Kong Island, Lantau Island, the Kowloon Peninsula and the New Territories. Hong Kong SAR's population was approximately 7.15 million in 2012. People of Chinese descent comprise the vast majority of the population, with foreign nationals comprising 5%.

2 Macao SAR consists of the Macao peninsula and the two islands of Taipa and Coloane and covers an area of 29.2 square kilometers. The population of Macao was estimated to be around 607,500 in 2013. More than 95% of the population speaks Chinese. Portuguese is spoken by about 0.6% and the remainder speaks English, Filipino or other languages.

3 Under the Convention for the Extension of Hong Kong Territory, which was a lease signed between Qing Dynasty and the UK in 1898, the territories north of Boundary Street and south of the Sham Chun River, and the surrounding islands, later known as the "New Territories" were leased to the UK for 99 years, expiring on 30 June, 1997 and became part of the crown colony of Hong Kong.

4 Throughout this book, the Mainland (China) purely serves as a geographic term to describe the geopolitical area under the jurisdiction of the People's Republic of China (PRC), generally excluding the PRC Special Administrative Regions of Hong Kong and Macao. The Mainland is located in the east of the Asian continent covering 9,600,000 square kilometers. The population was over 1.33 billion in 2010 according to the sixth national population census, which is the latest population census so far.

5 Basic Law of HKSAR, Article 19; Basic Law of Macao SAR, Article 19.

6 Basic Law of HKSAR, Article 81; Basic Law of Macao SAR, Article 84.

7 Basic Law of HKSAR, Article 58; Basic Law of Macao SAR, Article143.

8 Basic Law of HKSAR, Articles 8, 18; Basic Law of Macao SAR, Articles 8, 18.

9 Basic Law of HKSAR, Articles 16, 17, 19; Basic Law of Macao SAR, Articles 16, 17, 19.

10 Basic Law of HKSAR, Articles 106, 111, 114, 116, 151; Basic Law of Macao SAR, Articles 104, 106, 108, 115, 118.

11 The Treaty of Paris (European Coal and Steel Community, 1951); the Treaties of Rome (Euratom, EEC, 1957); the Treaty of Maastricht (the EU Treaty, 1992); the Treaty of Amsterdam (1997); the Constitutional Treaty (not entered into force, 2004); the Lisbon Treaty (TEU, TFEU, Charter, Euratom, 2007).

12 Basic Law of HKSAR, Article 5; Basic Law of Macao SAR, Article 5.

13 Basic Law of HKSAR, Article 1; Basic Law of Macao SAR, Article 1.

14 Case C-26/62, *NV Algemene Transport- en Expeditie Onderneming van Gend & Loos v Netherlands Inland Revenue Administration* [1963] ECR 1.

15 Ibid.
16 Basic Law of HKSAR, Article 19; Basic Law of Macao SAR, Article 19.
17 Case C-26/62, *NV Algemene Transport- en Expeditie Onderneming van Gend & Loos v Netherlands Inland Revenue Administration* [1963] ECR 1; Case C-93/71 *Leonesio v Italian Ministry of Agriculture and Forestry* [1972] ECR 287; Case C-403/98 *Azienda Agricola Monte Arcosu Srl v Regione Autonoma della Sardegna, Organismo Comprensoriale n° 24 della Sardegna and Ente Regionale per l'Assistenza Tecnica in Agricoltura (ERSAT)* [2001]; Case C-41/74 *Van Duyn v Home Office* [1974] ECR 1337; Case C-80/86 Criminal Proceedings against Kolpinghuis Nijmegen BV [1987] ECR 3969; Case C-9/70 *Grad v Finanzamt Traunstein* (1970) ECR 825.
18 Basic Law of HKSAR, Article 2; Basic Law of Macao SAR, Article 2.
19 Basic Law of HKSAR, Articles 106, 111, 114, 116, 151; Basic Law of Macao SAR, Articles 104, 108, 110, 112, 136.
20 L' Agence France-Presse (AFP), Taiwan expands shipping links with China, 18 June, 2008. http://archive.is/h78t#selection-315.0-315.50 (last accessed on 31 March, 2017).
21 Report from Ministry of Commerce of PRC, Chinese Mainland Registers Trade Deficit of More than $77 billion with Taiwan, visit: www.gwytb.gov.cn/lajm/lajm/201101/t20110121_1718251.htm (last accessed on 31 March, 2017).
22 Ma Ying-jeou, New Year's Day Celebratory Message (in Chinese), 1 January, 2009, available at www.mac.gov.tw/ct.asp?xItem=50076&ctNode=5909&mp=3&xq_xCat=2009 (last accessed on 31 March, 2017).
23 The list of the goods is available at www.ecfa.org.tw/90_2.htm (last accessed on 31 March, 2017).
24 Explanation Concerning the Signing of the Cross-Strait Economic Cooperation Framework Agreement, 24 June, 2010, available at www.mac.gov.tw/ct.asp?xItem=85683&ctNode=5921&mp=3 (last accessed on 31 March, 2017).
25 Supplement I – IX to CEPA, 1. Business Services, A. Professional Services, b. accounting, auditing and bookkeeping services.
26 SFC commences legal proceedings against Ernst & Young over access to accounting records, available at: www.sfc.hk/edistributionWeb/gateway/EN/news-and-announcements/news/doc?refNo=12PR92 (last accessed on 31 March, 2017).
27 CEPA Hong Kong & CEPA Macao, Article 19(3).
28 Ibid., Article 19(5).
29 ECFA, Article 11.
30 Ibid.
31 On 18 April, 2012, Ministry of Commerce of PRC and Ministry of Economic Affairs of Taiwan declared the implementation measures of establishment of offices across the Taiwan Strait, www.moeaic.gov.tw/system_external/ctlr?PRO=PrintFriendlyNews&id=823 (last accessed on 31 March, 2017).
32 The Basic Law of HKSAR, Articles 8, 160; Decision of the Standing Committee of the National People's Congress Concerning the Handling of the Laws Previously in Force in Hong Kong in Accordance with Article 160 of the Basic Law of the Hong Kong Special Administrative Region of the PRC.
33 Basic Law of HKSAR, Article 84.
34 Ibid., Article 92.
35 Ibid., Article 158.
36 For instance, *Ng Ka Ling & Another v Director of Immigration* [1999] HKCFA 72; *Tsui Kuen Nang v Director of Immigration* [1999] HKCFA 73; *Director of Immigration v Kan Hung Cheung and Others* [2004] HKCFA 83.
37 Basic Law of HKSAR, Article 158.
38 The population of Macao SAR can be divided into: Portuguese at the senior levels; Mecanese (descendants principally of marriages or liaisons between Portuguese and Chinese) at the middle level; these two groups make up around 3% of the total population in Macao and the rest are the local Chinese, who had been excluded from any role in policy or administration.
39 Decree No. 5/86/M, Article 3, 1986/1/25, visit http://bo.io.gov.mo/ (last accessed on 31 March, 2017).
40 The Basic Law of Macao SAR, Article 93.

41 For example, in 1999, there were over 300 cases heard by the intermediate courts. In 2008, there were more than 4,800 cases. Please see the annual report made by the director of the Court of Final Appeal, www.court.gov.mo/c/cdefault.htm (last accessed on 31 March, 2017) In accordance with the amendment to Macao Judicial Organic Law in 2009, the number of the judges has been increased, i.e. 32 judges in the courts of first instance, nine in the intermediate courts.

42 The Judicial Yuan is in charge of civil, criminal and administrative trial, the punishment of government officials and has the power of interpretation of the constitution and other laws.

43 The only exception is the administrative law, which has not been made into code. The administrative legal system in Taiwan is a law collection of internal affairs, land, finance, economy, education, personnel etc.

44 Mainland–Hong Kong Arrangement, Article 1.

45 Ibid., Article 3.

46 Ibid.

47 Please note that the Civil Procedure Law of the PRC was revised in 2007 and 2012. The version in effect at that time was Civil Procedure Law of the PRC (1991).

48 Civil Procedure Law of the PRC (1991), Article 141.

49 Ibid., Chapter 16, Articles 177, 178, 185.

50 *Chiyu Banking Corporation Ltd. v Chan Tin Kwun* [1966] 1 HKLR 395; *Tan Tay Cuan v Ng Chi Hung*, unrep. HCA 5477/2000 (5/2/2001); *Wu Wei v Liu Yi Ping* HCA 1452/2004.

51 *Lee Yau Wing v Lee Shui Kwan* [2005] HKCA 657, at 77.

52 Ibid., at 75.

53 *Shenzhen City Liangzi Jingshun Investment Management Co., Ltd. v Huang Binghuang and Another* [2011] HKCFI 70.

54 Mainland–Macao Arrangement, Articles 1, 3.

55 Ibid., Article 3.

56 Case 6/2010 of CFA, Macao SAR.

57 [2008] Judicial Interpretation No. 8.

58 [2002] Judicial Interpretation No. 5.

59 Cap.597, Section 5.

60 Ibid., Section 14.

61 Macao Civil Procedure Code, Article 1202-I.

62 Ibid.

63 Macao Civil Procedure Code, Article 1202-II.

64 The Judicial Opinions of the High Court of Macao, Vol. 1, 1998, p. 88.

65 Macao Civil Procedure Code, Article 1204.

66 [2015] Judicial Interpretation No. 13.

67 The repealed four judicial interpretations are: the Provisions of the Supreme People's Court on the People's Court's Recognition of the Verdicts on Civil Cases Made by Courts of Taiwan [1998] Judicial Interpretation No. 11; the Reply of the Supreme People's Court on whether the People's Court should Accept the Application for Recognition of Mediation Agreement Rendered by the Taiwan Court or the Authorities Concerned [1999] Judicial Interpretation No. 10; the Reply of the Supreme People's Court on whether the People's Court should Accept the Application for Recognition of Orders to Pay Rendered by the Taiwan Court [2001] Judicial Interpretation No. 13; Supplementary Provisions of the Supreme People's Court on the People's Courts' Recognition of Civil Judgments of the Relevant Courts of the Taiwan Region [2009] Judicial Interpretation No. 4.

68 [2015] Judicial Interpretation No. 13, Article 2.

69 Ibid., Article 4.

70 Ibid., Article 9.

71 Ibid., Article 15.

72 Taiwan High Court Family Ruling Appeal No. 316 (2003), Taiwan High Court Family Ruling Appeal No. 268 (2001), Taiwan High Court Family Ruling Appeal No. 179 (2001); Taiwan High Court Tainan Branch Court Family Ruling Appeal No. 63 (2004); Taiwan High Court Tainan Branch Court Family Ruling Appeal No. 31 (2001); Taiwan High Court Family Ruling Appeal No. 355 (2003); Taiwan High Court Family Ruling Appeal No. 366 (2002).

73 [2008] Judicial Interpretation No. 4, Article 3(5).

74 Taiwan Taipei District Court Application No. 2146 [2007].
75 Taiwan High Court Non-Ruling Appeal No. 76 [2008].
76 Taiwan Taoyuan District Court Application No. 1032 [2004]; Taiwan Taoyuan District Court Re-Action No. 208 [2005]; Taiwan High Court Re-Appeal No. 175 [2007]; Taiwan Supreme Court No. 2531 [2007]; Taiwan High Court Retrial No. 210 [2007]; Taiwan Supreme Court No. 2376 [2008].
77 Taiwan Supreme Court Appeal No. 2531 [2007].
78 Ibid.
79 IMF Legal Department, Orderly & Effective Insolvency Procedures: Key Issues, 1999, available at www.imf.org/external/pubs/ft/orderly/#genobj (last accessed on 31 March, 2017).

Reference list

In English

Banyan, "Students in the House", in: , *The Economist*, 20. Mar. ch, 2014, www.economist.com/blogs/banyan/2014/03/politics-taiwan

Chalmers, Damian, Davies, Gareth &, Monti, Giorgio, *European Union Law* (2nd ed.), Cambridge University Press, 2010

Chen Jianfu, *Chinese Law: Context and Transformation*, Leiden; Boston: Martinus Nijhoff Publishers, 2008

Ghai, Yash P., *Hong Kong's New Constitutional Order: The Resumption of Chinese Sovereignty and the Basic Law*, Hong Kong: HK University Press, 1999

Ghai, Yash P., "The Intersection of Chinese Law and the Common Law in the Hong Kong Special Administrative Region: Question of Technique or Politics?" in: 37 HKLJ 363, 2007

Huang Jie, Interregional Recognition and Enforcement of Civil and Commercial Judgments: Lessons for China from US and EU Laws, Duke Law Theses and Dissertations, Paper 1, 2010, available at http://scholarship.law.duke.edu/etd/1

Silk, Mitchell A., "Silent Partner", in: *China Business Review*, Vol. 17, 1990

Smart, Philip, "Finality and the Enforcement of Foreign Judgments under the Common Law in Hong Kong", 5 *Oxford University Commonwealth Law Journal*, 2005

Tang Jizong, *The Cross-strait Strait Economic and Scientific Cooperation and the Opportunities for Macao's Sustainable Development*, Macao: Chinese Culture Exchange Association, 2006

Tsang, Michelle, "A New Chapter in Reciprocal Enforcement of Judgments between the Mainland and Hong Kong", *Hong Kong Lawyer*, July 2008

Tu Guangjian, "Arrangement on Mutual Recognition and Enforcement of Judgments in Civil and Commercial Matters between China and Macau: Inherent Problems, Six Years' Experience and the Way Forward", 43 Hong Kong L. J., 349, 2013, p.349, 374

Wang Wei, "CEPA: A Lawful Free Trade Agreement under "One Country, Two Customs Territories?"", in: , 10 Law & Bus. Rev. Am. 647, 2004, p. 649

Wen Qing, "'One Country, Two Systems': The Best Way to Peaceful Reunification", in: , Beijing Review, 2009, available at: www.bjreview.com.cn/nation/txt/2009-05/26/content_197568.htm

Zhang Xianchu, "A New Stage of Regional Judicial Assistance in Civil and Commercial Matters: Implementation of the Mainland Judgments Ordinance and Certain Issues Beyond", in:, 39 HKLJ 3, 2009

In Chinese

Chen Li, "Mutual Recognition and Enforcement of the Cross-Strait Civil Judgments: Difficulty and Solution", *The Rule of Law Forum*, Vol. 17, issue 5, 2002

Chen Qichui, "Recognition and Enforcement of the Foreign Judgments", *Journal of New Perspectives on Law*, issue 75, 2001

Chen Rongzong, "Legal Issues of International Civil Procedural Law", *China Law Journal*, issue 162, 1996, p. 10

Gu Lixia, "The Culture and Public Policy of Social Associations in Macao", *Administration*, Vol. 70, 2005

Han Changyin, "The Development and Legal Issues of Chinese Bankruptcy Law", *Law Science Magazine*, Vol. 25, 2004

Huang Kuo-Chang, "A Beautiful Mistake: Has the Recognized Mainland Judgment Res Judicata?", *Taiwan Law Review*, issue 167, 2009

Jian Bingda, "The Laws under the Bilingual System", *Administration*, Vol. 26, 1994

Jiang Shi-ming, "Recognition and Enforcement of the Irrevocable Civil Judgments Rendered in the Mainland Area", *Taiwan Law Journal*, issue 123, 2009

Jiao Hongchang, "Studies of Macao SAR Basic Law", 1 *Tribune of Political Science and Law*, 1999

Liu Renshan, "Current Situation, Problems and Thinking regarding the Recognition and Enforcement of the Commercial Judgments between the Mainland and Taiwan", *Wuhan University Journal (Philosophy & Social Sciences)*, Vol. 62, issue 6, 2009

Liu Zuyun, "Case Study on the Political Function of Associations in Macao", *Studies on Hong Kong and Macao*, 2010/01

Mi Jian, *The Laws of Macao*, Beijing: China Friendship Publishing Company, 1996

Wang Shuwen, *Introduction to the Basic Law of the Hong Kong SAR*, Beijing: Central Committee of the CCP Party School Press, 1997

Wang Zejian, "The Reception of German Civil Law and the Development of Taiwan Civil Law", 6 *Journal of Comparative Law*, 2006

Wang Zhenmin, "The Analysis of the Constitutional Issues in the Implementation of the "One Country, Two Systems" Policy", 4 *Studies in Law and Business*, 2000

Wu Guochang, "The Localization of the Laws in Macao during the Late Transition Period", 28, *Administration*, 1995

Xian Peiwen, "Rights and Obligations in the Legal Language", *Administration*, Vol. 36, 1997

Xiao Weiyun, "The Relationship of the Constitution of PRC and the Basic Law of the Hong Kong SAR", in: Xiao Weiyun, *Theories of Hong Kong Basic Law*, Beijing: Peking University Press, 2003

Xie Huaishi, "Commentary of laws in force in Hong Kong and the Study of Issues on Laws of Hong Kong", 1 *Law Review*, 1988

Yu Fei, "The Appropriate Application of the Reservation of Public Order", *Taiwan Research Journal*, p. 11, issue 3, 2010

3 Diverse cross-border insolvency systems among the four regions

Introduction

The main topic of this chapter focuses on what the current cross-border insolvency systems among the four regions are. The chapter is composed of four sections, in which the individual cross-border insolvency system in each region will be introduced and analyzed. For each region, the introduction will start with a general overview of the local insolvency system. Following the introduction, the features and problems of the cross-border insolvency system in each region will be demonstrated in depth through legislation and case law. In the end, comparison and summary of the cross-border insolvency systems among the four regions will be presented in the pre-conclusion.

The Mainland approach

In the Mainland, the development of cross-border insolvency law is interrelated to the reform of the local insolvency system. In this section, the corporate insolvency system of the Mainland is reviewed first, including the history of the corporate insolvency system and a general description of the current insolvency system. Further, the development of the cross-border insolvency system is also briefly addressed. The current cross-border insolvency system is based on one article, the key elements of which are to be analyzed in detail by referring to relevant case law.

Brief introduction to national bankruptcy law

History of the corporate insolvency system of PRC

The former corporate insolvency system was a dual national bankruptcy system according to different types of debtors. It represented struggles between government control and market economy demand, national efforts and local initiatives. With the entry into effect in 2007 of the Enterprise Bankruptcy Law, a comprehensive corporate insolvency system was built up and an era of separate legislation on state and non-state owned corporation insolvency was over.

From 1986 to 2006 the bankruptcy legal system in the Mainland China was composed of the following:

(1) Enterprise Bankruptcy Law (for trial implementation, hereinafter the 1986 EBL);
(2) Civil Procedure Law and Company Law;

(3) Related judicial interpretations;
(4) Policy decrees and administrative regulations;
(5) Local rules and regulations.

These five components reveal that China's former bankruptcy law system was not uniform. Before 1986 there was no bankruptcy law in China. Due to the highly centralized planned economy, state-owned enterprises (hereinafter SOE), which existed and grew under the control of the government, were the main form of economic entity during that period. If a SOE did not do its business well, the government subsidized it to facilitate continued operations (Stevens, 1998). Therefore, it is not surprising that enterprises at that time had no idea about bankruptcy because it hardly happened. For instance, it was not until 3 August, 1986 that Shenyang Province Explosion-proof Equipment Factory became the first bankrupt enterprise in China just before the 1986 EBL was adopted. It is so-called an administrative bankruptcy in accordance with local government decree (1985 No. 24 Shenyang Government) and was in the form of the revocation of business license by the local administrative department for industry and commerce. Nevertheless, the government realized that it was not a long-term solution to keep rescuing SOEs with state finance (Peng, 1986). On 12 December, 1986, the 1986 EBL, the first bankruptcy law of PRC was adopted, which initiated an insolvency regime established on the basis of state-owned economy. First of all, considering the economic structure at that time, the 1986 EBL only applied to SOEs.[1] Secondly, pursuant to the 1986 EBL, the government played a significant role in the bankruptcy proceedings. For instance, a debtor can only apply for bankruptcy upon government approval.[2] Besides, the government was in charge of the whole reconciliation–readjustment procedure.[3] In addition, the government was the statutory member of the liquidation committee.[4] Last, but not the least, employees of the insolvent debtors were highly protected by the 1986 EBL. It was stated in the 1986 EBL that the government should arrange new jobs through various channels for the workers of bankrupt enterprises and guarantee their basic living necessities before they were reemployed.[5]

Due to economic reform, there were tremendous changes in ownership structure through the growth of non-state producers, including collective, private and foreign-invested firms. Chronic loss-making enterprises were closed down or sold off. For instance, the total number of industrial SOEs dropped from 120,000 in the mid-1990 to only 31,750 in 2004 (Naughton, 1995 & 2006). Consequently, the non-state-owned enterprises were gradually incorporated into the bankruptcy system. Adopted on 9 April, 1991, the Civil Procedure Law embraced one new chapter (Chapter XIX), entitled Procedure for Bankruptcy and Debt Repayment of Legal Person Enterprises, which provided the general legal foundation for the bankruptcy of non-state-owned enterprises. In addition, pursuant to Chapter VIII of the Company Law,[6] in which difference of ownership was no longer emphasized,[7] it was required that once the liquidation committee discovered the insolvency, it should apply to the court for a declaration of bankruptcy of the company. If the court declared that the company was bankrupt, the liquidation committee should hand over the liquidation affairs to the court.[8] The Supreme People's Court of PRC attempted to address these problems in practice by issuing several judicial interpretations. In particular, the 2002 Provisions on Bankruptcy Cases,[9] which contained 106 articles (almost three times as long as the bankruptcy law itself), was a very comprehensive interpretation with respect to the 1986 EBL. The highlight of the 2002 Provisions on Bankruptcy Cases was that it applied to both SOEs and non-SOEs,[10] which appeared to be an attempt by the Supreme People's Court to set uniform rules that govern the both (Chua, 2002). The government also promulgated a number of policy decrees and administrative regulations. Those decrees and administrative regulations mainly focused on placement of employees,[11] disposal of the bankruptcy property (especially the right to the use of land, secured claims and bank loans)[12] and rearrangement of the bankrupt enterprises of the SOEs.[13] Some local governments, including provinces and cities, enacted their own local rules and regulations to meet their local needs. For instance, from 1993 to 2006, there were 167 local bankruptcy decrees issued by various levels of governments, most of which related to employee rearrangement.[14]

Current corporate insolvency system of the Mainland and its problems[15]

THE CURRENT EBL

Adopted on 27 August, 2006, the current bankruptcy system in China is established based on the Enterprise Bankruptcy Law (hereafter the EBL), which replaced the former 1986 EBL and came into force on 1 June, 2007. After the EBL came into effect, Chapter XIX of the former Civil Procedure Law was repealed. The content involving bankruptcy was also removed from the former Chapter VIII of the Company Law in 2005. In accordance with Article 190 of the 2013 Company Law, where a company is declared bankrupt according to law, bankruptcy liquidation shall be conducted in accordance with the EBL. Evolving synchronously with economic reform in China, the EBL provides a unified bankruptcy system, covering all types of incorporated enterprises regardless of types of the ownership.[16] The current EBL is also a more debtor-friendly regime. In addition to the liquidation proceedings, it provides reorganization mechanisms for the purpose of giving a second chance to those economically viable but distressed businesses, by referring to the eminent models in other jurisdictions, including, Chapter 11 of the US Bankruptcy Code and German insolvency law (Shi, 2007). In addition, the current EBL introduced a new legal profession, bankruptcy administrators, into China's insolvency system, who are designated to undertake critical administrative functions and supervisory responsibilities.[17] The Supreme People's Court also issued a number of related judicial interpretations as important complementary legal references to the problems in practice, which thus play a crucial role in the current insolvency system. Nevertheless, according to the data released by the Supreme People's Court in 2014, from 2007 when the current EBL was implemented to 2012, the amount of the requests to open insolvency proceedings seized by the courts continue to decrease at an average rate of 12.23% every year (Ma, 2014). In 2012, there were 735,000 domestic enterprises in total that were deregistered or cancelled with the government bureau,[18] but only 20.52% of them utilized judicial insolvency proceedings and one decade ago it was 17.09% higher (Ma, 2014). With more specific and systematic arrangements under the current insolvency system, the reasons that the caseload of insolvency proceedings continues to decline on an annual basis are complicated and multifaceted.

THE COMPETING SYSTEM: PARTICIPATION IN DISTRIBUTION

The EBL, just like its literal meaning, only applies to an enterprise as a legal person (or a legal person enterprise). Liquidation of other organizations (that are not enterprise legal persons)[19] shall be governed mutatis mutandis by the procedure as prescribed under the EBL when they go bankrupt.[20] A natural person is excluded from the scope of the EBL. However, it is noteworthy that Article 57 of the Company Law provides the one-person company with limited liability where there is only one shareholder who is a natural person or a legal person. Pursuant to Article 63 of the Company Law, where the shareholder of a one-person company with limited liability cannot prove that the property of the company is independent of his own property, he/she assumes the joint and several liabilities for the debts of the company. In that circumstance, if this one-person company goes bankrupt and its natural person shareholder has the joint liability for the debts of the company, what will happen if his personal property is not enough to pay off the debts? The EBL does not provide any answer, whereas there is an alternative solution in practice. In 1992, prior to the current EBL that came into effect in 2007, the Supreme People's Court issued a judicial interpretation, Opinions of the Supreme People's Court on Some Issues Concerning the Application of the Civil Procedure Law of the People's Republic of China (hereinafter the 1992 Opinions),[21] which provides a so-called participation in distribution system.[22] Under the 1992 Opinions, the judgment debtors refer to natural persons and organizations other than the enterprises, which complemented the scope of application under the 1986 EBL. The participation in distribution system can be triggered when the assets of a judgment debtor are found insufficient to satisfy the judgment in the course of enforcement. The other creditors, after filing for petition against the same judgment debtor or having obtained the relevant enforcement basis, can apply for participation in distribution of the judgment debtor's assets seized in that enforcement proceeding.[23] In 1998, a u-turn occurred after the Supreme People's Court issued the Provisions of the Supreme People's Court on Several Issues Regarding Enforcement of the People's Courts For Trial Implementation (hereinafter the 1998 Trial Provisions).[24] In accordance with the 1998 Trial Provisions, the participation in distribution system can also apply to those enterprises dissolved, deregistered and shut down without liquidation, whose assets are not sufficient to pay off all the debts.[25] Moreover, in 2004, Provisions of the Supreme People's Court on Multiple Creditors that Participate in Distribution (Draft for Public Consultation) was released. Till now that judicial interpretation still has not come into effect and one of the key reasons is that it is difficult to achieve a consensus on the participation in distribution system within the Supreme People's Court (Chen, 2014). In accordance with the current EBL, only the creditors and the debtor can apply for bankruptcy. In practice, as pointed out by Wang and Xu, there are creditors who decline to file a bankruptcy petition but take advantage of the participation in distribution system in order to obtain more assets than they can receive through the insolvency proceedings (Wang & Xu, 2014). This is contradictory with the core function of bankruptcy law, which is, as remarked by Jackson, "a collective debt-collection device" (Jackson, 2001). Instead, it encourages the creditors to individually grab the assets under no obligation to "share with other creditors, who maybe slower to take action" (Bartell, 2011). That can lead to unfair distribution among the creditors as a whole. In addition, unlike the strict notice procedures as required under the EBL, some of the creditors cannot even know about the proceeding and then lose the opportunity to make claims. Besides, if the court seized the application for the opening of insolvency proceedings, the whole enforcement procedure can be stayed[26] and the participation in distribution can be stayed accordingly. If the debtor is declared bankrupt, the court should terminate the enforcement procedure.[27] Nevertheless, in accordance with Article 16 of the EBL, only payment to individual creditors that is done after the people's court seizes a request for bankruptcy shall be deemed as invalid. Therefore, even if the debtor or some creditors petition for opening of bankruptcy proceedings later, the assets that have been enforced through the participation in distribution system cannot be ordered to return because neither the EBL nor other legislation provide such a legal basis to revoke a legitimate action. Further, it will result in no possibility of rescue. Under the participation in distribution system, the courts do not have to take into consideration the conditions of the enterprise business but simply determine whether the debt is due. Plus, individual collection can consume the exhaustible assets of the debtors in an inefficient way, which leaves no resources to replenish the estate of the debtor. Therefore, the coexistence of the participation in distribution system is considered by most judges and academics as a leeway from formal insolvency proceedings and risks the sound development of the current EBL (Liu, 2014; Wang, 2014; Chen, 2014; Wang, 2014; Xu & Ou, 2014). The problem was partly solved on 4 February, 2015 when the judicial interpretation concerning application of Civil Procedure Law issued by the Supreme People's Court came into effect.[28] In accordance with the judicial interpretation, the court, upon the agreement of one of the applicants for enforcement or the respondent against whom the enforcement is sought, should stay the enforcement proceeding and transfer the case to the court at the domicile of the respondent, if the respondent, as enterprise legal person, meets the conditions set out under Article 2(1) of the EBL.[29] If the court at the domicile of the respondent accepts the insolvency case, the preservation measures on the property should be lifted. If the court at the domicile of the respondent orders the respondent bankrupt, the enforcement proceeding shall be terminated.[30] The judicial interpretation establishes a link between the enforcement procedure and initiation of insolvency proceedings so that the access to the corporate debtors' assets through the participation in distribution system is blocked. Nevertheless, it is noteworthy that Article 2 of the EBL is composed of two provisions. Article 2(1) stipulates the conditions concerning liquidation of debtor[31] and Article 2(2) provides the conditions of reorganization.[32] Compared to Article 2(1), Article 2(2) includes a less restrictive trigger condition based on likelihood of insolvency. Accordingly, under that judicial interpretation, enterprise debtors are ruled out of the participation in distribution system if they are considered subject to liquidation. Nevertheless, it seems that the judicial interpretation has not completely excluded enterprise debtors, which reach the lower threshold of reorganization pursuant to Article 2(2), from the participation in distribution system. In 2017, the Supreme People's Court issued a judicial interpretation, Guiding Opinions of the Supreme People's Court on Several Issues concerning the Transfer of Cases under Execution Proceeding to Bankruptcy Proceeding, which makes it clear that the transferred court is authorized to terminate the reorganization proceeding.[33] That would be meaningless if a reorganization could not be commenced in the first place. Therefore, the problem has been solved under that judicial interpretation.

INVOLVEMENT OF THE GOVERNMENT

Discussions about involvement of the Chinese government in handling insolvency cases often begin and end with a series of complaints about external interference. From the domestic perspectives, according to Li and Wang, involvement of the government, in particular the local government, in the insolvency proceedings, is regarded as "the most important factor influencing court's function in hearing bankruptcy cases" (Li & Wang, 2012) in the Mainland. Besides, as stated in Jiang's research, which was conducted based on statutory analysis and case studies, it is pointed out that involvement of government agencies in China's bankruptcy proceedings, especially the reorganization proceedings, is excessive, which contributed to a discouraging factor for bankruptcy filings (Jiang, 2014). From the international perspectives, the same concern arose. Early in 2007, it is acknowledged in an investigation report published by the United States International Trade Commission that the policy-led bankruptcy proceedings under the 1986 EBL was considered as "another instrument that China's government has used to satisfy its rationalization objectives",[34] which deviated from the market-oriented function of bankruptcy laws. In fact, a clear definition of bankruptcy laws is also one of five fundamental criteria,[35] based on which China has been seeking market economy status (MES) recognized by the EU but has been consistently rejected.[36] According to the EU, China has only met one of them, which excluded the bankruptcy laws criteria.[37] It seems that international confidence in a well-developed bankruptcy system under market economy conditions in China still requires time to be built up. Before that, the fear of foreign creditors to recover their investment and claims in the event of bankruptcy due to government interference can probably result in escape from the Mainland jurisdiction. I will discuss that point later in this section. Government involvement indeed exists in the course of China's insolvency proceedings. Nevertheless, in my view, those complaints also fail to capture the complex reality of China. Some of them do not merely have negative effects but a compromising choice in a transitional economy. In this section, I would like to explore the forms of and reasons for government involvement based on the relevant case law. In China, involvement of the government in the insolvency proceedings can exist in various forms. The most evident one is the liquidating committee. Under the current EBL, in addition to law firms, certified public accountant firms, bankruptcy liquidation firms or any other social intermediary agencies, the administrator can also be a liquidating committee,[38] which is an inheritance from the 1986 EBL.[39] In accordance with the judicial interpretation, the members of a liquidating committee can be appointed from the related government departments, from the social intermediary agencies included in the roster of administrators, from financial asset management companies as well as from the people's bank and the financial regulatory institution under relevant laws and administrative regulations.[40] For instance, the Tianyi (San-an) case involved reorganization proceeding of a listed company, 45.43% of whose equity structure is state-owned shares.[41] The liquidating committee was appointed, which was composed of the local State Assets Supervision and Administration Committee (SASAC), the local Labor and Social Security Bureau, the local central branch of the People's Bank of China, the local branch of China Banking Supervision and Administration Committee (CBSAC), in addition to an accounting firm and a law firm (Li & Wang, 2010). The same happened in the Huayuan case, which was a listed company directly subordinated to the State-owned Assets Supervision and Administration Commission of the State Council (SASAC). (Gao, Tang & Fu, 2010; please note that the authors are judges who participated in the reorganization proceedings of the Huayuan case.) The court designated a liquidating committee that was mainly composed of the CBSAC Shanghai Bureau, the China Securities Supervision and Administration Committee Shanghai Bureau, the Shanghai Financial Office, the SASAC Shanghai Branch (Zhang & Kuang, 2014). The judges, who participated in the Huayuan case, briefly explained the reason of that assignation. Reorganization of the listed company involved a series of complicated problems and had to coordinate with different government departments. For example, considering the state-owned shares in the debtor's capital structure, the reorganization should be subject to the supervision of the State Assets Supervision and Administration Committee. Meanwhile, the debtor was also a listed company, which should be regulated by the China Securities Regulating Commission. The main creditors of the debtor were banks and thus needed the assistance of the People's Bank of China and the China Banking Supervision and Administration Committee. However, the coordinating ability of the social intermediary agencies is relatively weak at this moment. That is why the judges understood that appointment of a liquidating committee might cause controversy but still found it necessary to include the related government departments into the liquidating committee in order to facilitate the reorganization proceedings, which was "in line with China's current national conditions" (Gao, Tang & Fu, 2010).

The government may also be requested to participate in insolvency proceedings that mostly relate to policy issues. Based on the case law, in particular, in the reorganization cases, the courts sought assistance from the government in matters of tax as well as all kinds of administrative approvals, such as concerning real estate, foreign merger and acquisition as well as employee replacement. Under the current EBL, tax is second on the rank of the order of paying off debts in the liquidation proceedings.[42] With respect to how to tackle tax issues in the course of reorganization, the current EBL does not provide specific rules but the tax authority itself issued the Measures for the Enterprise Income Tax of Enterprise Reorganizations.[43] In the case of Jiande Xuehong Home Textiles Co., Ltd., the debtor was reorganized by introducing an external investor. If the debtor was charged tax according to Measures for the Enterprise Income Tax of Enterprise Reorganizations, it would put more financial burdens upon the debtor's shoulder. In that case, the problem can be solved if the reorganization with the help of an external investor can be shifted into the category of investment promotion and capital attraction, which should be subject to preferential tax policy and consequently lower the costs. The court negotiated with the government several times and finally persuaded the government to accept the arrangement.[44] In the reorganization case of Zhoushan Huatai Petrol Company, a Hong Kong company was accepted as one of the strategic investors, who agreed to purchase the shares of the debtor. However, investment from Hong Kong was regarded as foreign investment in the Mainland, which had to go through time-consuming administrative procedures for approval. For the purpose of promoting the efficiency of the reorganization, the court persuaded the government to complete the administrative procedure as soon as possible.[45] In the case of Tang Ying Garment Co. Ltd., the government made an undertaking upon the request of the court, which was incorporated into the reorganization plan. The main capital of the debtor was its real estate, including land and buildings. However, the government did not issue related ownership certificates for that real estate, which meant the ownership of the debtor relating that real estate was in question and the interests of the creditor would accordingly be affected. The court held discussions with the government several times and the government finally agreed to issue related certificates as soon as possible and change the land status used for commercial purpose so as to raise the value of the land. Further, the reorganization plan included a written promise that the government would purchase the real estate if it failed to issue related certificates within two years, which enabled the reorganization plan to achieve a high pass rate.[46]

Sometimes the involvement of the government in the insolvency proceedings directly links to financial support or employee replacement. LDK, registered in Jiangxi Province, was a private company that manufactured photovoltaic (PV) products. According to the information published on the company's website, it was the first company of that province in China listed on the New York Stock Exchange and used to be a significant revenue contributor to that province (Li, 2009). Due to excess capacity and the anti-dumping and anti-subsidy investigation into China's photovoltaic products[47] imported into the United States and the EU, the solar power industry in China plunged since 2011 (Wei & Yu, 2013) and an array of photovoltaic enterprises went insolvent in China. The business of LDK also deteriorated in 2011. The salaries of employees had temporarily to be paid by the local government (Guo & Jian, 2012). In 2012, a budget bill was passed, which allowed the local government to pay for part of the debts of the private company with fiscal funds. The government had to delete the content of the bill from its official website in order to ease the media uproar (Guo, 2012). By the end of 2014, LDK has not filed the petition for bankruptcy in Mainland China, whereas its holding company applied for winding up in the Cayman Islands in February 2014. LDK is an extreme case. On 26 June, 2014, Shanghai No. 1 Intermediate People's

Court accepted the petition for reorganization concerning Shanghai Chaori Solar Energy Science & Technology Co. Ltd. (Chaori).[48] Chaori was a private company based in Shanghai, which also manufactured photovoltaic (PV) products and experienced financial distress. It is stated in the Chaori's draft reorganization plan that the court designated a law firm and an accounting firm as the administrators and the government participated in the proceedings in order to cooperate with the court in matters of employee replacement.[49] Another case concerning a company producing solar glass, it involved a reorganization proceeding in Zhejiang Province, which was filed in 2013. Considering the practical necessity arising from the reorganization case, the court sent a letter of request to the local government in order to discuss employee replacement and the replacement fees prepaid by the government, in which the court also suggested that the local government participate in the liquidating committee. The local government, however, refused to take the responsibility for prepaying the replacement fees and considered that it was more appropriate for qualified intermediary agencies to be appointed as administrator. As a result, the court dismissed the application for reorganization because the court considered that the feasibility of reorganization was not very high.[50] The reason behind that kind of government involvement is partly due to the lack of public funds related to wage guarantee. As mentioned by Wang and Yang, there are some local specialized funds for protection of labor claims established for limited purpose only available in Beijing and Shanghai (Wang & Yang, 2013). At national level, such a system that provides comprehensive financial support for labor claims incurred by insolvency of enterprises has not been set up. Consequently in 2009, the Opinions of the Supreme People's Court on Several Issues Concerning Correctly Trying Enterprise Bankruptcy Cases to Provide Judicial Protection for Maintaining the Order of Market Economy were published.[51] Problems, such as unpaid salaries and replacement of employee, are considered sensitive in nature and the courts are required to seek support from the local government.[52] It is further stated:

> if conditions permit, the government can set up stability funds or encourage the third parties to make advance payments to settle the employees of insolvent enterprises at the first place. The advance payments made by the government or any third party can be firstly repaid in the bankruptcy procedure according to the repayment sequence of employees' claims.[53]

China's insolvency proceedings involve frequent interplay between the courts and the government. Compared to the judiciary, the government has been given very extensive powers in administering affairs. Against that background, judicial independence alone is not sufficient to safeguard the sound and efficient operation of the insolvency proceedings and the courts have to seek cooperation from the government. For instance, problems like taxes, employee resettlement and policy-based loans cannot be settled without the proper support of the governments (Pan, 2011). The emerging consensus is that there is "minimal judicial independence, impartiality and integrity that countries of various political stripes should adhere to" (see also Henderson, 2010).[54] Nonetheless, an individual country, which is still in the course of judicial reform, should not simply be condemned before it meets the requirement because it is a long-term and complicated domestic process "involving different balance of struggle among competing interest groups" (Peerenboom, 2010). In addition, both the courts and the government in China share the same objective of cooperation. As pointed out by the Governor of the People's Bank of China (Central Bank of PRC), "in the process of reform, China attaches special importance to social stability" (Zhou, 2012). For example, maintaining social stability is a principle that has been incorporated into related judicial interpretations.[55] In the case of Wuxi Mingte Chemical Fiber Co., Ltd., which involved reorganization concerning a non-public company, the judge held the similar opinion as the judge in the Huayuan case, considering that involvement of government, by participating in the liquidating committee, has played an irreplaceable role in the reorganization case because the government can cooperate with the court in resolving the social conflicts and ensuring social stability.[56] Further, there are economic incentives for the government to get involved in insolvency proceedings. As pointed out by Zhou, the criteria of promotion of local officials have shifted from political achievements to economic contributions since 1980s (Zhou, 2004). Hence, local government is highly motivated to boost growth of local economy. In 1962, an economist, Arthur Melvin Okun, published his paper based on empirical observation, in which it is stated that for every 1% increase in unemployment, a country's gross domestic product (GDP) will decrease by 2% to 4% from its potential (Okun, 1962). His theory was later referred to as Okun's law. As pointed out by Knotek, Okun's law can be affected by a number of factors and consequently it might not be very precise, but is more useful as a forecasting tool to show the tendency (Knotek, 2007). In 2014, the IMF conducted empirical research based on the data of a group of advanced economies, the G7 economies plus Australia and New Zealand from 1989 to 2012, and confirmed that consistent with Okun's Law, forecasts of real GDP growth and change in unemployment are negatively correlated (Ball, Jalles & Loungani, 2014). Bankruptcy and unemployment are directly connected, which thus may have a direct influence on the political promotion of local officials. Nonetheless, the fact that the insolvency system only reminds the local government of unemployment or bad performance of the developing local economy is, according to Wang and Xu, nothing but a misunderstanding of the function of the insolvency system (Wang & Xu, 2014). The genuine purpose of establishing an insolvency system is to allow hopeless enterprise to exit the market in a prompt and efficient way and help to rescue economically viable but distressed businesses. It must be acknowledged that currently in the Mainland the advantages of the government in facilitating the insolvency proceedings are quite evident. Nevertheless, in the context of a market-oriented economy, the interference of the government in dealing with insolvency cases is also expected to be proportionate.

CAUTIOUS ATTITUDES OF THE COURTS TOWARDS INSOLVENCY CASES

In China, the courts usually hold cautious attitudes towards insolvency cases, which are mainly reflected in the reluctance to accept an application for insolvency proceedings. The first reason is that there is a lack of specific rules for the courts to refer to. In practice, in particular in the reorganization proceedings, the courts usually conduct a prior review before determining whether or not to open the proceeding. The first reorganization case of a listed company, the case of the Zhejiang Hai Na reorganization, after the current EBL came into effect, was such an example.[57] Despite the statutory threshold of rescue stipulated under the EBL,[58] the High Court of Zhejiang Province sent a notice to the lower court, i.e. the Intermediate Court of Hangzhou, to which the reorganization petition was filed, to conduct an evaluation prior to acceptance. The main concern of the High Court of Zhejiang Province related to the feasibility of the draft reorganization plan, the employee arrangement as well as the government opinions etc. (Yang, 2008), which were all included in the contents of the review of the lower court before the reorganization proceedings was decided to be commenced. In the case of Yiyang Tianye Real Estate Development Company (hereinafter the Tianye company), the shareholders of the Tianye company applied for reorganization but their application was dismissed by the court of the first instance, holding that the company was not qualified for entering into reorganization proceeding upon review.[59] The share-holders then appealed to the intermediate court. The intermediate court held a hearing and invited the members of the creditor committee, the representative of the creditors, the administrator and the government authorities in charge of real estate management to give their opinions on the reorganization application. The applicants contended that the court should only conduct a formal review instead of a substantial review on the reorganization application. The intermediate court held that examination on the reorganization application should include both a formal review and a substantial review. The substantial review mainly checked the possibility of whether or not the debtor could still be rescued, includ-ing the feasibility of the reorganization plan and the capability of the participants to realize the reorganization plan.[60] An application for reorganization of listed companies is subject to more pre-conditions. In 2012, the Supreme People's Court issued a notice concern-ing instructions on reorganization of listed companies.[61] When an applicant file a petition for reorganization of a listed company, in addition to the required documents set forth in Article 8 of the EBL, the applicant shall submit the report concerning the reorganization feasibility of the listed company, the briefing materials sent by the provincial people's gov-ernment at the place of the listed company's domicile to the securities regulatory authority, the opinions of the securities regulatory authority, the stability maintenance plans issued by the people's government at the place of the listed company's domicile. Where a listed company applies for reorganization on its own, it shall also submit a feasible employee resettlement plan.[62] The courts should hold a hearing before the courts decide to accept the application if the listed companies raise objections against the creditors' application or any creditor, the listed company and any contributor respectively present a liquidation petition and a reorganization petition. Considering the possible influence on social stability, the people's courts shall submit relevant materials level by level to the Supreme People's Court for examination before rendering a ruling to accept the reorganization applications of listed companies.[63] The second reason is that although they have been granted substantial and procedural power in accordance with the EBL (Li & Wang, 2012), the actual function of the courts in practice has been limited by external factors, such as the competing system of the participation in distribution system and government interference. The Supreme Peo-ple's Court has taken measures and tried to resolve this problem. In 2011, a judicial inter-pretation was issued,[64] which focuses on specifying the conditions of the courts to accept the application of insolvency cases so as to facilitate the courts to accept the insolvency petitions in a timely manner. It stipulated supervision of the higher courts on the courts at the lower level (Song, Zhang, Liu 2011; Wang, 2012). Suppose that a lower court did not even respond to the bankruptcy petition; it is stipulated that the applicant can present the petition to a higher court and the higher court shall order the court at the lower level to examine the application according to law and timely render a ruling on whether to accept the application. If the court at the lower level still does not render the ruling on whether to accept the application, the higher court may directly render a ruling to accept it and at the same time designate the court at the lower level to adjudicate this case.[65] In addition, the courts' reluctance to accept the bankruptcy application may also be attributed to the evaluation system of judges, which is quantity-based and dependent on how many cases the judges deal with. Due to its complexity, insolvency cases are usually very time-consuming. Hence, it is understandable that judges usually try to evade them and can spend more time in handling more ordinary civil and commercial cases, which can contribute to better evaluation results (Li & Wang, 2012). The further consequence is that the Mainland lacks professional judges in adjudicating insolvency cases. Fully aware of the problem, it has been advocated by the Supreme People's Court to promote the professionalism of judges, who are to be trained with relevant professional knowledge and specialized at handling bank-ruptcy cases.[66] Moreover, as remarked by Eisenberg in 1987, "Bankruptcy courts would not have arisen unless specialized knowledge was believed desirable" (Eisenberg, 1987). It has been suggested by the Supreme People's Court to establish special tribunals for bankruptcy cases or appoint special collegial panels to adjudicate bankruptcy cases and the judges, who are in charge of bankruptcy cases, shall be evaluated based on different criteria.[67] In prac-tice, instead of establishing special tribunals, jurisdiction over bankruptcy cases are centrally allocated to certain courts in some provinces, for instance Shenzhen Intermediate People's Court (since 2011) and Foshan Intermediate People's Court (since 2013) in Guangdong Province, Chongqing 5th Intermediate People's Court (since 2015) in Chongqing Munici-pality. Nevertheless, the actual effects of those special tribunals still need to be examined after a period of implementation.

Current cross-border insolvency law in the Mainland

There was no nationwide legislation concerning cross-border insolvency in the Mainland before the current EBL came into effect in 2007. Under the current EBL there are no rules governing international jurisdiction or choice of law. It only provides one single article (Arti-cle 5) concerning the criteria of recognition related to cross-border insolvency proceedings. First of all, Article 5(1) clearly indicates the effects of cross-border insolvency proceedings. A bankruptcy proceeding opened by the Mainland court shall have extra-territorial effect on debtors' assets situated outside the territories of the PRC; whereas a legally effective bankruptcy judgment or ruling rendered by a foreign court, involving a debtor's property within the territory of the PRC shall make an application for recognition and enforcement to the people's court. Therefore, China's insolvency proceedings are vested with outbound universal effect and inbound territorial effect. In addition, the EBL provides no special rules concerning ancillary proceedings to foreign insolvency proceedings involving assets in the Mainland (Wang, 2012). Secondly, Article 5(2) sets out the recognition criteria on foreign insolvency proceedings. To recognize and enforce an insolvency proceeding opened outside Mainland China, the following conditions shall be met:

(1) relevant international treaties between the country concerned and Mainland China have been concluded; or
(2) reciprocal relations between the country concerned and Mainland China have been established;
(3) the insolvency proceeding shall not violate the basic principles of the laws of the PRC;
(4) the insolvency proceeding shall not jeopardize the sovereignty and security of the State or public interests;
(5) the insolvency proceeding shall not undermine the legitimate rights and interests of creditors within Mainland China.

International treaties

From 1987 till now, China has signed over 30 mutual civil and commercial judicial assis-tance treaties or agreements.[68] The scope of those treaties covers generally all kinds of civil and commercial cases but some of them exclude recognition of insolvency proceedings, for instance those relating to Peru, Tunisia and Spain. In addition, some of them only apply to recognition of arbitral awards, such as Korea, Singapore and Belgium. Those treaties, if applicable, serve as a concrete foundation for the court to recognize foreign insolvency proceedings. In fact, before the 2007 EBL came into effect, there were already two cases that sought recognition of the insolvency proceedings based on the bilateral treaty. The first case involved an application from Italy, which is B&T Ceramic Group srl against E.N. Group spa (Liu, 2003). The E.N. Group spa was declared bankrupt by the Milan Court on 24 October, 1997. On 30 September, 1999, the Milan Court made a decision that all the property of the E.N. Group spa, including property overseas, shall be sold to the B&T Ceramic Group srl as a whole. In order to take over the debtor's assets located in China, on 18 December, 2000, B&T Ceramic Group applied to the Guandong Foshan Intermediate People's Court for recognition of the bankruptcy judgments made by the Italian court and restored the legal status of the applicant as the shareholder in Nassetti Ettore company and the shares of Nassetti Ettore company. The Foshan court formally and explicitly recognized the validity of the bankruptcy judgment rendered by the Italian court based on the Sino-Italy Mutual Civil Judicial Assistance Treaty.[69] The second application was filed by a French liquidator, Montier Antoine, on 1 April, 2005 to Guangzhou Intermediate People's Court for recognition of the insolvency of Pellis Corium (a French company) ordered by the French court in 1998. The Guangzhou Intermediate People's Court in accordance with Article 268 of the CPL[70] and the bilateral treaty recognized the effect of the bankruptcy proceeding (Wang & Lian, 2008). Sometimes recognition and enforcement rules can be found in other forms of state-to-state agreement but recognition cannot be guaranteed unless there is a specific arrangement. For instance, Australia has signed the Mutual Promotion and Protection of the Investment Agreement with the Chinese government in 1988, in which it is stated that the Contracting Party should make relevant recognition and enforcement rules in dealing with investment-related civil disputes,[71] which have not happened yet. In 2006, the High People's Court of Guangdong Province requested a reply from the Supreme People's Court to clarify whether or not recognition can be granted to a judgment rendered by an Australian court. This case involved a debt dispute between an Australian company and two Chinese citizens. The Supreme Court of Western Australia rendered the judgment in 2005 and then the Australian company sought recognition thereof in Shenzhen. Later in 2006 the case was appealed to the High People's Court of Guangdong Province and the High Court made a decision based on the Civil Procedural Law. Without a mutual civil and commercial judicial assistance treaty or reciprocity, the High Court considered that the application for recognition lacked legal basis and thus refused to grant recognition. In its reply to the High Court, the Supreme People's Court considered that there was no mutual civil and commercial judicial assistance treaty or reciprocity between China and Australia and thus that the application for recognition of a civil judgment rendered by an Australian court should be dismissed.[72] What will happen if there is no mutual civil and commercial judicial assistance treaty? The foreign judgment will probably not be recognized. In 2011, a judge from Shanghai Municipal High Court wrote an article about a case related to the Lehman Brothers insolvency proceeding (Zhang, 2011).[73] In *Hua An Funds v Lehman Brothers International Europe* (LBIE), a fund management firm of Mainland China filed petitions to the High People's Court of Shanghai Municipality based on the fund product cooperative agreement, claiming damage of US$96.4 million and sought an attachment of the assets of the defendant within the territory of the Mainland China soon after the business of Lehman Brothers collapsed in 2008. It is noteworthy that there is a fundamental block that cannot be bypassed, although the case was dealt in the form of a contract dispute, which is the effect of LBIE's insolvency proceeding in the UK. The judge declined to recognize the UK proceeding on the basis of the lack of a relevant international treaty between the UK and China.

Principle of reciprocity

Generally speaking, the principle of reciprocity is the idea that States will and should grant others recognition of judicial decisions only if, and to the extent that, their own decisions would be recognized (Michaels, 2009). Unlike international treaties, the principle of reciprocity is an ambiguous concept in China, which has neither been defined under legislation nor interpreted by the Supreme People's Court. In 1995, the Supreme People's Court made a reply to the request of the High Court of Liaoning Province, which was whether or not to recognize a Japanese judgment involving debt dispute. The Supreme People's Court held that China and Japan did not enter into any international treaties in matters of civil and commercial judgments and no reciprocity had been established, either. Therefore, the application should be dismissed.[74] In Japan, foreign judgments are automatically entitled to recognition in Japan if they fulfill the requirements without any formality or special procedure, such as an action for a judgment or summary judgment granting the recognition or registration of foreign judgments. At the time, the criteria for recognition of foreign civil and commercial judgments were governed by Article 118 of CCP Code of Civil Procedure (CCP), which was enacted since 1996 in Japan (Tada, 2003). Therefore, it seems that in terms of reciprocity the Supreme Court did not adopt the "would be" approach but a more concrete reciprocal basis, especially the precedents. In the aforementioned *Hua An Funds* case, with respect to reciprocity, the judge held that till now no relevant recognition had been given to China by the UK court and thus the effect of the UK insolvency proceeding could not be recognized on a reciprocal basis either (Zhang, 2011). The judge in fact made a "substantial" review by investigating in the precedents the counterpart foreign state in matters of recognition of China's civil or commercial judgments. Some foreign courts also realized this problem=. For example, in 2006 the Berlin High Court recognized a money judgment rendered by a Chinese court in accordance with Article 328 of German Code of Civil Procedure (Zivilprozessordnung) on a reciprocal basis.[75] The German court indicated that China and Germany had so far not entered into any bilateral treaties concerning recognition and enforcement in civil and commercial matters. Neither of them had before granted recognition to judgments rendered by the counterpart court on the reciprocal basis. On the contrary, there have been some precedents of refusal due to lack of a reciprocal basis. For instance, in 2001, a German company applied for recognition and enforcement of a judgment involving a finance lease contract dispute between the German company and a Chinese company, which was rendered by the court in Frankfurt. In matters of recognition, the Beijing Second Intermediate People's Court employed the same reasoning as in the aforementioned decision and refused to grant recognition.[76] Nevertheless, the court considered that without international treaties one side should probably start to grant recognition and thus solve the reciprocity deadlock. Once that obstacle was removed by Germany, China would probably follow.[77] As a concept arising from sovereignty, reciprocity is not set up as a requirement either under the EIR or the UNCITRAL Model Law. In EU reciprocity is not necessary because automatic recognition of insolvency proceedings is granted based on mutual trust between the Member States under the Union regime.[78] It is deemed outdated in matters of cross-border insolvency cooperation regarding business from the point view of the Model Law (Wessels, 2012), although a number of countries *de jure* or *de facto* apply the reciprocity requirement in the process of implementing the Model Law, which include the British Virgin Islands, Mauritius, Mexico, Romania and South Africa (Ho, 2012). However, it is noteworthy that in China, although each region has its own independent legal system, none of the legal cooperative arrangements in civil and commercial matters between the Mainland China and the other three regions contain reciprocity requirement for recognition. Considering the business motivated characteristic of cross-border insolvency and the current form of legal cooperation in China, the principle of reciprocity should not play an influential role in China's regional cross-border insolvency.

Public policy

Public policy does not literally appear in Article 5(2) of the EBL, but in the name of the fundamental principles of law, state sovereignty and security, socio-public interests as well as legitimate rights and interests of the creditors. The equivalent expressions can also be found in Article 282 of the current Civil Procedure Law, which stipulates the criteria for the recognition and enforcement of a legally effective civil or commercial judgment or written order rendered by a foreign court.[79] Such diverse expressions are regarded as considerable hurdles for understanding the concept of public policy in the course of China's international judicial cooperation, in particular in the matters of recognition and enforcement of foreign judgments and foreign arbitral awards (He, 2013). As public policy has long been acknowledged as "a very unruly horse" in practice,[80] it is the judges who get astride it by exercising discretion. To grasp the concept of public policy, the ideal way is to collect the relevant case law as much as possible and then make a summary. Nevertheless, the short time period of implementation of the system concerning publicity of judgments and the cross-border insolvency system altogether result in limited access to relevant information. In addition, insufficient rules and explanation in matters of cross-border insolvency and the reluctance of application thereof due to uncertainty are usually mutually reinforcing, which is to be discussed in the later section. On top of that, it is required by Article 4 of EBL that the provisions of the CPL should be applicable where the EBL does not provide the relevant provisions in dealing with bankruptcy proceedings, for example, international jurisdiction and applicable law. As a result, in the following sections, I sometimes have to refer to civil and commercial cases as expedient alternatives for comprehension of public policy in the judicial practice of the Mainland.

FUNDAMENTAL PRINCIPLES OF LAW

Due to lack of legislative and judicial interpretation, the concept of the fundamental principles of law is quite vague and broad. Considering it is stipulated in the wording of Article 5, most related law should be the EBL itself. What are the basic principles of the EBL? The EBL itself does not specify them. After the EBL came into effect, there has been only limited academic discussion concerning this issue (Qi, 2005; Xu, 2009). There seems to be some development in practice. In 2012, a district court in Shanghai heard a case between a local debtor and a local creditor involving individual debt-collection action after the debtor was declared bankrupt.[81] The action was considered invalid and the court clearly stated that protection of equal treatment of the creditors is the primary aim of the bankruptcy law and also serves as one of the basic principles thereof. However, without a nationalwide case registry system and standard criteria, a comprehensive understanding of the fundamental principles of law in the context of cross-border insolvency is missing.

STATE SOVEREIGNTY AND SECURITY

In the Mainland, sometimes the sovereignty requirement has something to do with the language. For example, some courts considered that the translation of relevant documents and supporting materials from the foreign language into Chinese was required, based on the principle of state sovereignty, which could help the Chinese court to make investigation and discover the facts.[82] As for Taiwan, the "One China" principle is firmly held by the Mainland courts in dealing with Taiwan-related case.[83] In 2004, an application for recognition of an arbitral award rendered by an arbitral tribunal in Taiwan was submitted to a Mainland court. It has been argued that the arbitral tribunal was inconsistent because the arbitral tribunal that appeared on the arbitral award submitted by the applicant was "the Arbitration Association of China"; but in fact, it was "the Arbitration Association of the Republic of China"[84] that rendered the award. The court noticed that the special heading appearing on the arbitral award was used in the Mainland area alone. Thus, the court considered that the arbitral tribunal changed the description of its title for the purpose of facilitating recognition and enforcement of its arbitral award in the Mainland China, which could be deemed as consistent with the "One China" principle and the award thus should be recognized.[85] Further, disputes concerning jurisdiction can cause concerns of the principle of state sovereignty. In order to guarantee the independent judicial power of each state or region, a Chinese court can still exercise its jurisdiction over the same dispute if it falls within the ambit of competence of the Chinese court, although there are parallel civil or commercial proceedings opened in other states or regions.[86]

SOCIO-PUBLIC INTERESTS

Socio-public interests play an important role in China's civil and commercial law. A civil act that violates the public interests shall be null and void.[87] For example, a contract is deemed invalid if it does harm to socio-public interests.[88] Nevertheless, socio-public interests, similar to other public policy provisions, do not have a concrete definition. The provision of socio-public interests function like a general principle in order to make up for legal blanks left behind by the statutes and thus remains flexible enough in order to facilitate judicial discretion. In practice, the provision of socio-public interests is not frequently utilized by the people's courts in handling bankruptcy cases if there are other specific provisions available. For instance, an employee filed a petition against his employer (a company) that was declared bankrupt for his salaries and compensations. The employee referred to the socio-public interests as one of the important legal bases for his claims. Without adopting the public interest argument, the court approved his claims simply pursuant to Article 48 of the EBL.[89] Nevertheless, it is noteworthy that public interests can be taken into account when it involves the state-owned company. In 2007, there was a case concerning debt-assignment disputes between a creditor and two state-owned companies, one of which was the parent company of the other.[90] Both of them were declared bankrupt and had been listed in the national bankruptcy plan of the year 2003, which is so-called policy-mandated bankruptcy (Booth, 2008). In accordance with the relevant administrative regulation,[91] once listed in the national bankruptcy plan approved by the State Council, the debt can no longer be transferred to external creditors. The creditor received the debt from a third party, who legally took over the debt from the two debtors. The appellate court had the same opinion as the court of first instance, holding that the agreement of debt assignment violated public interests and should be deemed as invalid. With respect to the socio-public interests, the court considered that policy-mandated bankruptcy aimed at improving the reform of state-owned companies and maintaining the social stability, which was undoubtedly related to the socio-public interests.

What are the legitimate rights of the creditors within the territory of PRC? It is a matter of applicable law. According to one of the drafters of the EBL, it depends on where the debtor's domicile is located. If the domicile of the debtor is in the Mainland and the Mainland court can exercise jurisdiction over the debtor's insolvency proceeding, the legitimate rights shall entail all the legitimate rights granted by the laws of the Mainland (*lex concursus*), including the EBL (Wang & Wang, 2008). In accordance with the EBL, they are mainly the right to apply for the opening of bankruptcy proceeding (liquidation or reorganization),[92] the right to declare the claims and to participate in the creditors' meeting[93] and the right to set off. During the insolvency proceeding, most of the influential rights are granted to the creditors' meeting, which generally include (1) checking the claims; (2) supervising the work of the administrator; (3) adopting plans for reorganization or adopting agreements for compromise; (4) adopting plans for management of the debtor's property, adopting plans for realizing the bankruptcy property into money and adopting plans for distribution of the bankruptcy property; (5) deciding on whether to have the debtor continue or discontinue his business operations.[94] If the debtor is domiciled outside the Mainland and the Mainland court is thus not competent to open the insolvency proceeding, the legitimate rights shall refer to the rights in accordance with the bankruptcy law in the foreign state and other laws except for the EBL in the Mainland (Wang & Wang, 2008). Accordingly, it seems that the applicability of the foreign *lex concursus* can be accepted indirectly under the current EBL. The EBL does not set a limitation on the scope of creditors, which means, in theory, foreign creditors can also apply for the opening of bankruptcy proceedings and enjoy the same legitimate rights. Nevertheless, in matters of cross-border insolvency, does a creditor, whose domicile or registered office is abroad, have the same rights as a domestic creditor under the EBL? Probably not. To recognize a foreign insolvency proceeding, only the legitimate rights and interests of the creditors "within the territory of PRC" is taken into consideration under Article 5 of the EBL. Also in the *Hua An* case, by referring to Article 5, the judge stated that, without relevant treaties and precedents of reciprocity, the court could protect the legitimate rights and interests of the creditors within the territory of PRC "in priority" by way of accepting the lawsuit (as an ordinary civil dispute) and ordering interim attachment on the assets (Zhang, 2011). Nonetheless, from the perspective of international insolvency law, domestic and foreign creditors should be equally treated. Without recognition, the court could not grant any relief to assist the foreign insolvency proceedings and thus the legitimate rights and interests of the foreign creditors in the foreign insolvency proceedings will be jeopardized.

In summary, the current EBL does not provide clear explanation with respect to those various expressions regarding public policy. Although some relevant civil and commercial case law has been found for reference, its reference value is limited because cross-border insolvency law has its own features and needs interpretation peculiar to its own characteristics. It is suggested to clarify the detailed public policy rules under the current EBL to prevent uncertainty in deciding insolvency cases and different understanding of the same norms on domestic level.

Consequences arising from insufficient rules[95]

Low caseload of cross-border insolvency

When the problems of the domestic insolvency system bring down the amount of national insolvency cases, the insufficient rules on cross-border insolvency law discourage filings of recognition and enforcement of foreign and regional insolvency proceedings before the Mainland courts at the same time. At the international level, Suntech Power is such a typical example.[96] In 2001, Wuxi Suntech was founded in Wuxi, Jiangsu Province, China. In 2005, Suntech Power Holdings Co. Ltd. was registered in the Cayman Islands (Suntech Power). The original purpose of establishing Suntech Power was to facilitate privatization of Suntech by purchasing state-owned stocks and the ultimate goal was to be listed on the New York Stock Exchange (NYSE), which was realized by the end of 2005 (Li, 2009). The aforementioned recession in the photovoltaic industry resulted in multiple cross-border insolvency proceedings concerning Suntech Power in China,[97] the Cayman Islands and the United States.[98] On 17 November, 2014, the United States Bankruptcy Court for the Southern District of New York (SDNY) recognized the Cayman proceeding as the foreign main proceeding.[99] However, as at the commencement of the Cayman proceedings, it was pointed out by Solyndra, one of Suntech Power's American creditors, that the headquarters, manufacturing facilities and primary assets of Suntech were in China.[100] The intent to shift COMI from China to the Cayman Islands was not hidden. I will turn to the COMI issue of this case later in Chapter 4. The attorney representing one of the debtor's largest creditor groups called China "the last place that one would go"[101] and indicated that: "The Chinese court's jurisdiction was in doubt, and China has different concepts of the rules of law and creditors' rights compared to those found in the Cayman Islands and the United States."[102] Interestingly in the same year, the United States Bankruptcy Court District of New Jersey in *Re Zhejiang Topoint photovoltaic Co. Ltd.*, considered all parties concerned in the United States had received due and proper notice of the petition and thus granted recognition of the joint bankruptcy proceedings pending in China[103] as the main proceedings and the relevant reliefs, including suspension on disposal of assets within New Jersey.[104] It seems that the opinions on China's insolvency system in the United States are not univocal. Nevertheless, in the course of cross-border insolvency cooperation, different insolvency systems are merely different options. The underlying consideration is that the parties concerned can choose a more favorable forum to his or her benefit, if the problems in one jurisdiction are considered unacceptable and its cross-border insolvency system deemed unpredictable.

Indirect way

On the regional level, as aforementioned in the Introduction (Chapter 1), there is no arrangement in resolving conflicts arising from cross-border insolvency between the Mainland and the SARs. How to recognize and enforce the interregional judgments of opening insolvency proceedings and interregional judgments, which are directly derived from insolvency proceedings, remains a problem. In practice, instead of submitting a request for recognition before the Mainland courts, the related judgments seek enforcement in an indirect way. In the case of *Gu Laiyun and others v Nardu Company Limited*,[105] a liquidator appointed by the Hong Kong High Court became a vice president of the company through a shareholders' resolution in the Mainland. In 1993, Nardu Company, registered in Hong Kong SAR, signed a joint venture contract with a local real estate company in Guangzhou Province of the Mainland and finally established the Fuyu Company in Guangzhou Province. On 22 June, 2005, Hong Kong High Court issued a winding-up order of Nardu Company Limited. On 15 February, 2006, two employees of Hong Kong Grant Thornton International Accounting Firm were appointed by the Hong Kong High Court as liquidators of Nardu Company Limited. On 2 March, 2006, one of the liquidators,

Ms. Li Fengying was elected as a vice president of Fuyu Company through a shareholders' resolution. It was stated in the same shareholders' resolution that the business license, seals, accounting records and properties, etc. of the company should be handed over to its new vice president. The advantages of that kind of arrangement are obvious. First of all, the liquidator could directly control the assets the Hong Kong debtor located in the Mainland without waiting for the recognition of the Mainland court. The other advantage of this arrangement was fully demonstrated when the former legal representative and the manager of Fuyu Company refused to return the items mentioned, and Nardu Company Limited, represented by Ms. Li, filed a lawsuit against them. Furthermore, due to the dual identity of Ms. Li who was both the liquidator appointed by the Hong Kong High Court and the vice president of Fuyu Company, the problem whether the legitimacy of Ms. Li's representation needed to be recognized or not, or whether the winding-up order of Hong Kong High Court should be recognized in advance or not, has been by passed. Instead, the Company Law of PRC was applicable to qualification of Ms. Li's actions in the Mainland[106] and the representation power of the liquidator was taken for granted on the same basis. That strategy, in which the liquidator appointed by the Hong Kong court becomes a member of the management or director of the company in the Mainland, seems ideal, but it is not satisfactory as a long-term solution. First of all, the status of the liquidator is confusing. They are both the liquidator appointed by the Hong Kong court and a member of the management or a representative of a Mainland company at the same time. This is a solution resulting in issues of conflicts of interests, for a liquidator of a Hong Kong wound-up company will have to act in the interest of the general body of creditors, whilst a member of the management or a representative of a local Mainland company is required to act to the benefit of the interests of the company. Secondly, it may be complicated and time-consuming. If the liquidators from Hong Kong SAR want to become a member of the management in order to control the relevant assets of the company in the Mainland, there are also a lot of requirements. Both the limited liability company and the public limited liability company, which are two main types of companies in the Mainland, have strict rules for the election of the members of the management stipulated either by the Company Law of PRC or by each company's own articles of association.[107] In the case of *Gu Laiyun and others v Nardu Company Limited*, the reason why the liquidator could successfully become the vice president of the Fuyu company in a short time was that the Nardu Company Ltd was the largest shareholder accounting for 80% of the Fuyu company. However, not all bankrupt shareholders in Hong Kong can have the same leading portion and the other shareholders may not agree to vote for the liquidator because the idea of enabling a liquidator to interfere with corporate governance may not be benefit to them. Even though the other shareholders are finally persuaded to vote for the liquidator, it still does not mean that the liquidator has substantial control over the relevant assets. Without the cooperation of the former management, the handover will probably be extended by one or more lawsuits. *First China Technology (Hong Kong) Limited v Yeung Chung-lung and Fuqing Longyu Food Development Co., Ltd.*[108] is such an example. A provisional liquidator appointed by the Hong Kong High Court was also designated by the Hong Kong High Court in the same order as the sole member of board of the wound-up Hong Kong company, which had a wholly owned subsidiary in the Mainland. The provisional liquidator passed a board resolution that replaced the board of its Mainland subsidiary, including its founder and former chairman, Yeung Chung-lung. The former chairman did not cooperate to facilitate the handover. Therefore, the provisional liquidator had to file a petition before the Mainland court in order to enforce the board resolution. Interestingly, the Mainland court acknowledged the validity of the board resolution, holding that the provisional liquidator exercised its power in a way that did not exceed the limits required under the order of appointment rendered by the Hong Kong High Court. Nevertheless, it did not indicate whether the winding-up order should be recognized in the first place as if the winding-up order had been deemed as effective in the Mainland. In fact, the appointment of a provisional liquidator or a liquidator as member of the management or representative of the Mainland subsidiaries is an indispensable part of the winding-up order. A winding-up order rendered by a Hong Kong court, which has independent jurisdiction, does not automatically have effect in the Mainland unless upon recognition. Prior to that, the provisional liquidators or liquidators do not have proper authority to take over the assets of the Mainland subsidiaries. Therefore, the indirect solution adopted in practice may seemingly bring some advantages at first sight, but in essence it is merely an evasion of the genuine problems, which involve uncertainty of recognition and lack of ancillary relief and coordination. That is why it is necessary to make regional cross-border insolvency arrangements, which can remove the uncertainty concerned eventually.

Hong Kong approach

In this section, I will firstly explain the difference between the corporate insolvency system and the individual bankruptcy system in Hong Kong. Then I will also briefly introduce the recent reform of the Companies Ordinance and its influence on insolvency law in Hong Kong. Further, the consultation conclusion on corporate insolvency law improvement, which was issued by the Legislative Council of Hong Kong in July 2014, is also referred to. I will focus on the development of cross-border insolvency in Hong Kong by reviewing the relevant legislative proposals and analyze the hesitation in accommodating a cross-border insolvency regime. In addition, the non-statutory feature of the Hong Kong insolvency system is presented. Key elements of the Hong Kong cross-border insolvency system, such as jurisdiction, recognition and coordination and communication, are discussed. Considering the common law characteristics of Hong Kong, they will be examined mainly on the basis of recent case law.

Brief introduction to local insolvency system

Hong Kong applies separate insolvency systems to companies and individuals. After the revision of the Companies Ordinance, its corporate insolvency system has been put on the reform agenda and a statutory company rescue regime is proposed. As for cross-border insolvency, although the adoption of the UNCITRAL Model Law has been taken into consideration, it is still a plan to establish a statutory cross-border insolvency system in Hong Kong, which will take time to come into reality.

Companies ordinance and bankruptcy ordinance

The insolvency system of Hong Kong is not a combined system. Personal insolvency is regulated under the Bankruptcy Ordinance, whereas the Companies Ordinance deals with corporate winding-up. It is noteworthy that the Bankruptcy Ordinance is also applied to insolvent companies from time to time. For example, over the years the Department of Justice, whose role is to provide legislative advice to the Legislative Council, have on numerous occasions drafted amendments to legislation by cross-referring parts of the Companies Ordinance to the Bankruptcy Ordinance (Briscoe & Booth, 2009). Another example is the Companies Ordinance relies on the cross-references to the provisions on unfair preferences under the BO with modifications to corporate winding-up cases,[109] which has been proposed for reform by introducing the relevant self-contained provisions into the Companies Ordinance.[110] Financial institutions are resolved pursuant to specialized legislation, for instance, the Banking Ordinance in matters of winding-up of a bank and the Insurance Companies Ordinance in case of winding-up of an insurance company.

Revision of Companies Ordinance and reform of insolvency law

The revised Companies Ordinance (Cap 622) was passed on 12 July, 2012, which came into effect in early 2014. Nevertheless, the content concerning the winding-up and insolvency provisions remained the same and merely through some format changes, which was entitled Companies (Winding-up and Miscellaneous Provisions) Ordinance (Cap 32). In 2013, the Financial Services and the Treasury Bureau issued a consultation paper on Improvement of Corporate Insolvency Law,[111] in which there are 46 legislative proposals to improve Hong Kong's current corporate insolvency law regime. The consultation lasted for about three months from April to July 2013.[112] In May 2014, the Financial Services and the Treasury Bureau briefed the outcome of the public consultation and the responses of the government[113] and an updated brief was submitted to the Legislative Council in July 2014.[114] It mainly covered the following topics:

(1) commencement of winding-up;
(2) appointment, powers, vacation of office and release of provisional liquidators and liquidators;
(3) conduct of winding-up;
(4) voidable transactions; and
(5) investigation during winding-up, offences antecedent to or in the course of winding-up and powers of the court.

On top of that, a new statutory company rescue regime was proposed.[115] Hong Kong lacked a statutory company rescue regime. Accordingly, a corporate rescue could only be brought about through the procedure of a scheme of arrangement.[116] Different from the winding-up proceeding, there was no such relief as moratorium or stay of proceedings against the company while a scheme of arrangement was being worked out. In other words, the fact that a company was pursuing a scheme of arrangement did not provide standstill to stay proceedings against the company generally or to give the company breathing space in respect of its obligations to creditors. To make up for the legislative blank in practice, a stay of proceedings against the company was usually brought about by Cap 32 s 186 with the appointment of a provisional liquidator. The Hong Kong courts seem to approve this approach so as to mitigate the difficulty of the lack of a moratorium while a restructuring proposal is being worked out, until there is new legislation for a corporate rescue procedure.[117] In 2009, the Hong Kong government formally announced a public consultation on the review of legislative proposals for a corporate rescue procedure. The proposed rescue procedure will not be a US-style Chapter 11. Instead, it is recommended to introduce a regime of "provisional supervision", which is similar to voluntary administration in the UK or Australia. (For more details of the "provisional supervision" proposal, see Booth & Lain, 2010.) In 2014, the provisional supervision approach was further detailed by the government in the proposal concerning the new statutory corporate rescue procedure, which mainly includes initiation of provisional supervision/appointment of provisional supervisor, effect of provisional supervision and rights of secured creditors, status, role, duty and powers of provisional supervisor, process and termination of the provisional supervision, process and termination of the voluntary arrangement.[118] In addition, problems concerning insolvent trading provisions,[119] safeguards for abuse of the special procedure set out in s 228A of the former Companies Ordinance[120] have also been addressed in the proposal. The Companies (Winding Up and Miscellaneous Provisions) (Amendment) Ordinance 2016 ("Amendment Ordinance") entered into effect on 13 February 2017. Nevertheless, the Amendment Ordinance does not include any provisions relating to corporate rescue. It is expected that the Financial Services Branch of the Financial Services and Treasury Bureau can draw up details of legislative proposals for introducing a statutory corporate rescue procedure and insolvent trading provisions, with a view to introducing an amendment bill into Legislative Council in 2017/2018.[121]

Pending development of cross-border insolvency law

As a region deeply influenced by common law, Hong Kong's current insolvency laws are based loosely on law from England that dates back to 1929. Only a few provisions in the Companies Ordinance can be referred to in matters of cross-border insolvency. Cap 32 Part X s 327 grants the court the authority to wind up the companies incorporated outside Hong Kong, which are non-Hong Kong companies in accordance with the Companies Ordinance.[122] The Law Reform Commission[123] considered the adoption of UNICTRAL Model Law into the Companies Ordinance in 1999. It was stated in the Commission's 1999 Report on the Winding-up Provisions of the Companies Ordinance that

> We note that there is some strong support for adoption of the UNCITRAL Model Law of Insolvency, . . . but we have been unable to find any jurisdiction which has adopted the Model Law and we are hesitant about recommending that Hong Kong, which is a relatively small jurisdiction, should pioneer the Model Law.
>
> (para 26.3)

> We do not reject the Model Law. We are simply exercising caution and a watch and wait approach. When the Model Law is adopted by leading jurisdictions, that would be the time to consider adopting the Model Law in Hong Kong, but until that happens we consider that there is no benefit in being the first to adopt the Model Law.
>
> (para 26.43)[124]

In the 2014 proposal, it has been well acknowledged that:

> At present, the court has the power to deal with certain cross-border insolvency cases under section 327 of the C(WUMP)O. However, there are certain limits to the extent to which a Hong Kong court will recognize the vesting and discharging effects of a non-Hong Kong order. We note that while some overseas jurisdictions have adopted the Model Law on Cross-Border Insolvency of the United Nations Commission on International Trade Law, many jurisdictions, particularly those in Asia (e.g. Singapore and the Mainland), still rely on the local legislation to handle such cases. We will closely monitor the international development in this regard and will consider how best to take forward the matter.[125]

In fact, due to the closer economic relationship between the Mainland and Hong Kong, the need for trans-regional cooperation in matters of cross-border insolvency has never been greater. For instance, many Hong Kong companies have set up branches in the Mainland. Some the local companies may transfer their assets to their associated enterprises in the Mainland instantly before winding-up. In the case of *Ocean Grand Holdings Limited v Ocean Grand Aluminum Industrial (San Shui) Ltd.*, Ocean Grand, which was a holding company incorporated in Bermuda, registered in Hong Kong. Its subsidiaries were mainly located in Nanhai and Zhuhai in the Mainland, and in Hong Kong. On 24 July, 2006, Ocean Grand presented a petition for its own winding up in Hong Kong and in Bermuda. Before the application, Ocean Grand announced in mid-July 2006 that a total of about US$840 million in funds in the four Mainland subsidiaries, including OG San Shui, had disappeared (Gong, 2011). Nevertheless, it is observed that Hong Kong still adopted a wait-and-see attitude towards the reform of its cross-border insolvency law. The Companies (Winding Up and Miscellaneous Provisions) (Amendment) Bill was passed in May 2016 and came into operation in February 2017,[126] in which cross-border insolvency provisions have not been included. Concerns have been expressed about the possibility of synchronous development of its major trading partners of Hong Kong (including the Mainland and Taiwan[127]), which have not signed and adopted the UNCITRAL Model Law. Therefore, it would instead closely monitor international development and the attitude of our major trading partners in this regard and will consider how best to take forward the matter.[128]

Current cross-border insolvency law in Hong Kong

In Hong Kong, it is the lack of a statutory regime that provides cross-border insolvency cooperation. This section will introduce the current cross-border insolvency system by referring to illustrative case law and touches on the topics of jurisdiction, methods of recognition and coordination and communication. It is noteworthy that owing to the lack of ancillary proceedings or relief for cross-border insolvency cooperation, rules of jurisdiction, which enables commencement of the parallel territorial insolvency proceedings, play a very important role in Hong Kong's current cross-border insolvency system.

Jurisdiction

A non-Hong Kong company, which is incorporated abroad, is called an "unregistered company" in Hong Kong;[129] it also includes an "oversea company" as a consequence of the decision of the court in the case of *Securities and Futures Commission v MKI Corporation*, which held that an "oversea company" might be wound up as an "unregistered company" in Hong Kong.[130] It is stipulated under Cap 32 s 327(1) that subject to the provisions of Cap 32 Part X, any unregistered company may be wound up. As a result, an insolvency practitioner appointed in the company's place of incorporation can also seek a winding-up order in Hong Kong to protect and realize the Hong Kong assets of an unregistered company. An unregistered company may be wound up in accordance with the Cap 32 s 327(3) on the following grounds:

(1) if the company is dissolved, or has ceased to carry on business, or is carrying on business only for the purposes of winding up its affairs;
(2) if the company is unable to pay its debts;
(3) if the court is of the opinion that it is just and equitable that the company be wound up.

The conditions set out in Cap 32 s 327(3), including inability to pay debts, are not very difficult to satisfy, which means the Hong Kong courts are conferred with a wide and unfettered jurisdiction to wind up unregistered companies. As explained by Lord Scott NPJ in the Court of Final Appeal in *Re Chime Corporation Limited*:

> The fact, however, that the terms of a statute create or confer a jurisdiction in very wide terms does not necessarily mean that the courts have an unlimited jurisdiction to make any orders that are within the wide statutory terms.[131]

There have been settled criteria adopted by the Hong Kong courts in exercising their power under Cap 32 s 327 to wind up a non-Hong Kong company, which are the so-called three core requirements:

(1) there is sufficient connection with Hong Kong, but this does not necessarily have to consist in the presence of assets within the jurisdiction;
(2) there is a reasonable possibility that the winding-up order would benefit those applying for it; and
(3) the court must be able to exercise jurisdiction over one or more persons interested in the distribution of the company's assets.

The three core requirements have been gradually developed by case law.[132] The wording embedded into the three requirements, such as "sufficient connection", "reasonable possibility" is considered to leave courts with a wide margin of discretion (Kwan, 2012). The Hong Kong court used to hold that the mere presence of assets in Hong Kong was sufficient to establish the jurisdiction, especially to satisfy the first two requirements. For instance, in *Re China Tianjin International Economic and Technical Cooperative Corporation*,[133] the court should decide whether or not the Hong Kong court had jurisdiction in winding up a company incorporated in the Mainland. The court considered that the presence of substantial assets, which are liable to be recovered in Hong Kong, constituted a solid ground for exercising jurisdiction.[134] In 2014, that point of view has been altered in *Re Yung Kee*.[135] The company involved is a company incorporated in the British Virgin Islands ("BVI") and is not registered under the Companies Ordinance. It is the ultimate holding company of a Hong Kong restaurant that is well known in Hong Kong for its roasted goose. It indirectly holds all of the group's businesses and properties, including the Hong Kong restaurant. The applicant sought two reliefs before the Hong Kong court. The principal relief is an order under Cap 622 s 724 (1) (former Cap 32 s 168A).[136] As an alternative, the applicant also sought a winding-up order under Cap 32 s 327(3)(c) that gives the Hong Kong court a discretionary jurisdiction to wind up an unregistered company on the just and equitable ground. It is noteworthy that the BVI company is still solvent. As to whether the court should assume jurisdiction to wind up a foreign company, it is held that:

> No single criterion, nor any prescribed combination of criteria, is to be considered as supplying an essential precondition for meeting this requirement: it is a matter of judgment to be made in the light of the evidence presented to the court in a particular case.[137]

Later in *Re Pioneer Iron and Steel*,[138] the three core requirements have been further explored in detail. It is stated in the judgment that the significance of each core requirement will vary from case to case.[139] For the first core requirement, the consideration of the court is different from other aforementioned cases. Without the presence of an asset in Hong Kong,[140] the court indicated that: "I accept that if the matter relied on by the Petitioners was the presence of assets in Hong Kong alone a sufficient connection would not have been demonstrated, but they are not."[141] The company's sole shareholder and also sole director, who was resident in Hong Kong, made major business decisions concerning the company's affairs from her base in Hong Kong.[142] Thus the court considered that "the controlling mind" of the company was based in Hong Kong, which constituted a "substantial connection" with Hong Kong.[143] As for the second core requirement, the court considered that it was satisfied through the use of the procedures provided for in the Companies Ordinance. For example, it is stipulated under Cap 32 s 221 that once Hong Kong proceeding commences, the liquidator will be enabled to have investigatory powers, which can be deemed as beneficial to the applicants.[144] With respect to the third core requirement, the court must be able to exercise jurisdiction over "a person who is concerned with the proper distribution of assets and over whom the Court can exercise jurisdiction other than by virtue of him being a creditor of the company".[145] The fact that the sole shareholder of the company asserted that she had a significant claim against the company was sufficient to satisfy the third requirement.[146] In addition, as indicated in *Re Pioneer Iron and Steel Group*, under the exceptional circumstance that the connection with Hong Kong is so strong and the benefits of a winding-up order for the creditors of a company are so substantial, the court would be willing to exercise its jurisdiction despite the third core requirement not being satisfied.[147] As for how properly to understand the exceptional circumstance, the court made some explanation later in *Re China Medical Technologies Inc.*[148] The debtor incorporated in the British Virgin Islands was the ultimate holding company of a group, through which it held three indirectly wholly-owned Hong Kong subsidiaries. Its principal business, involving manufacture of surgical and medical equipment, was located in the Mainland. There were three subsidiaries in the Mainland, which were held by the aforementioned three Hong Kong subsidiaries.[149] It used to be listed on the NASDAQ. The debtor did not carry on any business in the Cayman Islands or in the United States except, in the case of the latter, raising funds.[150] On 27 July, 2012 the company was wound up in the Cayman Islands. On 31 August, 2012, the company filed a bankruptcy petition in the United States Bankruptcy Court for the Southern District of New York. In order to be able to avail themselves of the investigatory powers granted to Hong Kong liquidators and make clear the Mainland subsidiaries-related fundraising process, on 26 November, 2012 the debtor filed a petition for an order of its winding-up in Hong Kong.[151] On 9 April, 2014, the Hong Kong court dismissed the petition because the third core requirement was not satisfied.[152] By referring to its decision in *Re Pioneer Iron and Steel*, the court stressed again that the third core requirement could not be omitted unless the connection with Hong Kong was sufficiently strong and the benefits of a winding-up order sufficiently substantial.[153] In *Re China Medical Technologies Inc.*, the court found it sufficient to satisfy the first core requirement on the basis of the presence of an office in Hong Kong and staff here, albeit leased and employed by a subsidiary, a certain amount of investor relations activities, occasional board meetings and, most significantly, the use of Hong Kong accounts for a substantial amount of its banking activity.[154] However, the court considered:

> it is clear that Hong Kong was peripheral to the Company's principal activities such as research and development, manufacturing and equity and debt fund raising. In my view, the court would only be justified in ordering a winding up if the third core

requirement is not satisfied if the court is satisfied that Hong Kong was clearly central to the Company's principal activities and in my view, it is not.[155]

Given the decisions in the recent case law, it can be briefly summarized that the presence of assets have been gradually replaced, for instance, by the location of the controlling mind, which can satisfy the first core requirement concerning sufficient connection with Hong Kong. That approach shares some similarities with the idea of central administration indicated in the decisions handed down by the CJEU.[156] The power of liquidators to undertake investigations under Cap 32 s 221 can be deemed as of benefit to those filing for the winding-up petition, through which the second requirement can be satisfied. The third requirement can be omitted only if the court is satisfied that Hong Kong was clearly central to the debtor's principal activities. Otherwise, the winding-up order will not be granted if one of the three core requirements has not been met.

Means of recognition

COMMENCEMENT OF WINDING-UP PROCEEDING

Recognition of foreign liquidation proceedings in Hong Kong is not governed by statutory laws. A foreign liquidator usually needs to start insolvency proceedings afresh even though insolvency proceedings are under way in another jurisdiction.[157] By doing so, a foreign liquidator is appointed pursuant to the Companies Ordinance to wind up an insolvent unregistered company, who actually does not seek recognition but indirectly attempts to achieve the effects of recognition through utilizing the reliefs available under the local insolvency regime, including collection of the assets in Hong Kong in accordance with Hong Kong law.[158] In *Re Information Security One Ltd*,[159] the company was incorporated in the Cayman Islands and registered in Hong Kong as an oversea company. In 2006, the court in the Cayman Islands ordered the company to be wound up and appointed the liquidators. Later the liquidators filed the new liquidation petition in Hong Kong to seek the assistance of the Hong Kong court to recover assets within its jurisdiction and to invoke the procedure under s 221 for the examination of various directors.[160] The Hong Kong court wound up the company by holding that there was sufficient connection with Hong Kong for the court to exercise its discretion.[161] With respect to possibility of opening ancillary proceeding to assist the liquidation in the company's state of incorporation, the judge in *Re Pioneer Iron* held that "[Unless] the three core requirements had been satisfied there was no independent basis for the Court to proceed to order an ancillary liquidation".[162] The attorney who presented on behalf of the provisional liquidators provided a number of authorities, which it was suggested supported the ancillary liquidation approach. However, the court considered that:

> It does not seem to me that the fact that in a particular case it is demonstrated that viewed objectively a liquidation in Hong Kong of an unregistered company will assist a foreign liquidator in carrying out his duties is a reason for making a winding-up order if the three core requirements have not been established. In my view, it would be inconsistent with the principles discussed earlier in the judgment to make an order which commenced the statutory regime for the liquidation of companies in order to enable a foreign liquidator to use that regime's investigatory procedures to obtain information about the affairs of a company, which had little connection with Hong Kong other than the presence here of one of its officers.[163]

Further, the judge made it even clearer that:

> It seems to me relevant that Hong Kong has not enacted an equivalent to section 426 of the Insolvency Act 1986 and is not a signatory to the UNCITRAL Model Law on Cross-Border Insolvency, which would have enabled orders to be made for the purpose of assisting liquidators of unregistered companies investigate in Hong Kong matters concerning their affairs despite the fact that the three core requirements referred to in paragraph 27 cannot be satisfied.[164]

In short, if an unregistered company is already in liquidation in its place of incorporation, a liquidator is required to be appointed in Hong Kong to wind up the insolvent unregistered company and the winding-up proceeding in Hong Kong is supposed to be treated as ancillary. Nevertheless, Hong Kong has not adopted the Model Law, which means there is no independent legal basis for the Hong Kong courts to open an ancillary proceeding. Accordingly, whether or not a foreign liquidator can seek assistance in Hong Kong will depend on whether or not the local jurisdiction rules (three core requirements) can be satisfied and the Hong Kong court can exercise its jurisdiction.

CIVIL ACTION

It is also possible that the effects of insolvency proceedings can be recognized by the Hong Kong court in the process of a civil action, which involves enforcement of judgments against a debtor that is subject to insolvency proceedings abroad. According to Smart, this kind of recognition shall be subject to two-stage analysis. The distinction has to be drawn between "whether a debt has been discharged and whether the creditor can levy execution" (Smart, 2004). First of all, the effect of the foreign insolvency proceeding is not binding on the creditor's claim in Hong Kong because the foreign discharge does not form part of the proper law, which governs the contract and gives rise to the claim (Smart, 2004). Nevertheless, in the second stage, it comes to the question of enforcing the civil judgment. To fulfill the objective of universal distribution on a comity basis, the Hong Kong court may refuse execution against such assets within Hong Kong (Smart, 2004). In the case of *CCIC Finance Ltd. v Guangdong International Trust & Investment Corporation* (GITIC),[165] CCIC applied for a garnishee order against GITIC, which was a company declared bankrupt by the Mainland court. The claim was based on a "letter of support" from GITIC to CCIC, which related to the loan agreement, entered into between the parties concerned and governed by the laws of Hong Kong.[166] The Hong Kong court considered the debt was due and allowed judgment to be entered against GITIC.[167] With respect to enforcement, the court turned to determine whether the Mainland insolvency proceeding had extra-territorial effect. The court consulted four expert witnesses from the Mainland, who provided their differing expert opinions to the court on this issue.[168] The Hong Kong court held that:

> It seems clear to me that whatever has been decided before and whatever may happen in the future, the GITIC liquidation is being pursued, without challenge, on the basis of a universal collection and distribution of assets and that the paramount principle of *pari passu* of distribution is strictly being adhered to.[169]

Hence, the court refused to allow CCIC's application for a garnishee order attaching the debtor's assets in Hong Kong, although the universalism of China's insolvency law asserted by the Hong Kong court was considered unconvincing because it was not until 2007 that the current EBL came into force, which adopted universalism on outbound transactions (Booth, 2008). Later in *Hong Kong Institute of Education (HKIE) v Aoki Corporation*,[170] HKIE, a Hong Kong company, filed a petition of enforcement of an arbitral award against a Japanese company (Aoki), which had completed the civil rehabilitation proceeding ordered by the Japanese court. Aoki alleged: "The enforcement of the Award would be repugnant to the fair and equitable debt restructuring scheme ['the Scheme'] in force [in relation to Aoki under the civil rehabilitation proceeding in Japan, the jurisdiction where Aoki was incorporated."[171] HKIE contended that HKIE was never invited to register its claim against Aoki in the Japanese civil rehabilitation proceedings and that it did not take part in the same.[172] After considering the authorities and academic commentaries, the court also adopted the two-stage analysis.[173] Firstly, the court held that judgment would be entered in HKIE's favor since Japanese law could not discharge a Hong Kong debt.[174] Secondly, the court did not allow HKIE to proceed immediately to execution and further emphasized that:

> Comity does not mean blind recognition of any corporate restructuring proceeding in any jurisdiction whatsoever, however bizarre or oppressive the result. . . . It is necessary to assess whether the foreign proceedings are on balance fair and equitable in all the circumstances. There would be an onus on the debtor to satisfy the Court that the Scheme approved by the foreign court was reasonable and just and was obtained through due process.[175]

There is a risk that the creditors may be able to enforce the debts owed to them in Hong Kong if the debts are considered discharged in the foreign proceedings but not recognized as having that effect in Hong Kong. To convince the Hong Kong courts, further evidences have to be submitted, in which the foreign proceedings should be proved reasonably and justly conducted through due process. Therefore, it can be concluded that recognition in the course of civil action is not a direct way of cooperation with the foreign insolvency proceedings but an alternative solution in order to prevent enforcement action brought by an individual creditor on local assets.

SANCTION OF SCHEMES OF ARRANGEMENT

In accordance with s 673(2) Cap 622, the power to sanction an arrangement or compromise is conferred upon the Hong Kong courts. In the UK, this power has been utilized by some companies, which have no clear links to the UK but would like to restructure their business through a scheme of arrangement instead of a formal insolvency proceeding. Pursuant to the recent case law, the connection between the UK courts and those foreign companies can be established either by COMI relocation[176] or by incorporating choice of law and choice of jurisdiction clauses into the underlying agreement.[177] That kind of restructure strategy has also become workable in Hong Kong since 10 December 2014, when the High Court of Hong Kong SAR handed down its decision on the sanction of the scheme of arrangements of LDK group.[178] As aforementioned, LDK is a photovoltaic products manufacturer based in the Mainland. In order to raise funds for its business and get access to the international capital market, LDK started to build up its offshore presence overseas. In 2006, LDK Solar, as the holding company of a group of companies, was incorporated in the Cayman Islands. In 2009, LDK Silicon, as a direct wholly-owned subsidiary of LDK Solar, was also incorporated in the Cayman Islands. In 2010, LDK Silicon Holding, as a direct wholly-owned subsidiary of LDK Silicon, was incorporated in Hong Kong.[179] As aforementioned, owing to the global recession of the photovoltaic market, the three afore-mentioned offshore companies filed a petition for winding-up. LDK Solar was ordered into provisional liquidation by the Grand Court of the Cayman Islands on 27 February, 2014.[180] There were three schemes, two of which were connected to LDK Solar and LDK Silicon respectively and approved by the Grand Court of the Cayman Islands.[181] The third one related to LDK Silicon Holding, which was sanctioned by the Hong Kong court.[182] All of them sought sanction before the Hong Kong court. Considering that LDK Solar and LDK Silicon were incorporated in the Cayman Islands, one of the creditors raised the question of the jurisdiction of the Hong Kong court to sanction schemes of arrangement in respect of foreign companies.[183] The Hong Kong court firstly considered that it was vested with broad jurisdiction to wind up any unregistered company in accordance with Cap 32 s 327.[184] Sec-ondly, the Hong Kong court acknowledged that:

> Like the jurisdiction to wind up a foreign company which has been said to be an exor-bitant power, the jurisdiction of the Hong Kong court to sanction a scheme of arrange-ment in relation to a foreign company ought also to be exercised only where there is sufficient justification for the Hong Kong court to do so.[185]

Further, the court identified the different criteria between the jurisdiction to wind up a company and the jurisdiction to sanction a scheme of arrangement.[186] The court indicated that the justification for exercising the power of sanctioning a scheme should not be gov-erned by exactly the same requirements regulating the exercise of the power of winding up.[187] By referring to English common law,[188] the court held that only the first core require-ment had to be fulfilled in the case of sanctioning a scheme of arrangement, which is, there is a sufficient connection of the scheme with Hong Kong.[189] In addition, the court referred to the UK High Court's decision in *Re Apcoa Parking Holdings*,[190] holding that the claims of the creditors are all or partly governed by Hong Kong Law and thus sufficient connection was established with Hong Kong.[191] Moreover, the court regarded the Hong Kong schemes as "part of a multi-jurisdictional restructuring exercise",[192] holding

> the Hong Kong schemes form part of a larger cross-border restructuring that includes the Cayman schemes and an application to the United States Bankruptcy Court for rec-ognition of certain aspects of the Cayman scheme in respect of LDK Solar. The Hong Kong schemes and the Cayman schemes are materially identical and inter-conditional in the sense that each takes effect only if the others are sanctioned and become effec-tive. As such they constitute a unitary restructuring exercise. It seems to me that, in these circumstances, in sanctioning the Hong Kong schemes, comity would be fostered and not thwarted.[193]

The LDK case is a typical example of the trans-regional company, which is structured into onshore operations and offshore operations separately. The onshore part consists of the principal business mainly located in the Mainland side, whereas the offshore part is usually composed of headquarters established in the haven jurisdictions, such as Cayman Islands, operations in North America and Europe in order to gain access to international capital markets to finance the company's activities. Due to the special tax arrangement, the Main-land has granted Hong Kong a more preferential tax rate than it did to other countries (Daljit, Susarla, 2011). Hence, Hong Kong is always chosen as an intermediate place of incorporation in order to connect onshore operations with the offshore operations for a more preferential tax rate, which can always be deemed as a sufficient connection. The *Re LDK Solar* decision enables the liquidators from the offshore jurisdictions to avail of the Hong Kong scheme of arrangement regime, which provides much more flexible jurisdiction criteria than formal insolvency proceedings and in fact further broadens the extent of the jurisdiction power of the Hong Kong court.

Cooperation and communication

By referring to case law in other common law jurisdiction, Hong Kong is the only region among the four that utilizes protocols and video conferencing to conduct coordination and communication in practice. If a company does no business in Hong Kong, it pays no tax in the territory on income derived from outside Hong Kong.[194] Although Hong Kong is not perceived to be an international tax haven, it has the *de facto* effect. Therefore, many companies that are based in Hong Kong are incorporated elsewhere and Hong Kong is also an ideal jurisdiction for holding companies since a Hong Kong-registered holding headquarters may accumulate tax-free profits gained by its subsidiaries outside Hong Kong. Against that background, it still took decades for the Companies Ordinance to be reformed in Hong Kong and cross-border insolvency is not yet included in the reform agenda. Without a statutory framework, how to cope with the ever-growing cross-border insolvency issues? In practice, the protocols are utilized by the Hong Kong court in the absence of international treaties or legislation on cross-border insolvency, which is indeed the "judicial innovation". In most of the cases the protocols deal with coordination of concurrent insolvency proceedings in the place of incorporation (usually offshore companies in Bermuda, BVI, etc.) and in Hong Kong[195] as well as group companies whose subsidiary is operating business in Hong Kong.[196] It can be concluded from those cases that the protocols should be consistent with comity without infringing on the jurisdictions of each court. Due to lack of statutory rules, the protocols should enable the liquidators to administer both liquidations in the most economical way, reducing the conflicts and complications that may arise in cross-border insolvency matters. As summarized in *Re Jinro*, the objectives of the protocols mainly focus on:

A. harmonizing and coordinating the proceedings in Hong Kong and in other jurisdictions if required;
B. ensuring the orderly and efficient administration of proceedings in the above jurisdictions;
C. identifying, preserving and maximizing the value of the debtor's worldwide assets for the collective benefit of the creditors and other interested parties, wherever located;
D. sharing of information and to minimize duplication of effort and costs;
E. complying with the laws of Hong Kong and foreign jurisdictions, and to satisfy the statutory and professional obligations of foreign representatives[197]

In *Re Chow Kam Fai David*,[198] the debtor was required to attend the hearing of the bankruptcy petition to be cross-examined on his affidavit. The debtor applied to the court to be permitted to be cross-examined using video conference facilities (VCF). The court of the first instance considered that the giving of evidence by VCF was an exception rather than the rule and that it would be a matter of privilege accorded to the respondent and not a matter of right for him to be allowed to do so.[199] This approach was supported by the Court of Appeal, which further indicated that:

> There is no doubt that VCF is a highly useful tool. It must be a question of judgment in each case as to whether VCF should be used for the taking of evidence. No doubt, on those occasions when the witness is giving evidence that is technical or purely factual, without important issues as to credibility, a court may be more disposed to allow evidence to be given by the use VCF. Questions of cost and convenience are no doubt also important considerations that the court will have to weigh in deciding whether to allow evidence to be given using VCF. But, first and foremost, it seems to me that the judge was correct in his approach that a party wishing to give evidence using VCF should establish a sound reason why that privilege should be accorded.[200]

The court held that the cross-examination of the respondent using VCF would be inappropriate in this case because both the court of the first instance and the Court of Appeal cast doubts on the honesty of the debtor, which can be clearly discerned from his avoidance of his contractual and legal obligations.[201] Moreover, the reason that the debtor applied for using VCF is because the debtor might be subject to arrest in Hong Kong for failure to observe the earlier order requiring his attendance for examination.[202] The Court of Appeal also indicated that the decision of the judge in this respect was clearly an exercise of his discretion. However, the facts of the *Re Chow Kam Fai David* case are rather extreme. It is suggested that in other cases, for example where a director is prepared to be examined by video-conference but not to come to Hong Kong, the discretion may well be exercised differently based on all the relevant circumstances (Kwan, 2012). Therefore, it is possible that the Hong Kong court applies video-conferencing to communication in the course of cross-border insolvency cooperation.

Macao cross-border insolvency system

Due to its territoriality approach, Macao's cross-border insolvency system is hardly established. This chapter will mainly focus on the exclusive jurisdiction exercised by Macao courts over foreign insolvency proceedings and its possible influences on practice.

Brief introduction to local insolvency system

According to the latest statistics released, from 2000 to 2014 the Court of First Instance of Macao accepted 88 insolvency cases in total,[203] whereas the annual total of winding-up orders made by the Hong Kong court in 2014 alone reached 271.[204] It is evident that insolvency cases in Macao relatively rarely happen. One of the reasons is the insolvency law is a bit outdated. The insolvency law of Macao is incorporated into the Civil Procedure Code of Macao (CPCM), which was enacted in 1999. As mentioned in the Chapter 2, Macao's legal system is deeply influenced by Portugal, which is based upon the tradition of European Civil Law countries. Although the CPCM has been revised due to Macao's reunification with PRC, the legacy of Portuguese laws still remains in the current code.[205] Even after the current CPCM came into effect, the Macao courts still substantially referred to the 1961 Civil Procedure Code of Portugal in handling insolvency cases.[206] Both companies and natural persons are governed by the CPCM. Commercial enterprises, which are companies or whoever commit commercial activities,[207] shall be regulated by the rules of bankruptcy in accordance with the CPCM.[208] Debtors, who are not commercial enterprises and not able to pay the debts when they fall due, can be declared insolvent and regulated pursuant to relevant rules under the CPCM.[209] Corporate insolvency proceedings in Macao are described as "cumbersome, inflexible, and time-consuming"(Kendall, 2004). In particular, lack of pre-liquidation asset protection under Macao's insolvency system has been condemned (Pace, 2006), which can also explain the scarcity of insolvency cases there.

Current cross-border insolvency law in Macao

Exclusive jurisdiction

There is no cross-border insolvency provision provided in the CPCM. In accordance with Article 20 of the CPCM, the Macao courts shall have exclusive jurisdiction over lawsuits concerning the bankruptcy or insolvency of legal persons, whose domicile is within Macao.[210] In accordance with the Commercial Code of Macao, the domicile of companies shall be established in a determined place,[211] which should be registered in accordance with the Commercial Registration Code of Macao.[212] Moreover, companies with their registered office in Macao cannot avoid the application of the provisions of Commercial Code of Macao against third parties by relying on the fact that they do not have their main administration here.[213] Therefore, it seems that the registered office is a decisive factor to the domicile of Macao companies. Foreign insolvency proceedings will not have effects in Macao, unless the foreign judgment is recognized according to the relevant rules.[214] With respect to affirmative requirements for recognition of civil judgments from outside Macao, it is stated under Article 1200-I of the CPCM that the court that rendered the judgment shall exercise jurisdiction over the case without fraud and the judgment does not fall into the ambit of the exclusive jurisdiction of the Macao court. In short, the territorial approach of Macao in matters of cross-border insolvency is quite self-explanatory. More importantly, even if foreign insolvency proceedings are recognized, they will only be able to affect the debtors' assets in Macao, after the claims of all Macao creditors, whose debt has its origin in Macao, have been satisfied (Garcia, 2015).

Treatment of priority under the Commercial Code of Macao

It is stated under Article 83 (Liability for obligations contracted outside Macao) of the Commercial Code of Macao that:

1. The assets of a foreign company, which are possessed by the representative office in Macao, are only liable for the debts abroad after all the debts incurred by operating business in Macao are paid off.
2. A decision of a foreign authority that orders a foreign company bankrupt shall only be binding on the assets mentioned in the previous paragraph after the payment obligation therein has been observed.

With respect to distribution of the local assets of a foreign company, according to Article 83 of the Commercial Code of Macao local claims in Macao have priority over foreign claims. In addition, if a foreign company is declared bankrupt by the court at its place of incorporation, the decision can be recognized but will not be enforced until the local debts have been paid off through the local assets. Besides, in accordance with Article 739 of the Civil Code of Macao, local fines[215] and tax claims[216] are ranked as the first priority. Moreover, it is stipulated under the Decree of Labor Relations in Macao that in the case of bankruptcy or judicial liquidation of assets, the employees as a creditor have priority over other creditors.[217]

Development in practice

Insolvency proceedings in Macao are hardly fully reported and the relevant information is released mostly through the judgments of other jurisdictions.

Re Zhu Kuan *case*

In *Re Zhu Kuan* case, Zhu Kuan Group (ZKG) had been incorporated in Macao since 1988. Zhu Kuan (Hong Kong) Company Limited (ZKHK) was incorporated in Hong Kong on 19 May, 1992. They were both established as "window companies" for the commercial activities of the Zhuhai Municipal Government ("ZMG") of the People's Republic of China ("the PRC"). In 2004, the companies were ordered to be wound up and the liquidators were appointed in each proceeding. To restructure the companies, the Hong Kong liquidator in the Hong Kong proceedings and the Macao liquidator have worked closely with regard to how the Hong Kong scheme of arrangement for the ZKG or application was to be followed in Macao.[218] Regardless of Macao's exclusive jurisdiction provision on insolvency, there is the possibility that cross-border cooperation can still be voluntarily achieved between the liquidators.

Central Steel Macao *case*

Being a free trade port with roughly 27 square kilometer territory, Macao continues to implement its low taxation policy, which is guaranteed by the Basic Law,[219] and attempts to become a haven of offshore commercial activities. Although there exists taxation of income in Macao, the level of taxation is significantly lower than that of industrialized Western countries. Macao makes active efforts to attract foreign investment, namely through the Macao Investment Promotion Board. There is a special procedure for investors to obtain permanent residence in Macao and a special regime for offshore industrial and financial activities (Godinho, 2006). There was a case involving Central Steel (Macao Commercial Offshore) Limited (hereinafter, Central Steel Macao) that was incorporated in Macao. It was an indirect wholly owned subsidiary of China Metal Recycling (Holdings) Limited (hereinafter China Metal) incorporated in the Cayman Islands and registered under s 333 of the repealed Companies Ordinance (Cap 32) as a non-Hong Kong company, which has numerous subsidiaries in other jurisdictions including the Mainland and Macao. In 2013, the Securities and Futures Commission of Hong Kong SAR (hereinafter the SFC) filed a petition at the Hong Kong High Court for the compulsory winding up of China Metal in light of evidence of fraud and dishonesty on the part of its senior management, in particular the existence of records of fictitious transactions, forged documents, and a round-robin of funds.[220] As the sourcing arm of the group for the acquisition of scrap metal from international markets for its operation in the Mainland, Central Steel Macao, as alleged by the SFC, was "at the center of a fraudulent scheme".[221] Upon the request of a winding-up order by the SFC, the Hong Kong High Court appointed two joint provisional liquidators for China Metal, who were also appointed as directors of Central Steel Macao on the same day in order to gain access to and take control of the subsidiary.[222] It seems that the same approach of appointing directors has been adopted to address the regional cross-border insolvency issues between Hong Kong SAR and Macao SAR. (Please refer to "Indirect Way" in Chapter 3.)

In summary, Macao's insolvency caseload stays at a very stable low level. Restricted by its territorial approach, Macao's cross-border insolvency system is a relatively closed system and lacks interactivity with other jurisdictions, although there might be the possibility of cooperation in some individual case. With respect to the distribution of local assets, local creditors will be treated with priority over foreign ones. Moreover, owing to employee protection and the superior ranks of certain local compulsory claims, foreign creditors probably will not have high expectation for the local assets. When the development of Macao's offshore activities is on the rise but the cross-border insolvency law does not make any progress, Macao can also become a forum that can be avoided, in particular on a regional level, by replacing the directors or management personnel in the local subsidiary.

Taiwan cross-border insolvency system

The current Bankruptcy Act of Taiwan (TBA) is decades old. That's why the insolvency system in Taiwan is undergoing reform. In this section, the revised draft of the Debt Clearance Act (the 2015 Draft), in particular, its new chapter concerning cross-border insolvency, is introduced. It further discusses the development of the current cross-border insolvency regime by referring to the case law. Due to the territorial approach adopted by the current TBA, discussion mainly covers the topic of jurisdiction and recognition. It will also be demonstrated in this section that the opinions of Taiwan courts with respect to the effect of foreign insolvency proceedings vary and different criteria of recognition have been applied in practice. In the end, the possible influences of parallel recognition rules of civil judgments to the Mainland and SARs on trans-regional insolvency proceedings will be examined.

Brief introduction to the local insolvency system

The current Bankruptcy Act of Taiwan (hereinafter TBA) was enacted in 1935. It applies to both legal persons and natural persons[223] with the exception of financial institutions.[224] Pursuant to TBA, there are two types of proceedings, one of which is reconciliation and the other is liquidation.[225] Reorganization is stipulated separately under Taiwan Corporate Act (hereinafter the TCA).[226] In accordance with TCA, the corporates, which issue stocks or corporate bonds with the possibility of revival, can apply to the court for reorganization.[227] Although insolvent natural persons may also use TBA to resolve their indebtedness, it has been seldom employed owing to its out-of-date provisions. After the breakout of the credit card debt crisis, in 2008 the Taiwan Consumer Debt Clearance Act came into effect (TCDCA). TCDCA aims at assisting debtors in restructuring their debts and maintaining their basic living standard in a more efficient way (TCDCA, Article 1; see also Shyuu, 2007). Nevertheless, none of the aforementioned laws, except for Article 4 under TBA, have anything to do with cross-border insolvency.

Current cross-border insolvency law in Taiwan

Jurisdiction

There are no specific rules concerning international insolvency jurisdiction under TBA. In practice, some courts refer to the doctrine of *forum non conveniens*. In the case of *Chinatrust Commercial Bank (CTCB) v Richard S. & Lehman Brothers Treasury Co., B.V.*, the plaintiff filed a damage claim against the defendants on the ground of their infringing acts by intentionally concealing important information and unjustified enrichment therefrom.[228] This case was lodged as a civil claim but indeed originated from Lehman Brother's global insolvency proceedings. As stated in the arguments of the defendants (Richard S. & Lehman Brothers Treasury Co., B.V.) in the first instance, on 26 January, 2010 CTCB withdrew the lawsuit against Lehman Brothers Holdings Inc. because it feared that its claim would be eliminated from the creditor list by the courts that opened the insolvency proceeding of Lehman Brothers Holdings Inc. if its individual actions continued. Instead, CTCB filed a petition against Lehman Brothers Treasury Co., B.V., which is a subsidiary of Lehman Brothers Holdings Inc., by referring to the theory of reverse piercing of the corporate veil.[229] The case went through three levels of adjudication and was treated as an ordinary civil petition and concentrated on how to determine the *locus delicti*.[230] Nevertheless, in an international scenario, if a creditor is still allowed to take individual enforcement action against a foreign debtor's assets in the local court after opening of a foreign proceeding, it will be inconsistent with the principle of *pari passu* among the creditors and jeopardize the collective insolvency regime. First Commercial Bank lodged a damages petition against Lehman Brothers Treasury Co., B.V. in 2010 as well. The lower court applied the doctrine of *forum non conveniens* and dismissed the application of the plaintiff. Later the High Court approved the decision of the lower court and dismissed the appeal.[231] Later in 2012, the Supreme Court reversed the ruling rendered by the High Court, holding:

> [I]t has been proved that the finance of Lehman Brothers is highly integrated, who took advantage of establishment of different entities in order to separate the responsibilities. The affiliated companies were set up and exploited as tools, which helped to evade or hide the responsibilities and make profits by issuing bonds. The respondent, together with Lehman Brother International (Europe), Lehman Brothers Holdings Inc. and Lehman Brothers Commercial Corporation Asia Limited shall take the joint liability for the damages . . . In addition, . . . the loss of the appellant occurred within Taiwan. . . . The High Court did not make investigation on the appellant's aforementioned arguments but considered that Taiwan did not have jurisdiction on this dispute. The ruling is questionable.[232]

By referring to the respondent's argument, the High Court seemed to be aware of the effects of foreign insolvency proceedings on the local civil lawsuit. Nevertheless, the Supreme Court again regarded this dispute as an ordinary civil case and thus assumed Taiwan's jurisdiction over this case without taking into consideration the existing bankruptcy proceeding commenced abroad.

Recognition

STATUTORY LIMITATION ON THE EFFECTS OF FOREIGN PROCEEDINGS

It is stipulated under Article 4 of TBA that: "If reconciliation or declaration of bankruptcy is rendered in a foreign country, it shall have no binding effect on the assets of the debtor or the bankrupt, which are located in Taiwan."[233] It is self-explanatory that Article 4 abides by the principle of territoriality in matters of cross-border insolvency. It was further explained by the Taiwan Supreme Court in its decision handed down in 1996 that, in accordance with Article 4 of TBA, reconciliation or declaration of bankruptcy rendered in a foreign country shall have no binding effect on the assets of the debtor within Taiwan. On the basis of reciprocity, the foreign courts can also refuse to recognize the effect of a Taiwanese bankruptcy order on the assets situated in the foreign states.[234] It is observed that the Supreme Court of Taiwan used to apply the principle of territoriality, not only to the inbound effects of the foreign bankruptcy orders in Taiwan, but also to the outbound effects of Taiwanese bankruptcy orders in the foreign states. However, if the declaration of bankruptcy rendered by foreign courts shall not be recognized, a parallel proceeding or derivative claims originating from foreign bankruptcy proceedings may occur, which can result in execution of the debtor's property located in Taiwan and thus damage the collectivity of insolvency proceedings.

FLEXIBLE INTERPRETATIONS IN PRACTICE

Some lower courts followed the aforementioned holdings of the Supreme Court,[235] whereas some inclined to interpret Article 4 in more flexible ways, adopting the optional recognition approach, considering that the limitation set up by Article 4 only applies to assets located within Taiwan but does not preclude all effects of the foreign proceedings from being recognized. In 1999, the Taipei District Court heard a case between a company registered in the Cayman Islands and a company registered in BVI. The former company was ordered to be wound up in Hong Kong. The debtor filed a petition for damages due to the provisional attachment initiated by the defendant after the commencement of the Hong Kong winding-up proceeding. With respect to the effect of the winding-up order of the Hong Kong court, the court held that Article 4 of TBA should be interpreted so that declaration of bankruptcy has no binding effect merely on the assets located in Taiwan. Therefore, the defendant argued that the declaration of winding-up rendered by the Hong Kong court had no binding effect at all in Taiwan, which is contrary to the legislative purposes of TBA and thus cannot be accepted.[236] The defendant appealed to the Taiwan High Court. The Taiwan High Court agreed with the lower court and dismissed the appeal.[237] In 2011, the Taiwan High Court recognized the power of liquidators appointed by the Hong Kong High Court in the Lehman Brothers insolvency proceeding (*Taipei Fubon Bank v Lehman Brothers Commercial Corporation Asia Limited*). The court also considered that that article of TBA only excluded the effect of the foreign insolvency proceedings on the assets located within Taiwan but did not deny the effects of all the actions done by foreign courts in foreign insolvency proceedings, especially the effect of appointment of legal agents or statutory representatives for the debtor rendered by the court. Otherwise, the debtor would not be able to participate in or respond to any suits due to the lack of a legal agent in Taiwan. Consequently, the creditors in Taiwan will not be able to make any property reservation or compulsory execution on the assets of the debtor in Taiwan and even their claims will not be able to be recognized and thus will be disadvantaged.[238] Generally speaking, the liquidators are appointed to administrate and coordinate the insolvency proceedings and one of their key functions is to realize all or part of the debtor's local assets, which is contrary to the purpose of Article 4. In that case, the mere recognition of the appointment of the liquidators, who will not be allowed to take any action on the local assets, is not very meaningful but only of some symbolic value.

POSSIBLE INFLUENCES OF PARALLEL RECOGNITION RULES

Some courts identify recognition of foreign insolvency proceedings as a non-litigation lawsuit and thus apply Article 49 of the Non-Litigation Law, instead of Article 4 of the TBA. In 2009, a Taiwan court recognized a ruling rendered by the Hong Kong High Court (In

the High Court of the Hong Kong Special Administrative Companies (Winding- Up) Proceeding No. 441 of 2008). In accordance with Article 42-I of the Hong Kong and Macao
Act,[239] the Taipei District Court identified the case as a "non-litigation lawsuit" and thus
applied Article 49 of the Non-Litigation Law.[240] Further, some courts held that Article
49 of the Non-Litigation Law adopted the automatic recognition approach. Accordingly,
the foreign insolvency proceedings are deemed as automatically effective and thus it is not
necessary for the Taiwan courts to grant recognition. In 2012, the Taipei District Court
handed down a decision concerning recognition of a Japanese insolvency proceeding.[241]
The Japanese liquidator, referring to the judgment of Taipei District Court in the former
Lehman Brothers decision (Taipei District Court Trial on Application No. 514 [2009]),
applied for recognition of a reorganization ruling rendered by the Tokyo District Court.
The Taipei District Court dismissed the application, holding:

> Except as otherwise provided by law or in pursuit of a ground for execution, the party
> concerned shall apply to the court in Taiwan who shall render a judgment for compul-
> sory execution of foreign judgments. Under any other circumstances, there is no legal
> ground for the court to grant recognition on the effect of foreign judgments. That's
> why the Non-Litigation Law only lists some exceptional conditions to refuse recogni-
> tion but it does not require that the foreign judgments can only be deemed as effective
> after the Taiwan courts grant recognition. Therefore, it is inconsistent with article 49
> of Non-Litigation Law that the applicant applied for recognition of reorganization
> proceeding ordered by Tokyo District Court.[242]

As for the relevance of its former judgment, the Taipei District Court pointed out that in the
case of Taipei District Court Trial on Application No. 514 [2009], it was a case related to
Hong Kong and accordingly recognition was rendered on the basis of Article 42 of the Hong
Kong and Macao Act, which thus did not apply to the Japanese insolvency proceeding.[243]
Therefore, it can be discerned from the judgment that Hong Kong and Macao proceedings
can be deemed as automatically effective in accordance with Article 42 of the Hong Kong and
Macao Act. As aforementioned in Chapter 2, Taiwan applies parallel recognition rules of civil
judgments to the Mainland and SARs. Since Article 42 of the Hong Kong and Macao Act
is regarded as the proper legal basis for recognition of Hong Kong insolvency proceedings,
the corresponding legal basis for recognition of the Mainland insolvency proceedings shall be
Article 74 of the Mainland Act, which requires a preliminary proceeding to be initiated for
the recognition of Mainland judgments. Besides, in accordance with the interpretation of the
Taiwan Supreme Court concerning Article 74 of the Mainland Act, civil rulings or judgments
rendered in the Mainland do not have res judicata in Taiwan and therefore should be subject
to substantial review when applying for recognition.[244] Consequently, the differential criteria
adopted by Taiwan to recognize civil judgments rendered by the Mainland and SARs can be
extended to insolvency proceedings under the current Taiwan legal system.

A new chapter of cross-border insolvency under the 2015 draft

Some new ideas concerning cross-border insolvency sprouted up in 2007 when the Judicial
Yuan issued a draft of the new bankruptcy law (also giving it a new name, the Debt Clearance Act). The draft integrated three types of proceedings – reconciliation, liquidation and
reorganization. It also provided a specialized chapter handling cross-border insolvency. In
February 2014, the Judicial Yuan released a revised draft of the Debt Clearance Act (the

2014 Draft) for public consultation. Under the 2014 Draft, Chapter VI is entitled Recognition of Debt Clearance Proceedings Rendered by the Foreign Courts. It is composed of 23 provisions, which covers key aspects of cross-border insolvency, including jurisdiction, recognition criteria, the effect of the foreign proceedings, the applicable law and the duty of cooperation. On 2 June, 2015, the Judicial Yuan approved the 2014 Draft, which will soon be moved forward into the legislative process. On 15 June, 2015, the Judicial Yuan published the approved draft (the 2015 Draft). The approved 2015 Draft will be used as the basic reference in this book.

Venue and international jurisdiction

The 2015 Draft designates a specialized court exclusively to adjudicate recognition of foreign debt-clearance proceedings in Taiwan, which is the Taipei District Court.[245] Besides, a debt-clearance proceeding comes under the venue of the Taiwanese court exclusively situated at the domicile of the debtor. If the debtor's head office or principal place of business is located abroad, the place where to adjudicate the debt-clearance proceedings is its head office or principal place of business in Taiwan.[246] In other words, the courts of foreign countries, within the territory of which the head office or principal place of business of the debtor is located, shall have jurisdiction to commence the foreign debt-clearance proceedings. Recognition of such foreign debt-clearance proceedings shall not preclude opening of the parallel debt-clearance proceedings in Taiwan,[247] where the local head office or local principal place of business of the debtor is situated. Besides, if the forum to adjudicate the debt-clearance proceedings within Taiwan cannot be ascertained based on the aforementioned factors, the proper venue for opening the local debt-clearance proceedings shall be the place where the debtor's principal assets is situated.

Recognition: restrictions and effects

Recognition is granted on a reciprocal basis under the 2015 Draft[248] and the court can refuse to recognize the foreign proceedings if

(1) in accordance with the laws of Taiwan, the foreign courts do not have jurisdiction;
(2) the interests of domestic creditors are inappropriately impaired in the foreign proceeding;
(3) recognition of the foreign proceeding is contrary to the public policy or *boni mores*.[249]

Moreover, after the Taiwan courts commence the debt-clearance proceedings, the foreign debt-clearance proceedings, upon which recognition has been granted, can be stayed.[250] In addition, the 2015 Draft also provides the conditions, upon which the courts can withdraw the recognition of the foreign debt-clearance proceedings:

(1) the foreign debt-clearance proceeding falls within the ambit of Article 299;
(2) the foreign debt-clearance proceeding has been terminated or rescinded;
(3) the documents submitted by the liquidator in accordance with Article 298-I and Article 300-I are forged, altered or involving other fraudulent behaviors;
(4) the liquidators, administrator or debtors seriously violate the statutory obligations.[251]

If there are debt-clearance proceedings against the same debtor pending before the Taiwanese court, the recognition of foreign debt-clearance proceedings should be ceased unless recognition will be more beneficial to the local creditors in Taiwan.[252] Except as otherwise provided, the effect of recognition dates back to the opening of debt-clearance proceedings ordered by foreign courts.[253] Once recognized, the foreign debt-clearance proceedings shall have effect on the assets of the debtor or interested party within Taiwan.[254] To dispose of, distribute and transfer the debtor's assets located within Taiwan, the petitions should be filed to the Taiwan court for approval.[255] The court shall refuse to grant approval if the petitions can inappropriately impair the interests of local creditors.[256] In addition, in order to ensure *pari passu* distribution among the creditors, the hotchpot rules have been introduced into the 2015 Draft. It is required that the creditors, who have, in the course of foreign debt-clearance proceedings, obtained a dividend on their claims shall share distributions made in the Taiwan proceeding only where creditors of the same ranking obtained an equivalent distribution.[257] Moreover, it is also stipulated that if creditors, who will in the course of foreign debt-clearance proceedings, obtain dividends on their claim, shall take distributions made in the Taiwan proceeding only where creditors of the same ranking have obtained an equivalent distribution or they can provide appropriate guarantee. If the guarantee cannot be provided, their distributions shall be held in escrow.[258]

Duty of cooperation

The 2015 Draft provides some general rules concerning the duty of the domestic and foreign liquidators or administrators to cooperate with each other. The liquidators or administrators appointed in the Taiwan debt-clearance proceedings can request the foreign liquidators or administrators for necessary cooperation and information as well as provide the foreign liquidators or administrators with necessary cooperation and information.[259] Further, it is stated that Chapter VI of the 2015 Draft shall apply mutatis mutandis to recognition of debt-clearance proceedings opened in Mainland China, Hong Kong and Macao.[260]

In summary, the 2015 Draft provides a relatively comprehensive cross-border insolvency regime. Nevertheless, several limitations have been set on recognition criteria of foreign insolvency proceedings. Protection of the interests of local creditors is emphasized, in particular, which may have an impact on the stay of recognition, approval of disposal of local assets and applicable law to the employment contract. Moreover, it is also observed that Taiwan tends to apply uniform rules in matters of recognition of cross-border insolvency proceedings regardless of its place of origin among China, Hong Kong, Macao and other foreign countries, which is a different approach from recognition of civil and commercial judgments.

Conclusion

The insolvency systems in the four regions have different characteristics, whereas the cross-border insolvency systems therein seem to share something in common since all of them are still under development. In the Mainland, the current EBL was adopted in 2006 covering all types of incorporated enterprises, although the former bankruptcy law to some extent still has its influence, especially with respect to involvement of government. In the Mainland, there are obvious advantages of government involvement in the insolvency proceedings. However, it is required by the market-oriented economy to reconsider the relationship between local government and local enterprises and the means of their involvement, which cannot touch the bottom line of the independence of the courts in insolvency proceedings. The EBL provides insufficient rules (Article 5) to deal with cross-border insolvency issues. In practice, for the countries, which have mutual civil and commercial judicial assistance treaties or agreements, it is more likely that the effects of the insolvency proceedings in those countries can be recognized in the Mainland. In addition to its ambiguity, the insufficient rule on cross-border insolvency law discourages filings of recognition and enforcement of the foreign and regional insolvency proceedings before the Mainland courts at the same time. Besides, the Chinese courts still hold quite restrictive reciprocity standards in rendering recognition of foreign civil and commercial judgments. On the international level, the Mainland jurisdiction has been intentionally avoided due to lack of confidence in its insolvency system and the uncertainty of its cross-border insolvency legislation. On the regional level, the absence of regional cross-border insolvency arrangements resulted in invention of substitutes based on company law, i.e. appointment of a provisional liquidator or liquidator as a member of the management or representative of the Mainland subsidiaries. Nevertheless, such a solution can bring complexity to the proceedings owing to the dual identities of the liquidators and delay the process because of the resistance of former members. Moreover, the solution, as an indispensable part of the effects of the parallel proceedings, which do not automatically have effect in the Mainland, is merely an evasion of the genuine problem.

Hong Kong SAR still holds a wait-and-see attitude towards the reform of its cross-border insolvency law. Although the UNCITRAL Model Law was published nearly two decades ago and over 40 countries and regions have adopted the Model Law as part of their domestic law, concerns have been expressed about the possibility of synchronous development in the neighboring jurisdictions, in particular, the Mainland. Thus, evolvement of Hong Kong's statutory cross-border insolvency system is still pending. The current Hong Kong cross-border insolvency law is greatly influenced by common law practice. Jurisdiction also plays an important role in recognition of foreign insolvency proceedings. There is no independent legal basis for Hong Kong courts to open an ancillary proceeding. To seek the assistance of the Hong Kong courts, a foreign liquidator usually needs to start insolvency proceedings afresh even though insolvency proceedings are under way in another jurisdiction. However, the purpose of seeking assistance alone does not suffice to be granted a winding-up order. The effects of insolvency proceedings can also be recognized by the Hong Kong court in the process of the civil action, which is subject to a two-stage analysis. The third means to seek recognition in Hong Kong is to utilize the power of the courts to sanction a scheme of arrangement as stipulated under Cap 622 s 673(2). By referring to the UK High Court's decision, the sanction of the Hong Kong scheme of arrangements as part of a multi-jurisdictional restructuring scheme enables Hong Kong to participate in the global unitary restructuring exercise on a comity basis. With respect to cooperation and coordination, video-conferencing may also be taken into consideration in matters of communication and coordination of concurrent insolvency proceedings.

Macao's insolvency caseload stays at a very stable low level. By adopting exclusive jurisdiction over insolvency proceedings of a company, Macao follows a territorialism approach in handling cross-border insolvency cases, which gives rise to interactivity with other jurisdictions. With respect to distribution of local assets, local creditors will be treated with priority over foreign ones. Moreover, owing to employee protection and the superior ranks of certain local compulsory claims, foreign creditors probably will not have high expectation for the local assets, although there might be the possibility of cooperation in some individual case. When the development of Macao's offshore activities is on the rise but the cross-border insolvency law does not make any progress, Macao can also become a forum that can be avoided, in particular on the regional level, by replacing the directors or management personnel in the local subsidiary.

In Taiwan, there are no specific rules concerning international insolvency jurisdiction under the current TBA. In addition, the current TBA (Article 4) sets a limitation on foreign insolvency proceedings, which shall have no binding effect on the assets of the debtor within Taiwan. The majority of courts opt to interpret the limitation in more flexible ways. Some courts adopt the optional recognition approach, considering that the limitation only applies to assets located within Taiwan but does not preclude all effects of the foreign proceedings, such as appointment of liquidators, from being recognized. In June 2015, the Judicial Yuan of Taiwan issued the approved draft of the Debt Clearance Act (the 2015 Draft) in order to conduct reform of the current decade-old Bankruptcy Act. The 2015 Draft provides one new chapter concerning cross-border insolvency, which is a relatively comprehensive cross-border insolvency regime, including rules of jurisdiction, recognition criteria, applicable laws and duty of cooperation. Moreover, it is observed that Taiwan tends to apply uniform rules in matters of recognition of cross-border insolvency proceedings regardless of its place of origin among China, Hong Kong, Macao and other foreign countries, which is a different approach from its current judicial practice on recognition of civil and commercial judgments.

For a sovereign state that has gone through reunification, to harmonize legal conflicts thereof is something inevitable in the process of further integration. Meanwhile, driven by economic interaction, legal cooperation also has to be carried out between Mainland China and Taiwan. Considering the special political composition and diverse cross-border insolvency systems among the four regions, the most urgent issues are concerning how to achieve efficient recognition by overcoming the jurisdictional hurdles and promote coordination of the concurrent insolvency proceedings opened in the four regions.

Notes

1 The 1986 EBL, Article 2: This law applies to the enterprises owned by the whole people. In pursuant to the Constitution Law of PRC, Article 7: The State-owned economy, namely, the socialist economy under ownership by the whole people. Therefore, EBL 1986 actually applied to state-owned enterprises alone.
2 EBL 1986, Article 8.
3 Ibid., Chapter 4 Reconciliation and Readjustment.
4 Ibid., Article 24.
5 Ibid., Article 4.
6 The Company Law was adopted on 29 December, 1993, revised on 25 December, 1999, 2005 and 2013.
7 Company Law (1993), Articles 1, 7.
8 Ibid.
9 2002 Provisions on Some Issues concerning the Trial of Enterprise Bankruptcy Cases of the Supreme People's Court, Interpretation No. 23 [2002], issued on 30 July, 2002. It superseded the earlier interpretations (the 1991 Several Opinions on EBL and the 1992 Several Opinions on CPL) if there was any inconsistency in the former.
10 The 2002 Provisions on Bankruptcy Cases, Articles 4, 5.
11 They are mainly: (A) Regulations on the Placement of Surplus Staff and Workers of State-owned Enterprises (1993, Decree No. 111); (B) Regulations on Unemployment Insurance for Staff and Workers of State-owned Enterprises (1993, Decree No. 110); (C) The Notice of Advancing the Problem-solving and the Reemployment of the Enterprise Employees (1997, Decree No. 166); (D) Supplementary Notice of the State Council on the Relevant Issues about the Pilot Implementation of the Merger and Bankruptcy of State-owned Enterprises

in Some Cities and the Reemployment of Workers (1997, Decree No. 10); (E) Notice of
the Central Committee of the Communist Party and the State Council on the Basic Living
Guarantee and the Reemployment of the Laid-off employees of the State-owned Enterprises
(1998, Decree No. 10).

12 They are mainly: (A) Rules on the Evaluation and Management of State Assets (1991);
(B) Notice of Stopping, Decreasing and Slowing the Return of the Interests of the Loans
for the Enterprises which are Suspended Operation for Consolidation, Merged, Dissolved
and Bankrupt (1993, Decree No. 113); (C) Notice of Several Issues on the Mortgage of the
Right to the Use of the Land (1997, Decree No. 2); (D) Several Opinions on Enhancing the
Land Asset Management and Promoting the Reform and Development of the State-owned
Enterprises (1999, Decree No. 433).

13 They are mainly: (A) Interim Measures on Enterprise Mergers (1989, Decree No. 38);
(B) Notice of the State Council on the Relevant Issues concerning the Pilot Implementation
of Bankruptcy of State-owned Enterprises in Some Cities (1994, No. 59); (C) Notice of
the Several Issues on the Pilot Implementation of the Merger and Bankruptcy of the State-
owned Enterprises (1996, Decree No. 492).

14 Data collected from www.vip.chinalawinfo.com (last accessed on 31 March, 2017).

15 Most part of this section has been derived from Xinyi Gong, Can the Day Understand the
Night? Brief Introduction into Problems of the Current Insolvency System in China, Norton
Journal of Bankruptcy Law and Practice, Volume 24, Issue 5, 2015.

16 The EBL 1986 still has some influence on the current EBL. Parallel to the normal bankruptcy
proceedings, so-called administrative closure is stipulated in the EBL, which means, certain
state-owned enterprises within the period and scope as are prescribed by the State Council
before the EBL is put into effect shall be handled according to the relevant regulations of
the State Council and therefore are excluded from the EBL (EBL, Article 133). The State-
Owned Assets Supervision and Administration Commission ("SASAC") of the State Council
estimated that roughly 2,000 SOEs might take advantage of this "administrative closure".
Not until the period for administrative closure expires will the new law truly harmonize the
bankruptcy treatment of all SOEs, including SOEs and non-SOE legal person enterprises.
See also Lan Xinzhen, Looking Forward to the New Bankruptcy Law (in Chinese), in: Beijing Review, 21 June, 2004, available at: www.bjreview.cn/Cn/2004-29/200429-jj2.htm
(last visited on 31 March, 2017).

17 EBL, Chapter III.

18 State Administration for Industry and Commerce of the PRC, Analysis Report on Domestic
Enterprises Life Circle (in Chinese), June 2013, p. 3, available at: www.saic.gov.cn/zwgk/
tjzl/zxtjzl/xxzx/201307/P020130731318661073618.pdf (last accessed on 31 March,
2017).

19 EBL, Article 2. In accordance with Article 2 of Regulations of the People's Republic of
China for Controlling the Registration of Enterprises as Legal Persons (effective as of July 1,
1988), not all kinds of enterprises are qualified as legal person.

20 EBL, Article 135.

21 The 1992 Opinions, No. 22 [1992] of the Supreme People's Court (in Chinese).

22 The 1992 Opinions (in Chinese), Articles 297–299.

23 Ibid., Article 297.

24 The 1998 Trial Provisions, No. 22 [1992] of the Supreme People's Court (in Chinese).

25 The 1998 Trial Provisions (in Chinese), Article 96.

26 Ibid., Article 102(1).

27 Ibid., Article 105.

28 Judicial Interpretation of the Supreme People's Court concerning Application of Civil Procedure Law [2015] Judicial Interpretation No. 5 (in Chinese).

29 [2015] Judicial Interpretation No. 5 (in Chinese), Article 513.

30 [2015] Judicial Interpretation No. 5 (in Chinese), Article 514.

31 The EBL, Article 2, para. 1.

32 Ibid., Article 2, para. 2.

33 [2017] Judicial Interpretation No. 2 (in Chinese), Article 20.

34 United States International Trade Commission, China: Description of Selected Government
Practices and Policies Affecting Decision-Making in the Economy, Investigation Nos. 332–492,
USITC Publication 3978, December 2007, p. 30.

35 To be considered a "market economy", a country must have a floating exchange rate, a free market, a non-intrusive government, effective business accounting standards and, lastly, a clear definition of property rights and bankruptcy laws. In Policy Department of European Parliament, Trade and Economic Relations with China 2015, June 2015, p. 24.

36 European Parliament, China and Granting of Market Economy Status thereto, 20 April, 2015, www.europarl.europa.eu/sides/getDoc.do?type=WQ&reference=E-2015-006250& language=EN (last accessed on 31 March, 2017).

37 Policy Department of European Parliament, Trade and Economic Relations with China 2015, June 2015, p. 24, www.europarl.europa.eu/RegData/etudes/IDAN/2015/549062/ EXPO_IDA(2015)549062_EN.pdf (last accessed on 31 March, 2017).

38 EBL, Article 24.

39 EBL 1986, Article 24.

40 Provisions of the Supreme People's Court on Designating the Administrator during the Trial of Enterprise Bankruptcy Cases (Interpretation No. 8 [2007], issued on 12 April, 2007, hereinafter Provisions of Designating the Administrator), Article 19.

41 Draft Report on Connected Transaction Concerning Tianyi's Acquisition of Assets through Issuing Stocks, 2008, available at: http://business.sohu.com/20080119/n254757501. shtml (last accessed on 31 March, 2017); [2007] Hubei Jinzhou Intermediate People's Court Civil Bankruptcy No. 14–5 (in Chinese).

42 EBL, Article 113.

43 [2010] Announcement of the State Administration of Taxation No. 4 (in Chinese).

44 2013 Top Ten Typical Enterprise-related Cases in Zhejiang Province, 13 January, 2014, available at: www.zjcourt.cn/content/20140113000001/20140113000008.html (last accessed on 31 March, 2017).

45 [2010] Zhoushan People's Court Ordinary Commercial Bankruptcy No. 1 (in Chinese).

46 [2011] Ningbo Fenghua People's Court Commercial Bankruptcy No. 1 (in Chinese).

47 Photovoltaic products generate electricity by converting solar energy through semi-conducting materials that exhibit the photovoltaic effect.

48 [2014] Shanghai No. 1 Intermediate People's Court Civil IV (Commercial) Bankruptcy No. 1–1 (in Chinese).

49 [2014] Shanghai No. 1 Intermediate People's Court Civil IV (Commercial) Bankruptcy No. 1–4 (in Chinese).

50 [2013] Zhejiang Huzhou Intermediate People's Court Bankruptcy Preliminary No. 1 (in Chinese).

51 [2009] Judicial Interpretation No. 36 (in Chinese).

52 Ibid., Article 5.

53 Ibid., Article 5.

54 For better understanding of "minimal judicial independence, impartiality and integrity", there are some examples, such as the UN Basic Principles on the Independence of the Judiciary (endorsed by General Assembly resolutions 40/32 of 29 November, 1985 and 40/146 of 13 December, 1985); IBA Minimum Standards of Judicial Independence (adopted by the International Bar Association in 1982).

55 [2009] Judicial Interpretation No. 36 (in Chinese); [2012] Judicial Interpretation No. 261 (in Chinese).

56 [2010] Jiangsu Wuxi Intermediate People's Court Bankruptcy No. 6 (in Chinese).

57 [2007] Hangzhou Civil II First Instance No. 184 (in Chinese).

58 EBL, Articles 70, 95 and 96.

59 [2012] Yiyang Heshan Civil Bankruptcy Civil Verdict No. 3–2 (in Chinese).

60 [2013] Yiyang Civil II Final No. 168 (in Chinese).

61 [2012] Judicial Interpretation No. 261 (in Chinese).

62 Ibid., Article 3.

63 Ibid., Article 4.

64 Provisions (I) [2011] Judicial Interpretation No. 22 (in Chinese).

65 Ibid., Article 9.

66 [2011] Judicial Interpretation No. 281, Article 2.

67 [2011] Judicial Interpretation No. 281, Articles 2, 3.

68 These countries that signed the civil and commercial judicial assistance treaties with China are (in chronological order): France, Poland, Belgium, Mongolia, Romania, Italy, Spain,

Russia, Turkey, Ukraine, Cuba, Belarus, Kazakhstan, Bulgaria, Thailand, Egypt, Greece, Cyprus, Hungary, Morocco, Kirghizstan, Tajikistan, Singapore, Uzbekistan, Vietnam, Laos, Tunisia, Lithuania, Argentina, Republic of Korea, Democratic People's Republic of Korea, United Arab Emirates, Kuwait, Peru, Brazil, Algeria. Information collected from the database Chinalawinfo.

69 The Chinese proceeding involved a third party, a Hong Kong company. On 2 May, 1999, E.N.Group s.p.a. agreed to sell the share it held of the Nassetti Ettore company, which was located in China to a Hong Kong company. On 21 July, 1999, the agreement was approved by the local government and then the Hong Kong company, replacing E.N.Group s.p.a., became the shareholder of Nassetti Ettore. B&T Ceramic Group argued that E.N.Group s.p.a. had no rights to do that. Therefore, the court dismissed the enforcement request because the court held that the third party (the Hong Kong company) involved, which should be solved in another lawsuit.

70 CPL (1991), Article 268.

71 Sino-Australian Mutual Promotion and Protection of the Investment Agreement, Article 5(3).

72 [2006] Civil Division IV of the Supreme People's Court Others No. 45.

73 The dispute was settled by way of mediation. Unlike judgments, in China, the results of mediation are not required to be disclosed. Nevertheless, in his article the judge provided quite detailed information and analysis on that case because as judge who made decision on that case, he found it necessary to disclose some information as reference for improvement of the legislation involved.

74 [1995] Civil Division of the Supreme People's Court Others No. 17.

75 Kammergericht-Berlin-Aktenzeichen: 20 SCH 13/04, Beschluss von 18.05.2006. Leitsatz: 1. Eine rechtskräftige Entscheidung eines Volksgerichts (in China) kann gemäß §328 ZPO anerkannt werden. Available at: www.juraforum.de/urteile/kammergericht-berlin/kammergericht-berlin-beschluss-vom-18-05-2006-az-20-sch-1304 (last accessed on 31 March, 2017).

76 [2003] First Instance of Beijing Second Intermediate People's Court Civil Mediation No. 00002.

77 Kammergericht-Berlin-Aktenzeichen: 20 SCH 13/04, Beschluss von 18.05.2006, para. 2(a).

78 The EC Regulation, Recital (22).

79 Article 282 of CPL (2012).

80 *Richardson v Mellish* (1824) 2 Bing. 228; (1824–34) All ER Rep 258.

81 [2012] Shanghai Pudong New Area District Court Civil Litigation Second Division (Commercial) First Instance No. 1119.

82 [2009] Wuhan Intermediate People's Court of Hubei Province Intellectual Property First Instance No. 519.

83 [2004] Xiamen Intermediate People's Court of Fujian Province Civil Recognition No. 20.

84 Republic of China was originally founded in 1912. After the establishment of the People's Republic of China in 1949, Republic of China relocated its government to Taiwan and its surrounding areas. Since 1971 the People's Republic of China restored its position in United Nations, whose representatives are "the only lawful representatives of China" and expelled the unlawful representatives of Republic of China.
    See United Nations General Assembly Resolution 2758, Restoration of the Lawful Rights of the People's Republic of China in the United Nations, visit http://daccess-dds-ny.un.org/doc/RESOLUTION/GEN/NR0/327/74/IMG/NR032774.pdf?OpenElement (last accessed on 31 March, 2017).

85 [2004] Xiamen Intermediate People's Court of Fujian Province Civil Recognition No. 20 (in Chinese).

86 [2003] Xiamen Intermediate People's Court of Fujian Province Economic First Instance No. 146. In that case, the Xiamen Intermediate People's Court of Fujian Province also made detailed explanation on *forum non conveniens*. The case was regarded as model case in that regard and thus published in Gazette of Supreme People's Court Vol. 7, 2004, pp. 32–34.

87 General Principles of Civil Law of PRC, Article 58(5).

88 Contract Law of PRC, Article 52(4).

89 EBL, Article 48; [2011] Shenzhen Intermediate People's Court Civil Division VI Final Instance No. 94.

90 [2007] Hainan High People's Court Civil Division I Final Instance No. 28.
91 [2005] Ministry of Finance Financial No. 74, Article 2.
92 EBL, Article 7.
93 EBL, Chapter VI and Article 59.
94 EBL, Article 61.
95 Part of this section has been derived from my publication Gong, Xinyi, When Hong Kong Becomes SAR, Is the Mainland Ready? – Problems of Judgments Recognition in Cross-border Insolvency Matters, in: International Insolvency Review, Wiley-Blackwell, Vol. 20, Issue 1, 2011, pp. 63–64; and also Gong Xinyi, Can the Day Understand the Night? Brief Introduction into Problems of the Current Insolvency System in China, Norton Journal of Bankruptcy Law and Practice, Vol. 24, Issue 5, 2015.
96 In *Re Suntech Power Holdings Co., Ltd.*, Case No. 14-10383(SMB), Written Opinion Signed On 17 November, 2014.
97 On 20 March, 2013, the Mainland court accepted the application for the reorganization of Wuxi Suntech (the Wuxi proceeding). See Wu Xi Intermediate Court Successfully Concluded the Suntech Reorganization Proceeding, the Reorganization Plan Has Been Almost Completely Implemented (in Chinese), 7 January, 2014, p. 4, available at: http://wxzy.chinacourt.org/public/detail.php?id=5228 (last accessed on 31 March, 2017).
98 On 5 November, 2013, provisional liquidation of Suntech Power was initiated in Cayman Islands (the Cayman proceeding). On 21 February, 2014, a petition was filed for recognition of Suntech Power's provisional liquidation proceeding pending in Cayman Islands as a foreign main proceeding or non-main proceeding before the United States Bankruptcy Court for the Southern District of New York (SDNY) In *Re Suntech Power Holdings Co., Ltd.*, Case No. 14-10383(SMB), Written Opinion Signed On 17 November, 2014, available at www.nysb.uscourts.gov/sites/default/files/opinions/247366_67_opinion.pdf (last accessed on 31 March, 2017).
99 In *Re Suntech Power Holdings Co., Ltd.*, Case No. 14-10383(SMB), Written Opinion Signed On 17 November, 2014, p. 3.
100 Objection of the Solyndra Residual Trust to Chapter 15 Petition of *Suntech Power Holdings Co., Ltd.* (in provisional liquidation) for Recognition of Foreign Main Proceeding Pursuant to §1517 of the Bankruptcy Code, In *Re Suntech Power Holdings Co., Ltd.* (in Provisional Liquidation), Case No. 14-10383 (SMB), Related Docket Nos. 1, 2, 3, 4, p. 2.
101 In *Re Suntech Power Holdings Co., Ltd.*, Case No. 14-10383(SMB), Written Opinion Signed On 17 November, 2014, at Background, B. Foreign Proceeding, p. 6; C. COMI, p. 29.
102 In *Re Suntech Power Holdings Co., Ltd.*, Case No. 14-10383(SMB), Written Opinion Signed On 17 November, 2014, at Background, B. Foreign Proceeding, pp. 5–6.
103 [2014] Jiaxing Haining Bankruptcy(Pre) No. 4 (in Chinese).
104 The bankruptcy proceedings involved Zhejiang Topoint Photovoltaic Co. Ltd. and its three affiliates, Zhejiang Jiutai New Energy Co. Ltd., Zhejiang Yutai Solar Materials Co. Ltd. and Zhejiang Willsolar Photoelectric Materials Co. Ltd. Recognition was granted altogether on 12 August, 2014. Their jointly administered proceedings are (i) *Zhejiang Topoint Photovoltaic Co., Ltd.*, Case No. 14-24549-GMB; (ii) *Zhejiang Jiutai New Energy Co., Ltd.*, Case No. 14-24555-GMB; (iii) *Zhejiang Yutai Solar Materials Co., Ltd.*, Case No. 14-24557-GMB; and (iv) *Zhejiang Willsolar Photoelectric Materials Co., Ltd.*, Case No. 14-24559-GMB.
105 [2007] Guangzhou Intermediate People's Court Civil Fourth Tribunal Final Instance No. 7 (in Chinese).
106 Company Law of PRC (2005), Article 152.
107 Company Law of PRC (2013), Article 105.
108 [2009] Fuzhou Intermediate People's Court Civil First Instance No. 166 (in Chinese).
109 Cap 32, ss 266, 266A and 266B refer to ss 50–51B of the BO.
110 Financial Services and the Treasury Bureau, Improvement of Corporate Insolvency Law Legislative Proposal (consultation paper), April 2013, at 5.16.
111 Financial Services and the Treasury Bureau, Improvement of Corporate Insolvency Law Legislative Proposal (consultation paper), April 2013.
112 Legislative Council Panel on Financial Affairs Meeting on 7 July, 2014, Updated background brief on review of corporate insolvency law and introduction of a statutory corporate rescue procedure, LC Paper No. CB (1)1668/13–14(02), 7 July 2014, p. 1.

113 Financial Services and the Treasury Bureau, Improvement of Corporate Insolvency Law Legislative Proposals Consultation Conclusions, 28 May, 2014.

114 Legislative Council Panel on Financial Affairs, Consultation Conclusions on Corporate Insolvency Law Improvement Exercise and Detailed proposals on a new Statutory Corporate Rescue Procedure, CB (1)1536/13–14(01), 7 July, 2014.

115 Legislative Council Panel on Financial Affairs, Consultation Conclusions on Corporate Insolvency Law Improvement Exercise and Detailed proposals on a new Statutory Corporate Rescue Procedure, CB (1)1536/13–14(01), 7 July, 2014, pp. 3–10 and Annex B.

116 Cap 622, ss 668–670, 673, 674, 677.

117 See for example: *Re Keview Technology (BVI) Ltd.* [2002] 2 HKLRD 290; *Re Luen Cheong Tai International Holdings Ltd.* [2002] 3 HKLRD 610; *Re I-China Holdings Ltd.* [2003] 1 HKLRD 629; *Re Fujian Group Ltd.* [2003] HKEC 266.

118 Legislative Council Panel on Financial Affairs, Consultation Conclusions on Corporate Insolvency Law Improvement Exercise and Detailed proposals on a new Statutory Corporate Rescue Procedure, CB (1)1536/13–14(01), 7 July, 2014, Annex B.

119 Legislative Council Panel on Financial Affairs, Consultation Conclusions on Corporate Insolvency Law Improvement Exercise and Detailed proposals on a new Statutory Corporate Rescue Procedure, CB (1)1536/13–14(01), 7 July 2014, Annex C.

120 Legislative Council Panel on Financial Affairs, Consultation Conclusions on Corporate Insolvency Law Improvement Exercise and Detailed proposals on a new Statutory Corporate Rescue Procedure, CB (1)1536/13–14(01), 7 July, 2014, Appendix III-B.

121 SFST's (Secretary for Financial Services and the Treasury) Speech on Financial Services at LegCo Finance Committee Special Meeting, Tuesday, April 5, 2016, available at: http://www.fstb.gov.hk/en/docs/sp20160405_e.pdf; see also Speech by SFST at opening of Corporate Governance Roundtable, March 13, 2017; available at: http://www.fstb.gov.hk/en/docs/sp20170313_e.pdf (latest accessed on 25 August 2017)

122 Cap 622, s 2: non-Hong Kong company means a company incorporated outside Hong Kong that: (a) establishes a place of business in Hong Kong on or after the commencement date of Part 16; or (b) has established a place of business in Hong Kong before that commencement date and continues to have a place of business in Hong Kong at that commencement date.

123 The Law Reform Commission of Hong Kong was established in January 1980. The Commission considers for reform those aspects of the laws of Hong Kong, which are referred to it by the Secretary for Justice or the Chief Justice.

124 The Law Reform Commission of Hong Kong, 1999 Report on the Winding-up Provisions of the Companies Ordinance, available at: www.hkreform.gov.hk/en/publications/rwind.htm (last accessed 31 March, 2017).

125 Legislative Council Panel on Financial Affairs, Consultation Conclusions on Corporate Insolvency Law Improvement Exercise and Detailed proposals on a new Statutory Corporate Rescue Procedure, CB (1)1536/13–14(01), 7 July, 2014, p. 65.

126 Companies (Winding Up and Miscellaneous Provisions) (Amendment) Ordinance 2016 (Commencement) Notice 2016, LN190 of 2016.

127 Trade and Industry Department of Hong Kong SAR, Hong Kong's Principal Trading Partners in 2015, available at: www.tid.gov.hk/english/trade_relations/mainland/trade.html (last accessed on 31 March, 2017).

128 Bills Committee on the Companies (Winding Up and Miscellaneous Provisions) (Amendment) Bill 2015, Summary of views of submissions and Government's responses, CB (1)481/15–16(04), 25 January, 2016, Government's responses No. 59.

129 Cap 32, s 326(2), Companies Ordinance.

130 *Securities and Futures Commission v MKI Corporation* [1995] 2 HKC 79.

131 *Re Chime Corporation Limited* [2004] 7 HKCFAR 546, at 40.

132 The three core requirements were adopted in several cases in Hong Kong. For instance, *Re Zhu Kuan Group Co. Ltd.* [2004] HKCFI 795; HCCW874/2003 (2 August 2004), at 22; *Re Information Security One Ltd* [2007] HKCFI 848; [2007] 3 HKLRD 780; [2007] 4 HKC 383; HCCW212/2007 (13 August, 2007) at 8; *Re Beauty China Holdings Ltd* [2009] 6 HKC 351, at 23; *Re Yung Kee Holdings Limited* [2012] 6 HKC 246, at 70; *Re Pioneer Iron and Steel Co. Ltd.* [2013] HKCFI 324, at 27.

133 Zoneheath Associates Ltd., as creditor, which was a UK company, sought a winding-up order in Hong Kong against China Tianjin International Economic and Technical Cooperative

Corporation, which was incorporated in the Mainland and therefore was a non-Hong Kong company. In *Re China Tianjin International Economic and Technical Cooperative Corporation* [1994] HKCFI 114; [1994] 1 HKLR 327; [1995] 1 HKC 720; HCCW438/1994.

134 *Re China Tianjin International Economic and Technical Cooperative Corporation* [1995] 1 HKC 720, at 3,6.
135 *Re Yung Kee* [2014] 2 HKC 556.
136 Cap 622, s 724(1).
137 *Re Yung Kee* [2014] 2 HKC 556, at 42.
138 *Re Pioneer Iron and Steel Group Co. Ltd.* [2013] HKCFI 324.
139 Ibid., at 28.
140 Ibid., at 34.
141 Ibid., at 35.
142 Ibid., at 36.
143 Ibid., at 38.
144 Ibid., at 41.
145 Ibid., at 43.
146 Ibid., at 43.
147 Ibid., at 28.
148 *Re China Medical Technologies Inc.* [2014] HKCFI 656.
149 Ibid., at 1, 12.
150 Ibid., at 13.
151 Ibid., at 21, 22.
152 Ibid., at 54.
153 *Re Pioneer Iron and Steel Group Co. Ltd.* [2013] HKCFI 324, at 27.
154 Ibid., at 57,58.
155 Ibid., at 58.
156 Case C-341/04 *Eurofood IFSC Ltd* [2006] ECR I-03813 (*Eurofood*), para. 34; Case C-396/09 *Interedil Srl (in liquidation) v Fallimento Interedil Srl, Intesa Gestione Crediti SpA* [2011] ECR I-09915 (*Interedil*), para. 51; Case C-191/10 *Rastelli Davide e C. Snc v Jean-Charles Hidoux* [2011] ECR I-13209 (*Rastelli*), para. 35.
157 The Law Reform Commission of Hong Kong, 1999 Report on the Winding-up Provisions of the Companies Ordinance, para. 26.24 available at: www.hkreform.gov.hk/en/publications/rwind.htm (last accessed on 31 March, 2017).
158 See *Re Bank of Credit and Commerce International SA (No 2)* BCLC 579 and *Re B.C.C.I. SA (No 3)* [1993] BCLC 1490.
159 *Re Information Security One Ltd* [2007] HKCFI 848.
160 Ibid., at 6.
161 Ibid., at 11.
162 *Re Pioneer Iron and Steel Group Co. Ltd.* [2013] HKCFI 324, at 44.
163 Ibid., at 44.
164 *Re Pioneer Iron and Steel Group Co. Ltd.* [2013] HKCFI 324, at 44.
165 *CCIC Finance Ltd. v Guangdong International Trust & Investment Corporation* (GITIC) [2005] 2 HKC 589.
166 Ibid., at 12.
167 Ibid., at 47.
168 Ibid., Shi Jingxia at 67; Wang Xinxin at 83; Zou Hailia, at 75; Wang Weiguo at 76.
169 Ibid., at 84.
170 *Hong Kong Institute of Education v Aoki Corporation* [2004] 2 HKC 397.
171 Ibid., at 108.
172 Ibid., at 120.
173 Ibid., at 123–124, 160.
174 Ibid., at 159.
175 *Hong Kong Institute of Education v Aoki Corporation* [2004] HKCFI 33; [2004] 2 HKLRD 760; [2004] 2 HKC 397; HCCT109/2003, at 149, 151.
176 *Re Zlomrex International Finance SA* [2013] EWHC 4605 (Ch), at 13.
177 *Re Apcoa Parking (UK) Ltd and others* [2014] EWHC 997 (Ch), at 39.
178 *Re LDK Solar Co. Ltd.* [2014] HKCFI 2234.
179 Ibid., at 5–10.

180 Ibid., at 17.
181 Ibid., at 2.
182 Ibid., at 2.
183 Ibid., at 25.
184 Ibid., at 36.
185 Ibid., at 39.
186 Ibid., at 36.
187 Ibid., at 41.
188 *Re Drax Holdings Ltd* [2004] 1 BCLC 10, at 25; *Re LDK Solar Co. Ltd.* [2014] HKCFI 2234, at 43.
189 *Re LDK Solar Co. Ltd.* [2014] HKCFI 2234, at 44.
190 *Re Apcoa Parking Holdings GmbH* [2014] 2 BCLC 285, at 19.
191 *Re LDK Solar Co. Ltd.* [2014] HKCFI 2234, at 55,56.
192 Ibid., at 63.
193 Ibid., at 62.
194 Hong Kong Economic and Trade Office, Tax Regime and Regulations, www.hongkong-eu.net/pg.php?id_menu=88 (last accessed on 31 March, 2017).
195 *Re Peregrine Investments Holdings Ltd.* [1998] HKCFI 643, *Greater Beijing First Expressways Ltd.* [2000] HKCFI 755, *Re Kong Wah Holdings Ltd.* [2000] HKCFI 21, *Re Akai Holdings Ltd.* [2004] HKCFI 346.
196 *Re Jinro (HK) International Ltd.* [2003] HKCFI 239.
197 Ibid., para. 32.
198 *Re Chow Kam Fai David* [2004] HKCA 111.
199 Ibid., at 16.
200 Ibid., at 19.
201 Ibid., at 25.
202 Ibid., at 21.
203 Data collected from www.court.gov.mo/zh/subpage/statisticstjb?report=2013 (last accessed on 31 March, 2017).
204 Data collected from www.oro.gov.hk/cgi-bin/oro/stat.cgi?stat_type=W&start_year=2009&start_month=1&end_year=2014&end_month=12&Search=Search (last accessed on 31 March, 2017).
205 Feng Wenzhuang, Brief Introduction into the Compositions of Macao Civil Proceedings (in Chinese), in: www.dsaj.gov.mo/macaolaw/cn/data/prespectiva/issued/VASCO.pdf (last accessed on 31 March, 2017).
206 Case No. 84/2001.
207 Commercial Code of Macao, Article 1.
208 CPCM, Articles 1043–1184.
209 Ibid., Articles 1185–1198.
210 Ibid., Article 20.
211 Commercial Code of Macao, Article 181.
212 Commercial Registration Code of Macao, Article 5.
213 Commercial Code of Macao, Article 175-II.
214 CPCM, Article 1199.
215 Macao Rules of Court Litigation Fees, Article 102.
216 Macao Civil Code, Article 739 (a).
217 Decree of Labor Relations in Macao, Decree-Law No. 24/89/M, 3 April 1989 (With amendments introduced by the Decree-Law No. 32/90/M, 9 July 1990), Article 32.
218 *Re Zhu Kuan (Hong Kong) Co Ltd.* [2007] HKCFI 1119, paras. 1, 4, 5, 12.
219 Basic Law of Macao SAR, Article 106.
220 *Re China Metal Recycling (Holdings) Ltd.* [2014] HKCFI 2404, paras. 1, 2, 11.
221 *Re China Metal Recycling (Holdings) Ltd.* [2015] HKCFI 332, paras. 9, 10.
222 *China Metal Recycling (Holdings) Ltd. and Another v Chun Chi Wai and Others* [2013] HKCFI 1305, para. 7.
223 TBA, Article 3.
224 The ways of resolution of the Taiwanese financial institutions are scattered in relevant laws and regulations, such as the Insurance Act, the Insurance Deposit Act, the Banking Act, the Financial Institutions Merger Act, the Financial Holding Company Act etc.
225 TBA, Chd. II and III.

226 TCA, Articles 282–314.
227 Ibid., Article 282.
228 Taiwan Taipei District Court Litigation No. 1807 [2010].
229 Ibid.
230 Taiwan High Court Appeal from Ruling No. 215 [2011]; Taiwan Supreme Court Appeal from Ruling No. 1022 [2011].
231 Taiwan High Court Appeal from Ruling No. 286 [2012].
232 Taiwan Supreme Court Appeal from Ruling No. 529 [2012].
233 In the process of translation, the author has made some technical modification in the wording of this article. In the original Chinese version of Article 4 TBA, it is stated China instead of Taiwan. Please note that the Act was enacted in 1935, i.e. before the establishment of PRC. Nowadays, it might cause misunderstanding if China is being utilized here. In order to make clear the effective geographic extent of this article, the corresponding context is thus translated into Taiwan.
234 Taiwan Supreme Court No. 1592 [1996].
235 Banqiao District Court Bankruptcy No. 9 [2012].
236 Taipei District Court International Trade No. 9 [1999].
237 Taiwan High Court International Trade Appeal No. 9 [2002].
238 Taiwan High Court Important Appeal No. 23 [2011].
239 In accordance with Article 42-1 of the Hong Kong and Macao Act, in determining the conditions for the validity, jurisdiction, and enforceability of civil judgments made in Hong Kong or Macao, Article 402 of the Code of Civil Procedure and Article 4, para. 1 of the Compulsory Execution Law shall apply mutatis mutandis.
240 Taipei District Court Trial on Application No. 514 [2009].
241 Taipei District Court Trial on Application No. 355 [2012].
242 Ibid.
243 Ibid.
244 Taiwan Supreme Court Appeal No. 2376 (2008).
245 The 2015 Draft, Article 297(1).
246 Ibid., Article 7(2).
247 Ibid., Article 315(1).
248 Ibid., Article 299(2).
249 Ibid., Article 299.
250 Ibid., Article 315(2).
251 Ibid., Article 310.
252 Ibid., Article 314(1).
253 Ibid., Article 309(1).
254 Ibid., Article 304(1).
255 Ibid., Article 305(1).
256 Ibid., Article 305(3).
257 Ibid., Article 318(1).
258 Ibid., Article 318(2).
259 Ibid., Article 317(1).
260 Ibid., Article 319.

Reference list

In English

Ball, Laurence, Jalles, João Tovar, Loungani, Prakash, "Do Forecasters Believe in Okun's Law? An Assessment of Unemployment and Output Forecasts" (IMF Working Paper), February 2014, available at: www.imf.org/external/pubs/ft/wp/2014/wp1424.pdf (last accessed on 31 March, 2017)
Bartell, Laura B., *Visualizing Bankruptcy*, Lexis Nexis, 2011, Chapter 1 [1/2]
Booth, Charles D., *The 2006 PRC Enterprise Bankruptcy Law: The Wait is Finally Over*, 20 Singapore Academy of Law Special Issue 275, 2008, pp 275, 311–312
Booth, Charles D., Lain, Trevor N., "Rescuing Hong Kong Companies with Provisional Supervision: Proposals That Workers and Management Can Support", 40 HKLJ 271, 2010

Briscoe, Stephen, Booth, Charles D, *Hong Kong Corporate Insolvency Manual* (2nd ed.), Hong Kong Institute of Certified Public Accountants, 2009, p. 5

Chua Eu Jin, "The Reform of the PRC Corporate Bankruptcy Law: Slowly but Surely", 16 (8) *China Law and Practice*, 2002 Oct., p. 19

Daljit, Kaur, Susarla, Kamesh, "Anti-Tax Avoidance Developments in Selected Asian Jurisdictions", *Asia-Pacific Tax Bulletin*, Volume 17, No 4, 2011, p. 261

Eisenberg, Theodore, "Bankruptcy in the Administrative State", *Law and Contemporary Problems*, Vol. 50, No. 2, 1987, p. 5

Garcia, Augusto Teixeira, *Macao Insolvency Law and Cross-border Insolvency Issues*, New Zealand Association for Comparative Law: hors série (Wellington) Vol. XIX, 2015, p. 341

Godinho, Jorge A.F., *Macao Business Law and Legal System*, LexisNexis Hong Kong, 2006, pp. 18–20

Gong, Xinyi, "When Hong Kong Becomes SAR, Is the Mainland Ready? – Problems of Judgments Recognition in Cross-border Insolvency Matters", *International Insolvency Review*, Wiley-Blackwell, Vol. 20, Issue 1, 2011

He Qisheng, "Public Policy in Enforcement of Foreign Arbitral Awards in the Supreme People's Court of China", 43 *Hong Kong Law Journal* 1037, 2013, p. 1037

Henderson, Keith E., "Halfway Home and a Long Way to Go: China's Rule of Law Evolution and the Global Road to Judicial Independence, Judicial Impartiality, and Judicial Integrity", in: Randall Peerenboom (ed.), *Judicial Independence in China: Lessons for Global Rule of Law Promotion*, Cambridge University Press, 2010, p. 24

Ho, Look Chan, *Cross-border Insolvency* (2nd ed.), Global Law and Business, 2012, p. 8

Jackson, Thomas H., *The Logic and Limits of Bankruptcy*, Beard Books, 2001, p. 8

Jiang Yujia, "The Curious Case of Inactive Bankruptcy Practice in China: A Comparative Study of U.S. and Chinese Bankruptcy Law", *Northwestern Journal of International Law & Business*, Vol. 34, Issue 3, 2014, pp. 569–570

Kendall, Sue, "Winding Up Macanese Companies in Macau – The Zhu Kuan Experience Brings Positive Development", *Out of Court*, Autumn 2004, p. 3

Knotek, Edward S., II, "How Useful is Okun's Law?" 2007, pp. 73–103, available at: www.kc.frb.org/publicat/econrev/pdf/4q07knotek.pdf (last accessed on 31 March, 2017)

Kwan, Susan (ed.-in-chief), *Company Law in Hong Kong – Insolvency*, Sweet & Maxwell, 2012, pp. 529, 559

Li Shuguang , Wang Zuofa, "Review of the PRC Bankruptcy Law in 2009", *INSOL International Technical Series* Issue No. 11, March 2010, p. 5

Li Shuguang, Wang Zuofa, "The Function of China's Court in Enterprise Bankruptcy and the Future Trend – Observations from the Background of the Four-Year Implementation of China's Existing Bankruptcy Law", *INSOL World, the Quarterly Journal of INSOL International*, Fourth Quarter, 2012, pp. 8–11, 13

Michaels, Ralf, Recognition and Enforcement of Foreign Judgments, in Rüdiger Wolfrum (ed.), *Max Planck Encyclopedia of Public International Law*, Oxford University Press, 2009, para.7

Naughton, Barry, Growing out of the Plan: Chinese Economic Reform, 1978–1993, Cambridge University Press, 1995, pp. 137–168

Naughton, Barry, *The Chinese Economy: Transitions and Growth*, The MIT Press, 2006, pp. 105–106

Okun, Arthur M., *Potential GNP: Its Measurement and Significance, American Statistical Association*, Proceedings of the Business and Economics Statistics Section, 1962, pp. 98–104

Pace, Vincent A., "The Bankruptcy of the Zhu Kuan Group: A Case Study of Cross-border Insolvency Litigation against a Chinese State-owned Enterprise", 27 U. Pa. J. Int'l L. 517, 2006, p. 565

Peerenboom, Randall, "Judicial Independence in China: Common Myths and Unfounded Assumptions", in: Randall Peerenboom (ed.), *Judicial Independence in China: Lessons for Global Rule of Law Promotion*, Cambridge University Press, 2010, p. 88

Shi Jingxia, "Twelve Years to Sharpen One Sword: The 2006 Enterprise Bankruptcy Law and China's Transition to a Market Economy", 16 *Norton Journal of Bankruptcy Law and Practice*, Vol. 16, No. 5, October 2007, p. 666

Smart, "Recognition of Japanese Reorganization Proceedings", *International Corporate Rescue*, Vol. 1, issue 4, 2004, pp. 187–188

Stevens, Neal, "Confronting the Crisis of Insolvency in China's State-owned Enterprises: Can the Proposed Bankruptcy Law Erase the Red Ink?" *Wisconsin International Law Journal*, 1998, 554

Tada, Nozomi, "Enforcement of Foreign Judgments in Japan Regarding Business Activities", *Japanese Annual of International Law*, No. 46, 2003, pp. 75–94

Wang Weiguo, "National Report for the People's Republic of China", in: Faber, Dennis, Vermunt, Niels, Kilborn, Jason, Richter Tomáš (ed.), *Commencement of Insolvency Proceedings*, Oxford University Press, 2012, 6.7.2

Wessels, Bob, *International Insolvency Law* (3rd ed.), Kluwer, 2012, at 10385

Zhang Haizheng, Kuang Jingting, "Corporate Reorganization Case Analysis under China's New Bankruptcy Law", *International Corporate Rescue*, Vol. 11, issue 3, 2014, p. 177

In Chinese

Chen Zhixin, "Dilemma and Way Out of Civil Participation in Distribution System", *Journal of Shanghai University of Political Science and Law (The Rule of Law Forum)*, Vol. 29, No. 6, Nov. 2014, pp. 82–87

Gao Changjiu, Tang Zhengyu, Fu Wang, *Legal Dilemmas Encountered in the Course of Listed Corporation Reorganization: Taking ST Huayuan as Example*, Nomocracy Forum, 2010, pp. 45–46

Guo Fang, Jian Wenchao, "Saiwei and the "Kidnapped" Government", *China Economic Weekly*, Issue 30, 2012, p. 25

Guo Ruyi, "Xinyu Government Deleted from Its Website the Bill to Pay Saiwei's Debt with Fiscal Funds", 19 July, 2012, available at: http://business.sohu.com/20120719/n348571532.shtml (last accessed on 31 March, 2017)

Lan Xinzhen, "Looking Forward to the New Bankruptcy Law, Beijing Review", 21 June, 2004, available at: www.bjreview.cn/Cn/2004-29/200429-jj2.htm (last accessed on 31 March, 2017)

Li Yulong (ed.), *Legal Analysis of Private Equity Cases*, Law Press, 2009, pp. 3–4

Liu Guixiang, "Distribution of Functions of Participation in Distribution System and Insolvency System", *People's Court Daily*, 30 April, 2014, at 8

Ma Jian, "Statistic Analysis on Insolvency Cases Accepted by People's Court from 2003–2012", *Legal Information*, 2014 (03), pp. 23–24

Pan Junfeng, "Study of Judicial Reorganization Practice: from the perspective of reorganization cases handled by the courts in Jiangsu Province", in: Wang Baoshu (ed.), *Chinese Yearbook of Commercial Law*, Law Press, 2011, p. 209

Peng Zhen, "The Bankruptcy Law is also the Promotion Law", *People's Daily*, 30 November, 1986, at 01

Qi Shujie, *Research of Bankruptcy Law*, Xiamen University Press, 2005, pp. 62–91

Shyuu, Shu-Huan, *Basic Structures of Debt Clearance Law*, Yuanzhao Press, 2007, p 18

Song Xiaoming, Zhang Yongjian, Liu Ming, "Understanding and Application of Several Issues concerning the Application of the Enterprise Bankruptcy Law of the People's Republic of China", *People's Judicature*, 2011(21), p. 028

Wang Guanghua, "Participation in Distribution System and Insolvency System are Different in Nature", *People's Court Daily*, 30 April, 2014, at 8

Wang Meiying, Lian Changren, "The Recognition and Enforcement of the Foreign Judgments: The Recognition of a French Bankruptcy Case", 2008, available at: www.ccmt.org.cn/shownews.php?id=8413 (last accessed on 31 March, 2017)

Wang Xinxin, "Wang Jianbin, Analysis About China's Acknowledging Extraterritorial Effect System of Foreign Bankrupt Procedure and Its Improvement", *Law Science Magazine*, Issue 6, 2008, p. 12

Wang Xinxin, "Transforming Ideas and Improving Legislation, Accepting the Bankruptcy Cases According to Law II: to understand the judicial interpretation of the EBL in depth", *People's Court Daily*, 15 February, 2012, p. 07

Wang Xinxin, Yang Tao, "Study on Protection of Labor Claims of Insolvent Enterprises: Tolerance and Share of Costs during Social Reform", *Research on Rule of Law*, 2013 (01), p. 29

Wang Xinxin, "Participation in Distribution System Should Not Conflict with Insolvency System", People's Court Daily, 30 April, 2014, at 8

Wang Xinxin, Xu Yangguang, "Dilemmas and Solutions to China's Bankruptcy Law: Reasons of Decrease on the Numbers of Acceptance of Bankruptcy Cases and the Relevant Treatment", 19 November 2014, available at www.chinaqingsuan.com/news/detail/7702/page/2 (last accessed on 31 March, 2017)

Wei Zheng, Yu Bingqing, "Study of the Current Photovoltaic Development in China and Its Solutions", *Sino-Global Energy*, Vol. 18, Issue. 6, 2013, pp. 15–16

Xu Defeng, "Rethinking Basic Principles of Bankruptcy Law", *Legal Science*, issue 8, 2009, pp. 49–59

Xu Haoshang, Ou Yuanjie, "Separation of Functions of Participation in Distribution System and Insolvency System: Restructuring the Participation in Distribution System", *People's Judicature*, 2014 (17), pp. 102–107

Yang Zhengyu, *Application of Reorganization to the Listed Companies, in: Guide on Civil and Commercial Trial*, People's Court Press, 2008, p. 209

Liu Jianhong, "Application for Recognition and Enforcement of an Italian Insolvency Judgment", 2003, available at: http://www.pkulaw.cn/fulltext_form.aspx?Gid=1510089690&Db=qikan (last accessed on 25 August, 2017)

Zhang Fengxiang, *The Needs for Improvement of Relevant Laws Arising from the Financial Derivative Products Cooperative Disputes between Hua An Funds and Lehman Brothers International Europe*, Frontier of Financial Law, 2011, pp. 33–45

Zhou Xiaochuan, "Debate on Rescue in the Midst of Financial Crisis", *Journal of Financial Research*, No. 9, 2012, p. 5

Zhou Lian, "The Incentive and Cooperation of Government Officials in the Political Tournaments: An Interpretation of the Prolonged Local Protectionism and Duplicative Investments in China", *Economic Research Journal*, 2004(06), p. 34

4 Regulation versus model law
A comparative review on key aspects

Introduction

On 20 May, 2015, the European Parliament approved the final text of the recast of the European Insolvency Regulation, 12 years after it came into effect. In this chapter, the Regulation on insolvency proceedings (Council Regulation (EC) 1346/2000, hereinafter EC Regulation), the Regulation of the European Parliament and of the Council on insolvency proceedings (recast) (Regulation (EU) 2015/848 of the European Parliament and of the Council of 20 May 2015 on insolvency proceedings (recast), hereinafter the EU Regulation (recast)) and the UNCITRAL Model Law on Cross-border Insolvency (1997) with Guide to Enactment and Interpretation (2013) (hereinafter the Model Law and the Guide and Interpretation) will be compared to each other in order to figure out the similarities and differences of the two regimes on key aspects through literature review and case analysis. In the following sections, the comparative discussion about the Regulation and the Model Law will cover the key topics concerning cross-border insolvency law, in particular, jurisdiction, recognition and enforcement, cooperation and communication. Nevertheless, following the referendum held in the UK, negotiations will be held for the UK to leave the European Union and "the now famous Article 50 of the Treaty on European Union ('TEU')"[1] will be put into practice for the first time. As the recast EU Regulation is applicable from 26 June, 2017, to what extent the EU Insolvency Regulation can be effective in the UK becomes an open question. I will have a brief discussion on that topic at the end of this chapter.

Both the Regulation and the Model Law are outstanding examples in the area of cross-border insolvency. Before the Regulation and the Model Law began to play the leading role in dealing with issues arising from cross-border insolvency, there have been a few multilateral initiatives, either on the international level or on the regional level, most of which failed to gain wide and active acceptance. For instance, in Latin America, some relevant efforts have been made, for example, through the Treaty of Montevideo 1940. However, with limited provisions it was not that successful (Wood, 2007; Wessels, 2012). In Europe, some related conventions were replaced or partly replaced by the EC Regulation, such as the Nordic Bankruptcy Convention of 1933 partly replaced except that it is still applicable in the case of Denmark because Denmark falls beyond the scope of the Regulation. The Model Law was developed in the mid 1990s, at a time when trade and investment increasingly expanded across the world. The administration of cross-border insolvencies at that time, however, were conducted in a fragmented way subject to national insolvency laws prevailingly based on territoriality.[2] By then, the text of the EC Regulation 1346/2000 was merely available in the preliminary form of a draft convention (Moss, Fletcher & Isaacs, 2009) and "best practice" guidelines served as earlier initiatives to address global cross-border insolvency problems.

For example, Committee J of the Section on Business Law of International Bar Association (IBA), the Model International Insolvency Cooperation Act (MIICA), the International Bar Association Cross Border Insolvency Concordat. During 1995 and 1997, a project was launched by UNCITRAL with the participation of "seventy-two states, seven intergovernmental organizations and 10 non-governmental organizations" in order to work out a draft model law on cross-border insolvency (Mohan, 2012). Therefore, the drafting procedure of the Model Law found wide acceptance on a global level and accordingly the Model Law was established based on international consensus.[3] Now, there are over 40 jurisdictions in the world that have incorporated the Model Law into their insolvency systems,[4] five of which are Member States of the EU – Greece (2010), Poland (2003), Romania (2002), Slovenia (2007) and the UK (2006). Unlike the Regulation, the worldwide agreement on adoption of the Model Law is not guaranteed by any regional legal instrument but achieved by its own flexible nature, which tolerates a wide range of legal diversity.

Generally speaking, the Regulation, a binding regional framework, and the Model Law, a soft law mechanism, are different in most aspects. Nonetheless, the Model Law has taken into consideration the content of the EC Regulation by adopting some key concepts stipulated under the EC Regulation, such as COMI and establishment.[5] With respect to cooperation and communication, it is also explicitly stated under the EU Regulation (recast) that European insolvency practitioners and courts shall refer to "relevant guidelines prepared by UNCITRAL".[6] Besides, they also share something in common in treating corporate groups. For example, both suggest the actors involved to cooperate and communicate with each other properly through use of cross-border insolvency agreements[7] or appointment of a single insolvency practitioner to conduct coordination,[8] although in the EU context such an appointment may also be affiliated with the opening of group coordination proceedings.[9] In pursuit of a suitable solution for China's cross-border insolvency cooperation, it is of significance to discover the difference and similarity from those leading international regimes, which are both potentially relevant models.

COMI

COMI is the term relating to determination of the main proceedings, which has been employed both by the Regulation and the Model Law. In this section, I will start with its origin and then move on to explain the reasons of ambiguity of the concept and the problems incurred by application of the overlapping concepts. I will further explore the development of interpretation under the EU Regulation (recast) as well as under the Model Law based on the legal texts and the case law.

Before I discuss about COMI, I would like to address something about establishment. In the EU, there are two types of territorial proceedings that can be opened on the basis of establishment under the Regulation: territorial insolvency proceedings and secondary proceedings. Owing to pre-existing rights created under diverse local laws as well as different priority rules governed by various domestic insolvency systems, territorial proceedings are considered as "a necessary evil" (Pottow, 2011) and they must be subordinate to the main proceedings under the Regulation. The reason is that the ideal of the Regulation is to achieve "a single exclusive universal form of insolvency proceedings for the whole of the Community",[10] which are established on the basis of the principle of unity, i.e. "concentrating cross border insolvencies within a single proceeding" (Arts, 2015), and the principle of universality ("extending those proceedings to all the debtor's assets, wherever they may be situated"[11]).[12] Commencement of territorial proceedings inevitably disrupts these underlying principles of the Regulation. For instance, the opening of territorial insolvency proceedings is subject to restrictions[13] because they serve the sole purpose of protection of local interests (Viimsalu, 2011). Moreover, territorial insolvency proceeding shall be transferred into secondary proceedings as soon as the main insolvency proceedings are opened.[14] As for the secondary proceedings, intervention with the secondary proceedings has been further strengthened under the recast EU Regulation. First of all, the duties of cooperation and communication have been broadened for insolvency practitioners and extended to the courts involved (Wessels, 2014). Secondly, the EU Regulation (recast) has introduced so-called synthetic secondary proceedings, which are framed in a way that insolvency practitioners can promise to local creditors in the form of an undertaking that they will be treated as if secondary proceedings had been opened.[15] It aims at preventing the potential opening of secondary proceedings (Dammann and Menjucq, 2008; Janger, 2010; Pottow, 2011). In addition to an undertaking, the court can temporarily stay the opening of secondary insolvency proceedings for the purpose of preservation of the efficiency of the moratorium granted in the main proceedings,[16] which allows for negotiations between the debtor and its creditors in order to promote the prospects of a restructuring of the debtor's business.[17] Besides, the main insolvency practitioner shall be given an immediate notice and an opportunity to be heard if a request to open secondary insolvency proceedings is presented to a court,[18] which functions as a procedural guarantee for the intervention. The concept of establishment pursuant to the Model Law is not related to the opening of local proceedings (jurisdiction) but is a factor in determining recognition of a non-main proceeding.[19] It is held under the Guide and Interpretation that proceedings commenced on the presence of assets without establishment would not qualify for recognition under the Model Law scheme.[20] Therefore, I will not have in-depth discussion on establishment.

Origin

By incorporating COMI into the respective texts,[21] the Regulation and the Model Law literally utilize the same terminologies to indicate jurisdiction in cross-border insolvency. In fact, it is the EC Regulation that inspired both the contents and the formulations of COMI under the Model Law.[22] Therefore, to find the origins of the two concepts, it is necessary to trace the relevant sources in the EU context. The EC Regulation does not contain a definition of COMI. Instead, it offers a presumption, which is rebuttable. What is the reason behind that kind of arrangement? It can be deemed as a balance between the real seat theory of the civil law and the state of incorporation theory of the common law (Fletcher, 2005). In Europe, there are two competing doctrines with respect to the domicile of companies,[23] incorporation and real seat. The place of incorporation prevailed in common law system. Its reflection on cross-border insolvency law is that, according to this theory, if there were to be proceedings in more than one country, the main proceedings would take place in the jurisdiction of the place of registration of the company, and proceedings in other jurisdictions would be ancillary to the main proceeding.[24] On the other hand, the real seat theory of jurisdiction espoused by the civil law prevails in Europe (Moss, Fletcher & Isaacs, 2009). In the case of *Überseering BV v Nordic Construction Company Baumanagement GmbH (NCC)*,[25] the CJEU mentioned the points of view of Germany's Bundesgerichtshof with respect to the weakness of the place of incorporation. By choosing the place of incorporation, the company's founding members can choose the legal system that suits them best. Hence, the place of incorporation fails to take account of the fact that a company's incorporation and activities also affect the interests of third parties and of the State in which the company has its actual center of administration, where that is located in a State other than the one in which the company was incorporated.[26] By contrast, if the actual center of administration is taken to be the connecting factor, that can prevent the provisions of company law in the State in which the actual center of administration is situated, which are intended to protect certain vital interests, from being circumvented by incorporating the company abroad.[27] It is considered that it will be of more advantage to lay emphasis on substance instead of formality so that insolvency cases can be dealt with in a more appropriate court where the debtor has a genuine connection. Accordingly, it seems that the theory of real seat is most likely the idea behind the "center of main interests" concept. However, it is not directly applicable but a possibility of replacement to the place of incorporation under the EC Regulation. It is designed in such a way, which implied that a consensus was hard to be reached between the common law and the civil law at the beginning and thus a compromise was a must.

Rebuttal of presumption

The aforementioned compromise gives rise to a controversial problem concerning the meaning of COMI, which is how to rebut the presumption of registered office. In the EU, the elusive nature of COMI used to result in different points of view between theory and practice. As Wessels observed, the legal literature has suggested that presumption is strong and difficult to be rebutted "under very specific circumstances" (Wessels, 2012). Nevertheless, in accordance with the empirical research conducted based on 104 cases collected from all over the EU from 2002 to 2009, more than 80% of Member State courts whose decisions form the basis of this study rebutted the presumption of the cases (Mevorach, 2010) since the factors that could determine COMI were diverse (Marshall, 2013; Moss & Smith, 2009). The tension was firstly eased by the CJEU in the *Eurofood* case.[28] Eurofood is an Irish subsidiary wholly owned by an Italian company, Parmalat. The Italian court also opened an insolvency proceeding against Eurofood in Italy, determining that the COMI was in Italy. Later the Irish court also opened insolvency proceeding against Eurofood, ruling that the COMI was in Ireland, where it was registered. The CJEU affirmed the jurisdiction of the Irish court by indicating that:

> the presumption . . . whereby the center of main interests of that subsidiary is situated in the Member State where its registered office is located, can be rebutted only if factors which are both objective and ascertainable by third parties enable it to be established that an actual situation exists which is different from that which location at that registered office is deemed to reflect. That could be so in particular in the case of a company not carrying out any business in the territory of the Member State in which its registered office is situated. By contrast, where a company carries on its business in the territory of the Member State where its registered office is situated, the mere fact that its economic choices are or can be controlled by a parent company in another Member State is not enough to rebut the presumption laid down by that Regulation.[29]

In its decision in *Eurofood*, the CJEU set very high threshold to rebut the presumption, which could therefore be understood to equate COMI with the registered office (McCormack, 2009). However, in later case law, the CJEU gradually deviated from the strict approach adopted by *Eurofood* with respect to Article 3(1). The *Interedil* case is the most significant. In 2001, Interedil transferred its registered office from Italy to the UK. In 2002, the company ceased all activity and was removed from the UK register. One year later,

Intesa Gestione Crediti SpA filed insolvency proceedings against Interedil in Italy. Interedil challenged the jurisdiction of the Italian court on the ground that only the UK courts would have jurisdiction following the company's transfer to the UK. The CJEU was asked to provide guidance on how the COMI under Articles 2 and 3 was to be interpreted. The court indicated that a debtor company's main center of interests must be determined by attaching greater importance to the place of the company's administration. This place must be identified by reference to criteria that are both objective and ascertainable by third parties, in particular by the company's creditors. Importantly, the court held that if the bodies responsible for the company's management and supervision are in the same place as its registered office, the presumption in Article 3(1) cannot be rebutted. Under the circumstance that a company's central administration is not to be found in the same place as its registered office, the CJEU concluded that the presence of objective factors, such as

> immovable property owned by the debtor company, lease agreements, and the existence in that Member State of a contract concluded with a financial institution . . . may be regarded as objective factors and, in the light of the fact that they are likely to be matters in the public domain, as factors that are ascertainable by third parties[30]

can be taken into consideration. However, these elements cannot be regarded as sufficient factors to rebut the presumption, unless

> a comprehensive assessment of all the relevant factors makes it possible to establish, in a manner that is ascertainable by third parties, that the company's actual center of management and supervision and of the management of its interests is located in that other Member State.[31]

Following the *Interedil* decision, the CJEU rendered another judgment involving similar issues in the *Rastelli* case. The Commercial Court of Marseille (Tribunal de commerce de Marseille) opened a main proceeding of Médiasucre, the registered office of which is located in France. The liquidator of Médiasucre filed the application in order to put Rastelli, an Italian registered company, together into the liquidation proceeding because the property of the two companies were intermixed. The request was approved by the French Court of Appeal (Cour d'appel d'Aix-en-Provence), holding that the liquidator's application was not intended to open insolvency proceedings against Rastelli but to join it to the judicial liquidation already opened against Médiasucre.[32] The Cour de cassation decided to stay the proceedings and to refer to the Court of Justice for a preliminary ruling on the questions of the effectiveness of national substantive consolidation rules in the case of cross-border insolvency and the possibility of joining one company into another company's main proceeding because of intermix of companies property. With respect to the matter of COMI, the CJEU held that:

> That presumption may be rebutted where, from the viewpoint of third parties, the place in which a company's central administration is located is not the same as that of its registered office. In that event, the simple presumption laid down by the European Union legislature in favor of the registered office of that company can be rebutted if factors which are both objective and ascertainable by third parties enable it to be established that an actual situation exists which is different from that which locating it at that registered office is deemed to reflect.[33]

From *Eurofood* to *Interedil* and *Rastelli*, it seems that the CJEU, when assessing rebuttal of the registered office presumption, has attached more importance to the place where the company has its central administration (Marshall, 2013) on the basis of a comprehensive assessment of all the relevant factors. Ascertainability by third parties, in particular the creditors, is also a crucial factor that needs to be taken into account.

Corresponding to the term in the Regulation, COMI is also contained in Article 16 of the Model Law, which provides that "in the absence of proof to the contrary, the debtor's registered office, or habitual residence in the case of an individual, is presumed to be the center of the debtor's main interests".[34] Although it serves a different purpose,[35] it is stated in the Guide and Interpretation of the Model Law that the jurisprudence with respect to interpretation of COMI in the EC Regulation may be relevant to its interpretation in the Model Law.[36] Nevertheless, the practice told a different story of "maybe not". The overlapping concepts are actually subject to divergent interpretation in different jurisdictions. The Model Law was introduced into the UK via Sch. 1 to the Cross-Border Insolvency Regulations 2006 (CBIR), which enacted almost verbatim the Model Law. In the *Re Standford* case,[37] there were parallel insolvency proceedings concerning the group in the United States and in Antigua and Barbuda, where the key entity (Stanford International Bank Ltd) was registered. Due to disagreement between the American receiver and the Antiguan liquidators, they both applied for recognition under the CBIR in the UK, which enacted almost verbatim the Model Law, in order to control assets in the UK. With respect to the concept of COMI, the British Court of Appeal determined the meaning of COMI in accordance with the CJEU's decision in *Eurofood*[38] based on the Regulation and held that:

> if there is any difference in the test promulgated by the ECJ in *Eurofood* and that applied by the courts in the US then it is right that the court in England should apply the *Eurofood* test.[39] . . . There is nothing in it to suggest that the COMI of SIB alone was not in Antigua.[40]

However, the flexibility inherent in the Model Law allows the enacting State to make adjustments to its uniform text. In the US, on the contrary, as indicated in *Re Tri-Continental Exchange Ltd.*:

> Congress chose to substitute 'evidence' for 'proof' and otherwise to adopt the Model Law provision word-for-word. The explanation was that the substitution conformed to United States terminology and made clear that the burden of proof of 'center of main interests' is on the foreign representative who is applying for recognition of a foreign proceeding as a main proceeding. This comports with the concept of a rebuttable presumption for purposes of Federal Rule of Evidence 301. FED.R.EVID. 301.[41]

By replacing the word "proof" with "evidence" in the equivalent provision for the COMI presumption, the US courts began to part from the *Eurofood* approach. Especially in *Re Bear Stearns*, Judge Lifland distributed the burden of proof on the person who was asserting that particular proceedings were main proceedings[42] and considered that the registered office presumption would be rebutted if there was any evidence to the contrary, regardless of an objection raised by any interested parties.[43] According to the empirical study conducted by Westbrook, "the COMI requirement had reduced forum shopping after Bear Stearns primarily because of the rejection of haven filings" (Westbrook, 2013). In the *Re Stanford* case,[44] by referring to Judge Lifland's opinion in *Re Bear Stearns*,[45] Lewison J, the judge of the UK High Court of Justice, also pointed out that:

> except where there is no contrary evidence the registered office does not have any special evidentiary value. This change in language of the enactment, as it seems to me, may well explain why the jurisprudence of the American courts has diverged from that of the ECJ.[46]

As States that both enacted the Model Law,[47] the literal distinction of COMI under the legislation of the United States and the UK is visible. Although there are obvious similarities between the Model Law and the Regulation, both in the definitions and the rebuttable presumptions, there are differences, too. For instance, there is nothing in the Model Law comparable to clarification of COMI under the EC Regulation, which indicates that "the 'centre of main interests' should correspond to the place where the debtor conducts the administration of his interests on a regular basis and is therefore ascertainable by third parties".[48] The definition of foreign main proceeding in the Model Law is wider than that of "insolvency proceedings" in the EC Regulation. The former comprehends at least some types of receivership but the latter does not. Bearing the difference in mind, the US receiver submitted that Lewison J should have applied the head office functions test he had recognized in *Re Lennox Holdings Ltd* and not the objective and ascertainable test adopted by *Eurofood* that he applied in this case. The US proceedings were not the end of the story. In 2009, the Superior Court of Quebec reached conclusions opposite to the UK decision in *Stanford*.[49] The Quebec court recognized the US receiver as the "foreign representative", holding that the center of interest was in Houston, which was indisputable.[50] Later the Quebec Court of Appeal dismissed the appeal of the Antiguan liquidators because "the Court is of the view that petitioners' efforts to have this conclusion set aside shows no reasonable chance of success".[51]

Time to determine COMI

The EC Regulation literally sets up the aim of prevention of forum shopping[52] and the EU Regulation (recast) further attempts to rule out forum shopping in a fraudulent or abusive manner.[53] Such an arrangement is tied to the characteristics of cross-border insolvency law and the requirement of the effective functioning of the internal market. As summarized by Bell, forum shopping is possible: first, there are potential parallel forums that are available to be selected; second, the legal systems in those potentially available forums must be heterogeneous (Bell, 2003). In international insolvency law, the debtor's center of main interests (COMI) is the criterion to determine the jurisdiction of the main proceedings. It is not defined and shall be assessed based on the facts. COMI's fact-dependent feature provides opportunities for shift and manipulation of forum (Eidenmüller, 2009). Change of forum would not be necessary if the insolvency system was the same everywhere. On the contrary, the fact is that each Member State in the EU has its own insolvency law, which can be perceived through Annex A to the Regulation. In accordance with the Heidelberg-Luxembourg-Vienna Report as well as the Impact Assessment issued by the EU Commission, for example, the UK is deemed as an attractive venue because it provides flexible restructuring tools for corporates in default[54] as well as a shorter time period of discharge for indebted individuals.[55] In the EU, the freedom of establishment of companies is regarded as one of the fundamental principles guaranteed currently by the TFEU,[56] which is of central significance to the effective functioning of the internal market.[57] Following its interpretation in *Centros*,[58] the CJEU continues in case law to support the freedom of establishment in case of allegedly abusive conduct[59] and embrace a very liberal and "pro-free market" point of view (Tridimas, 2009), which might facilitate COMI shift (Eidenmüller, 2009). The EU Regulation (recast) thus introduced a look-back period of three months to ease the tension between the freedom of establishment and the avoidance of COMI shift.[60] It is also required that a study on the issue of abusive forum shopping shall be submitted by the Commission to the European Parliament, the Council and the European Economic and Social Committee no later than three years after the EU Regulation (recast)'s entry into enactment.[61]

The Model Law does not set up prevention of forum shopping as its objective and actually it is a concept that has not been mentioned in its main text. Instead, there is an equivalent concept of forum shopping stated under the Guide and Interpretation Law, which is abuse of process.[62] Under the circumstance that an applicant falsely claims the center of main interests to be in a particular State, whether or not that constitutes a deliberate abuse of the process and accordingly provides a ground to decline recognition is not governed by the Model Law but by domestic law or procedural rules.[63] Therefore, prevention of abuse of the process will bring two consequences to the Model Law regime. One is refusal of recognition and the other non-uniformity in its application. Recognition is one of the core objectives of the Model Law. Refusal of recognition will undermine its function, i.e. "to foster international cooperation as a means of maximizing outcomes for all stakeholders".[64] Therefore, it is suggested that domestic law or procedural rules applied to abuse of process should be narrowly construed.[65] In addition, unlike the Regulation, which is a Union legal instrument binding in its entirety, uniformity in its application is the goal the Model Law shall strive for.[66] Without a uniform criteria of abuse of process, the enacting State should apply its domestic law with due consideration and regard being given to the international origins of the Model Law.[67] In sum, although the courts are not prevented from applying domestic law or procedural rules in response to an abuse of process,[68] the two overriding purposes of the Model Law – reducing the possibility of non-recognition to the minimum and promoting uniformity in application on international level – outweigh the necessity to set up prevention of abuse of process as a key objective.

Although fraudulent or abusive forum shopping is not allowed in general, it is not forbidden to relocate COMI to somewhere else. In practice, to evaluate whether or not the relocation is effective largely depends on the COMI's time of establishment. In the EU, the EC Regulation did not explicitly set up rules on the timing issue. It is the CJEU that gradually made the relevant interpretation. The first case is the *Staubitz-Schreiber*,[69] which involved individual insolvency. Ms. Staubitz-Schreiber used to be resident in Germany and filed for opening of insolvency proceedings regarding her assets before a German court. After her request for the opening of insolvency proceedings was lodged, she moved to Spain before the court decided to open the proceedings.[70] Hence, the main issue of this case is whether the COMI of Ms. Staubitz-Schreiber should be assessed at the time of the filing of the request. If not, the German court should no longer have jurisdiction to open the main proceedings since the COMI of the applicant was shifted to Spain. The CJEU decided in favor of the time of the request for the opening of proceedings.[71] The reasons are mainly twofold. The first reason is to achieve the objective of preventing forum shopping and the second concerns legal certainty and the power to adopt preservation measures.[72] As pointed out by AG Colomer:

> to hold that it is legitimate for a debtor to transfer his center of main interests in the period between the request for the opening of proceedings and the opening of

insolvency proceedings would undermine the foundations of the whole scheme of the Regulation. In graphic terms, that would ultimately lead to creditors and courts continually having to pursue insolvent debtors in a vicious circle of requests for the opening of insolvency proceedings and transfers of centers of main interests which would never reach a satisfactory conclusion. Such a fate would have more in common with the legend of the Flying Dutchman than with the proper application of the Regulation on insolvency proceedings.[73]

The second case is regarding corporate insolvency, the aforementioned *Interedil* case. With respect to the relevant date for the purpose of locating the COMI of the company, the court followed the *Staubitz-Schreiber* approach, holding that "in principle, it is the location of the debtor's main center of interests at the date on which the request to open insolvency proceedings was lodged that is relevant for the purpose of determining the court having jurisdiction."[74] The Model Law itself does not provide any rules concerning the date to determine COMI. It is stipulated under the Guide and Interpretation that the date relevant to COMI determination is the date of commencement of the foreign proceeding,[75] which is an approach different from European one. In accordance with the Model Law, COMI is utilized to facilitate the recognition of foreign insolvency proceedings. Although there can be a pending period between the time of the application for commencement and the actual commencement of those proceedings, a request for recognition of foreign proceedings can only be made for existing proceedings, which are effectively opened. Hence, in the case of the Model Law, it is more appropriate to refer to the date of commencement of the foreign proceeding to determine the COMI.[76] In practice, the instruction is not always obeyed by the enacting States. For example, there is a split concerning the timing issue among the bankruptcy courts in the United States. Some courts followed the Guide and Interpretation of the Model Law[77] but some did not, which considered that the COMI should be determined as of the date of petition for recognition.[78]

The first case that set rules on the date is *Re Ran*, which involved an individual insolvency case. Ran was an Israeli businessman, who was put into an involuntary bankruptcy proceeding in 1997. Before the involuntary bankruptcy proceeding was commenced, Ran left Israel and moved to the United States and worked there. He has never returned to Israel. Nearly a decade after Ran's emigration, the receiver of Israeli insolvency proceeding filed a petition seeking recognition of the Israeli bankruptcy proceeding as a foreign main or nonmain proceeding under Chapter 15 of the Bankruptcy Code in the US Bankruptcy Court for the Southern District of Texas. The petition was dismissed and then it was appealed to the Court of Appeals for the Fifth Circuit.[79] In addition to the extreme fact in *Re Ran* that almost a decade lapsed between the commencement of the foreign bankruptcy proceeding and the petition for recognition,[80] the Court of the Fifth Circuit emphasized the grammar of the statute, holding: "Congress's choice to use the present tense requires courts to view the COMI determination in the present, i.e. at the time the petition for recognition was filed."[81] Moreover, the Court of Appeals for the Fifth Circuit considered that it would be contrary to Congress's purpose for implementing Chapter 15, if COMI had to be assessed by focusing upon the debtor's operational history, indicating:

> a meandering and never-ending inquiry into the debtor's past interests could lead to a denial of recognition in a country where a debtor's interests are truly centered, merely because he conducted past activities in a country at some point well before the petition for recognition was sought.[82]

Later in *Re Kemsley*, Mr. Kemsley, who is British, had also been living and working in the United States for an extended period of time. He was ordered personal bankruptcy in London in January 2012 and his bankruptcy trustee filed a petition in the United States under Chapter 15, seeking an order recognizing the UK proceeding as a foreign main or non-main proceeding. Judge Peck held that the date of commencement of a foreign insolvency proceeding is the proper date for determining the COMI for a foreign debtor and refused to grant recognition accordingly.[83] In his analysis with respect to the timing issue, Judge Peck considered that the date of opening the bankruptcy proceeding is "a fixed and readily verifiable date. In contrast, the date for filing a petition for recognition can vary greatly depending on circumstances and the diligence of the foreign representative".[84] With respect to corporate insolvency, the two options concerning the date to determine .COMI also co-exist. In *Re Betcorp Ltd.*, the court, by referring to *Re Ran*, used the time of the petition for recognition as the date for determining the COMI of an Australian company.[85]

Nevertheless, in *Re Millennium*, Judge Groppe rejected the reasoning in *Re Ran*. The case involved two funding companies, which were incorporated in Bermuda and was put into liquidation there three years prior to their Chapter 15 petitions. First of all, Judge Gropper considered that the "plain words" of the statute did not control the date to make the COMI determination.[86] He further pointed out that the petition for recognition under Chapter 15 was ancillary or secondary in nature and thus the date of the petition for recognition was "a matter of happenstance",[87] whereas the substantive date for the determination of the COMI issue should be "at the date of the opening of the foreign proceeding for which recognition is sought".[88] Secondly, Judge Gropper referred to the decision in *Re Tri-Continental Exchange Ltd.* and determined that the term COMI "generally equates with the concept of principal place of business' in United States law".[89] Considering that a debtor does not continue to have a place of business after liquidation is ordered since the business stops operating, it is obvious that an entity's principal place of business should be determined before it was placed into liquidation.[90] Thirdly, Judge Gropper took into account the international origin of Chapter 15, which adopted the Model Law almost verbatim. The term of COMI under the Model Law corresponds to the formulation in Article 3 of the EC Regulation. Judge Gropper indicated that the date of the opening of initial insolvency proceeding is the only date that the original drafters of the term of the EC Regulation could have contemplated.[91] Fourthly, contrary to the opinions in *Re Ran*,[92] Judge Gropper found inquiry "in the past" consistent with the "plain words of the statute" and stood in line with the stated purpose of Chapter 15, "to promote cooperation with foreign proceedings".[93] In particular, Judge Gropper mentioned that the fact the liquidator appeared before the US court 10 years after the commencement of the foreign proceeding could prevent him from being granted substantive relief, instead of using the date of the Chapter 15 petition to deny recognition.[94] Fifthly, Judge Gropper considered that the COMI determination as of the time of the petition for recognition could result in forum shopping because it "gives *prima facie* recognition to a change of residence between the date of opening proceedings in the foreign nation and the chapter 15 petition date".[95]

In *Re Fairfield Sentry Ltd.*, the Court of Appeals for the Second Circuit, reaffirmed that "a debtor's COMI is determined as of the time of the filing of the Chapter 15 petition".[96] The Second Circuit first pointed out that the statute text of the Chapter 15 did not invite the courts to take into consideration the debtor's entire operational history but signified the proper time, i.e. the filing date of the Chapter 15 petition, to trigger the COMI analysis.[97] Then the Second Circuit looked into the relevant case law of the federal courts, noting "Most courts in this Circuit and throughout the country appear to have examined a debtor's COMI as of the time of the Chapter 15 petition."[98] The Second Circuit further referred to *Re Millennium*, in which the court attempted to equate COMI with principal place of business and consequently raised the expectation of the debtor's operational history check at the time of commencement of the foreign proceedings.[99] The Second Circuit considered that the "principal place of business" approach, however, was intentionally abandoned by the Congress in enacting Chapter 15.[100] Besides, the Second Circuit also noticed that the Congress suggested to take into account the international origin of Chapter 15 in the event of interpretation. The Second Circuit turned to the Guide and Interpretation and the EC Regulation but indicated that international interpretation was of limited use in resolving the timing problem the US courts met, especially pointing out "the EU Regulation does not operate as an analog to Chapter 15".[101] In the end, the Second Circuit tried to reconcile the split on the timing issues among the federal courts (Adler, 2014). By taking into consideration the EC Regulation and other international interpretations, it is suggested "a court may consider the period between the commencement of the foreign insolvency proceeding and the filing of the Chapter 15 petition to ensure that a debtor has not manipulated its COMI in bad faith."[102]

Development of COMI

It has been a well-acknowledged problem that the crucial concept of COMI is not defined under the EC Regulation.[103] In accordance with the EU Regulation (recast), the former Recital (13) under the EC Regulation,[104] which provided an explanatory statement to COMI, is relocated to Article 3(1) of the EU Regulation (recast) with slight modification.[105] Such a "relocation" can at least be deemed as a formal introduction of clarification concerning COMI into the main text. Moreover, the registered office presumption regarding a company or legal person has gone through tremendous content alteration. First of all, a look-back period has been set on the presumption in order to restrict the improper reincorporation of a company.[106] Reincorporation of less than three months prior to the application for insolvency proceedings is viewed as fraudulent or abusive forum shopping (Rudbordeh, 2016). Accordingly, the registered office presumption can possibly be rebutted (Moss, Fletcher, Isaacs, 2016). Besides, it seems that the EU Regulation (recast) changed the tone set on the presumption, which no longer shall be applied but is possible to be rebutted if certain conditions are met.[107] The EU Regulation (recast) offers in its renewed recitals additional explanations on those key conditions, which were left unresolved under the EC Regulation. It is noteworthy that the EU Regulation (recast) sets up all those conditions by literally codifying the case law handed down by the CJEU.[108] The first decisive condition is what constitutes administration. In accordance with the EU Regulation (recast), it refers to the central administration of a company where it conducts the "actual center of management and supervision and of the management of its interests".[109] The second condition is COMI should be assessed comprehensively based on all the relevant factors.[110] Given the third condition that COMI shall be ascertainable by third parties, the EU Regulation (recast) also specifies that the creditors and their perception deserve special consideration – for instance, the timely notification to the creditors in the case of relocation of COMI through appropriate means.[111]

In order to provide guidance concerning the interpretation of COMI, the Guide has been revised in accordance with the request of UNCITRAL at its 43rd session (2010)[112] and was adopted by the Commission as the "Guide to Enactment and Interpretation of the UNCITRAL Model Law on Cross-Border Insolvency" on 18 July, 2013.[113] It is stipulated that the key indicators, considered as a whole, to determine the location of COMI are (1) central administration of the debtor; (2) ascertainability by creditors; (3) the date at which these factors should be analyzed,[114] which is the date of commencement of the foreign proceeding.[115] In case the three indicators are not sufficient to locate COMI, the Model Law also allows additional factors, including "an unexhaustive list of relevant factors",[116] to be taken into consideration in individual cases. Further, the Model Law emphasizes that: "In all cases, however, the endeavor is an holistic one, designed to determine that the location of the foreign proceeding in fact corresponds to the actual location of the debtor's center of main interests, as readily ascertainable by creditors."[117] Regardless of COMI under the two instruments serving different purposes,[118] the Model Law lays out nearly identical criteria to the EU Regulation (recast) with respect to determination of COMI. In reality, however, the enacting States do not strictly abide by those common rules. The *Re Suntech Power* case,[119] which was mentioned in Chapter 3, should be recalled. It involved parallel cross-border insolvency proceedings pending in China, the Cayman Islands and the United States. On 5 November, 2013, the provisional liquidation of Suntech Power was initiated in the Cayman Islands (the Cayman proceeding). On 21 February, 2014, a petition was filed for recognition of Suntech Power's provisional liquidation proceeding pending in the Cayman Islands as a foreign main proceeding or non-main proceeding.[120] One of Suntech Power's American creditors, Solyndra, who brought antitrust litigation against the debtor, objected to the request.[121] On 17 November, 2014, the United States Bankruptcy Court for the Southern District of New York (SDNY) recognized the Cayman proceeding as the foreign main proceeding.[122] The case was filed in New York merely based on a New York bank account established one day prior to the petition for recognition.[123] Solyndra contended that neither was Suntech Power's venue properly in New York, nor could Suntech Power be qualified as a debtor under s 109(a) of the Bankruptcy Code (Seife and Vazquez, 2014; Swick and Harle, 2014).[124] By referring to *Re Octaviar Admin. Pty Ltd.*[125] and *Re Yukos Oil Co.*,[126] the court considered the New York bank account as the only asset of the debtor in the United States,[127] sufficed to render the eligibility of the debtor under 11 U.S.C. § 109(a) through the establishment of the bank account in New York.[128] Solyndra further argued that the debtor's COMI was not located in the Cayman Islands. As of the commencement of the Cayman proceeding,

- *Suntech* was headquartered in China;
- All of Suntech's managers and employees resided outside of the Cayman Islands
- Suntech's (technically, those of its wholly-owned subsidiaries) manufacturing facilities were located in China;
- All of Suntech's creditors, suppliers, and customers were located outside the Cayman Islands;
- As the debtor's primary assets, all of Suntech's bank accounts were maintained in Hong Kong and the Mainland China.[129]

By referring to its former decisions on the similar issues, the United States Bankruptcy Court for the Southern District of New York considered that the following non-exhaustive list of factors, singly or combined, could be relevant to determining a debtor's COMI:

the location of the debtor's headquarters; the location of those who actually manage the debtor (which, conceivably could be the headquarters of a holding company); the location of the debtor's primary assets; the location of the majority of the debtor's creditors or of a majority of the creditors who would be affected by the case; and/or the jurisdiction whose law would apply to most disputes.[130]

First of all, the court admitted that up to 5 November, 2013, when the Cayman proceeding was commenced, Suntech Power did "not conduct any activities in the Cayman Islands and maintained its principal executive offices in Wuxi, China from where it managed the Suntech Group".[131] Nevertheless, the court followed the decision of the Court of Appeal for the second circuit in *Re Fairfield Sentry Ltd.*,[132] holding that a debtor's COMI should be determined based on its activities at the time the Chapter 15 petition is filed, i.e. on 21 February, 2014. Secondly, the court laid emphasis on the liquidation activities of the Joint Provisional Liquidators by quoting *Re Fairfield Sentry Ltd.*, holding that "any relevant activities, including liquidation activities and administrative functions may be considered in the COMI analysis".[133] The court indicated that the appointment order entered by the Cayman Court, which commenced the Cayman proceeding, appointed and authorized the Joint Provisional Liquidators to do all acts on behalf of the debtor, enabled the shift of COMI from China to the Cayman Islands. Within less than four months between the initiation of the foreign liquidation proceeding and the filing of the Chapter 15 petition, necessary steps have been taken by the Joint Provisional Liquidators to centralize the administration of the proceeding in the Cayman Islands.[134]

Coleman and Johnson have done comprehensive analysis on the timing issue concerning COMI in the American jurisprudence, which highlighted that "at its core, COMI is a pre-insolvency concept" (Coleman & Johnson, 2014). I agree and would like to add a few points from a comparative perspective. Despite the complex cross-border insolvency scenarios, COMI is an international standard, upon which a certain degree of consensus has been reached between the two international instruments specializing in cross-border insolvency law, i.e. the Regulation and the Model Law. Although those two instruments diverge from each other in many ways, with respect to the time to determine COMI, the EU Regulation (recast) provides that it should be assessed at the date of the request for opening of insolvency proceedings[135] and it is required pursuant to the Guide and Interpretation of the Model Law (2013) that it shall be at the date of commencement of the foreign proceeding.[136] It is evident that both of them opt for a pre-insolvency approach. Moreover, based on objective observation, to allow assessment of COMI to start later after the commencement of insolvency proceedings, it will breed expansion of the scope of factors that can be taken into account to determine COMI so that liquidation activities and administrative functions can be validated as effective factors for the COMI determination. Consequently, more factors can be actually utilized for COMI relocation. The United States has adopted the Model Law almost verbatim by incorporating Chapter 15 into its Bankruptcy Code, including the concept of COMI, which can be deemed as a commitment to an international standard. If there is inconsistency between the rule of domestic statutory and a particular section of Chapter 15, the problem of proper interpretation arises. Deviation from its original international approach on proper interpretation of a common concept would compromise the goal of achieving uniformity and facilitating cross-border cooperation in insolvency matters and would reduce certainty and predictability in the application of the international standard.

Recognition and reliefs

Upon request for recognition of a foreign judgment, a receiving court has to determine (1) Whether or not to recognize a foreign judgment. (2) Once recognized, to what extent the effect of the foreign judgment should be accorded. (3) If the judgment is recognized, how to enforce it. This section will answer the three questions in the context of cross-border insolvency and identify the difference concerning recognition, effects and enforcement between the Regulation and the Model Law.

Automatic recognition and universal effects under the Regulation

The recognition system under the Regulation is based on a singular criterion, which is directly linked to jurisdiction. A judgment commencing a main insolvency proceeding rendered by a court of a Member State shall be automatically recognized in all other Member States as long as the court that opened the proceeding has jurisdiction pursuant to Article 3.[137] To understand that kind of arrangement, it should be explained from three aspects. First of all, that arrangement accords with the general rule concerning recognition under private international law, which is "no state recognizes the judgment of another state rendered without jurisdiction over the judgment debtor".[138] Secondly, from the perspective of cross-border insolvency, the aim of the Regulation is universalism, though with some compromise.[139] The rationale behind that principle is to administer all of the assets and debts of the debtor through one central jurisdiction. Accordingly, the Regulation provides a system of automatic recognition concerning the main proceeding throughout the EU. Thirdly, that arrangement is peculiar to the EU because automatic recognition is guaranteed by the principle of mutual trust.[140] It requires that grounds for non-recognition should be reduced to the minimum necessary. In the case that the courts of two Member States both claim competence to open the main insolvency proceedings, the principle of mutual trust should also serve as the proper foundation for jurisdiction dispute settlement in the course of recognition.[141] In the *Eurofood* case, the CJEU makes clear that "the principle of mutual trust requires that the courts of the other Member States recognize the decision opening main insolvency proceedings, without being able to review the assessment made by the first court as to its jurisdiction".[142] On the ground of the principle of mutual trust, the effects flowing from automatic recognition are universal to the extent the exception applies, which means without further formalities, the effects of the main proceeding are extended to all other Member States.[143] Besides, the scope of the effects of cross-border insolvency proceedings is also connected with choice of law rules. In order to approach the universal effect, the Regulation adopted *lex fori concursus* as the fundamental rule of its uniform choice of law system, which requires that the law of the State of the opening of proceedings shall determine the conditions for the opening, conduct and closure of insolvency proceedings.[144] Meanwhile, aware of the fact that it is difficult to implement a single exclusive regime of universality without modifying,[145] the effects of the main proceedings will be limited by the opening of secondary proceedings in another Member State.[146] Although the rule of applicable law on the secondary proceedings is also *lex fori concursus*,[147] the effects, instead of being universal, are restricted to the assets located in the State of the opening of secondary proceedings (hence, in fact, *lex fori concursus secondarii*).[148] Upon recognition, the effects are mainly realized by the insolvency practitioners, who exercise the powers vested in them under the Regulation.[149] If an insolvency practitioner is appointed by the opening of the main proceedings, the nature, content and extent of his power is determined subject to the *lex fori concursus* automatically exercisable in other Member States.[150] There are also built-in exceptions. First of all, if the main insolvency practitioners exercise the powers in foreign Member States, they shall be subject to both substantive and procedural restrictions. For instance, there are explicit bars on coercive measures and rights to rule on legal proceedings and disputes. In addition, they should take action according to the local law.[151] Secondly, the power of the main insolvency practitioners to remove the debtor's assets from the territory of the Member State in which they are situated is deemed as "the most common reason for attempting to exercise powers and perhaps the most sensitive in terms of local interests" (Moss, Fletcher, Isaacs, 2016). Therefore, it is stipulated under the Regulation that third parties' rights in rem and rights involving reservation of title are not affected by the effects of the main proceedings[152] and accordingly fall out of the reach of the powers of the main insolvency practitioners. Thirdly, if a preservation measure has been taken in order to open secondary proceedings, the main insolvency practitioners cannot exercise their powers conflicting with those measures.[153] Last, but not least, once the secondary proceedings are opened, the powers of the main insolvency practitioners will no longer be effective as against those local assets. The secondary insolvency practitioners have the power to claim in any other Member State that moveable property was removed from the State where the territorial proceedings were commenced after the opening of those insolvency proceedings[154]

Recognition and reliefs under the model law

Recognition

Instead of establishing a comprehensive framework as under the Regulation, the Model Law narrowed its scopes and goals to some of the most crucial issues concerning cross-border insolvency, including facilitation of recognition of foreign insolvency proceedings.[155] Under the Model Law, recognition will be "granted as a matter of course"[156] if recognition is not contrary to the public policy of the enacting States and if the application meets the basic criteria set out in Article 17(1), including:

(1) the proceeding must be a foreign proceeding (within the meaning of Article 2(a));
(2) applied for by a foreign representative (within the meaning of Article 2(d));
(3) the application meets the requirements (provided under Article 15(2));
(4) has been submitted to the competent court (Article 4).

Those simple recognition criteria reflect the core philosophy of the Model Law, which is "there is no time to waste, as the recognition must take place as expeditiously as possible" (Berends, 1998). In particular, it is advised that based on any of those criteria a proceeding could be deemed a main proceeding. If more than one criterion is included, it "would raise the risk of competing claims from foreign proceedings for recognition as the main proceeding".[157] The receiving court is not given the opportunity to judge the merits of the foreign proceedings.[158] Further, it has been stressed that to obtain early recognition is often the guarantee for effective protection of the assets of the debtor from dissipation and concealment. For that reason, the court is obliged to decide on the application "at the earliest possible time".[159] In addition, the Model Law also uses the jurisdictional basis, i.e. COMI and establishment, for the court to distinguish recognition of the foreign proceedings as the main or non-main proceedings.[160]To be recognized as the main or non-main proceeding differ quite substantially in the legal consequences because the effects and reliefs flowing from recognition may depend upon the category into which a foreign proceeding falls.

Reliefs

Due to various insolvency systems from State to State influenced by respective social, political, financial and other considerations, UNCITRAL found it difficult to provide uniform choice of law rules on a global level in the process of drafting the Model Law and thus choice of law rules fall outside of the ambit of the Model Law (Clift, 2014). Without harmonized choice of law rules, the applicable law that governs the effect of recognition is unpredictable and uncertain. To fill in the gap and give necessary support to the recognized proceedings, the Model Law introduced a "minimum" list of automatic or discretionary effects and measures that would be triggered by recognition, while at the same time leaving room for the recognizing court to provide additional effects or measures.[161] Those effects or measures are addressed as reliefs in the context of the Model Law.

Automatic reliefs are mandatory and solely granted upon recognition of main proceedings alone. The types of those automatic reliefs are certain and specific under Article 20(1) of the Model Law, including:

(1) Commencement or continuation of individual actions or individual proceedings concerning the debtor's assets, rights, obligations or liabilities is stayed;
(2) Execution against the debtor's assets is stayed; and
(3) The right to transfer, encumber or otherwise dispose of any assets of the debtor is suspended.[162]

As emphasized in the Guide and Interpretation, recognition of the main proceedings set under Article 20 has its own effects rather than importing the consequences of the foreign law into the insolvency system of the enacting State. That entails the imposition on the insolvent debtor of the consequences of Article 20 in the enacting State is justified, even if the automatic effects of the insolvency proceeding in the country of origin are different from the effects of Article 20 in the enacting State.[163] Meanwhile, notwithstanding the "automatic" or "mandatory" nature, the automatic reliefs upon recognition of the main proceedings might be subject to certain exceptions, limitations, modifications or termination in accordance with the law of the enacting State.[164]

In addition to the automatic reliefs under Article 20, the Model Law also provides discretionary reliefs. The scope of discretionary reliefs are much wider, including provisional reliefs under Article 19 of the Model Law and any appropriate relief available upon recognition under the laws of the Enacting State.[165] Provisional relief deals with "'urgently needed' relief that may be ordered at the discretion of the court and is available as of the moment of the application for recognition".[166] Provisional reliefs include stay of execution against the debtor's assets, transfer of the administration or realization of the debtor's assets to the foreign representative or another person designated by the court, suspension of the right to transfer, encumber, or dispose of any assets of the debtor, providing for the examination of witnesses, the taking of evidence or the delivery of information concerning the debtor's assets etc., and granting additional relief.[167] Unless granted extension in accordance with Article 21(f), provisional reliefs terminate when the application for recognition is decided upon.[168] Following the recognition of main or non-main proceedings, the court may, at the request of the foreign representative, grant any appropriate relief,[169] which means the court may "subject the relief granted to any conditions it considers appropriate".[170] Unlike a representative of a foreign main proceeding, who normally seeks to gain control over all assets of the insolvent debtor, a representative of a foreign non-main proceeding normally have narrower interests and limited authority.[171] Relief granted to a foreign non-main proceeding should be limited to assets that are to be administered in that non-main proceeding, and if the foreign representative seeks information concerning the debtor's assets or affairs, the relief must concern information required in that non-main proceeding.[172] In order not to interfere with the administration of another insolvency proceeding, in particular the main proceeding, the court is advised when granting relief in favor of a foreign non-main proceeding, the court "should not give unnecessarily broad powers to the foreign representative".[173] Moreover, it is stipulated under the Model Law "granting any additional relief that may be available under the laws of this State".[174] In accordance with the Guide and Interpretation of the Model Law:

> The proviso 'under the law of this State' reflects the principle underlying the Model Law that recognition of a foreign proceeding does not mean extending the effects of the foreign proceeding as they may be prescribed by the law of the foreign State. Instead, recognition of a foreign proceeding entails attaching to the foreign proceeding consequences envisaged by the law of the enacting State.[175]

The Model Law did not specify whether "the law" includes private international law of the enacting state. Nevertheless, a few relevant recommendations concerning discretionary reliefs find their ways into the Legislative Guide.[176] If private international law is included in "the law", a question arises whether the recognizing court can grant the reliefs on the basis of *lex fori* or *lex fori concursus*. The general rule adopted by the Legislative Guide to apply to the insolvency proceedings is the *lex fori concursus*, which entails insolvency proceedings shall be governed by the law of the State in which those proceedings are commenced.[177] In the meantime, it also provides a couple of exceptions to the *lex fori concursus* in order to respect the rights and claims established under the domestic law,[178] to maintain the certainty of ordinary transactions relying on a determined legal environment[179] or to safeguard certain rights subject to special protection.[180] It is pointed out under the Legislative Guide that the general application of the *lex fori concursus* can better achieve the goal of maximizing the value of the debtor's assets and an exception to the *lex fori concursus* may distort the universal insolvency effects on similarly situated creditors owing to varied applicable law.[181] The Model Law aims at fairly and efficiently administering cross-border insolvency proceedings for the benefit of all creditors on an equal basis rather than specific individual creditors.[182] Hence, any exception to the general rule of the *lex fori concursus* is suggested to be limited and clearly elaborated.[183] In the UK, it is stated under the Sch. I of the UK Cross-border Insolvency Regulations 2006, "references to the law of Great Britain include a reference to the law of either part of Great Britain (including its rules of private international law)".[184] As indicated by Ho, there is the possibility that choice of law rules may direct an English court to use (foreign law) *lex fori concursus* when granting relief (Ho, 2010). *Cambridge Gas Transportation Corporation v Official Committee of Unsecured Creditors of Navigator Holdings (Cambridge Gas)*[185] is such a typical example. The UK Privy Council granted relief in accordance with Chapter 11 of the US Bankruptcy Code instead of a scheme of arrangement under s 152 of the Companies Act 1931. There are two main conditions that enabled the UK Privy Council to grant a relief in accordance with the US Bankruptcy Code: (1) the underlying principle of the common law in matters of judicial assistance in international insolvency is the principle of universality, which entails universal application;[186] (2) In the present case, exactly the same result could have been achieved by a scheme of arrangement under s 152 of the Companies Act 1931 as under the Chapter 11 plan.[187] Nevertheless, the decision in *Cambridge Gas* was overturned by the Supreme Court in the case of *Rubin v Eurofinance*.[188] The principal issue is whether the rules at common law or under the foreign law regulating those foreign courts, which are to be regarded as being competent for the purposes of enforcement of judgments, apply to judgments in avoidance proceedings in insolvency.[189] The main finding in *Rubin* was that orders in insolvency matters are either in personam or in rem[190] "but not *sui generis* in terms of the private international law rules of insolvency" (Dessain, 2014). When enforcing foreign insolvency orders at common law in England, the principles in the *Dicey* rules are applicable unless the judgment is considered subject to a separate rule.[191] It was pointed out that prior to *Cambridge Gas* and the present cases, there had been no suggestion that there might be a different rule for judgments in personam. in insolvency proceedings and other proceedings.[192] (The avoidance orders in the present case were held in personam. The judge in the Court of Appeal accepted that the judgment was in personam and the *Rubin* respondents have not sought to argue that it was not an in personam judgment.)[193] Further, the Supreme Court held that there was no reason to class avoidance judgments relating to insolvency proceedings any differently to any other type of foreign judgment in the interests of the universality of bankruptcy.[194] Accordingly, the decision in *Cambridge Gas* was deemed as "a radical departure from substantially settled law"[195] and wrongly decided.[196] On 10 November, 2014, the Privy Council handed down its decision in *Singularis Holdings Limited (Singularis) v PricewaterhouseCoopers (PwC)*.[197] *Singularis*, incorporated in the Cayman Island, was ordered by the Grand Court of the Cayman Islands to be wound up. The Bermudan court issued an order recognizing in Bermuda the status of the Cayman liquidators. The Bermudan court then exercised what it termed a common law power "by analogy with the statutory powers contained in section 195 of the Companies Act" to order PwC to provide information under s 195.[198] The Court of Appeal set aside this order on the basis that this was not an appropriate exercise of discretion because this would be an order made in support of a Cayman liquidation, which could not have been made by the Cayman court. In deciding this case, the Privy Council addressed the apparent conflict between the *Cambridge Gas* case and the *Rubin* case and gave guidance as to whether the principle of modified universalism as articulated by Lord Hoffman in *Cambridge Gas* was correct. The Privy Council considered

> The primary way in which the case was put by the liquidators was that the common law develops to meet changing circumstances and that in international insolvencies the common law should be developed by the adoption of a principle that where local legislation does not provide for relevant assistance to a foreign officeholder, the legislation should be applied by analogy "as if" the foreign insolvency were a local insolvency. This argument was accepted by the Chief Justice. But it involves a fundamental misunderstanding of the limits of the judicial law-making power, and should not go unanswered.[199]

Although the aforementioned cases involved different kinds of reliefs, such as recovery of assets, transaction avoidance and access to information, there is no material difference on the principal issue invoked among them. In each case, the main issue was whether the local legislation should be applied and, if so, to what extent. The Privy Council in *Singularis* held that the principle of modified universalism is a recognized principle of the common law.[200] However, the principle is much more limited in scope than articulated in *Cambridge Gas*. This is because the principle of modified universalism is subject to local law and local public policy and the domestic court can only ever act within the limits of its own statutory and common law powers.[201] To that extent, *Cambridge Gas* is overruled.[202] As indicated by Lord Collins:

> It is a principle of the common law that the court has the power to recognize and grant assistance to foreign insolvency proceedings . . . Those powers can be extended or developed from existing powers through the traditional judicial law-making techniques

of the common law . . . The very limited application of legislation by analogy does not allow the judiciary to extend the scope of insolvency legislation to cases where it does not apply.[203]

As a result, the appeal was dismissed because the liquidators would not have had the power to require PwC to produce the requested documentation under Cayman Islands law.[204] In the United States, *lex fori concursus* used to be applied when granting relief. In *Re Schimmelpenninck*,[205] a Dutch curator, a position akin to a trustee in a United States bankruptcy proceeding, filed an ancillary proceeding in the United States Bankruptcy Court in the Northern District of Texas, requesting declaratory and injunctive relief in order to preserve for the debtor's estate value.[206] The United States Court of Appeals for the Fifth Circuit overturned the decision made by the bankruptcy court and the district court on appeal, granting declaratory and injunctive relief to the Dutch curator. After having examined the related Dutch law, the court adopted the comity-based approach for application of the foreign law, considering

> the foreign laws need not be identical to their counterparts under the laws of the United States; they merely must not be repugnant to our laws and policies . . . As we have already found sufficient congruity between Dutch and American bankruptcy laws to eschew such repugnance, we conclude that principles of comity weigh in favor of granting the injunction sought by the Curators.[207]

The case was heard in 1999 on the basis of §304 of the US Bankruptcy Code, which has been replaced by Chapter 15. Case law applying that section remains relevant. Some of the American courts continuously followed that point of view after 2005 when Chapter 15 came into effect[208] but some courts do not. *Re Vitro*[209] is such a notable example. In *Re Vitro*, it involved recognition and enforcement of a Mexican reorganization plan (the Concurso Approval Order).[210] The United States Court of Appeals for the Fifth Circuit pointed out "whether any relief under Chapter 15 will be granted is a separate question from whether a foreign proceeding will be recognized by a United States bankruptcy court"[211] and recognized the Mexican reorganization proceeding as a foreign main proceeding.[212] However, it denied the enforcement of the reorganization plan, which would discharge obligations held by non-debtor guarantors and did not provide the protections afforded to creditors under the Bankruptcy Code.[213] The Fifth Circuit admitted that comity is central to Chapter 15[214] and "an important factor in determining whether relief will be granted".[215] Nevertheless, the Fifth Circuit also found that: "Chapter 15 does impose certain requirements and considerations that act as a brake or limitation on comity, and preclude granting the relief requested by a foreign representative."[216] It therefore developed a hierarchical three-step framework of statutory analysis, which governs whether a relief should be granted or precluded.[217] They are:

> Step (1): a court should check whether the relief requested falls within the ambit of one of the explicit provisions enumerated under § 1521(a)(1)–(7).
> Step (2): if § 1521(a)(1)–(7) and (b) does not list the requested relief, a court should decide whether it can be considered "appropriate relief" under § 1521(a).
> Step (3): if the requested relief goes beyond the relief afforded under § 1521, a bankruptcy court then should consider whether "additional assistance" is appropriate under § 1507.[218]

As addressed by the Honorable Justice Louise De Carl Adler, with §304 of the Bankruptcy Code replaced by Chapter 15 in 2005, comity has been elevated from one of six factors under §304(c) to the introductory text of §1507 (Adler, 2014). Nevertheless, the three-step framework adopted by the Fifth Circuit in *Re Vitro* gives more weight to the law of the United States (*lex fori*), who seems to depart from its former *lex fori concursus* approach on the basis of comity. Besides, Chapter 15 instructs the US courts to take into account its international origin and the need to promote an application of this chapter that is consistent with the application of similar statutes adopted by foreign jurisdictions,[219] whereas the restricted interpretation of Chapter 15 in *Re Vitro* are more subordinate to the peculiarities of jurisprudence in the United States. Moreover, to seek relief, extra requirements are set for foreign representatives to satisfy, which previously have not been required by Chapter 15.

Public policy

Public policy in the context of cross-border insolvency

Public policy is applied in both the Regulation and the Model Law to refuse the recognition of the foreign insolvency proceedings. Public policy is the only ground for refusing recognition under the EC Regulation[220] and the EU Regulation (recast) follows this approach,[221] which reflects the fact that the Regulation is based on a presumption that a judgment opening insolvency proceedings is valid (Moss, Fletcher, Issacs, 2016). Hence, public policy is interpreted by the CJEU in a very restrictive manner and is expected to be applied in exceptional cases. The CJEU set the tone with respect to public policy in the *Eurofood* case, in which it directly referred to its case law on the Brussels Convention (*Bamberski v Krombach*.[222] As stated in *Bamberski v Krombach*, the CJEU based on the Brussels Convention (Brussels I and II) ruled that:

> recourse to that clause can be envisaged only where recognition or enforcement of the judgment delivered in another Contracting State would be at variance to an unacceptable degree with the legal order of the State in which enforcement is sought inasmuch as it infringes a fundamental principle. The infringement would have to constitute a manifest breach of a rule of law regarded as essential in the legal order of the State in which enforcement is sought or of a right recognized as being fundamental within that legal order.[223]
>
> . . .
>
> . . . on a proper interpretation of Art. 26 of the Regulation, a Member State may refuse to recognize insolvency proceedings opened in another Member State where the decision to open the proceedings was taken in flagrant breach of the fundamental right to be heard, which a person concerned by such proceedings enjoys.[224]

In practice, courts of the Member States often refer to the case law of the CJEU in matters of the public policy exception in a consistent way (Hess/Pfeiffer, 2011). In addition, based on the national reports collected in the Study of Interpretation of the Public Policy Exception, the policy exception is applied narrowly at the national level.[225] Public policy has not been defined in Article 6 of the Model Law on purpose since the notion of public policy is "grounded in national law and may differ from State to State".[226] It is emphasized under the Guide and Interpretation that the genuine intent of Article 6 was expected to "be invoked under exceptional circumstances".[227] Nonetheless, Wessels indicated that the scope under Article 6 of the Model Law is wider than that under the Regulation because the latter only involves the negative condition of recognition whereas Article 6 of the Model Law "provides the possibility of invoking public policy against any decision of a foreign court" (Wessels, 2012). A notable example is that public policy is not only an exception for recognition but also has been frequently applied to entitlement to relief in the American jurisprudence. In *Re Cozumel Caribe*,[228] the dispute involved the effect of insolvency proceedings opened against *Cozumel Caribe*, a Mexican corporation, in Mexico (the *concurso*). The debtor, *Cozumel Caribe*, together with its non-debtor Mexican affiliates, was jointly under an obligation of debt payment in connection with a $103 million secured loan. The loan was guaranteed through the cash management account governed by New York law. The account was controlled by CTIM, as special servicer for the loan. When the debtor and the non-debtor affiliates had defaulted on the loans, CTIM sought to recover some or all of the funds in the cash management account before the United States District Court for the Southern District of New York. Meanwhile, the foreign representative filed a petition for recognition of the *concurso* and a stay of the adversary proceeding brought by the foreign representative. Although the US Bankruptcy Court for the Southern District of New York recognized the *concurso* as foreign main proceedings and granted a stay of the adversary proceeding, Judge Glenn considered that a bankruptcy court can grant the relief if it "sufficiently protects parties in interest in accordance with §1522",[229] and must deny the relief if it is "manifestly contrary to United States public policy under §1506".[230] Judge Glenn is not the first American bankruptcy judge, and will not be the last one, who has extended the public policy exception to granting relief.

Basic content of public policy

The content of public policy is left to each Member State to decide and has not been unified by the Regulation. As explained in the Virgós-Schmit Report, public policy under the Regulation is governed by fundamental principles of both substance and procedure.[231] Thus public policy can embody procedural and substantive contents. With respect to procedural contents, the importance of due process has been highlighted. Failure to observe due process, including the adequate opportunity to be heard and the rights of participation in the proceedings, will consequently incur the violation of the equality of arms principle, which probably hamper the substantial rights of the parties concerned. What constitutes public policy is also an unanswered question under the Model Law but governed by various national laws.[232] It has been acknowledged that the majority limits the public policy exception to fundamental principles of law, in particular constitutional guarantees.[233] Whether or not due process will be considered manifestly contrary to public policy is not resolved by the Model Law but also depends on the laws of the enacting states.[234] Although the Model Law does not mandate due process, it is also emphasized "in a number of jurisdictions, fundamental principles of due process, in some cases enshrined in the constitution".[235] For instance, in *Re Silvec*, an Italian debtor did not give a US creditor notice of Italian insolvency proceedings. The US court noted that there were no procedures in Italy that would allow for the protection of the creditor's rights of notice and opportunity to be heard. Consequently, the court modified the automatic stay of the Italian insolvency proceedings, holding that fundamental public policy under US law is that parties in a legal proceeding are entitled to due process and notice and denying those rights, therefore, is manifestly contrary to that policy.[236]

Procedural contents are more foreseeable, whereas substantive contents are more variable. As incorporated into the systematic context of the Regulation, the public policy exception shall also be guided by the principle of universality[237] and of equal treatment of creditors,[238] which are "opposed to any unnecessary fragmentation of insolvency proceedings based on a non-recognition of foreign insolvency proceedings" (Hess, Oberhammer & Pfeiffer, 2014). Accordingly, the threshold set out by the Regulation for the Member States to refuse to recognize insolvency proceedings is very high (Moss, Fletcher, Isaacs, 2016). According to Hess and Pfeiffer's statistical information, there are only a few cases where the public policy exception was raised successfully out of substantive contents (Hess/Pfeiffer, 2011). For instance, in the case of *Re Rover France SAS*,[239] it involved a British holding company, MG Rover, which had subsidiaries registered in different European countries. The holding company, together with some of its subsidiaries, applied for the opening of the main insolvency proceedings in the UK in order to put the entire group into joint administration.[240] The effects of the English main proceedings met resistance in France, where the French Public Prosecutor attempted to initiate parallel main insolvency proceedings.[241] The French Public Prosecutor considered the English main proceedings should not be recognized because recognition, which could amount to the negative influences on the rights of French employees, would constitute a manifest breach of French public policy.[242] As pointed out by Norris QC:

> In general, in striking the balance between the interests of employees on the one hand and the interests of finance and trade creditors on the other, English insolvency law treats the claims of employees less favourably than the law of other Member States.[243]

Nevertheless, the Commercial Court of Nanterre (the Tribunal de commerce, Nanterre) and the Court of Appeal of Versailles (Cour d'Appel, Versailles) held against the French Public Prosecutor and did not think the public policy objection could be properly raised in this case. First of all, in accordance with the Regulation, the employment contract was governed by the law of contract, i.e. French law, which required that the works committee and the staff representatives should be consulted where insolvency proceedings affected contracts of employment and labor relations.[244] The fact that the British court had the jurisdiction to open main proceedings would not change the applicable law or consequently undermine the adequate protection of employees. Secondly, the English administrators gave certain undertakings to ensure that the French employees would receive the same treatment as they could receive under French law (Samad, 2013). There are no related statistics or survey into all the enacting States of the Model Law on how they interpret public policy with respect to the substantive contents on the international level. The case law in American jurisprudence can be viewed as an exemplar, which illustrates the scope of substantive contents concerning the public policy exception. Substantive rights, which are guaranteed under the constitution, are included. In *Re Toft*,[245] it involved a request applied by the foreign representative in a Germany insolvency proceeding to get access to the debtor's e-mail accounts under Chapter 15, which were stored on servers in the United States. While German law permitted such mail interception,[246] the ex parte interception of electronic communications is illegal under two US statutes.[247] The Court held that the relief sought would be manifestly contrary to public policy because "the relief sought would directly compromise privacy rights subject to a comprehensive scheme of statutory protection, available to aliens, built on constitutional safeguards incorporated in the Fourth Amendment as well as the constitutions of many [s]tates."[248] In addition, the public policy exception is also extended to the fundamental policy of the United States. In the aforementioned *Re Vitro* case, the U.S. court refused to grant reliefs to the Mexican reorganization plan (the *concurso* approval order), holding:

> The expression by Congress in §524, paired with the case law in this Circuit, lead this Court to conclude that the protection of third party claims in a bankruptcy case is a fundamental policy of the United States. The *Concurso* Approval Order does not simply modify such claims against non-debtors, they are extinguished. As the *Concurso* plan does not recognize and protect such rights, the *Concurso* plan is manifestly contrary to such policy of the United States and cannot be enforced here.[249]

The other typical instance related to fundamental policy is *Re Qimonda AG*, which was appealed to the Supreme Court of the United States. In *Re Qimonda AG*, a German manufacturer of semiconductor memory devices (Qimonda) obtained recognition of the German proceeding as a foreign main proceeding in the United States under Chapter 15.[250] The specific question presented was whether Chapter 15 permits a foreign administrator to avoid the application of §365(n) of the Bankruptcy Code, which was enacted by Congress with the explicit goal of furthering the public policy of supporting the high-tech industry by providing protection for intellectual property license agreements (Chung, 2013). The court concluded that Congress enacted §365(n) to protect American technology, and that this is direct evidence of a "strong" U.S. policy favoring technological innovation.[251] In reaching this conclusion, the Court conducted a balancing test between the relief that may be granted to the foreign representative and the interests of the persons that may be affected by such relief. The Court noted that failure to apply §365(n) would "slow the pace of innovation, to the detriment of the U.S. economy" and "would severely impinge an important statutory protection . . . and thereby undermine a fundamental U.S. public policy".[252] Accordingly, the bankruptcy court denied the motion of the foreign administrator, who then appealed to the United States Court of Appeals for the Fourth Circuit. The Fourth Circuit affirmed the Bankruptcy Court's decision and concluded that the Bankruptcy Court reasonably exercised its discretion in balancing the interests of the licensees against the interests of the foreign debtor and finding that the application of §365(n) of the Bankruptcy Code was necessary to protect the licensees' rights under Qimonda's US patents.[253] The Fourth Circuit recognized both the importance of Chapter 15 of the Bankruptcy Code to the global economy and the United States' commitment to cooperate with foreign insolvency proceedings. Nevertheless, such commitment, according to the Fourth Circuit, was not untempered.[254] The Fourth Circuit held that a bankruptcy court is required to ensure sufficient protection of creditors under §1522(a) of the Bankruptcy Code, and, at a more general level, a bankruptcy court may refuse to grant comity or take an action that would be manifestly contrary to the United States' public policy under §1506 of the Bankruptcy Code.[255] The foreign administrator then appealed to the Supreme Court of the United States for review of the decision of the Fourth Circuit. On 6 October, 2014, the Supreme Court denied the petition for a writ of certiorari.[256] It seems that public policy under the Model Law could be interpreted in a much broader way if it might relate to any mandatory rule of the local law or protection of the interests of local creditors, although it is expected that the public policy exception will be rarely used and shall be understood more restrictively than domestic public policy.[257]

Cooperation and communication

Single debtor

For single debtor, the EC Regulation designed the cooperation model through the liquidators from both main proceeding and secondary proceeding, which reduces the overall complexity in order to achieve the effective realization of the total assets.[258] Article 31 provides that as a general principle the liquidator in the main proceedings and the liquidators in any secondary proceedings should communicate information to each other and in particular should immediately communicate any information that might be relevant to the other proceedings. The information to be communicated includes information relating to the lodging and verification of claims and relating to the termination of the proceedings.[259] However, it is merely a duty without specific measures. Moreover, the EC Regulation does not allow cooperation and direct communication between the courts as well as between the courts and the foreign representatives,[260] whereas in EU's practice, the cooperation and communication has been extended to courts.[261] After revision, the EU Regulation (recast) has incorporated rules of cooperation and communication between the actors involved in all the concurrent proceedings, including the courts and insolvency practitioners.[262] The insolvency practitioners in the main proceedings and secondary proceedings shall at the earliest opportunity communicate to each other any relevant information about the other proceedings and discover the rescue potential of the debtor by preparing a restructuring plan if possible.[263] Different from the Model Law, the main proceedings have the dominant role under the Regulation. Therefore, in the process of coordination, the insolvency practitioner in the main proceedings is given "an early opportunity" to submit proposals on the administration of the realization or use of the debtor's assets and affairs.[264] The courts in the main and territorial or secondary insolvency proceedings are required to cooperate and communicate with each other to the extent such cooperation is not incompatible with the rules applicable to each of the proceedings.[265] The courts can directly request information or assistance from each other unless that direct communication may jeopardize the procedural rights of the parties to the proceedings or the confidentiality of information.[266] Besides, the courts may not charge costs to each other in the course of cooperation and communication.[267] With respect to cooperation and communication between the insolvency practitioners and the courts, it is required that the insolvency practitioner in the main proceedings shall cooperate with any courts that open or receive a request to open the secondary proceedings.[268] Accordingly, the insolvency practitioner in the territorial proceedings (including territorial insolvency proceedings and secondary proceedings) shall cooperate with the court that opens or receives a request to open the main proceedings.[269]

Considering the lack of cooperation and communication between different jurisdictions in matters of cross-border insolvency, the Model Law provides a legislative framework for cooperation between the courts and the insolvency representatives from two or more countries in order to "prevent dissipation of assets, to maximize the value of assets or to find the best solutions for the reorganization of the enterprise".[270] For national laws lacking rules providing a legal basis for cooperation by local courts with foreign courts in dealing with cross-border insolvencies, the Model Law mandates cross-border cooperation by stating that the court and the insolvency representative "shall cooperate to the maximum extent possible".[271] The phrase "cooperate to the maximum extent possible" provides a sufficient degree of flexibility (Berends, 1998). For States that has already established the cross-border judicial cooperation framework, regardless of its legal basis that is either comity or reciprocity, Chapter IV of the Model Law may serve as a model for the development of such international cooperation. In the process of cooperation, the courts are left with discretion in matters of appropriate involvement of the parties, in either a direct or indirect way.[272] In accordance with Articles 25 and 26 of the Model Law, cooperation and communication can be established between courts, between courts and foreign representatives and between insolvency representatives. The participation of the courts in cooperation and communication has been emphasized because their involvement can significantly contribute to efficiency, which can "help to simplify the formalities and get rid of the use of time-consuming procedures, such as letters rogatory".[273] In case of urgency, it is even recommended by UNCITRAL that the enacting State may consider to include "an express provision, which would authorize the courts, when they engage in cross-border communications, to forgo use of the formalities".[274] Article 27 of the Model Law merely provides a list of possible forms of cooperation on a general basis. Therefore, in 2009, UNCITRAL released Practice Guide on Cross-Border Insolvency Cooperation (Practice Guide on Cooperation), which aims at the introduction of information relating to cooperation and communication based on a collection of sources relating to global development in recent years, including case law.

In addition to the Model Law and the Regulation, there are two sets of soft laws, which are specialized at providing generally accepted guidance with respect to cross-border insolvency cooperation and communication. Each of them is established based on consultation of opinions of related experts (including scholars, judges, insolvency practitioners). The first one is the American Law Institute (ALI) and International Insolvency Institute (III) Transnational insolvency: global principles for cooperation in international insolvency cases published in 2012 (hereinafter, the Global Principles). The second one is the EU Cross-Border Insolvency Court-to-Court Cooperation Principles (hereinafter, EU JudgeCo Principles) published in 2015.

Enterprise groups

The Model Law itself does not address the issue of the group of companies but in 2010, UNCITRAL released the Legislative Guide on Insolvency Law, Part III Treatment of enterprise groups in insolvency, hereinafter the Legislative Guide Part III, to assist States in handling cross-border insolvency of enterprise groups.[275] Both the EU Regulation (recast) and the Legislative Guide Part III attached importance to cooperation of insolvency proceedings concerning different entities of the same group by utilizing cooperation and communication measures. In fact, the relevant provisions under the EU Regulation (recast) have been greatly influenced by the Legislative Guide Part III, which share quite a lot in common with the latter. Generally speaking, the actors, involved in the process of cooperation and communication concerning members of a group of companies, include insolvency practitioners[276] (insolvency representatives, as addressed under the Model Law[277]) and the courts.[278] Cooperation is deemed necessary as long as such cooperation is appropriate to facilitate the fair and effective administration of the proceedings, is not incompatible with the rules applicable to them and does not entail any conflict of interests.[279] The contents of cooperation and communication between insolvency practitioners (insolvency representatives) mainly include:

(1) timely communication of any relevant information concerning the group members subject to insolvency proceedings, provided appropriate arrangements are made to protect confidential information;[280]

(2) coordination of the administration and supervision of the affairs of the group members subject to insolvency proceedings;[281]
(3) coordination of the proposal and of reorganization plans;[282]
(4) allocation of powers or responsibilities between insolvency representatives;[283]
(5) by means of agreements or protocols.[284]

With respect to cooperation and communication involving courts, it is suggested under the Legislative Guide Part III that the proper time to cooperate and communicate shall not depend on the formal recognition of foreign proceedings, which allows communication to take place before, or irrespective of whether, an application for recognition is made.[285] In accordance with the EU Regulation (recast), cooperation and communication with the participation of the courts shall be initiated based on a pending request for the opening of proceedings or the proceedings that have been commenced.[286] Courts can communicate with each other or request information or assistance from each other on a direct basis.[287] They can communicate and cooperate with each other by any appropriate means they consider appropriate.[288] They can cooperate in matters of coordination of the administration and supervision of the assets and affairs of the members of the group,[289] coordination of the conduct of hearings[290] as well as coordination in the approval of protocols where necessary.[291] Between the insolvency practitioners (insolvency representatives) and the courts, the insolvency practitioners (insolvency representatives) are given the rights to directly request information or seek assistance from the courts concerning the proceedings regarding the other member of the group.[292] Under the EU Regulation (recast), insolvency practitioners can only request assistance concerning the proceedings in which they have been appointed.[293] As for the costs, the Legislative Guide Part III merely raised some concern about the costs of cooperation and communication in proceedings concerning members of a group of companies,[294] whereas it is stipulated under the EU Regulation (recast) that costs and expenses incurred in the process of cooperation and communication shall be borne by the respective proceedings.[295]

The single insolvency practitioner approach has been introduced into the EU Regulation (recast), which further substantiates that approach by establishing the system of group coordination proceedings.[296] A group coordinator has been vested with substantial rights and obligations.[297] The main tasks of the group coordinator are to outline recommendations for the coordinated conduct of the insolvency proceedings and propose a group coordination plan.[298] The insolvency practitioners appointed in relation to members of the group and the group coordinator are required to cooperate with each other.[299] Not all of the members of a group of companies have to participate in the group coordination proceedings but it is the duty of the insolvency practitioners to communicate any information that is relevant for the coordinator to perform his tasks.[300] With respect to the costs, they are estimated and proposed by the insolvency practitioner, who requests the opening of the group coordination proceedings.[301] The estimated costs and shares to be paid by each member concerned will be decided by the court that opens the group coordination proceedings.[302] UNCITRAL drafted an "enterprise group insolvency solution", which means a proposal for coordinated reorganization, sale as a going concern or liquidation of the whole or part of the business or assets of two or more members of an enterprise group that would, or would be likely to, either maintain or add value to the enterprise group as a whole or to those group members.[303] It is also stipulated that a single or the same insolvency representative can be appointed so as to facilitate coordination of multiple insolvency proceedings of the same group in different States as a whole.[304] In light of that recommendation, whether or not the coordination can be carried out successfully depends greatly on the level of integration of its members and its business structure as well as the qualification of that single or the same insolvency representative.[305]

Instruments of cooperation and communication

General introduction

The EC Regulation does not have specific provisions concerning means of cooperation but they are incorporated into the EU Regulation (recast). Some of them are literally are identical to those under the Model Law or carry a similar sense, including:

(a) communication of information by any means considered appropriate by the court;[306]
(b) coordination of the administration and supervision of the debtor's assets and affairs;[307]
(c) coordination in the approval of protocols, where necessary/[308]approval or implementation by courts of agreements concerning the coordination of proceedings;[309]
(d) appointment of a person or body to act at the direction of the court;[310]
(e) coordination of the conduct of hearings/[311]coordination of concurrent proceedings regarding the same debtor.[312]

In addition, the EU Regulation (recast) also provides the possibility of appointment of a single insolvency practitioner for several insolvency proceedings concerning the same debtor or for different members of a group of companies.[313] As aforementioned, appointment of a single insolvency representative is recommended only in the context of an enterprise group under the Legislative Guide Part III by referring to some existing case law.[314] Generally speaking, it is quite difficult to reconcile the various requirements concerning qualification and licensing of the insolvency representatives under the national law, in particular, on the international level. Hence, it is not surprising that the appointment of a single insolvency representative concerning a single debtor has not been suggested under the Practice Guide on Cooperation. Instead, the Practice Guide on Cooperation compiles practice and experience with the use of cross-border insolvency agreements. Among all those instruments available to achieve cooperation and communication, discussion will be expanded only on three of them in this section, which are considered to be helpful in China's context and the reasons will be explained in Chapter 5. In addition to the EU Regulation (recast) and relevant guidelines prepared by UNCITRAL as well as other related soft law rules, in particular, the Global Principles and the EU JudgeCo Principles will also be taken into consideration.

Cross-border insolvency agreements (protocols)

What are cross-border insolvency agreements (protocols)? In accordance with Chapter III of Practice Guide on Cooperation, this refers to "an oral or written agreement intended to facilitate the coordination of cross-border insolvency proceedings and cooperation between courts, between courts and insolvency representatives and between insolvency representatives, sometimes also involving other parties in interest".[315] Before UNCITRAL adopted the specific term, a number of other titles have been used, including "protocol"(most commonly), "insolvency administration contract", "cooperation and compromise agreement" and "memorandum of understanding".[316] The diversity of titles exemplifies that cross-border insolvency agreements were inventions developed through individual attempts of the insolvency profession to resolve practical cross-border insolvency coordination issues in the absence of relevant national or international laws.[317] The earliest reported case involving use of cross-border insolvency agreement dated back to 1908.[318] A firm went bankrupt in England and India. The trustee in bankruptcy in England and the official assignee in India entered into an agreement for pooling and distributing the assets amongst English and Indian creditors. Considering it is "clearly a proper and common-sense business arrangement to make, and one manifestly for the benefit of all parties interested",[319] the English court held that it had jurisdiction "to sanction such an agreement, notwithstanding that the Bankruptcy Act, 1883, contained no express provisions authorizing such a scheme".[320]

The standardization of cross-border insolvency agreements is mostly rooted in common law jurisdictions, in particular, between the United States and Canada. The first guidelines for cross-border insolvency agreements were prepared by insolvency practitioners, the Committee J-Insolvency and Creditors' Rights of the International Bar Association, which issued a Cross-border Insolvency Concordat in 1995. The Cross-Border Concordat "helped to rebut concerns that it would be difficult and expensive to develop *ad hoc* protocols" (Bellissimo and Johnston, 2010). In the *Everfresh* case, the courts of the United States and Canada entered into the first insolvency agreement based on the Cross-border Insolvency Concordat.[321] The development of cross-border insolvency agreements did not stop there. Instead, they have been continuously streamlined and improved in practice. Practice Guide on Cooperation especially addresses the issues of use of cross-border insolvency agreements. The Annex I to Practice Guide on Cooperation, UNCITRAL has collected some 44 relevant cases, which related to utilization of cross-border insolvency agreements. In addition to 26 cases between the United States and Canada, the application of cross-border insolvency agreements has been extended to jurisdictions such as Switzerland,[322] Bermuda,[323] Bahamas,[324] Germany,[325] France,[326] UK,[327] British Virgin Islands,[328] the Cayman Islands,[329] Israel[330] and Hong Kong SAR.[331] In particular, in the *Lehman Brothers* case, there were over 75 separate proceedings with more than 16 official representatives.[332] Ten of those official representatives signed the cross-border insolvency protocol for Lehman Brothers, representing Australia, the Netherlands, the Netherlands Antilles, Hong Kong, Germany, Luxembourg, Singapore, Switzerland, and the United States.[333] The possible content of cross-border insolvency agreements has also been suggested in a more extensive way. It has been stressed that cross-border insolvency agreements should coordinate "procedural, rather than substantive, issues between jurisdictions" (Farley, Leonard and Birch, 2006). Later it is further summarized in the Practice Guide on Cooperation that the basic contents of the cross-border insolvency protocol.[334] Do all the cross-border insolvency agreements address all the issues? Actually not. Protocols vary in form and scope and are tailored to address the specific issues of a case and the needs of the parties involved. For example, in *the United Pan-Europe Communications N.V.* case, which involved the United States and the Netherlands, there was no written agreement between the two sides. The insolvency representatives from the both sides worked closely with each other and enabled the parallel proceedings closed on the same day.[335] In the Lehman Brothers protocol, besides the regular provisions such as court-to-court communication, a special procedure was formulated to promote the consistency of the calculation and adjudication of intercompany claims.[336] A Procedures Committee is allowed to be established so as to reconcile the possible conflicts incurred by those intercompany claims.[337]

In the EU, it has been observed by Maltese (2013) that protocols do not play a role as active as they do in common law countries. Although there are a few examples of protocols applied also in civil law jurisdictions, such as *Daisytek*, *SENDO* and *Swissair*, protocols are more frequently used and more developed in common law jurisdictions (Pannen, 2007). The significant reason is that the EC Regulation does not specify the legal basis of cross-border insolvency agreements. To reach a cross-border insolvency agreement, "the active participation of judges" is usually required (Paulus, 2006). Nevertheless, Article 31 of the EC Regulation merely establishes the duty of liquidators to cooperate and communicate information but it does not provide the legal basis of cooperation and communication between courts. That is why the reluctance of the judges, most of whom are from the civil law jurisdictions, to conduct cooperation through a binding agreement is understandable. In addition, the intra-EU cross-border insolvency agreements also have limited contents, which do not address any matters related to jurisdiction or recognition (Maltese, 2013). As stated in the *SENDO* Protocol:

> this protocol . . . is not intended to create a binding precedent and should not be considered appropriate for all other secondary proceedings in France pursuant to the EC Regulations, however may be regarded indicative of achieving good practice. It is established for the purposes of implementing such operating means by the Joint Administrators and the French Liquidators agreeing to act in conformity with the following principles:
>
> • mutual trust,
> • Adherence to the duty to communicate information and to cooperate as defined by Article 31 of the (EC) regulation,
> • Precedence of the main proceedings over the secondary proceeding.
>
> (Pannen, 2007)

The Regulation itself provides comprehensive procedural rules in matters of cross-border insolvency, especially concerning jurisdiction and recognition. It does not leave a lot of space for the courts and insolvency practitioners to exercise their discretion in that regard. To address that issue, Virgós and Wessels provide customized solutions, which fit into the characteristics of the EC Regulation. It incorporates the basic requirements with respect to the protocols, the liquidators, the debtor and the proceedings. In addition, it provides more detailed discretionary indications of what a protocol may contain in the form of a checklist (Virgós & Wessels, 2007). As result, although agreements or protocols do find their way into the EU Regulation (recast) and becomes the official legal instrument for cooperation and communication in the EU, they have not been defined in the text of the EU Regulation (recast). Nevertheless, it has been pointed out the objective of protocols is to facilitate cross-border cooperation of multiple insolvency proceedings in different Member States concerning the same debtor or members of the same group of companies.[338] The form and scope of protocols are not limited. However, the EU Regulation (recast) gives an example of simple generic agreements, which do not address specific issues but establish a framework of principles to govern multiple insolvency proceedings for the purpose of close cooperation between the parties concerned.[339]

Joint hearing

What is joint hearing? In accordance with the Practice Guide on Cooperation, a joint or coordinated hearing enables the courts to solve the complex problems of different insolvency proceedings directly and in a timely manner and bringing relevant parties in interest together at the same time for direct contact and the opportunity to share information and discuss and resolve outstanding issues or potential conflicts in other jurisdictions.[340] How should the joint hearing be conducted? Neither the Model Law nor the Regulation gives a clear answer. The EU Regulation (recast) merely provides the general legal basis for courts to conduct coordination of hearings.[341] UNCITRAL has collected a list of cases, in which joint hearings have been contemplated or implemented.[342] Interestingly, all those examples were United States–Canadian insolvency cases and the use of the joint hearing was referred to in the insolvency agreements (protocols). On 12 May, 2014, in the latest case, which is *Nortel Networks Corp.*, a joint hearing was simultaneously conducted also between the Delaware court in the United States and the Toronto court in Canada (Wessels, 2014). The earliest case occurred in 1995[343] and later the *Livent* case and *Loewen* case in 1999, which were prior to "the Court-to-Court Guidelines" coming into existence. It seems that the joint hearing was developed based on common law practice, in particular, the experience between the United States and Canada. In the meantime, the application of the joint hearing has been mutually recommended by both the Global Principles and the EU JudgeCo Principles. In particular, the EU JudgeCo Principles have to a great extent reached consensus with the Global Principles on the contents of the relevant guidelines. According to both of them, a court may conduct a joint hearing with another court that shall be conducted in the following manner:

(a) Each Court should be able to simultaneously hear the proceedings in the other Court.

(b) Evidentiary or written materials filed or to be filed in one Court should, in accordance with the Directions of that Court, be transmitted to the other Court or made available electronically in a publicly accessible system in advance of the hearing. Transmittal of such material to the other Court or its public availability in an electronic system should not subject the party filing the material in one Court to the jurisdiction of the other Court.

(c) Submissions or applications by the representative of any party should be made only to the Court in which the representative making the submissions is appearing unless the representative is specifically given permission by the other Court to make submissions to it.

(d) Subject to Global Guideline 8(b)/[344]EU JudgeCo Guideline 8(ii),[345] the Court should be entitled to communicate with the other Court in advance of a joint hearing, with or without counsel being present, to establish Guidelines for the orderly making of submissions and rendering of decisions by the Courts, and to coordinate and resolve any procedural, administrative, or preliminary matters relating to the joint hearing.

(e) Subject to Global Guideline 8(b)/EU JudgeCo Guideline 8(ii), the Court, subsequent to the joint hearing, should be entitled to communicate with the other Court, with or without counsel present, for the purpose of determining whether coordinated orders could be made by both Courts and to coordinate and resolve any procedural or non-substantive matters relating to the joint hearing.[346]

Due to the lack of specific rules, it is expected that the provisions concerning the conduct of joint hearings under the Global Guidelines and the EU JudgeCo Guidelines will be of great reference value. In reality, the joint hearing was developed based on common law practice, in particular the experience between the United States and Canada. The latest example is the *Nortel Networks* case. The affiliates of Nortel Networks Corporation, who is the ultimate corporate parent, filed Chapter 11 of the Bankruptcy Code in the United States, filed an application with the Canadian court in accordance with the Companies' Creditors Arrangement Act and also 19 of Nortel's European affiliates were put into administration by the High Court in the UK. The American, Canadian and English courts recognized each proceeding as the main proceeding in their own jurisdictions. An "Interim Funding and Settlement Agreement" (IFSA) has been reached among the UK, US and Canadian proceedings and was approved by the US court. Pursuant to s 12 of the IFSA, the parties agreed that the proceeds of any sale of their material assets (less taxes and costs) would be held in escrow until the parties either reached a consensual allocation of the proceeds, or

> in the case where the Selling Debtors fail to reach agreement, determination by the relevant dispute resolver(s) under the terms of the Protocol . . . applicable to the Sale Proceeds . . . which Protocol shall provide binding procedures for the allocation of Sales Proceeds . . ..[347]

Nevertheless, the parties concerned cannot enter into an agreement that could govern the allocation process. Instead, they attempted to reach agreement on the proper way of resolving allocation disputes. Unfortunately, as pointed out by Judge Gropper, there was no single cross-jurisdictional forum acceptable to all of the parties or able to assume control over the dispute despite extensive negotiations and formal mediations (Gropper, 2012). Nortel's US and Canadian debtors opted for judicial proceedings,[348] whereas Nortel's UK joint administrators opted for arbitration,[349] which was opposed by the US and Canadian creditors.[350] In the end, the US and Canadian courts agreed to hold a cross-border coordinated joint hearing on allocation.[351] Moreover, the conditions for conducting such a joint trial have been clarified. First of all, both the US court and the Canadian court have jurisdiction in a joint hearing pursuant to the IFSA.[352] Secondly, although it was fully acknowledged that a joint hearing "will confront practical and logistical difficulties" and the courts could arrive at inconsistent decisions on allocations,[353] it is believed that the parties concerned, very ably represented, would assist the courts in minimizing any practical problems to "avoid the travesty of reaching contrary results which would lead to further and potentially greater uncertainty and delay" and in reaching the correct decision to seek timely solutions in the best interest of all parties concerned.[354] Thirdly, both the US court and the Canadian court have worked through numerous difficulties on the Nortel case for years based on shared information, coordinated pre-trial discovery and schedule (Miller, 2012). That generated "enormous respect" between the courts from both sides, which further fueled confidence in the courts' ability to "continue to work together seamlessly".[355] Fourthly, the practical difficulties, such as distance in space, were overcome through simultaneous hearings by using closed-circuit video, which both the US and Canadian courts can afford.[356]

Independent intermediaries

Who are intermediaries? According to the Practice Guide on Cooperation, independent intermediaries can be regarded as the medium through which communication between the courts can be conducted indirectly.[357] For the single debtor, the EU Regulation (recast) provides that the courts may appoint an independent person or body acting on its instructions if that is not incompatible with the rules applicable to them,[358] which corresponds to the form of cooperation stipulated under Article 27(a) of the Model Law.[359] For enterprise groups, both the EU Regulation (recast) and Legislative Guide Part III stipulate that courts can also appoint a court representative, acting on their behalf, to fulfill its duties in case of any hesitance or reluctance with respect to direct communication with courts from different jurisdictions.[360] In *Maxwell Communications Corporation plc* (the *Maxwell* case), an examiner was appointed by the US court in order to harmonize the proceedings between the United States and the UK and "permit a reorganization under U.S. law which would maximize the return to creditors".[361] In *Re Joseph Nakash*, the US bankruptcy court entered an order, appointing an examiner to develop a protocol for harmonizing and coordinating the US Chapter 11 proceedings before the courts of the United States and the State of Israel.[362] In the *Matlack* case, the Canadian court appointed an information officer to summarize the status of the US proceeding and such other information in reports, which were periodically or upon request delivered to the court.[363] Wessels has also suggested a further expansion of Article 27(a) of the Model Law by introducing a so-called independent intermediary as an alternative or an addition to court-to-court communication (Wessels, 2012). The suggestion later became Global Principle 23, which created "a new professional function to overcome any hurdles in global communication" (Wessels, 2013). It is stated in the comment to the Global Principle 23 that:

> Under certain circumstances, the court may wish to refrain from conducting direct communication with another foreign court . . . The court could consider appoint an independent intermediary, whose task is to ensure that an international insolvency case is operated in accordance with these Global Principles and with any specific provisions that are either set out in a protocol or specified in the order made by the court.[364]

It has been addressed that Global Principle 23 "fully fits within the structure of UNCITRAL Model Law"[365] because appointment of an independent intermediary is consistent with the appropriate means stipulated under Article 27(a) of the Model Law, which is the appointment of a person or body to act at the direction of the court. In addition, the UNCITRAL Legislative Guide, Part Three: Treatment of enterprise groups in insolvency (Legislative Guide Part III) has adopted a "court representative".[366] The potential functions of the court representative are regarded as similar as those of an independent intermediary.[367] As the latest outcome of the development in the field of international insolvency, it is noteworthy that the EU Regulation (recast) also permits appointment of an independent person or body to act on the instructions of the court, who is authorized to deal with the cooperation and communication concerning the same debtor or the different members of a group of companies.[368] Moreover, the Global Principles and the EU JudgeCo Principles also provide special rules for the independent intermediary.[369]

Interconnection of insolvency registers

In the EU, the accessibility of the information about insolvency proceedings to the public also varies considerably. According to the Heidelberg-Luxembourg-Vienna Report, the most effective way of notification is through the internet but not all the Member States provide for online registers in which the opening of insolvency proceedings is published.[370] The transparency problems result in the parallel opening of main proceedings[371] and raise difficulty of lodging of claims for creditors.[372] In order to avoid the opening of parallel insolvency proceedings and facilitate due notification of creditors, the EU Regulation (recast) requires Member States to establish one or several insolvency registers, which publish information of insolvency proceedings as soon as possible after they are opened.[373] As the European Commission observed, information about insolvency proceedings is hardly collected at a central point on the national level.[374] Hence, the EU Regulation (recast) establishes a system in a decentralized way by interconnecting the individual insolvency registers on the basis of the implementing act.[375] The EU-wide interconnection of insolvency registers system is composed of central public electronic access point through the European e-Justice Portal, which provides links to information of the individual insolvency registers through a search service in all the official languages of the institutions of the Union.[376] The EU Regulation (recast) provides mandated information,[377] which has to be made publicly available in the insolvency registers and the optional information that the Member States can choose to make available through the European e-Justice Portal.[378] Costs incurred by the establishment, maintenance and future development concerning the system of interconnection of insolvency registers shall be covered by the general budget of the Union.[379] As for the establishment and improvement of national insolvency registers, the costs shall be borne by each Member State.[380] Besides, the Member States have to make sure that access to the mandated information published on insolvency registers shall be free of charge.[381]

Brexit and its influences

A special partnership

Due to the referendum held in the United Kingdom, the UK triggered its retreat negotiation in accordance with Article 50 of the Treaty on European Union on 29 March 2017. At the end of March, the British government presented to its Parliament a White Paper, in which it is explained how to convert EU law into UK law by introducing a Great Repeal Bill (hereinafter, the Bill). In the foreword delivered by British prime minister Theresa May, it is hoped to establish "a new deep and special partnership with the European Union".[382] On 22 August 2017, the British government issued a policy paper, "Providing a Cross-border Civil Judicial Cooperation Framework – a future partnership paper" (hereinafter, the Paper), to outline the UK's position on cross-border civil judicial cooperation in the future partnership. In the first page of the Paper, it also indicated the special partnership with the EU.[383] However, a clear definition of the special relationship is still not crystallized. According to Basedow, there is one possible solution that the UK could consider – membership of the EFTA Pillar of the EEA, which brings together the EU and the three EEA EFTA states in a single market (EEA Agreement, article 2). However, it also ensures the free movement of persons that the UK rejects.[384] In order to guarantee the legal homogeneity of the EEA law and the constantly evolving EU law related to internal market, the corresponding new EU legislation is continuously incorporated into the EEA Agreement through decisions of the EEA Joint Committee by amending its annexes and protocols (EEA Agreement, article 102). In more than 20 years, the EFTA States have only negotiated substantive exemptions to the relevant EU legal acts "in a very limited number of cases" (Fredriksen and Franklin, 2015). Political agreements on continuous updating of EEA law have always been reached between the EU and the EEA (Jónsdóttir, 2013). The EFTA court also contributes to legislative homogeneity between EU and EEA law, which has "consistently taken into account the relevant rulings of the ECJ given".[385] Early in 2017, Wolfgang Schäuble, Germany's finance minister, suggested the UK to look to the Swiss model. He also pointed out "Switzerland still faces pressure from Brussels to give the EU courts oversight of migration and its large financial services sector does not have access to the single market" (Waterfield, 2017), which might be a less attractive prospect for Britain. Nevertheless, according to the UK's plan, as stated in the Bill and the Paper, after Brexit officially enters into force, it will resume its own legislative power and independent judicial power to escape the CJEU's influence.[386]

In 1984, as aforementioned in Chapter 2, China and the UK signed an agreement, the Sino-British Joint Declaration, in pursuit of integration between the Mainland and Hong Kong. That agreement was based on the "one country, two systems" principle and created the Special Administrative Region in China. The principle established, within its own territory, a special independent jurisdiction where its own state law almost cannot be applied except for those listed in Annex III to the Basic Law. Since 2003, the Mainland and Hong Kong entered into CEPA and annual complementary agreements thereof in order to promote bilateral economic cooperation and market integration. However, the Mainland has not made any amendment or expansion of Annex III to the Basic law since 2005. In addition, for entry into the Hong Kong SAR, people from other parts of China must apply for approval. Among them, the number of persons who enter the SAR for the purpose of settlement shall be determined by the competent authorities of the Central People's Government after consulting the government of the SAR.[387] It seems that the "one country, two systems" principle is more inclusive in nature. The principle is also deemed as a courageous innovation. Similar to the UK's plan under the Bill and the Paper, the SAR is vested with independent judicial power. Accordingly, China's interregional legal cooperation is accompanied with co-existence of judicial authorities with the power of final adjudication. After Brexit, the continued legal cooperation between the EU and the UK, who proposed to establish a special relationship with its estranged neighbours, may also have to confront the same problem.

Common law vis-à-vis civil law

The landscape of EU law would be changed after Brexit. With the retreat of one of its most influential common law countries, the EU legal system would be mainly composed of civil law countries, with the exception of Ireland, which "has inherited both the common law method and the substance of many laws from its connection with the United Kingdom".[388] Most of Chinese scholars and researchers, who conduct comparative study on private interregional law, usually choose the EU legal system as one of the comparative models because of its ability in coordinating common law and civil law in addition to its historical link with both SARs (Tang and Xiao, 2016; Yu, 2009; Zhang, 2007; Li, 2006). Considering Hong Kong SAR's common law ties with the UK, the potential reference value of the EU law for legal cooperation between the Mainland and Hong Kong after Brexit is uncertain. Having conducted comparative study between the EU and China for years, the author feels reluctant to draw any premature conclusion. The answer is pending.

The future framework

It is stated, according to the article 4(3) of TEU, pursuant to the principle of sincere cooperation, that the Union and the Member States shall, in full mutual respect, assist each other in carrying out tasks which flow from the Treaties. The principle of sincere cooperation (sometimes also addressed as the principle of loyalty) is regarded to have produced "some of the strongest 'ties that bind' the Member States within the European Union".[389] Even during the Brexit negotiation, it has been emphasized in the European Council (Art. 50) guidelines following the United Kingdom's notification under Article 50 TEU that the principle of sincere cooperation is still binding on the UK as long as it is still a member.[390]

In *Hedley Lomas*, the CJEU connected the principle of sincere cooperation with the notions of trust.[391] In AG's Opinion in *Bourquain*, it is believed that mutual trust as "fulfilling a role similar to that of loyal cooperation".[392] It seems that mutual trust can be deemed as reflection of sincere cooperation in European legal cooperation. Unfortunately, the outcome of the Brexit vote entails that the EU and UK no longer live enmeshed in such thick trust relationships as the EU legal system used to rely on.

Brexit will bring an end of authority of EU law and the jurisdiction of the CJEU in the UK.[393] Legislation is relatively fixed and solid, whereas judicial decision is relatively flexible and fluid, which makes the latter far more challenging to be harmonized. For example, the role of the CJEU in safeguarding the coherent interpretation on COMI has been emphasized in this chapter, while the different points of view of the US jurisprudence on COMI and its deviation from the genuine intents of the Model Law have also been provided as a contrast. The Bill makes it clear that EU regulations – as they applied in the UK the moment before the UK left the EU – will be converted into domestic law by the Bill and will continue to apply until legislators in the UK decide otherwise.[394] Nevertheless, given the *de facto* split circumstances, even if the EU Regulation (recast) would be literally converted into UK law, to what extent the new domestic law could reflect the genuine spirit of sincere cooperation and mutual trust,[395] which are fundamental principles underlying the EU Regulation (recast), and to what extent the UK courts would be allowed to depart from its previous decisions "when it appears right to do so",[396] remain unsolved problems.

As aforementioned in this chapter, the insolvency profession, faced with the daily necessity of dealing with insolvency cases, created an interconnected network structure via cooperation and communication between the judges and practitioners from various jurisdictions. In the Paper, the UK has indicated its continued active participation in the UNCITRAL, including the UNCITRAL Model Law on Cross-Border Insolvency,[397] and the cooperation and communication provisions have also found their way into the recast EU Regulation.[398] Therefore, that coordinated approach might help the UK and the EU to focused on judicial interaction rather than attempting the unification of insolvency legislation and respect the differences among national procedural laws in the future. As pointed out in the following Chapter 5, such a coordinated approach is not based on a solid trust relationship but out of pragmatic necessity. Despite the uncertainties of the future relationship between the Union and the UK, cooperation has to continue between the neighbors.

Conclusion

As leading international insolvency regimes assisting States in operating transnational insolvency systems in an efficient, fair and cost-effective manner, the Regulation attempts to provide comprehensive private international law rules, including jurisdiction, applicable law, recognition and enforcement, cooperation and communication on the Union level, whereas the Model Law, as a soft law mechanism on the global level, covers less ground and mainly focuses on simplified recognition, through which jurisdiction is considered indirectly, and cross-border cooperation and communication between courts and insolvency representatives. After revision, the Regulation and the Model Law were brought together, by extending the obligation of cooperation and communication between liquidators to insolvency practitioners and courts and expanding its scope by adding rescue measures into the existing European cross-border insolvency regime.

The Regulation and the Model Law employ the same terminologies, i.e. COMI and establishment, both of which can find their origins from the relevant sources in the EU context. COMI is designed in a way of rebuttable presumption, which reflects a compromise between the theory of real seat and the place of incorporation. How to rebut the presumption of registered office has raised quite a few problems in the EU as well as on the global level. In the EU, with the continuous efforts made by the CJEU, the relevant factors to rebut the COMI presumption has been gradually made clear at the Union level, which has attached more importance to the place where the company has its central administration on the basis of a comprehensive assessment of all the relevant factors. Those decisions handed down by the CJEU, in particular *Interedil*, have been literally codified into the EU Regulation (recast), which help to sets up all those conditions to rebut the presumption if possible. When the countries that have adopted the Model Law interpreted COMI, some of them chose to follow the European approach and some opted for different understandings, which resulted in incoherence among the enacting States. That is particular the case with respect to the timing COMI. In addition, the EC Regulation alone literally sets up the aim of prevention of forum shopping and the EU Regulation (recast) further attempts to rule out forum shopping in a fraudulent or abusive manner by introducing a look-back period of three month for companies. Such an arrangement is tied to the characteristics of cross-border insolvency law and the requirement of the effective functioning of the internal market. Based on case law, the EU Regulation (recast) provides that the COMI assessment shall be initiated at the time of the request for the opening of insolvency proceedings and adds a restriction of a look-back period of three months on the presumption to make sure that the registered office has not been shifted for the purpose of fraudulent or abusive forum shopping. However, according to the case law of the United States, an enacting State of the Model Law, the American jurisprudence not only holds different opinions from the Regulation and the Model Law, but also has split views on the timing issues among the federal courts. The majority considers that the time to determine COMI shall be the date of the filing of the Chapter 15 petition, which allows assessment of COMI to start later after the opening of insolvency proceedings. That directly results in expansion of the scope of factors that can be taken into account to determine COMI so that liquidation activities and administrative functions are validated as effective factors for the COMI analysis. Consequently, more factors can be manipulated for COMI relocation.

The EU insolvency regime is an international jurisdiction dominant system. The effect of international recognition is closely related to the jurisdiction. Once the insolvency proceedings are opened as the main proceedings, the automatic and universal effects throughout the EU will be incurred. That arrangement is peculiar to the EU because automatic recognition is guaranteed by the principle of mutual trust. Accordingly, more restrictive requirements are set up for the Member States to refuse to recognize insolvency proceedings based on substantive contents. The Model Law is a recognition dominant system. One of its key objectives is to establish simplified procedures for recognition of qualifying foreign proceedings. In addition, the Model Law also uses the jurisdictional basis, i.e. COMI and establishment, for the court to distinguish recognition of the foreign proceedings as the main or non-main proceedings. To be recognized as the main or non-main proceeding differ quite substantially in the legal consequences because the effects and reliefs flowing from recognition may depend upon the category into which a foreign proceeding falls. Due to various insolvency systems from State to State influenced by respective social, political, financial and other considerations, UNCITRAL found it difficult to provide uniform choice of law rules on the global level. To fill in the gap and give necessary support to the recognized proceedings, the Model Law introduced a "minimum" list of effects or measures that would be triggered by recognition, while at the same time leaving room for the recognizing court to provide additional effects or measures. Those effects or measures are addressed as reliefs in the context of the Model Law. The public policy exception is more frequently incurred in the context of the Model Law for the sake of protection of the interests of local creditors, although it is expected that the public policy exception will be rarely used and shall be understood more restrictively than domestic public policy.

The EU Regulation (recast), by referring to international best practice in matters of cooperation and communication, in particular, the relevant guidelines prepared by UNCITRAL (e.g. the Practice Guide on Cooperation), has stressed cooperation between courts, courts and insolvency practitioners in the insolvency proceedings involving the same debtor and group companies. The approach the EU Regulation (recast) and the Legislative Guide Part III have chosen is to attach importance to cooperation of insolvency proceedings concerning different entities of the same group by utilizing cooperation and communication measures. The single insolvency practitioner approach has been introduced into the EU Regulation (recast), which further substantiates that approach by establishing the system of group coordination proceedings. It is also recommended by the Working Group V as well as under the Legislative Guide Part III that a single or the same insolvency representative can be appointed so as to facilitate coordination of multiple insolvency proceedings of the same group as a whole. The forms of cooperation incorporated into the EU Regulation (recast) are literally identical to those under the Model Law. Cross-border insolvency agreements (protocols) are the most common means that facilitate cross-border cooperation and coordination of multiple insolvency proceedings in different States, which have found their way into the Model Law and the EU Regulation (recast). The joint hearing is a means of direct cooperation, which is developed from common law practice. The merit of the joint hearing is to promote the efficiency of current proceedings, by enabling the courts to solve the complex problems of different insolvency proceedings directly and in a timely manner and bringing relevant parties in interest together at the same time. Both the Model Law and the EU Regulation (recast) provides the basis for the coordination of hearings without specific rules. Under certain circumstances, the court may wish to refrain from conducting direct communication with another foreign court. In such a case, intermediaries, which are furnished by the Global Principle 23, can be appointed by the courts as a medium. Through intermediaries, communication between the courts can be conducted indirectly, which is thus consistent with the appropriate means stipulated under the Model Law and also permitted in accordance with the EU Regulation (recast). In order to avoid opening of parallel insolvency proceedings and facilitate the due notification of creditors, the EU Regulation (recast) requires Member States to establish one or several insolvency registers, which publish information of insolvency proceedings. A decentralized EU-wide interconnection of insolvency registers system will be established, which is composed of a central public electronic access point through the European e-Justice Portal and is linked to information of the individual insolvency registers through a search service in all the official languages of the institutions of the Union.

After Brexit, it is expected that a special relationship would be established between the EU and the UK. Like the Mainland and Hong Kong SAR, however, such special relationship may encounter problems caused by lack of a united final dispute resolver. Due to the withdrawal of one of the most influential common law countries, the potential reference value of the EU for legal cooperation between the Mainland and Hong Kong SAR, with which the UK used to have a close connection, is in question. In the future, cooperation and communication measures adopted both by international instruments and the EU might help the UK and the EU to establish a new cross-border insolvency cooperation regime that is not based on a solid trust relationship but out of pragmatic necessity.

Notes

1 Bob Wessels, Brexit and Insolvency – A View from the Continent, 1 August, 2016, available at: www.law.ox.ac.uk/business-law-blog/blog/2016/08/brexit-and-insolvency-view-continent (last accessed on 31 March, 2017).
2 UNCITRAL, A/CN.9/398 – Cross-border Insolvency: Report on UNCITRAL – INSOL Colloquium on Cross-Border Insolvency, 1994, paras. 5–6.
3 See the report of UNCITRAL on the work of its thirtieth session (Official Records of the General Assembly, Fifty-Second Session, Supplement No. 17 (A/52/17), paras. 12–225).
4 Please note that the number of the Enacting States of the Model Law is subject to changes. For instance, in September 2015, the 17 Member States (Benin, Burkina Faso, Cameroon, Central African Republic, Chad, Comoros, Republic of the Congo, Côte d'Ivoire, Equatorial Guinea, Gabon, Guinea, Guinea-Bissau, Mali, Niger, Senegal, Togo and Democratic Republic of the Congo) of OHADA (the Organisation pour l'Harmonisation en Afrique du Droit des Affaires) adopted the UNCITRAL Model Law.
5 Guide and Interpretation, paras. 10, 82.
6 EU Regulation (recast), recital (48).
7 EU Regulation (recast), recital (49), Article 56; Part III to the Legislative Guide (treatment of enterprise groups), III, paras. 48–54.
8 EU Regulation (recast), Article 71; Part III to the Legislative Guide (treatment of enterprise groups), III, paras. 43–47.
9 EU Regulation (recast), recital (55), Article 61(1)(a).
10 Virgós/Schmit Report (1996), para. 12.
11 Case C-328/12, *Ralph Schmid v Lilly Hertel* [2013] Opinion of Advocate General Sharpston, ft.6.
12 Ibid., para. 22.
13 EC Regulation, recital (17); EU Regulation (recast), recital (37).
14 EC Regulation, recital (17), Article 3(4); EU Regulation (recast), recital (38), Article 3(4).
15 EU Commission Staff Working Document the Impact Assessment Accompanying the document Revision of Regulation (EC) No 1346/2000 on insolvency proceedings, Strasbourg, 12.12.2012, SWD (2012) 416 final, p. 36.
16 EU Regulation (recast), recital (45).
17 Ibid., Article 38(3), para. 1.
18 Ibid., Article 38(1).
19 Guide and Interpretation, para. 85.
20 Ibid., para. 32.
21 EC Regulation, recital (13), Article 3(1); EU Regulation (recast), recital (28), (30), Article 3(1); the Model Law, Article 2.
22 Guide and Interpretation, paras. 81, 88.
23 Brussels I Regulation, Article 60(1).
24 *Re English Scottish and Australian Chartered Bank* [1893] 3 Ch 385, 394 (UK).
25 *Überseering BV v Nordic Construction Company Baumanagement GmbH (NCC)*, C-280/00, 5 November, 2002.
26 Ibid., para. 15.
27 Ibid., para. 16.
28 Case C-341/04 *Eurofoods IFSC Ltd* [2006] ECR I-03813 (*Eurofood*).
29 *Eurofood*, paras. 34–36.
30 Case C-396/09 *Interedil Srl (in liquidation) v Fallimento Interedil Srl, Intesa Gestione Crediti SpA* [2011] ECR I-09915 (*Interedil*).
31 *Interedil*, para. 53.
32 Case C-191/10 *Rastelli Davide e C. Snc v Jean-Charles Hidoux* [2011] ECR I-13209 (*Rastelli*), para. 11.
33 *Rastelli*, para. 35; *Eurofood*, para. 34, and *Interedil*, para. 51.
34 The Model Law, Article 16(3).
35 Guide and Interpretation, para. 141.
36 Ibid., para. 141.
37 *Re Stanford International Bank* [2010] EWCA Civ 137; [2011] Ch 33.

38 *Eurofood*, para. 34.
39 *Re Stanford International Bank* [2010] EWCA Civ 137; [2011] Ch 33, at 54.
40 Ibid., at 63; Critism to confusion with respect to the COMI in *Re Stanford* case (Wessels, 2012).
41 *Re Tri-Continental Exchange Ltd* [2006] 349 BR 629, at 635.
42 *Re Bear Stearns High-Grade Structured Credit Strategies Master Fund Ltd* 374 BR 122, at 127.
43 Ibid., at 130.
44 *Re Stanford International Bank* [2010] EWCA Civ 137; [2011] Ch 33.
45 *Re Bear Stearns High-Grade Structured Credit Strategies Master Fund Ltd* 374 BR 122.
46 *Re Stanford International Bank* [2009] EWHC 1441 (Ch), at 65.
47 The Model Law was introduced into the UK via the Sch. 1 to the Cross-Border Insolvency Regulation 2006 (CBIR). The US enacted the Model Law as Chapter 15 of the Federal Bankruptcy Code.
48 EC Regulation, recital (13).
49 *Stanford International Bank Ltd.* (Syndic de), 2009 QCCS 4109.
50 Ibid., at 36, "L'importance du centre névralgique de Houston est incontestable. Et le plus équitable est que le Tribunal reconnaisse comme *foreign proceeding* le *Receivership* et comme représentant étranger le US Receiver Janvey" (in French).
51 *Stanford International Bank Ltd.* (Dans l'affaire de la liquidation de), 2009 QCCA 2475, at 31.
52 EC Regulation, recital (4).
53 EU Regulation (recast), recital (5), (29), (31).
54 EU Commission Staff Working Document Impact Assessment Accompanying the document – Revision of Regulation (EC) No 1346/2000 on insolvency proceedings, Strasbourg, 12.12.2012, SWD (2012) 416 final, at 3.4.1.2, p. 21.
55 Ibid., p. 20.
56 TFEU, Article 49 (ex Article 43 TEC), Article 54 (ex Article 48 TEC); Case C-55/94, *Reinhard Gebhard v Consiglio dell'Ordine degli Avvocati e Procuratori di Milano* [1995] ECR I-4165, Case C-2/74, *Jean Reyners v Belgian State* [1974] ECR 631.
57 European Commission, the EU Single Market: freedom to provide services/ freedom of establishment, at: http://ec.europa.eu/internal_market/top_layer/living_working/services-establishment/index_en.htm (Last visited on 31 March, 2017).
58 Case C-212/97, *Centros Ltd v Erhvervs- og Selskabsstyrelsen* [1999] ECR I-01459, at 27.
59 Case C-208/00, *Überseering BV v Nordic Construction Company Baumanagement GmbH* [2002] ECR I-09919, at 95; Case C-411/03, *Sevic Systems AG* [2005] ECR I-10805, at 19; Case C-210/06, *Cartesio Oktató és Szolgáltató bt* [2008] ECR I-09641, at 124; Case C-378/10, *VALE Építési Kft.* [2012], at 41.
60 EU Regulation (recast), recital (31).
61 Ibid., Article 90(4).
62 Guide and Interpretation, paras. 161–162.
63 Ibid., para. 162.
64 Ibid., para. 161.
65 Ibid., para. 161.
66 Ibid., para. 22.
67 Ibid., para. 161.
68 Ibid., para. 162.
69 Case C-1/04, *Susanne Staubitz-Schreiber* [2006] ECR I-00701 (*Staubitz-Schreiber*).
70 Ibid., paras. 15–16.
71 Ibid., para. 29.
72 Ibid., paras. 25, 27, 28.
73 *Staubitz-Schreiber* Opinion of AG Colomer, para. 82.
74 *Interedil*, para. 55.
75 Guide and Interpretation, paras. 141, 149, 159.
76 Ibid., para. 159, ft.34.
77 *Re Kemsley*, 489 BR 346 (Bankr SDNY 2013); *Re Millennium Global Emerging Credit*, 458 BR 63 (Bankr SDNY 2011); *Re Gerova Fin. Grp., Ltd.*, 482 BR 86 (Bankr SDNY2012).

78 *Re Ran*, 607 F3d 1017 (5th Cir. 2010); *Re Betcorp Ltd.*, 400 BR 266 (Bankr D Nev 2009); *Re British American Isle of Venice (BVI), Ltd.*, 441 BR 713 (Bankr S D Fla 2010); *Re Fairfield Sentry Ltd.*, 440 BR 60, 64 (Bankr SDNY 2010), aff'd, 714 F3d 127(2d Cir. 2013).

79 *Re Ran*, 607 F3d 1017 (5th Cir. 2010), at 1020.

80 Ibid., at 1026.

81 Ibid., at 1025.

82 Ibid.

83 *Re Kemsley*, 489 BR 346 (Bankr SDNY 2013), at 354.

84 Ibid.

85 *Re Betcorp Ltd.*, 400 BR 266 (Bankr D Nev 2009), at 292.

86 *Re Millennium Global Emerging Credit*, 458 BR 63 (Bankr SDNY 2011), at 72.

87 Ibid.

88 Ibid.

89 *Re Tri-Continental Exchange Ltd.*, 349 BR 627 (Bankr E.D.Cal.2006), at 634.

90 *Re Millennium Global Emerging Credit*, 458 BR 63 (Bankr SDNY 2011), at 72.

91 Ibid., at 74.

92 *Re Ran*, 607 F3d 1017 (5th Cir. 2010), at 1025; see also *Re Betcorp Ltd.*, 400 BR 266 (Bankr D Nev 2009), at 291–292.

93 *Re Millennium Global Emerging Credit*, 458 BR 63 (Bankr SDNY 2011), at 75.

94 Ibid., at 76.

95 Ibid., at 75.

96 *Re Fairfield Sentry Ltd.*, 714 F3d 127(2d Cir. 2013), at 134.

97 Ibid., at 135.

98 Ibid., at 136.

99 *Re Millennium Global Emerging Credit*, 458 BR 63 (Bankr SDNY 2011), at 72.

100 *Re Fairfield Sentry Ltd.*, 714 F3d 127(2d Cir. 2013), at 137.

101 Ibid., at 137.

102 Ibid., at 138.

103 EU Commission Staff Working Document the Impact Assessment Accompanying the document Revision of Regulation (EC) No 1346/2000 on insolvency proceedings, Strasbourg, 12.12.2012, SWD (2012) 416 final, p. 19.

104 EC Regulation, recital (13).

105 EU Regulation (recast), Article 3(1).

106 Ibid., Article 3(1), para. 2.

107 Ibid., recital (30).

108 *Interedil*, para. 53.

109 EU Regulation (recast), recital (30).

110 Ibid., recital (30).

111 Ibid., recital (28).

112 Official Records of the General Assembly, Sixty-Fifth Session, Supplement No. 17 (A/65/17), para. 259.

113 Guide and Interpretation, para. 18.

114 Ibid., para. 145.

115 Ibid., paras. 141, 149, 159.

116 Ibid., para. 147.

117 Ibid., para. 146.

118 Ibid., para. 141.

119 *Re Suntech Power Holdings Co., Ltd.*, Case No. 14-10383(SMB), Written Opinion Signed On 17 November, 2014.

120 Ibid., p. 14.

121 Objection of the Solyndra Residual Trust to Chapter 15 Petition of *Suntech Power Holdings Co., Ltd.* (in provisional liquidation) for Recognition of Foreign Main Proceeding Pursuant to §1517 of the Bankruptcy Code, In *Re Suntech Power Holdings Co., Ltd.* (in Provisional Liquidation), Case No. 14-10383 (SMB), Related Docket Nos. 1, 2, 3, 4.

122 *Re Suntech Power Holdings Co., Ltd.*, Case No. 14-10383(SMB), Written Opinion Signed On 17 November, 2014, p. 3.

123 Objection of the Solyndra Residual Trust to Chapter 15 Petition of Suntech Power Holdings Co., Ltd. (in provisional liquidation) for Recognition of Foreign Main Proceeding Pursuant to §1517 of the Bankruptcy Code, *Re Suntech Power Holdings Co., Ltd.* (in Provisional Liquidation), Case No. 14-10383 (SMB), Related Docket Nos. 1, 2, 3, 4, at D Suntech Has Not Qualified as a Debtor Under 11 USC § 109(a), ii Suntech Cannot Rely on $500,000 Recently Placed in the KCC Trust Account as "Property"; See also Findings of Fact and Conclusions of Law Granting Petition for Recognition as Foreign Main Proceeding and Denying Cross-motion to Change Venue, *Re Suntech Power Holdings Co., Ltd.*, Case No. 14-10383(SMB), Written Opinion Signed On 17 November, 2014, at D New York Proceeding, 2. The Chapter 15 Case.

124 Objection of the Solyndra Residual Trust to Chapter 15 Petition of Suntech Power Holdings Co., Ltd. (in provisional liquidation) for Recognition of Foreign Main Proceeding Pursuant to §1517 of the Bankruptcy Code, *Re Suntech Power Holdings Co., Ltd.* (in Provisional Liquidation), Case No. 14-10383 (SMB), Related Docket Nos. 1, 2, 3, 4, at Factual Background, p. 7.

125 511 BR 361, 372–73 (Bankr SDNY 2014). It has been suggested by the United States Court of Appeals Second Circuit in *Re Barnet* that §109(a) of the Bankruptcy Code should be applied to cases filed under the Chapter 15. (See In *Re Barnet*, 737 F3d 238 (2ᵈ Cir. 2013). *Re Octaviar* is the remand case of *Re Barnet* and thus followed the holding in *Re Barnet*. Chapter 15 adopted the UNCITRAL Model Law almost in verbatim. Nonetheless, there is no threshold under the Model Law, requiring a foreign debtor must have a business or property in the state, where the petition of recognition is filed. The Second Circuit's conclusion that §109(a) applies in Chapter 15 cases has received criticism from commentators. It has been argued that the decision in *Re Barnet* "limits international cooperation under chapter 15" and "is ill-suited for deciding the jurisdictional requirements for a chapter 15 case". The decision is contrary to the former case law. For example, in *Re Toft*, 453 BR 186 (Bankr, SDNY 2011), at 193 and in re Fairfield, 458 BR 665 (Bankr SDNY 2011), at 679, No. 5. Later in *Re Bemarmara*, it is held that "This Court does not agree with the decision of the Second Circuit. And it is the Court's belief that there is a strong likelihood that the Third Circuit, likewise, would not agree with that decision." In *Re Bemarmara Consulting A.S.*, No. 13-13037 (KG) (Bankr D Del, 17 December, 2013) *Re Barnet* will still have the binding effect on any court within the Second Circuit until the Bankruptcy Code is revised or the Supreme Court reconsiders the issue, although the Second Circuit has forwarded copies of its opinion of *Re Barnet* to Congress in order to report the technical deficiencies in the Bankruptcy Code (*Re Barnet*, 737 F3d 238 (2nd Cir. 2013), at Conclusion). In accordance with the Long-Range Plan for the Federal Courts adopted by the Judicial Conference, 91e: All courts of appeals should be encouraged to participate in the pilot project to identify technical deficiencies in statutory law and to inform Congress of same. In: Report of the Proceedings of the Judicial Conference of the United States, 19 September, 1995, p. 62.

126 321 BR 396, 407 (Bankr SD Tex, 2005).

127 In *Re Suntech Power Holdings Co., Ltd.*, Case No. 14-10383(SMB), Written Opinion Signed On 17 November, 2014, at Discussion A Eligibility to be a Debtor, p. 18.

128 Ibid., pp. 18–19.

129 Objection of the Solyndra Residual Trust to Chapter 15 Petition of *Suntech Power Holdings Co., Ltd.* (in provisional liquidation) for Recognition of Foreign Main Proceeding Pursuant to §1517 of the Bankruptcy Code, *Re Suntech Power Holdings Co., Ltd.* (in Provisional Liquidation), Case No. 14-10383 (SMB), Related Docket Nos. 1, 2, 3, 4, p. 2.

130 In *Re SPhinX, Ltd.*, 351 BR 103 (Bankr SDNY 2006), at 117; *Re Bear Stearns High-Grade Structured Credit Strategies Master Fund, Ltd.*, 389 BR 325 (SDNY 2008), at 336; *Re Basis Yield Alpha Fund (Master)*, 381 BR 37 (Bankr SDNY 2008), at 47.

131 *Re Suntech Power Holdings Co., Ltd.*, Case No. 14-10383(SMB), Written Opinion Signed On 17 November, 2014, at Discussion C. COMI, p. 25.

132 *Re Fairfield Sentry Ltd.*, 714 F3d 127, (2d Cir. 2013), at 133, 137.

133 Ibid., at 137.

134 *Re Suntech Power Holdings Co., Ltd.*, Case No. 14-10383(SMB), Written Opinion Signed On 17 November, 2014, at Discussion C. COMI, p. 27.

135 The EU Regulation (recast), recital (31), Article 3(1), para. 2.
136 Guide and Interpretation, para. 141, 149, 159.
137 The EC Regulation, Article 16(1); the EU Regulation (recast), Article 19(1).
138 American Law Institute, Restatement of the Law Third: The Foreign Relations Law of the United States, Vol. 1, American Law Institute Publishers, 1987, p. 591.
139 Virgós/Schmit Report (1996), para. 12; the EC Regulation, recital (11), (12); the EU Regulation (recast), recital (22), (23).
140 EC Regulation, recital (22); EU Regulation (recast), recital (65).
141 EC Regulation, recital (22); EU Regulation (recast), recital (65).
142 *Eurofood*, para. 42; EU Regulation (recast), recital (65).
143 EC Regulation, Article 17(1); EU Regulation (recast), Article 20(1).
144 EC Regulation, recital (23), Article 4; EU Regulation (recast), recital (66), Article 7.
145 Virgós/Schmit Report (1996), para. 12.
146 EC Regulation, Article 3(2)(3); EU Regulation (recast), Article 3(2)(3).
147 EC Regulation, recital (23); EU Regulation (recast), recital (66).
148 EC Regulation, recital (12); EU Regulation (recast), recital (23).
149 EC Regulation, Article 18; EU Regulation (recast), Article 21.
150 EC Regulation, Article 18(1); EU Regulation (recast), Article 21(1).
151 EC Regulation, Article 18(3); EU Regulation (recast), Article 21(3).
152 EC Regulation, Articles 5, 7; EU Regulation (recast), Articles 8, 10.
153 EC Regulation, Article 18(1); EU Regulation (recast), Article 21(1).
154 EC Regulation, Article 18(2); EU Regulation (recast), Article 21(2).
155 UNCITRAL Secretariat, Report on UNCITRAL-INSOL Colloquium on Cross-Border Insolvency, UN Doc A/CN.9/398 (19 May, 1994), paras.17–18.
156 Guide and Interpretation, para. 150.
157 Ibid., para. 155.
158 Ibid., para. 151.
159 The Model Law, Article 17(3); see also the Guide and Interpretation, para. 163.
160 The Model Law, Article 17(2)(a)(b).
161 UNCITRAL, Working Group on Insolvency Law, Report on its 18th Session, 30 October–10 November, 1995, U.N Doc A/CN.9/419 (1 December, 1995), paras. 55–56.
162 The Model Law, Article 20 (1).
163 Guide and Interpretation, para. 178.
164 The Model Law, Article 20(2).
165 The Model Law, Article 21.
166 Guide and Interpretation, para. 170.
167 The Model Law, Articles 19(1), 21 (c), (d), (g).
168 Guide and Interpretation, para. 174.
169 The Model Law, Article 21(1).
170 Guide and Interpretation, para. 191.
171 Guide and Interpretation, para. 193.
172 The Model Law, Article 21(3).
173 Guide and Interpretation, para. 193.
174 The Model Law, Article 21(1)(g).
175 Guide and Interpretation, para. 194.
176 The Legislative Guide, Part Two, I, Recommendations 30–34.
177 Ibid., paras. 83–84; Recommendation 31.
178 Ibid., paras. 81–82; Recommendation 30.
179 Ibid., paras. 85–86, 88–90; Recommendation 32.
180 Ibid., para. 87; Recommendation 33.
181 Ibid., para. 91.
182 Ibid., para.91.
183 Ibid., Recommendation 34.
184 Schedule I UNCITRAL Model Law on Cross-border Insolvency, Article 2(q).
185 *Cambridge Gas Transportation Corporation v Official Committee of Unsecured Creditors of Navigator Holdings* [2006] UKPC 26; [2007] 1 AC 508.
186 Ibid., para. 16.

187 Ibid., para. 24.
188 *Rubin v Eurofinance* [2012] UKSC 46.
189 Ibid., at 87.
190 Ibid., at 103–104.
191 Ibid., at 106.
192 Ibid., at 107.
193 Ibid., at 104, 105.
194 Ibid., at 115.
195 Ibid., at 129.
196 Ibid., at 132.
197 *Singularis Holdings Limited v PricewaterhouseCoopers* [2014] UKPC 36. (This case is closely connected with its decision in *PricewaterhouseCoopers v Saad Investments Company Limited* [2014] UKPC 35.)
198 Ibid., at 6.
199 Ibid., at 3–7.
200 Ibid., at 23.
201 Ibid., at 15, 25.
202 Ibid., at 18.
203 Ibid., at 38.
204 Ibid., at 30, 31.
205 *Re Schimmelpenninck*, 183 F3d 347 (5th Cir. 1999).
206 Ibid., at 350.
207 Ibid., at 365; see also *Overseas Inns S.A. P.A. v United States*, 911 F2d 1146 (5th Cir. 1990), at 1149; *Re Petition of Garcia Avila*, 296 BR 95 (Bankr SDNY 2003), at 112.
208 *Re Metcalfe & Mansfield Alternative Investments*, 421 BR 685 (Bankr SDNY 2010), at 697; *Re Qimonda AG*, 462 BR 165 (Bankr E.D.Va. 2011), at 184 n.17; *Re Sivec SRL*, 476 BR 310 (Bankr E.D. Okla. 2012), at 324.
209 *Ad Hoc Grp of Vitro Noteholder v Vitro SAB de CV*, 12-10542 (5th Cir. 2012).
210 *Re Vitro, SAB De CV*, 455 BR 571 (Bankr ND Tex, 2011), at 575.
211 *Ad Hoc Grp of Vitro Noteholder v Vitro SAB de CV*, 12-10542 (5th Cir. 2012), at 16.
212 Ibid., at 16.
213 Ibid., at 2.
214 Ibid., at 14, 31.
215 Ibid., at 32.
216 Ibid., at 32.
217 Ibid., at 36,39.
218 Ibid., at 36–38.
219 11 US Code § 1508.
220 EC Regulation, Article 26.
221 EU Regulation (recast), Article 33.
222 Case C-7/98 *Dieter Krombach v André Bamberski* [2000] ECR I-1935.
223 Case C-7/98, *Dieter Krombach v André Bamberski* [2000] ECR I-01935, paras.23, 37.
224 *Eurofood, para.* 67.
225 This result was confirmed by the national reports from Austria, France, Germany, Italy, Netherlands, Poland, Portugal and the UK. According to the Austrian Report, the narrow approach is supported by Annexes A and B to the Regulation as the proceedings listed there are generally recognized (Hess/Pfeiffer, 2011).
226 Guide and Interpretation, para. 101.
227 Guide and Interpretation, para. 104.
228 *Re Cozumel Caribe, S.A de C.V.*, 482 BR 96 (2012).
229 Ibid., at 113.
230 Ibid., at 113.
231 Virgós/Schmit Report (1996), para. 206.
232 Guide and Interpretation, para. 30, 101.
233 Ibid., para. 102.
234 Ibid., para. 136.
235 Ibid., para. 135.

236 *Re Sivec SRL*, WL 3651250 (ED Okla, 18 August, 2011), para. 7.
237 EC Regulation, recital (11); EU Regulation (recast), recital (21).
238 EC Regulation, recital (21); EU Regulation (recast), recital (59).
239 *Re Rover France SAS* [2005] EWHC 874.
240 *Re Rover France SAS* [2006] BCC 599.
241 *Public Prosecutor v Segard (As Administrator for Rover France SAS)* [2006] IL Pr 32, at H3.
242 Ibid., at H5.
243 *Re Rover France SAS* [2006] EWCH 3426 (Ch), at 8.
244 *Public Prosecutor v Segard (As Administrator for Rover France SAS)* [2006] IL Pr 32, at H5.
245 In *Re Toft*, 453 BR 186 (SDNY 2011).
246 Ibid., paras. 197–198.
247 The two statutes referred to the Wiretap Act, 18 USC § 2511 (2012) and the Privacy Act, 18 USC § 2701 (2012). See *Re Toft*, 453 B.R at 196–197.
248 *Re Toft*, 453 BR 186 (SDNY 2011), para. 198.
249 *Re Vitro, S.A.B. de C.V.*, 473 BR 117 (Bankr ND Tex, 2012), at 1070.
250 *Re Qimonda AG*, 433 BR 547 (Bankr ED Va, 2010), at 552.
251 In *Re Qimonda AG*, 462 BR 165 (Bankr ED Va, 2011), para. 185.
252 Ibid.
253 *Jaffé v Samsung Electronics Co.*, 737 F3d 14 (4th Cir. 2013), at 6.
254 Ibid., at 41.
255 Ibid., at 27, 33.
256 *Jaffé v Samsung Electronics Co.*, 135 S.Ct. 66 (2014).
257 Guide and Interpretation, paras. 21(e), 30, 103–104.
258 Virgós/Schmit Report (1996), at 34.
259 Virgós/Schmit Report (1996), at 230.
260 The Model Law, Articles 25, 26.
261 *Re Stojevic*, 9 November, 2004, 28 R 225/04w.
262 EU Regulation (recast), recital (48).
263 EU Regulation (recast), Article 41(2)(a)(b).
264 EU Regulation (recast), Article 41(2)(c).
265 EU Regulation (recast), Article 42(1).
266 EU Regulation (recast), Article 42(2).
267 EU Regulation (recast), Article 44.
268 EU Regulation (recast), Article 43(1)(a).
269 EU Regulation (recast), Article 43(1)(b).
270 Guide and Interpretation, para. 211.
271 The Model Law, Articles 25, 26.
272 Guide and Interpretation, para. 217.
273 Guide and Interpretation, para. 40.
274 Guide and Interpretation, para. 218.
275 Legislative Guide Part III, para. 4(a).
276 EU Regulation (recast), Article 2(5); Annex B.
277 The Model Law, Article 2(d).
278 EU Regulation (recast), Articles 56–58; Legislative Guide Part III, Ch.3, para. 7.
279 EU Regulation (recast), Articles 56(1), 57(1), 58 last paragraph; Legislative Guide Part III, Ch.3, para. 7.
280 EU Regulation (recast), Article 56(2)(a); Legislative Guide Part III, Recommendation 250(a).
281 EU Regulation (recast), Article 56(2)(b); Legislative Guide Part III, Recommendation 250(d).
282 EU Regulation (recast), Article 56(2)(c); Legislative Guide Part III, Recommendation 250(e).
283 EU Regulation (recast), Article 56(2), second paragraph; Legislative Guide Part III, Recommendation 250(c).
284 EU Regulation (recast), Article 56(1); Legislative Guide Part III, Recommendation 250(b).
285 Legislative Guide Part III, para. 15.
286 EU Regulation (recast), Article 57(1), 58(a).

287 EU Regulation (recast), Article 57(2); Legislative Guide Part III, Recommendation 241(c).
288 EU Regulation (recast), Article 57(3)(b); Legislative Guide Part III, Recommendation 241(a).
289 EU Regulation (recast), Article 57(3)(c); Legislative Guide Part III, Recommendation 241(b).
290 EU Regulation (recast), Article 57(3)(d); Legislative Guide Part III, Recommendation 245.
291 EU Regulation (recast), Article 57(3)(e); Legislative Guide Part III, Recommendation 241(d).
292 EU Regulation (recast), Article 58(b); Legislative Guide Part III, Recommendation 248.
293 EU Regulation (recast), Article 58(b);.
294 Legislative Guide Part III, Ch.3, para. 33.
295 EU Regulation (recast), Article 59.
296 Ibid., recital (50), Ch.5, Section II.
297 Ibid., Articles 69(2), 72.
298 Ibid., Article 72(1)(a)(b).
299 Ibid., Article 74(1).
300 Ibid., Article 74(2).
301 Ibid., Article 61(3)(d).
302 Ibid., Article 68(1)(c).
303 Working Group V (insolvency law), UNCITRAL, Facilitating the Cross-border Insolvency of Multinational Enterprise Groups, A /CN.9/WG.V/WP.128, 2015, Article 2(i).
304 Ibid., Article 18(1); Legislative Guide Part III, Recommendation 251.
305 Ibid., Ch.3, para. 44.
306 EU Regulation (recast), Article 42(3)(b), the Model Law, Article 27(b).
307 Ibid., Article 42(3)(c), the Model Law, Article 27(c).
308 Ibid., Article 42(3)(e).
309 The Model Law, Article 27(d).
310 EU Regulation (recast), Article 42(1), the Model Law, Article 27(a).
311 EU Regulation (recast), Article 42(3)(d).
312 The Model Law, Article 27(e).
313 EU Regulation (recast), recital (47); Article 42(3)(a).
314 Legislative Guide Part III, para. 46; Recommendation 251.
315 Practice Guide on Cooperation, Introduction-Glossary, 2(i).
316 Ibid., Introduction, para. 9.
317 Ibid., II, para. 12.
318 *Re P MacFadyen & Co, ex parte Vizianagaram Company Limited* [1908] 1 KB 675.
319 Ibid.
320 Ibid.
321 Ontario Court of Justice, Toronto, Case No. 32-077978 (20 December 1995), and the United States Bankruptcy Court for the Southern District of New York, Case No. 95 B 45405 (20 December, 1995).
322 Practice Guide on Cooperation, Annex I, No. 3, No. 41.
323 Ibid., No. 4, No. 30.
324 Ibid., No. 6.
325 Ibid., No. 8, No. 14.
326 Ibid., No. 8, No. 38.
327 Ibid., No. 10, No. 13, No. 14, No. 20, No. 24, No. 30, No. 38, No. 41.
328 Ibid., No. 12, No. 21.
329 Ibid., No. 13.
330 Ibid., No. 26.
331 Ibid., No. 4, No. 12, No. 30.
332 Alvarez & Marsal Holdings LLC. Lehman Brothers International Protocol Proposal, 11 February, 2009, p. 4, available at: http://dm.epiq11.com/LBH/Document#maxPerPage=25&page=1 (last accessed on 31 March, 2017).
333 Lehman Bros. Holdings Inc., Cross Border Insolvency Protocol for the Lehman Brothers Group of Companies, approved on 17 June, 2009, p. 2 available at: http://dm.epiq11.com/LBH/Document#maxPerPage=25&page=1 (last accessed on 31 March, 2017).

334 Practice Guide on Cooperation, at 28.
335 Ibid., No. 44 case.
336 Proposed Cross-border Insolvency Protocol for the Lehman Brothers Group of Companies, para. 9, 2009, available at: www.ekvandoorne.com/files/CrossBorderProtocol.pdf (last accessed on 31 March, 2017).
337 Ibid., paras. 9.3, 9.4.
338 EU Regulation (recast), recital (46).
339 Ibid., recital (46).
340 UNCITRAL Legislative Guide on Insolvency Law, Part Three: Treatment of enterprise groups in insolvency (2010), para. 38; Practice Guide on Cooperation, at 154.
341 The EU Regulation (recast), Articles 42(3), 57(3).
342 Practice Guide on Cooperation, Annex I: No. 2 *AgriBioTech Canada Inc.*(2000); No. 9 *Everfresh* (1995); No. 11 *Financial Asset Management* (2001); No. 15 *Laidlaw* (2001); No. 17 (1999); No. 18 *Loewen* (1999); No. 25 *Mosaic* (2002); No. 27 *360Networks* (2001); No. 33 *Pope & Talbot* (2007); No. 34 *Progressive Moulded* (2008); No. 35 *PSINet* (2001); No. 36 *Quebecor* (2008); No. 40 *Solv-Ex* (1998); No. 42 *Systech* (2003).
343 Practice Guide on Cooperation, Annex I, No. 9 *Everfresh* (1995).
344 Global Guidelines, Guideline 8(b).
345 EU JudgeCo Guidelines, Guideline 8(ii).
346 Global Principles, Section III Global Guidelines for Court-to-Court Communication (Global Guidelines), Guideline 10; EU JudgeCo Principles, 3. EU Cross-Border Insolvency Court-to-Court Communications Guidelines (EU JudgeCo Guidelines), Guideline 10.
347 *Re Nortel Networks Corp*, 426 BR 84 (Bankr D Del 2010).
348 Motion, *Re Nortel Networks, Inc.* (25 April, 2011), ECF No. 5307.
349 Opposition & Cross-Motion to Compel Arbitration, In *Re Nortel Networks, Inc.* (19 May, 2011), ECF No. 5444.
350 Reply, *Re Nortel Networks, Inc.* (2 June, 2011), ECF No. 5571.
351 *Re Nortel Networks, Inc.*, Case No. 09-10138(KG), Re Dkt No. 13208 (Bankr D Del Apr. 3, 2013); *Nortel Networks Corp.* (Re), 09-CL-7950, 2013 O.N.S.C. 1757 (Can Ont Sup Ct J, 3 April, 2013).
352 *Re Nortel Networks INC*, 737 F3d 265 (2013), at 269.
353 *Re Nortel Networks, Inc.*, No. 09-10138, 2013 WL 1385271 (Bankr D Del, 3 April, 2013), at 4; see also *Nortel Networks Corp.* (Re), 09-CL-7950, 2013 ONSC 1757 (Can Ont Sup Ct J, 3 April, 2013), at 35–37.
354 *Re Nortel Networks, Inc.*, No. 09-10138, 2015 WL 2374351 (Bankr D Del, 12 May, 2015), at 27; *Nortel Networks Corp.* (Re), 09-CL-7950, 2015 ONSC 2987 (Can Ont Sup Ct J, 12 May, 2015), at 10.
355 *Re Nortel Networks, Inc.*, No. 09-10138, 2013 WL 1385271 (Bankr D Del, 3 April, 2013).
356 See Order Entering Allocation Protocol, In *Re Nortel Networks, Inc.*, No. 09-10138 (17 May, 2013), ECF No. 10565, at Ex. 1¶ 4(e).
357 Practice Guide on Cooperation, at III-152–153.
358 EU Regulation (recast), Article 42(1).
359 The Model Law, Article 27(a).
360 EU Regulation (recast), Article 57(1), 57(3)(a); Legislative Guide Part III, Ch.3, para. 37.
361 *Re Maxwell Communication Corp. Plc*, 170 BR 800 (Bankr SDNY 1994).
362 *Re Joseph Nakash*, United States Bankruptcy Court for the Southern District of New York, Case No. 94 B 44840 (23 May, 1996).
363 *Matlack, INC.*, Superior Court of Justice of Ontario, Case No. 01-CL-4109.
364 ALI/III, Transnational insolvency: global principles for cooperation in international insolvency cases: report to the ALI, Philadelphia. PA: Executive Office, The American Law Institute, 2012, the Comment to Global Principle. 23.
365 Ibid., ft. 111.
366 Legislative Guide Part III, para. 37.
367 ALI/III, Transnational insolvency: global principles for cooperation in international insolvency cases: report to the ALI, Philadelphia. PA: Executive Office, The American Law Institute, 2012, the Comment to Global Principle, ft. 112.
368 The EU Regulation (recast), Articles 42(1), 57(1).

369 Global Principles, Principle 23; EU JudgeCo Principles, Principle 17.
370 The Member States that provide online registers (with websites) include Austria, Czech Republic, Estonia, France, Germany, Italy, Latvia, Luxembourg, Malta, Netherlands, Slovenia and Spain. (Hess, Oberhammer, Pfeiffer, 2014).
371 Case example: County Court Croydon 21/10/2008 1258/08, NZI 2009, 136. See EU Commission Explanatory Memorandum, Proposal for a Regulation of the European Parliament and of the Council amending Council Regulation (EC) No. 1346/2000 on insolvency proceedings, Strasbourg, 12.12.2012, COM (2012) 744 final, p. 25.
372 See all National Reports on Q37 of the Heidelberg-Luxembourg-Vienna Report, in particular, Austria, Belgium, Czech Republic, Estonia, Ireland, Italy, Lithuania, Malta. (Hess, Oberhammer, Pfeiffer, 2014).
373 EU Regulation (recast), Article 24(1).
374 EU Commission Explanatory Memorandum, Proposal for a Regulation of the European Parliament and of the Council amending Council Regulation (EC) No. 1346/2000 on insolvency proceedings, Strasbourg, 12.12.2012, COM (2012) 744 final, p. 28.
375 EU Regulation (recast), Article 25(1).
376 EU Regulation (recast), Article 25(1).
377 EU Regulation (recast), Article 24(2).
378 EU Regulation (recast), Article 25(1).
379 EU Regulation (recast), Article 26(1).
380 EU Regulation (recast), Article 26(2).
381 EU Regulation (recast), Article 27(1).
382 Department for Exiting the European Union, Legislating for the United Kingdom's withdrawal from the European Union, March 2017.
383 Department for Exiting the European Union, Providing a Cross-border Civil Judicial Cooperation Framework – a future partnership paper, August 2017.
384 Jürgen Basedow, Brexit and Business Law, Max Planck Institute for Comparative and International Private Law - Research Paper Series, No. 17/1, 2017.
385 Case E-9/07, L'Oréal (2008) EFTA Ct. Rep. 258, para 28; see also Skouris, 2014.
386 Department for Exiting the European Union, Legislating for the United Kingdom's withdrawal from the European Union, March 2017, para. 2.12; Department for Exiting the European Union, Providing a Cross-border Civil Judicial Cooperation Framework – a future partnership paper, August 2017, para. 2, 20.
387 Basic Law, article 22(4); see also the Interpretation by the Standing Committee of the National People's Congress of Articles 22(4) and 24(2)(3) of the Basic Law of the Hong Kong Special Administrative Region of the People's Republic of China after a series of right of abode cases involving the rights of residence of the mainland-born children to stay in Hong Kong. For detailed discussion on the series of cases, please refer to Chen Youqing, 2007.
388 Connolly, Niamh, The Prospective and Retrospective Effect of Judicial Decisions in Ireland, in: Steiner, Eva, Comparing the Prospective Effect of Judicial Rulings Across Jurisdictions, Springer, 2015, p. 29.
389 Klamert, Marcus, The Principle of Loyalty in EU, Oxford University Press, 2014, p. 1
390 European Council, European Council (Art. 50) guidelines for Brexit negotiations, Press Release 220/17, 29/04/2017, para.25
391 Case C-5/94, *The Queen v Ministry of Agriculture, Fisheries and Food, ex parte: Hedley Lomas (Ireland) Ltd.* [1996] ECR I-02553, para.19
392 Case C-297/07, *Staatsanwaltschaft Regensburg v. Klaus Bourquain* [2008] ECR I-09425, Opinion of Advocate General Ruiz-Jarabo Colomer, delivered on 8 April 2008, para.45
393 Ibid., para. 2.12.
394 Ibid., para. 2.8.
395 TEU, Article 4(3); Council of the European Union, Draft guidelines following the UK's notification under Article 50 TEU, 31 March, 2017, paras. 23–25; TFEU, Article 81(1).
396 Department for Exiting the European Union, Legislating for the UK's withdrawal from the European Union, March 2017, para. 2.16.
397 Department for Exiting the European Union, Providing a Cross-border Civil Judicial Cooperation Framework – a future partnership paper, August 2017, pp. 6, 9.
398 EU Regulation (recast), Articles 42–44; Chapter V, Section I.

Reference list

Adler, Louise De Carl, *Managing the Chapter 15 Cross-Border Insolvency Case (A Pocket Guide for Judges)* (2nd ed.), Federal Judicial Center, 2014, p. 22; ft.48

Arts, Robert, "Main and Secondary Proceedings in the Recast of the European Insolvency Regulation – The Only Good Secondary Proceeding is a Synthetic Secondary Proceeding", 2015, p. 2, available at: http://iiiglobal.org/iii-prize-in-insolvency.html (last visited on 31 March, 2017)

Bell, Andrew, *Forum Shopping and Venue in Transnational Litigation*, Oxford, 2003, pp. 5, 25

Bellissimo, Joseph J., Johnston, Susan Power, *Cross-Border Insolvency Protocols: Developing an International Standard*, Norton Annual Review of International Insolvency, 2010, Art.2, p. 2

Berends, André, "The UNCITRAL Model Law on Cross-border Insolvency: A Comprehensive Overview", 6 Tul. J. Int'l & Comp. L.309, 1998, pp. 320, 357

Chen Youqing, "1997–2007: Jurisprudential Observation on Rule of Law Practice of One Country, Two Systems – from a Conflict of Law Perspective" (doctoral dissertation in Chinese), Southwest University of Political Science & Law, 2007, pp. 45–67, available at: http://eng.oversea.cnki.net.ezproxy.leidenuniv.nl:2048/kns55/brief/result.aspx?dbPrefix=CDFD

Chung, John J., "In Re Qimonda AG: The Conflict between Comity and the Public Policy Exception in Chapter 15 of the Bankruptcy Code", 32 B.U. Int'l L.J. 2013, p. 91

Clift, Jenny, "Choice of Law and the UNCITRAL Harmonization Process, Brooklyn Journal of Corporate", *Finance & Commercial Law*, Vol. 9, Issue 1, 2014, p. 22

Coleman, Sarah, Johnson, Jen, "Journey to the Center of the Economic Universe: How the Current U.S. COMI Timing Determination Misses the Mark", 23 No. 6 J. Bankr. L. & Prac. NL Art. 4, December 2014, p. 6

Dessain, Anthony, Wilkins, Michael, "How Strong and How Long Is "the Golden Thread"? Jurisdictional Issues in a Globalized World", *The Jersey & Guernsey Law Review*, Issue 1, 2014, p. 74

Eidenmüller, Horst, "Abuse of Law in the Context of European Insolvency Law", 6 ECFLR 1, 2009, pp. 4, 12

Farley, J.M, Leonard, Bruce, Birch, John M, "Cooperation and Coordination in Cross-Border Insolvency Cases" (paper delivered on the INSOL conference in May 2006), p. 9 available at www.iiiglobal.org/component/jdownloads/viewcategory/362.html (last accessed on 31 March, 2017)

Fletcher, Ian, *Insolvency in Private International Law*, Oxford University Press, 2005, supplement 2007, p. 367

Fredriksen, Halvard Haukeland, Franklin, Christian N.K., "Of Pragmatism and Principles: The EEA Agreement 20 Years on", *Common Market Law Review*, vol. 52(3), 2015, p. 631

Gropper, Allan L., "The Arbitration of Cross-border Insolvencies", 86 Am. Bankr. L.J., 201, 2012, p. 211

Hess, Burkhard, Oberhammer, Paul, Pfeiffer, Thomas, European *Insolvency Law: The Heidelberg-Luxembourg-Vienna Report on the Application of Regulation No. 1346/2000/EC on Insolvency Proceedings* (External Evaluation JUST/2011/JCIV/PR/0049/A4), C.H.Beck.Hart.Nomos, 2014, paras. 121; 175; 679–685; 943; 976

Hess/Pfeiffer, *Interpretation of the Public Policy Exception* (IP/C/JURI/IC/2010–076), 2011, p. 30 et seq. & pp. 119–120; 167–168, ft.713

Ho, Look Chan, "Applying Foreign Law-Realising the Model Law's Potential", JIBLR 552, 2010, p. 557

Janger, Edward, "Virtual Territoriality", 48 Colum. J. Transnat'l L. 401, 2010

Jónsdóttir, Jóhanna, *Europeanization and the European economic area: Iceland's participation in the EU's policy process*, Routledge, 2013, p. 107

Klamert, Marcus, *The Principle of Loyalty in EU*, Oxford University Press, 2014

Li Ji, "A Study on China's Interregional Judicial Assistance in Civil and Commercial Matters" (doctoral dissertation in Chinese), China University of Political Science and Law, 2006, p. 44–46, available at: http://eng.oversea.cnki.net.ezproxy.leidenuniv.nl:2048/kns55/brief/result.aspx?dbPrefix=CDFD (last accessed on 5 October 2017)

Maltese, Michele, "Court-to Court Protocols in Cross-border Bankruptcy Proceedings: Differing Approaches between Civil Law and Common Law Legal Systems", 2013, p. 39 http://iiiglobal. org/images/pdfs/maltese_michele%20submission.pdf (last accessed on 31 March, 2017)

Marshall, Jennifer (ed.), *European Cross-border Insolvency Looseleaf*, Allen & Overy, Sweet & Maxwell, December 19, 2013, at 1.8.225; 2.4.250

McCormack, Gerard, "Jurisdictional Competition and Forum Shopping in Insolvency Proceedings", 68 *Cambridge Law Journal* 169, 2009, p. 189

Menjucq, Michael, Dammann, Reinhard, "Regulation No. 1346/2000 on Insolvency Proceedings: Facing the Companies Group Phenomenon", 9 Bus. L. Int'l. 145, 2008, p. 154

Mevorach, Irit, "Jurisdiction in Insolvency, A Study of European Courts' Decisions", *Journal of Private International Law*, Vol. 6, No. 2, 2010, p. 343

Miller, Robert W., "Economic Integration: An American Solution to the Multinational Enterprise Group Conundrum", 11 Rich. J. Global L. & Bus. 185 (2012), at p. 217

Mohan, S. Chandra, "Cross-border Insolvency Problems: Is the UNICITRAL Model Law the Answer?" *International Insolvency Review*, Vol. 21, 2012, p. 202

Moss, Gabriel, Fletcher, Ian F., Isaacs, Stuart (ed.), *The EC Regulation on Insolvency Proceedings: A Commentary and Annotated Guide* (2nd ed.), Oxford University Press, 2009, paras.1.01–1.25; 3.12; 8.81

Moss, Gabriel, Fletcher, Ian F., Isaacs, Stuart (ed.), *The EU Regulation on Insolvency Proceedings* (3rd ed.), Oxford University Press, 2016, at 8.560–8.561

Pannen, Klaus (ed.), *European Insolvency Regulation*, De Gruyter Recht, 2007, pp. 660–666

Paulus, Christoph, "Judicial Cooperation in Cross-Border Insolvencies-An outline of some relevant issues and literature", p. 1, available at http://siteresources.worldbank.org/GILD/Resources/GJF2006JudicialCooperationinInsolvency_PaulusEN.pdf (Last accessed on 31 March, 2017)

Pottow, John A.E., "A New Rule for Secondary Proceedings in International Bankruptcies", 46 Tex. Int'l L.J. 579, 2011, pp. 582, 585

Rudbordeh, Amir Adl, "An analysis and hypothesis on forum shopping in insolvency law: From the European Insolvency Regulation to its Recast", 2016, p. 51, available at: www.iiiglobal. org/node/1932 (last accessed on 31 March, 2017)

Samad, Mahmud, *Court Application under the Company Acts*, Dublin: Bloomsbury, 2013, p. 1251

Seife, Howard and Vazquez, Francisco, "The Octaviar Saga: The Chapter 15 Door Opens, Closes, and then Reopens on the Foreign Representatives", *Norton Journal of Bankruptcy Law and Practice*, Vol. 23, No. 5, October 2014, p. 576

Skouris, Vassilios, "The Role of the Court of Justice of the European Union (CJEU) in the Development of the EEA Single Market: Advancement through Collaboration between the EFTA Court and the CJEU", in *The EEA and the EFTA Court – Decentred Integration*, Hart Publishing, 2014, p. 5

Swick, R. Adam, Harle, Paul, "Section 109(a)'s Jurisdictional Requirements Applied to Chapter 15", 33-MAR Am. Bankr. Inst. J. 30, 2014, p. 32

Tang, Zheng Sophia, Xiao Yongping, Chapter 13 "Interregional Conflicts and Cooperation between Mainland, Hong Kong, Macao and Taiwan", in Tang, Zheng Sophia, Xiao Yongping, Huo Zhengxin (ed.), *Conflict of Laws in the People's Republic of China*, Edward Elgar Publishing, 2016, p. 357

Tridimas, P. Taski, "Abuse of Right in EU Law: some reflections with particular reference to financial law", 2009, p. 15, available at: http://papers.ssrn.com/sol3/papers.cfm?abstract_id=1438577 (Last visited on 31 March, 2017)

Viimsalu, Signe, *The Meaning and Functioning of Secondary Insolvency Proceedings* (doctoral dissertation), Tartu University Press, 2011, pp. 23–25

Virgós & Wessels, *European Communication and Cooperation Guidelines for Cross-border Insolvency*, Developed under the aegis of the Academic Wing of INSOL Europe, July 2007, Appendix I

Waterfield, Bruno, "Copy the Swiss Model, Schäuble Advises Britain", *The Times*, 23 January, 2017, T1

Wessels, Bob, *International Insolvency Law* (3rd ed.), Vol. X, Kluwer, 2012, paras. 10066, 10247, 10283e, 10334d, 10568,

Wessels, Bob, "A Global Approach to Cross-border Insolvency Cases in a Globalizing World", *Eleven Journals*, 2013, Issue 1, p. 23

Wessels, Bob, "Contracting out of Secondary Insolvency Proceedings: The Main Liquidator's Undertaking in the Meaning of Article 18 in the Proposal to Amend the EU Insolvency Regulation", *Brooklyn Journal of Corporate, Finance & Commercial Law*, Vol. 9, issue 1, 2014, p. 87

Wessels, Bob, "Nortel Network Joint hearing as a test case for EU JudgeCo Principle 10?", 13 May 2014, http://bobwessels.nl/2014/05/2014-05-doc8-nortel-network-joint-hearing-as-a-test-case-for-eu-judgeco-principle-10/ (last accessed on 31 March, 2017)

Westbrook, Jay L., "An Empirical Study of the Implementation in the United States of the Model Law on Cross-Border Insolvency", 87 Am. Bankr. L. J. 247, (2013), p. 252

Wood, Philip, *Principles of International Insolvency* (2nd ed.), Sweet & Maxwell, 2007, 29–081

Yu Zhihong, "On the Reciprocal Recognition and Enforcement of the Judgments Made by Courts of the Mainland and Hong Kong Special Administrative Region" (doctoral dissertation in Chinese), Wuhan University, 2009, p. 156, available at: http://eng.oversea.cnki.net.ezproxy.leidenuniv.nl:2048/kns55/brief/result.aspx?dbPrefix=CDFD (Latest accessed on 5 October 2017)

Zhang Shudi, "A Study on Conflict of Jurisdiction on Civil and Commercial Matters between the Mainland and Hong Kong" (doctoral dissertation in Chinese), East China University of Political Science and Law, 2007, p. 94, available at: http://eng.oversea.cnki.net.ezproxy.leidenuniv.nl:2048/kns55/brief/result.aspx?dbPrefix=CDFD (last accessed on 5 October 2017)

5 Solutions tailored to a Chinese context

A balanced way[1]

Introduction

Based on the analysis in the former parts, Chapter 5 attempts to find a balanced way between the Model Law and the Regulation and tailor them to China's context. It provides 10 Recommendations to China's Inter-regional Cross-border Insolvency Arrangement (hereinafter referred to as CICIA), including the Guiding Principle, the Overriding Objectives, Form and Scope, Recognition and Reliefs, Public Policy, Cooperation and Communication (single debtor and enterprise groups), Cross-border Insolvency Agreements, the Functional Dispute Settlement Mechanism, the Inter-regional Case Register and the Independent Intermediary (a separate arrangement for cross-strait insolvency cooperation).

Recommendation 1 – guiding principle

> *Acknowledging lack of cooperation in matters of cross-border insolvency despite the increasingly closer economic relationship, the guiding principle that embodies the entire arrangement is designed to promote fair and efficient administration of China's interregional cross-border insolvency proceedings in a coordinated manner.*

Comments on recommendation 1

As a to-be-established interregional legal cooperation regime, CICIA cannot stand firm without any guiding legal principles that serve as the foundation. Among all those classic jurisdiction-oriented principles, Recommendation 1 explains the reasons for choosing a coordinated approach based on cooperation and communication between the courts and insolvency practitioners.

Universalism v territorialism

When God first made people, everyone spoke the same language. No one had any trouble understanding one another. People started to build the city and the tower (Babel). Because of this, God created new languages, and different people began speaking these languages. People couldn't understand each other anymore. Groups of people had to move away to different parts of the world and start their own cultures (Genesis 11:1-9). According to semiotician Umberto Eco, there has been a long struggle in the West to overcome the perceived problems which stem from language and worldwide heterogeneity and highlights efforts on developing universal ontologies and artificial languages (Eco, 1995). However, in accordance with the latest statistics released by the UNESCO, there are estimated 6000 languages spoken in the world.[2]

The underlying principle of Recommendation 1 is related to an enduring struggle in the world of international insolvency law between the ideal and the reality over a hundred years, i.e. universalism and territorialism (Lowell, 1888; LoPucki, 2005). In an ideal picture painted by the universalists in its purest form, there would have been a single insolvency regime (principle of unity) that collects, administers and then distributes all the debtor's assets wherever these assets may be situated throughout the world (principle of universality) (Trautman, 1993; Westbrook, 2000). It reflects a principle that a person (a debtor) owns the undivided entirety of property (Wessels, 2012). From the economic perspective, it is also easy to explain since debt collection inherently involves transaction costs (Bufford 2009). Bankruptcy systems are designed to reduce these collection costs through collective action (Jackson, 2001). In addition, when browsing through the legal literature, one cannot escape the impression that jurists are "slightly (at least) biased against divergence. Convergence, harmonization and even stronger phenomena like unification are often perceived as positive developments in and of themselves" (Larouche, 2013). Universalism has been and still is well acknowledged as the fundamental principle of cross-border insolvency law.[3] Unfortunately, the reality is that we do not live in a world with a single insolvency regime. Each jurisdiction runs its own insolvency system under its sovereignty and the differences are often dramatic. Those specialized rules that govern the proper liquidation or reorganization of insolvent entities are usually closely interrelated to some local policies, for instance tax and pension scheme. That is why, in practice, universalism has had to give way to pragmatic realities (McCormack, 2012).

Development in practice

Before any influential global or regional solutions came into effect, tentative measures were taken by sovereign States in accordance with domestic legislation. For example, in the United States, once a bankruptcy proceeding is opened, an automatic stay prevents creditors from instituting or continuing any action to obtain assets from the bankruptcy estate or to collect a debt owed by the debtor.[4] If a creditor violates the stay, whether in the United States or abroad, that creditor is liable to penalties in the US bankruptcy courts, which may include denial of the creditor's claim.[5] As for the foreign insolvency proceedings in pursuit of assistance in the United States, before 2005 it was §304 (repealed) of the US Bankruptcy Code that provided the possibility. That section, for the first time, codified US notions of comity and cooperation with foreign courts in bankruptcy matters. The model is referred to as "modified universalism".[6] Modified universalism shares the view that there should be a single main case for an international business in its home country, mostly subject to the laws of the home country. Nevertheless, the modified universalism in the context of extra-territoriality is effective solely in a single direction. Upon the inbound request, the ancillary proceeding was opened in the requested State merely for assistance purposes. As for the outbound proceeding, the effect relied on the vast extent of jurisdiction stated beforehand under the domestic legislation, which would probably meet challenge and uncertainty since it may have difficulty being enforced if the foreign State refuses to recognize it where this effect is inconsistent with the domestic law of the relevant foreign country (McCormack, 2012).

In pursuit of approaching universalism in a round-about form (principle of unity and principle of universality), a system of parallel jurisdictions has been invented within the EU, each of which can open an independent insolvency proceeding. What is the relationship between them to realize the goal of "a single forum" (principle of unity)? Some specialized terminology has been developed to establish specialized rules of choice of forum for cross-border insolvency cases. It attempts to allocate cross-border insolvencies to a single proceeding, which is called the "main" proceeding and shall be granted automatic recognition in other Member States without the need for an exequatur or of prior publication.[7] There is also some compromise because secondary proceedings can be opened without reference to the main proceedings, which was regarded as a deviation from the principle of unity. Accordingly, the universal effect of the main proceedings has also to be restricted for the sake of local interests, which departs from the principle of universality. With the reform of the Regulation, there are two main solutions to that kind of deviation: one is to avoid the opening of the secondary proceedings;[8] the other is to reinforce the duties of cooperation and communication among the actors involved.[9]

Compared to the Regulation, the Model Law is a less ambitious regime, which does not aim at concentrating cross-border insolvency within one jurisdiction. The key objective of the Model Law is to facilitate recognition of insolvency proceedings via simplified procedures and emphasizes access, recognition, relief, cooperation and coordination. The similarity is that the Model Law, like the Regulation, also allows local concurrent proceedings opened parallel to the main proceedings. Nevertheless, the Model Law avoids establishing a rigid hierarchy between the main proceedings and the non-main proceedings because that would unnecessarily hinder the ability of the court to cooperate.[10] The consequence is that the Model Law does not provide any rules to intervene or prevent the opening of concurrent proceedings, which eventually result in more than one single proceeding. Considering the differences between the Regulation and the Model Law, if the Regulation approaches the principle of universalism in a way acknowledged by many universalists or even territorialists (Rasmussen, 1999; Buxbaum, 2000; LoPucki, 2000; Westbrook, 2005; Janger, 2007 & 2010; Clark, 2011; Wessels, 2012), can the Model Law still be labeled as the same universalism as described under the Regulation? According to Wessels, who highlighted some major ingredients of the Model Law that reflect both universality and territoriality (Wessels, 2012), the answer is no (Wessels, 2012). It is further indicated that the Model Law has chosen a "middle road" between the aspiration of universalism and a concession to the essential influence of pragmatism (Clift, 2014).

Universalism in a coordinated manner

The traditional discussion between the pros and cons of universalism and territoriality usually leads to a "struggle over jurisdiction" (Wessels, 2012). In particular, the possibility of opening of non-main (territorial/secondary) proceedings is deemed as "essentially a territorial system with universalist pretensions" (Tung, 2001). However, non-main proceedings (territorial/secondary) cannot be totally given up. First of all, as aforementioned, the birth of non-main proceedings (territorial/secondary) is a result of compromise between local interests and the principles of unity and universality from the beginning. Secondly, as remarked by Pottow, allowing only one single proceeding running worldwide could lead to a "fight over who gets to be the COMI in any given bankruptcy", whereas non-main proceedings (territorial/secondary) can make the foreseeable competition far less intensive (Pottow, 2011). Thirdly, the non-main proceedings (territorial/secondary) are still relevant proceedings in the context of group insolvency. Under the Regulation, a secondary proceeding can be commenced in respect of a subsidiary at its place of operation if the COMI of a subsidiary is located at the registered office of the parent company.[11] In addition, in the proposal of Working Group V (insolvency law) of UNCITRAL, which deals with the cross-border insolvency of multinational enterprise groups, the proceedings for group members on the basis of criteria such as the location of an establishment or the presence of assets, which is akin to non-main proceedings under the Model Law, is recommended as the coordinating center of the group insolvency solution if the COMIs of those group members are not located in the same jurisdiction.[12]

If the parallel non-main proceedings (territorial/secondary) cannot be removed from both international cross-border insolvency regimes, what is the solution to the deviation from universalism? Despite the differences, there is a common measure shared by both the Regulation and the Model Law, which is cooperation and communication. Under the EC Regulation, it provides the mandatory cooperation and communication between the liquidators of main proceedings and secondary proceedings.[13] The current EU Regulation (recast) extends the duties of cooperation and communication to all the actors involved, which greatly refers to the relevant provisions under the Model Law concerning cooperation and communication between the courts and representatives of the parallel proceedings.[14] Besides, the landscape of cross-border insolvency has been changed by the enterprise groups. It has been accepted by both the EU and UNCITRAL that coordination of concurrent insolvency proceedings involving single debtors and multiple debtors based on cooperation and communication is a more pragmatic approach,[15] which is capable of easing the tension caused by competition among jurisdictions. Under the circumstances that it is getting more and more difficult to identify a "home" for multiple debtors, a neutral and efficient mechanism is needed on the basis of respect for the independence and authority of each competent court.

In addition to the EU and UNCITRAL, more supportive references are available now in regards to cooperation and communication. One of the most prevailing sources are the *Global Principles for Cooperation in International Insolvency Cases* (the Global Principles) contributed by Fletcher and Wessels, who were appointed by the American Law Institute (ALI) and the International Insolvency Institute (III) to prepare a report. The report is based on a global research and survey and aims at a worldwide acceptance of the ALI-NAFTA Principles, in which the Guidelines Applicable to Court-to-Court Communications in Cross-Border Cases ("Court-to-Court Guidelines") are also included. These Guidelines in their original form were included in Appendix B of the ALI-NAFTA Principles and represent procedural suggestions for increasing communications between courts and between insolvency administrators in cross-border insolvency cases. These ALI-NAFTA Guidelines have already been used in many cross-border cases, recently in such cases as *Lehman Brothers* involving some 70 insolvency proceedings in 17 countries around the world.[16] Even the key supporter of territorialism, LoPucki, also advocates in his theory of "cooperative territorialism" that every State can administer the bankruptcy asset located within its jurisdiction and meanwhile courts and representatives should cooperate and communicate (LoPucki, 1999). In an era when business goes global, it is cooperation that matters: "The barren choice of either universality or territoriality of bankruptcy has almost lost its meaning" (Balz, 1996). Moreover, pursuant to the Basic Law, which provides China's legal foundation of interregional legal cooperation, it is the judicial organs of the Mainland and the SARs that shall maintain juridical relations with each other through consultations.[17] Accordingly, cooperation and communication between the courts is consistent with the fundamental legal basis. Therefore, I submit to adopt the coordinated approach to resolve the conflicts between universalism and co-existence of parallel proceedings under CICIA, which attaches importance to cooperation and communication among the proceedings involving both single debtors and multiple debtors. In particular, the courts are suggested to cooperate and communicate with each other to resolve cross-border insolvency cooperation-related disputes together at the regional level. I will come back to that point later in Recommendation 8.

Recommendation 2 – overriding objective

Aware of restrictions set by the constitutional arrangements and lack of functioning fundamental principles, the overriding objective of the arrangement is to facilitate recognition of interregional insolvency proceedings.

Comments on recommendation 2

Recommendation 2 attempts to determine the proper main line of CICIA, i.e. jurisdiction oriented or recognition oriented. A balanced solution is sought on the basis of comparison of the underlying legal foundations and principles of different relevant regimes.

Jurisdiction or recognition as the main line

To address the issues raised by cooperation in cross-border insolvency cases, the Regulation and the Model Law have different focuses. The former is able to establish a compulsory jurisdiction system for cross-border cooperation in insolvency cases within the EU, whereas the latter has adopted a streamlined formulation, which does not contain choice of forum rules but provisions concerning recognition of foreign insolvency proceedings. From the perspective of private international law, choice of forum, choice of law and recognition and enforcement constitute the three central themes of private international law (Woelki, 2010). Among the three central themes, to provide for uniform rules on jurisdiction is deemed as one of the most difficult tasks because that might incur sovereignty concerns. For example, from 1996 to 2001, the Hague Conference conducted intense negotiations on a Convention concerning recognition and enforcement of judgments in civil and commercial matters, excluding insolvency matters, which ultimately failed.[18] The most unresolved area was the possible ground of jurisdiction at the international level.[19] Later, the project was scaled down to focus on international cases involving choice of court agreements, which led to the conclusion of the Hague Convention of 30 June 2005 on Choice of Court Agreements ("Choice of Court Convention"). The Choice of Court Convention is thus based on party autonomy, entered into force on 1 October, 2015 following approval by the EU on 11 June, 2015. As for China, rules of jurisdiction also used to be one of the biggest problems for the Mainland and the Hong Kong SAR to reach consensus on reciprocal enforcement of judgments in civil and commercial matters (Jiang, 2007). In order to break the deadlock, the exercise of jurisdiction based on a choice of forum agreement served as a useful guide and model in the arrangement between the Mainland and the Hong Kong SAR, who in the end entered into the Arrangement on Reciprocal Recognition and Enforcement of Judgments in Civil and Commercial Matters by the Courts of the Mainland and of the Hong Kong Special Administrative Region Pursuant to Choice of Court Agreements between Parties Concerned (Chen and Shen, 2006).[20]

Nonetheless, both the Brussels I Regulation (recast) and Choice of Court Convention exclude insolvency cases from their scopes of application. That implies rules of jurisdiction in the context of cross-border insolvency cannot be properly governed by party autonomy. In the field of cross-border insolvency, it is the principle of unity (concentrating on cross-border insolvencies within a single proceeding) that dominates the rule of choice of forum, which is, as stated by Westbrook, "perhaps no other principle of choice of forum has been so generally accepted for so long" (Westbrook, 1991). In the EU, the principle of unity with regards to the main insolvency proceeding has been preserved as much as possible. For example, the EU Regulation (recast) allows the opening of synthetic proceedings so as to contract out the commencement of the secondary proceedings.[21] Contrary to the EU's insistence on the principle of unity, the Model Law imposes no limitations on the jurisdiction of the courts in the enacting State to commence or continue concurrent insolvency proceedings, which can be initiated either on the basis of establishment or mere presence of assets.[22] To understand the reasons behind the differences between the Regulation and the Model Law, it is necessary to identify why a compulsory jurisdiction system is possible in the EU. Above all, the legal foundation underlying the Regulation is based on the principle of mutual trust,[23] flowing from the principle of sincere cooperation under the EU Treaties, which is the fundamental support for a compulsory jurisdiction system. In addition, the establishment of a compulsory jurisdiction system alone will become meaningless if the dominant effects of the main proceedings cannot be recognized in other jurisdiction. It is also the principle of mutual trust that generates the automatic effects of recognition throughout the EU,[24] which are governed by a set of uniform choice of law rules. The Model Law also accords the main proceedings with a sort of automatic effect.[25] Without equivalent legal foundations, the automatic effect granted under the Model Law is relatively limited. First of all, the Model Law does not provide uniform rules of applicable law but introduced a "minimum" list of automatic reliefs while at the same time leaving room for the recognizing court to provide additional effects or measures. Secondly, those automatic effects are triggered by recognition, the extent of which is limited between the state where the proceeding is opened and the state where the petition for recognition is sought. In summary, considering the fundamental differences between the Regulation and the Model Law, to choose a main line between a jurisdiction-oriented approach or a recognition-oriented approach relies on whether or not the equivalent legal basis is available.

Sincere cooperation and mutual trust

Function of sincere cooperation and mutual trust under the Regulation

To properly understand the function of the principles of sincere cooperation and mutual trust, how those two principles operate under the Regulation should be made clear at first. It is stated according to the Article 4(3) of the TEU that "pursuant to the principle of sincere cooperation, the Union and the Member States shall, in full mutual respect, assist each other in carrying out tasks which flow from the Treaties". The principle of sincere cooperation (sometimes also addressed as the principle of loyalty) is regarded to have produced "some of the strongest 'ties that bind' the Member States within the European Union" (Klamert, 2014), among which one of the derivatives is the principle of mutual trust. According to Guzman, international law works based on "three Rs of compliance", i.e. reciprocity, retaliation, and repudiation (Guzman, 2007). However, he also noted that there is a "single greatest example of international cooperation, which is the European Union that substituted reciprocity and retaliation by a complete system of remedies and a centralized jurisdiction to enforce them" (Guzman, 2007). In the context of cross-border insolvency cooperation, reciprocity was replaced by mutual trust. It is specified in Article 81(1) of TFEU that:

the Union shall develop judicial cooperation in civil matters having cross-border implications, based on the principle of mutual recognition of judgments and of decisions in extrajudicial cases. Such cooperation may include the adoption of measures for the approximation of the laws and regulations of the Member States.

On the basis of Article 81(1) and the underlying principle of sincere cooperation, the Regulation provides "automatic and universal recognition (throughout the EU) of insolvency proceedings opened in accordance with the jurisdictional scheme of Article 3"(Moss, 2009), which stipulates the rules of the allocation of international jurisdiction with respect to insolvency proceedings (Moss, 2007). In the *Eurofood* case and the *MG Probud* case, the following remarks are repeatedly used by the CJEU, which were originally quoted from the Court's decision regarding the Brussels Convention (now the Brussels I Regulation):

> It is that mutual trust which has enabled a compulsory system of jurisdiction to be established, which all the courts within the purview of the Convention are required to respect, and as a corollary the waiver by those States of the right to apply their internal rules on recognition and enforcement of foreign judgments in favor of a simplified mechanism for the recognition and enforcement of decisions handed down in the context of insolvency proceedings [see by analogy, in relation to the Convention of 27 September 1968 on Jurisdiction and the Enforcement of Judgments in Civil and Commercial matters.[26]

The principle of mutual trust also constitutes the main basis of the Brussels I regulation. Van Calster concluded, "the theme of mutual trust runs through European private international law, extending from Brussels I into the Insolvency Regulation" (Van Calster, 2013). In practice, it is evident that the CJEU has repeatedly referred to the principle of mutual trust to safeguard the uniform understanding of the EU legislation and coordinate the conflicting or competitive opinions as held by the courts of the Member States. The principle of mutual trust entails that a court may not refuse to recognize the foreign judgment on the ground that "it would be more appropriate for the case to be dealt with in proceedings opened in another Member State" (Virgós & Garcimartín, 2004), i.e. *forum non conveniens*. Besides, in the case of *Bank Handlowy*,[27] the French court opened insolvency proceedings of a Polish company, the COMI of which was situated in France. The *sauvegarde* proceedings were opened in France, which had a protective nature. In the event that the judgment of the French court was held to be in breach of public policy in accordance with Article 26 of the Regulation, an alternative application was made by *Bank Handlowy* for the opening of winding-up proceedings in Poland. Thereafter, the French court approved a rescue plan for the Polish company, pursuant to which debts would be paid off in installments over a 10-year period. The debtor contended that Bank Handlowy's application for the opening of secondary proceedings in Poland should be dismissed on the basis that such proceedings would be contrary to the objectives of the French insolvency proceedings and argued that the secondary proceedings should be discontinued since the main proceedings had closed once the French court approved the rescue plan.[28] Although the *sauvegarde* is incorporated into Annex A to the EC Regulation, concerns have been raised as to whether they comply with the definition of insolvency proceedings. The CJEU considered that the court having jurisdiction to open secondary proceedings could not examine the main insolvency of a debtor opened in another Member State, which has a protective purpose, holding:

> It should be noted, however, that when a court before which an application for secondary proceedings has been made draws conclusions from the finding of insolvency

in the main proceedings, it must have regard to the objectives of the main proceedings and take account of the scheme of the Regulation as well as the principles on which it is based.[29]

Moreover, in the case of *Bank Handlowy*, the court allowed the opening of the secondary proceedings, which conformed to Article 27 of the EC Regulation. As aforementioned, the sole liquidation nature of the secondary proceedings has received a lot of criticism in the process of amendment to the EC Regulation[30] since they might derogate from the protective purpose of the main proceedings. Therefore, the CJEU, according to the principle of sincere cooperation laid down in Article 4(3) TEU, stressed that the court of the secondary proceedings had to take into account the objectives and the scheme of the EC Regulation and encouraged "the mandatory coordination of the main and secondary proceedings guaranteeing the priority of the main proceedings".[31] By relying on the principles of sincere cooperation and mutual trust, the CJEU attempted to make up for deficiencies left by the EC Regulation.

Sincere cooperation and mutual trust under construction in China

INTERPRETATION OF THE BASIC LAW

It is equally essential to check out whether or not there is sincere cooperation and mutual trust among the three jurisdictions in China. The first issue that has to be addressed is the interpretation of the Basic Law. Governed by the constitutional framework between the Mainland and the two SARs, interpretation of the Basic Law directly demonstrates the relationship between the central authority and the two regions. In accordance with the Basic Law, the interpretation of the Basic Law shall be requested through the Court of Final Appeal of the Region to the Standing Committee of the National People's Congress (NPC, the Central Legislator) under certain circumstances.[32] After China's resumption of sovereignty over Macao, it has never occurred that the Court of Final Appeal seeks interpretation of the Basic Law from the Standing Committee of the NPC. According to Zheng Wei, Advisor of the Legislative Council of the Macao SAR, so far there have not been "any conflicts and debates arising due to the interpretation of the Basic Law by the Standing Committee of the NPC in SAR as the cases in the Hong Kong SAR" (Zheng, 2009). In 2012, the Hong Kong government issued a report to celebrate the 15th anniversary of reunification, in which it was stated that there are several occasions that incurred the interpretation of the Basic Law and each of them might have challenged the smooth implementation of the Basic Law. These occasions include the right of mainland-born children to reside in Hong Kong SAR, the selection of the Chief Executive and the length of office of the Chief Executive (Tam, 2012) and whether or not the PRC's policy on absolute state immunity also applies to Hong Kong in the *DR Congo* case.[33] I will mainly focus on the *DR Congo* case by comparing it with the right of abode[34] of the mainland children cases. In respect of selection of the Chief Executive and the length of office of the Chief Executive, it falls outside the ambit of the research topic of this book and thus will not be discussed.

The right of abode cases involved a series of cases involving the rights of residence of Mainland-born children to stay in Hong Kong. One of the most important decisions is *NG Ka Ling and Another v The Director of Immigration*,[35] which was handed down by the Court of Final Appeal of the Hong Kong SAR in 1999. In matters of interpretation of the Basic Law, the Court of Final Appeal of the Hong Kong SAR made the following statement in its decision:

Article 158 has been quoted in full earlier in this judgment. Article 158(1) provides that the power of interpretation of the Basic Law shall be vested in the Standing Committee of the National People's Congress. Article 158(2) provides that the Standing Committee "shall authorize" the courts of the Region "to interpret on their own, in adjudicating cases, the provisions of this Law which are within the limits of the autonomy of the Region.

It is clear, as is accepted by both counsels, that this contains the constitutional authorization. The words "on their own", in our view, emphasize the high degree of autonomy of the SAR and the independence of its courts but the jurisdiction of the courts of the SAR is not limited to interpreting such provisions. For Article 158(3) provides that the courts of the SAR "may also interpret other provisions of the Basic Law in adjudicating cases."[36] Further, the Court of Final Appeal considered that it did not have a duty to make a reference to the Standing Committee of the National People's Congress unless both the classification condition and the necessity condition were met.[37] From the point of view of the Court of Final Appeal:

> it is for the Court of Final Appeal and for it alone to decide, in adjudicating a case, whether both conditions are satisfied. It is for the Court, not the National People's Congress, to decide whether the classification condition is satisfied, that is, whether the provision is an excluded provision. This is accepted by both counsel for the applicants and counsel for the Director.[38]

After having examined both conditions, the Court of Final Appeal did not refer the issue to the Standing Committee of the National People's Congress but made an interpretation on its own. On 20 May, 1999, the Chief Executive of the Hong Kong SAR in accordance with Articles 43 and 48(2) of the Basic Law submitted a report to the State Council seeking the assistance of the Central People's Government in resolving the problems encountered in the implementation of the relevant provisions of the Basic Law. It was stated in the report "the Court's interpretation of Articles 22(4) and 24(2)(3) differed from the Hong Kong SAR Government's understanding of the relevant provisions".[39] On 26 June, 1999, the Standing Committee of the National People's Congress issued the interpretation. In the preamble, it is stated that:

> The issue raised in the Motion related to the interpretation of the relevant provisions of the Basic Law by the Court of Final Appeal of the Hong Kong SAR dated 29 January 1999. Those provisions concerned affairs, which are the responsibility of the Central People's Government and concerned the relationship between the Central Authorities and the Hong Kong SAR. Before making its judgment, the Court of Final Appeal of the Hong Kong SAR had not sought an interpretation of the NPCSC in compliance with the requirement of Article 158(3) of the Basic Law. Moreover, the interpretation of the Court of Final Appeal is not consistent with the legislative intent.[40]

The reaction of the Court of Final Appeal of the Hong Kong SAR can be found in the case of *Lau Kong Yung and Others v The Directors of Immigration*,[41] which was also one of the right of abode series cases. The Court of Final Appeal of the Hong Kong SAR summarized its views on the interpretation issued by the Standing Committee of the National People's Congress as following:

(1) The Standing Committee has the power to make the Interpretation under Article 158(1).

(2) It is a valid and binding Interpretation of Article 22(4) and Article 24(2)(3) which the courts in the Hong Kong SAR are under a duty to follow.

(3) The effect of the Interpretation is:

    (a) . . .

    (b) . . .

(4) The Interpretation has effect from 1 July 1997.[42]

It is also noteworthy that in accordance with Article 158(3), judgments previously rendered shall not be affected by the interpretation, which might cause inconsistency in those rights of abode cases, since the interpretation does not bind the former ones.

In 2011, in *Democratic Republic of the Congo and Others v. FG Hemisphere Associates LLC* (the *DR Congo* case),[43] the case involved an application by an American company for enforcement of arbitral awards against DR Congo in Hong Kong. The case was appealed to the Court of Final Appeal and the core question is whether the Hong Kong court shall follow the Mainland's rule of policy on state immunity, which is different from Hong Kong's doctrine that recognizes a commercial exception to absolute immunity, after China's resumption of the exercise of sovereignty on 1 July, 1997. The Court of Final Appeal found it necessary to adopt the doctrine of the Mainland rule on state immunity. The opinions of the Court of Final Appeal on that specific issue are summarized as follows:

(1) The doctrine of state immunity, both in international law and at common law, is a matter of relations between states, which constitutes "an important component in the conduct of a nation's foreign affairs in relation to other States".[44]

(2) The responsibility for laying down the policy to be adopted on state immunity is allocated to a government organ or exceptionally to a province on the basis of the respective constitutional arrangements of each country.[45] As to Hong Kong, it has no responsibility for foreign affairs in accordance with the Article 13(1) of the Basic Law. Hong Kong "lacks the very attributes of sovereignty", which might enable it to establish its own policy or practice of state immunity.[46]

(3) In accordance with the common law, the doctrine adopted by the courts of the UK and the United States was that the courts and the executive should "speak with one voice".[47] Considering the constitutional arrangements governing the position in the Hong Kong SAR, "it is self-evident that any attempt by such a region or municipality to adopt a divergent state immunity policy would embarrass and prejudice the State in its conduct of foreign affairs".[48] Hence, the Court of Final Appeal accepted the "one voice principle" and followed the executive's lead in this case.

In addition, for the first time the Court of Final Appeal decided to take the initiative to make a reference to the Standing Committee for the interpretation of the Basic Law before the final decision was handed down.[49] Nevertheless, the decision of the Court of Final Appeal was not adopted without debate. There were five judges, who participated in adjudication of this case, and two of the justices dissented from the majority. I focus on the dissenting opinions of Justice Bokhary PJ because Justice Mortimer NPJ agreed with Mr Justice Bokhary PJ's judgment "in its conclusions and its reasoning".[50] Justice Bokhary PJ considered that the aim of the Basic Law was to ensure "continuity between the pre-handover and present judicial systems".[51] Justice Bokhary further referred to Justice Chan's statement in the earlier judgment *Hong Kong SAR v Ma Wai Kwan*, which was also rendered altogether by him and Justice Mortimer NPJ:

> In my view, the intention of the Basic Law is clear. There is to be no change in our laws and legal system (except those which contravene the Basic Law). These are the very fabric of our society. Continuity is the key to stability. Any disruption will be disastrous.[52]

Justice Bokhary PJ considered that by virtue of Article 13(3) of the Basic Law, Hong Kong was allowed to deal with its external affairs. He went on to point out: "Whether the immunity available in the courts of Hong Kong is absolute or restrictive is a question of Hong Kong common law for Hong Kong's independent judiciary to adjudicate upon, independently of course."[53] Indeed, the SARs are empowered with independent judicial competence. It is also correct that the Basic Law intends to maintain continuity of the legal system and the law in each region. Nevertheless, that kind of continuity cannot be granted without any restrictions. The restrictions are two-fold.

The first restriction is regarding the rank of the legislation. A regional legal system is established under the Basic Law, in which parallel legal systems are effective in the respective jurisdiction. The legislation convergences are either listed in the Annex to the Basic Law or the interpretation of the Central Authority in respect of the responsibility of the Central People's Government and concerning the relationship between the Central Authorities. It is obvious that that legislations or those rules have supremacy over the other regional laws and are binding throughout China.

The second restriction is placed on the discretion of the courts of the SAR. The judicial intersection occurs when the courts of the SARs are required to make a reference to the Central Authority in order to interpret the relevant provisions of the Basic Law. It is at the discretion of the courts of the SAR to determine whether the specific provisions in the individual case fall within the ambit of interpretation. The problem is to what extent the courts of the SAR can apply their discretion. It has been well acknowledged that Hong Kong operates under the common law system, which can result in deviation from the legal system of the Mainland, such as understanding of state immunity. The majority of justices in the *DR Congo* case have precisely indicated that Hong Kong SAR is also bound by the constitutional arrangements with Mainland China since 1997. While the Mainland Authority is obliged not to intervene in the continuity of the legal system and the law in the Hong Kong SAR, the courts of the Hong Kong SAR shall also adhere to the principles set under the Basic Law and use their discretion accordingly in a self-restrained way. I think the restrictions under the Basic Law are mutual. From the rights of abode cases to the *DR Congo* case, it is observed that the Court of Final Appeal began to cooperate with the Standing Committee of the NPC to carry out tasks of interpretation, which flow from the Basic Law. Nevertheless, the dissenting opinions disclosed that cooperation was not conducted in "one voice". I would like to go a bit further to address something about evolvement of the new regional legal system in China. It is a scheme that has to resolve the constitutional conflicts between the Central Authority and the Regions as well as promote cross-border judicial cooperation in matters of civil and commercial disputes. Thus, one of the main problems concerning the regional legal system is how to coordinate "the coexistence autonomous legal orders in the same time–space context" (Twining, 2010), i.e. the legal pluralism between the Mainland and the SARs in order to ensure compliance with the Basic Law. In China's context, it is more difficult to be solved because there is no regional supreme court to adjudicate the disputes caused by the legal pluralism (Chan, 2011). It is expected that the fight will continue because "victory is determined by the shifting loyalties of officials in each particular instance" (Tai, 2002) at their own discretion.

TRUST TOWARDS THE MAINLAND COURTS

Mathews, Ma and Lui remarked that:

> Many people in the world take for granted their national identity, and thus cannot easily examine it critically; they may disagree with their country's policies but their subliminal feeling of rooted attachment to their country – the unexamined sense that they 'naturally' belong to their country.
>
> (Mathews, 2008)

Nevertheless, that is not the case between the Mainland and the SARs. People in the SARs did not acquire their Chinese nationality in a natural way but through political and constitutional arrangements. Against that background, it is unlikely that these "new citizens" can get used to their new identity immediately and have confidence in the Chinese legal system right away, on which they used to cast doubt. When the Mainland and Hong Kong entered into the arrangement of recognition of civil and commercial judgments in 2006, Zhang and Smart mentioned that there had been "deep worries of Hong Kong businessmen" about the rulings rendered by the Mainland courts through questionable means, even through corruption. They also indicated that it was not that easy to prove that kind of foul play, "even when it is obvious" (Zhang & Smart, 2006). Besides, lack of recognition of the judgments rendered in the other regions also poses problems. For instance, in the aforementioned *ML v YJ* case (in Chapter 2), it is evident in the reasoning of the Court of Final Appeal of Hong Kong SAR that non-recognition is a big concern of Hong Kong courts towards the Mainland courts, even in case of a doubt, which can be deemed as one of the legitimate reasons to open parallel civil proceedings in Hong Kong. Nonetheless, China's judicial reform is difficult but ongoing. For instance, Li has conducted empirical research on court corruption in China and, according to her, the latter half of the 1990s witnessed an increase in court corruption and in 1998 the number of court personnel investigated and punished for corruption reached a peak, 2,512 cases in total. But Li also pointed out that the situation is undergoing change and improvement. In the first half of the first decade of the 21st century the number of corruption cases declined (Li, 2010). In 2016, it is stated in the annual work report of the Supreme Court that 575 judges were investigated and punished for corruption and poor performance of their duties and the authorities made a commitment to adhere to zero tolerance and to continue to fight against judicial corruption.[54] In addition, China has taken some measures to improve the quality in handling foreign-related cases and safeguard better judicial independence (Li, 2014). In 2002, the Provisions of the Supreme People's Court on Some Issues Concerning the Jurisdiction of Civil and Commercial Cases Involving Foreign Elements[55] came into effect, which centralized jurisdiction over foreign-related civil and commercial cases to a few designated intermediate people's courts and basic courts. In accordance with that judicial interpretation, the jurisdiction of the people's courts over civil and commercial cases involving parties from Hong Kong, Macao or Taiwan shall refer to this judicial interpretation.[56] Later incorporated into the specialized bilateral arrangements between the Mainland and the SARs, jurisdiction over the recognition and enforcement of a civil or commercial decision rendered by the Hong Kong and Macao courts is designated only to the intermediate people's courts in the Mainland.[57] Therefore, these bilateral arrangements apply a higher threshold to the Mainland courts, which are allowed to exercise jurisdiction over interregional recognition and enforcement petitions. In my view, it reflects the cautious attitude adopted by the Mainland towards the interregional legal cooperation. It is widely accepted that the courts at the basic level are the ones most affected by local protectionism mainly for their reliance on the local financial support from local government (Peerenboom, 2010). The intermediate people's courts, which are at the higher level, can perform a correctional function that is designed to remedy some of the wrongs upon appeal perpetrated at the lower levels. With that kind of function, according to the findings of one of the latest empirical study, Chinese courts at the higher level gain fruitful experience on reducing likely influence caused by judicial local protectionism (Long & Wang, 2015). Accordingly, concentrating jurisdiction over interregional recognition and enforcement in civil and commercial matters to the intermediate people's courts can better ease the concern on the capability and impartiality of the Mainland courts in trying such cases.

Recognition as the main line

As mentioned above, the principles of sincere cooperation and mutual trust are pretty much at the primary stage in China's regional legal system. The compulsory jurisdiction and automatic recognition under the Regulation is built upon those two fundamental principles. Since they are still under construction in China, it is premature to make a direct allocation of jurisdiction under CICIA. In addition, it may not be wise frequently to trigger conflicts of jurisdiction in a country that is undergoing resumption of sovereignty and integration. Instead, the recognition approach on a more flexible basis adopted by the Model Law should thus be regarded as the proper main line. Meanwhile, considering the decisive roles played by those jurisdiction-related concepts, such as COMI, in pursuit of recognition, a functional dispute settlement mechanism is to be set up under CICIA (see Recommendation 8) to ease the possible tension between the rules of recognition and the rules of jurisdiction.

Having taken into consideration recent developments under the EU Regulation (recast), the crucial concepts, such as COMI and establishment, will be introduced into CICIA (Recommendation 4). However, a look-back period as stipulated under the EU Regulation (recast) has not been introduced to assess abusive forum shopping. The reasons are two-fold. First of all, a look-back period is set up for the purpose of prevention of abusive forum shopping under a jurisdiction-dominant regime, which is not a key objective under the Model Law or CICIA. (For the detailed reasons, please refer to Chapter 4, p. 88.) Secondly, to what extent a look-back period can prevent abusive forum shopping and how long a look-back period can be effective and proper still needs to be tested. The look-back period actually has a direct effect on company reincorporation rather than a quick relocation of assets or business. Therefore, if a company was to shift its COMI instead of its registered office within a period of three months prior to a request for insolvency proceedings, it would fall outside the scope of Article 3(1) EIR Recast. That, according to Rudbordeh, would puncture the functionality of the look-back period (Rudbordeh, 2016). Therefore, it is sufficient to define COMI as a pre-insolvency concept to facilitate its assessment. Besides, considering that there may be a gap between the date of the application for commencement of insolvency proceedings and the date of commencement of insolvency proceedings, it is appropriate to refer to the date of commencement for the purposes of COMI determination because CICIA, as a recognition-oriented regime, is concerned only with existing insolvency proceedings. Especially under certain insolvency systems, the effects of commencement are backdated to the date of the application for commencement.[58] Moreover, it has been clearly indicated in the Guiding Principle that CICIA lays emphasis on cooperation and coordination between the main and the non-main proceedings and thus the effect of the opening of the main proceedings is not as extensive as under that the EU Regulation (recast).

Recommendation 3 – form and scope

(1) *Considering China's complex internal structure and desiring more predictability and more legal certainty at the regional level, an interregional cross-border insolvency arrangement (CICIA) is to be established.*

(2) *CICIA is binding on the Mainland and the two SARs altogether. In accordance with CICIA, cross-strait insolvency cooperation between the Mainland and Taiwan is subject to a separate arrangement.*

(3) *CICIA applies only to proceedings where the center of the debtor's main interests (COMI) is located within the Mainland and the two SARs.*

(4) *CICIA shall apply to public collective proceedings, including interim proceedings, in accordance with laws relating to insolvency in which proceedings the assets and affairs of the debtor are under the control or supervision of a court for the purpose of rescue, reorganization or liquidation.*

(5) *CICIA shall not apply to insolvencies concerning natural persons and financial institutions, which are governed by special insolvency regimes in the three regions.*

Comments on recommendation 3

Recommendation 3 examines the proper form of CICIA against China's special political composition and gives the reasons of the extent and the limits of such an arrangement.

A comprehensive interregional arrangement

China in a "group" context

In the course of cross-border insolvency cooperation, convention used to be regarded as the proper form of achieving the goal. Prior to the EU Insolvency Regulation, efforts had been made to introduce conventions into Europe, which were the European Convention on Certain International Aspects of Bankruptcy (i.e. the Istanbul Convention) and the Convention on Insolvency Proceedings. The former was only ratified by one State, Cyprus. The latter did not come into effect due to the retreat of the UK (Fletcher, 2005). Nowadays, it still remains a prominent option. Upon the proposal of the Union, the Internationale des Avocats and support of the International Bar Association (IBA), Working Group V of UNCITRAL has taken into consideration the possibility of developing an international convention in matters of cross-border insolvency.[59] Now the related project is continuing and has been put in the current mandate of Working Group V.[60] Nevertheless, UNCITRAL also raised the concern with respect to "the feasibility of reaching agreement, particularly in view of the difficulties encountered in the past in the area of international insolvency law",[61] such as the aforementioned EU experience. Suppose that the international convention on cross-border insolvency was adopted by UNCITRAL, to which the Mainland, the SARs and

Taiwan all became parties, cooperation on cross-border insolvency among those regions could be solved. Nevertheless, after the People's Republic of China resumed its sovereignty over Hong Kong and Macao respectively in 1997 and 1999, China becomes a country composed of peculiar political compounds, which include Mainland China, Hong Kong SAR and Macao SAR. From then on, Hong Kong and Macao can no longer be treated as "foreign" jurisdictions. As for Taiwan, although there is still political uncertainty, the cross-strait relationship is undergoing changes due to closer economic cooperation (Ramzy, 2014). Consequently, as a "group" composed of four regions, the landscape of China gets complicated when entering into international conventions. For instance, it involves "four Chinas" in the WTO Agreement, i.e. the People's Republic of China, "Hong Kong, China", "Macao, China" as well as "Chinese Taipei", which all enjoy full membership of WTO (HSIEH, 2005; Wu, 2012).

As for conventions concerning legal cooperation, in accordance with the Basic Law, the relationship of China and its SARs to the convention is briefly introduced as follows. (1) If the conventions are implemented in the two SARs prior to the reunion, they may continue to be implemented in the two SARs even if the Mainland is not a party,[62] such as some of the Hague Conventions. (2) There are conventions implemented in the Mainland and also applied to Hong Kong and Macao based on declarations filed by the UK or Portugal prior to the reunification. Whether or not the application of those kinds of conventions can be extended to the SARs should be decided by the Central People's Government, in accordance with the circumstances and needs of the Region, and after seeking the views of the government of the Region.[63] The 1958 New York Convention on the Recognition and Enforcement of Foreign Arbitral Awards (hereinafter the New York Convention) is such an example. Upon resumption of sovereignty over Hong Kong on 1 July, 1997, the Government of China extended the territorial application of the New York Convention to Hong Kong, Special Administrative Region of China, subject to the statement originally made by China upon accession to the Convention. On 19 July. 2005, China declared that the New York Convention shall apply to the Macao SAR of China, subject to the statement originally made by China upon accession to the New York Convention.[64] (3) In addition, there are also conventions that prior to the reunification have applied to the Mainland China but not to Hong Kong and Macao. For example, the United Nations Convention on Contracts for the International Sale of Goods (CISG). As stated on the website of the CISG, so far there is no related depositary notification for the CISG having been filed with the Secretary-General of the United Nations by the People's Republic of China.[65] Therefore, it is still uncertain whether or not the effect of the CISG is extended to the two SARs and there is a risk that the opinions of the courts of other jurisdictions, including the Mainland courts, may vary on the effect of CISG on Hong Kong and for Macao (Schroeter, 2004). With respect to Taiwan, its legal identity is always a problem. Conventions are usually only open for the accession of sovereign states. That is why Taiwan is neither a signatory to the New York Convention[66] nor a member of CISG.[67] Under some circumstances, as stated in the CISG, if a contracting state has two or more territorial units in which, according to its constitution, different systems of law are applicable in relation to the matters dealt with in the convention, it may declare that the convention is to extend to all its territorial units or only to one or more of them.[68] However, it depends on China's consent to granting such an extension and Taiwan's willingness to being China's territorial unit.

Evidently, legal cooperation in the form of an international convention is not that easy to be accepted by China in a "group" context. Even under the circumstances that the international conventions can be implemented in both the Mainland and the two SARs, it is still necessary to make specific regional arrangements since those conventions are only applicable to the "States", which is deemed as inappropriate to deal with the relevant domestic issues and the content should be subject to relevant adjustment. A typical example is the New York Convention. Although both the Mainland and the two SARs are contracting "States" to the New York Convention, mutual arrangements are signed in dealing with the enforcement of arbitral awards among the three regions.[69] It is noteworthy that only one of the most important provisions, Article V of the New York Convention, is almost copied and pasted in each of the three arrangements.[70] However, the rest of the content is different.

Problems of adopting a soft law instrument

As a soft law instrument, although the word "State" occurs in the Model Law regularly, as explained in the Guide to Enactment, the word "State" refers to the entity that enacts the Law.[71] It seems that the neutral explanation of the word "State" under the Model Law is flexible enough to be incorporated into a local legal system. Unlike accession to a convention, once an entity would like to enact the Model Law, it can simply introduce the Model Law into the local legal system without sending related depositary notification to the UN or some other countries. If the four regions adopted the Model Law respectively, a certain degree of harmonization could be achieved. However, for a region that is undergoing integration, would that kind of arrangement be satisfactory? Probably not. The Model Law is not designed for regional cooperation but aims at promoting the efficiency of dealing with cases of the cross-border insolvency on a global level. Considering the diversity of national legislation, the drafters placed text in italics between square brackets to "instruct" the national legislators to complete the text in their own way (Berends, 1998). Although the spirit of the Model Law and the intention of its drafters is that States should make as few changes as possible in incorporating the Model Law into their legal systems to ensure a degree of certainty and predictability, a satisfactory degree of certainty achieved in relation to harmonization is likely to be lower than that resulting from a binding regime[72] since the character of the Model Law, as a soft law instrument, is a recommendation in essence. Moreover, owing to the legislative autonomy of each region in China, it will be up to local authority to decide to what extent they would like to adopt the Model Law and one jurisdiction cannot interfere even if there is deviation from the Model Law in the process of its enactment in others within one country.

A regional cooperation instrument

In Europe, a successful regional cross-border insolvency cooperation regime has been established on the basis of some prerequisites that need to be satisfied in advance. Bariatti remarked that "public international law is at the basis of both the European Law and of many developments of private international law that is comprised of uniform rules established through treaties and international conventions" (Bariatti, 2011). The legislation competence concerning interregional judicial cooperation in civil matters at the Union level gradually derogates from the development of EU treaties. In 1957, it was stipulated in the Treaty establishing the European Economic Community (EEC, repealed, Article 220)

> Member States shall, so far as is necessary, enter into negotiations with each other with a view to securing for the benefit of their nationals.

- the simplification of the formalities governing the reciprocal recognition and execution of judicial decisions and of arbitral awards.

Later in 1992, it was provided in the Treaty of Maastricht on European Union that:

> Article K Cooperation in the fields of justice and home affairs shall be governed by the following provisions.
>
> Article K.1 For the purposes of achieving the objectives of the Union, in particular the free movement of persons, and without prejudice to the powers of the European Community, Member States shall regard the following areas as matters of common interest:
>
> . . .
>
> 6. judicial cooperation in civil matters;
>
> . . .

Later in 1997, pursuant to the Treaty of Amsterdam, the EC acquired legislative competence in cross-border judicial cooperation with respect to civil and commercial cases. Measures in the field of judicial cooperation in civil matters having cross-border implications, to be taken in accordance with Article 67 and in so far as necessary for the proper functioning of the internal market, shall include:

(1) improving and simplifying:

- the system for cross-border service of judicial and extrajudicial documents;
- cooperation in the taking of evidence;
- the recognition and enforcement of decisions in civil and commercial cases, including decisions in extrajudicial cases;

(2) promoting the compatibility of the rules applicable in the Member States concerning the conflict of laws and of jurisdiction;
(3) eliminating obstacles to the good functioning of civil proceedings, if necessary by promoting the compatibility of the rules on civil procedure applicable in the Member States.[73]

In 2012, in accordance with the Treaty on the Functioning of the EU (TFEU), it has been stressed that "The Union shall facilitate access to justice, in particular through the principle of mutual recognition of judicial and extrajudicial decision in civil matters."[74] Moreover, the legislation competence of EU in private international law has been standardized and extended. It is stipulated under the TFEU that

> The Union shall develop judicial cooperation in civil matters having cross-border implications, based on the principle of mutual recognition of judgments and of decisions in extrajudicial cases. Such cooperation may include the adoption of measures for the approximation of the laws and regulations of the Member States.[75]

From a mere possibility to consolidated competence, the evolvement of the Treaties texts has illustrated the growth of "judicial cooperation in civil matters having cross-border implications" at the European Union level. The whole process took over 50 years and is to be continued. Meanwhile, in accordance with the Basic Law, which entered into force over 15 years, the SAR may, through consultations and in accordance with law, maintain juridical relations with the judicial organs of other parts of the country, and they may render assistance to each other.[76] That text of the Basic Law reminds me of the aforementioned text of the EEC signed in 1957, which only provided a possible reference for China's inter-regional legal cooperation.

In the EU, legal cooperation in matters of cross-border insolvency has been achieved in the form of regulation, although there are also other instruments available. Wessels summarized the development of insolvency law on the European level in three periods (Wessels, 2014). In the early period prior to 2002, when the Regulation came into effect, there were only individual national attempts of some Member States by referring to the Directives respectively,[77] which provided some insolvency rules on the EC level. The implementation of the Regulation opened the era of the cross-border period, which enabled interaction between the Regulation and national insolvency law of the Member States as well as inter-connection in matters of cross-border insolvency between the Member States since they are required to grant automatic recognition to the main proceedings opened in other Member States and cooperate and communicate in accordance with the EC Regulation. Recently the third period, proposed by the European Parliament to harmonize the national insolvency law on EU level, has started.[78] Under the Basic Law, both SARs have been granted a high degree of autonomous legislative powers[79] and the three independent jurisdictions are operating parallel to each other with very limited interference from the central authority in one country. In China, the legal instruments available at the regional level include Annex III to the Basic Law and bilateral arrangements. The laws listed in the Annex III are those applicable in the Mainland and shall be applied in the SARs through local promulgation or legislation procedures. Currently the legislation listed in Annex III to the Basic Law of Hong Kong SAR and in Annex III to the Basic Law of Macao SAR have very limited scope, which only covers the matters outside the limits of the autonomy of the SARs, mainly including defense and foreign affairs.[80] Legal cooperation in the field of civil and commercial cases does not fall within the ambit of the mandatory uniform legislation system (Annex III to the Basic Law) in China. Although the Basic Law leaves a window open, which allows the Mainland and the SARs to maintain juridical relations with the judicial organs of each other and may render assistance to each other through consultations,[81] the Basic Law does not specify the proper forms of interregional legal cooperation or provide equivalent instruments as under the EU legal system. That gives rise to the consequence that it is conducted in the form of bilateral arrangements in practice. Those bilateral arrangements take measures on service of judicial documents, exchange of evidence as well as recognition and enforcement of judgments and arbitral awards.

China's complex internal structure, as reflected from its relations with international conventions, makes it necessary to make arrangements for legal cooperation at China's regional level. It is also noteworthy that the word "arrangement" is applied in almost all the agreements, economic or legal, entered into between the Mainland and SARs. As pointed out by Wang, the choice of word is deliberate.

> From the negotiating history of the CEPA, it appears the use of the term 'arrangement' was the result of an understanding between Mainland China and Hong Kong SAR negotiators that most FTAs [Free Trade Agreements] in the world are preferential agreements among states, while the negotiated trade agreement between Mainland China and the Hong Kong SAR was under one country, China. Therefore, based on the principle of the 'one country, two systems,' the agreement [of CEPA] was entitled arrangement.
>
> (Wang, 2004)

Accordingly, CICIA is also entitled "Arrangement". CICIA will not adopt the soft law approach. The reasons are two-fold. First of all, more considerate arrangements can be made exclusively on a region-wide scenario because there are common constitutional arrangements, which provide the legal basis for regional judicial cooperation. Secondly, more predictability and more legal certainty is a reasonable expectation within one country through uniform rules at the regional level for the purpose of maximization of the debtor's assets and protection of the interests of all creditors. The Regulation is an indispensable part of the whole EU legal system. To achieve a comprehensive regional arrangement as the Regulation, there are certain obstacles, such as restricted regional legislation competence and limited regional legislation instruments, that China will have to overcome. Although the Basic Law provides some legal instruments, there is no equivalent mandatory instrument like regulation under the EU law, which is directly applicable throughout the whole region. In China, the relevant measures with respect to legal cooperation can be taken upon consensus and it is also noteworthy that it takes time for the consensus to be reached. The arrangement concerning recognition and enforcement of arbitral awards is such an example. In 1999, the Mainland and Hong Kong SAR entered into the Arrangement Concerning Mutual Enforcement of Arbitral Awards between the Mainland and Hong Kong SAR. Meanwhile, Hong Kong considered that arrangements for mutual enforcement of arbitral awards between Hong Kong and Macao "should be finalized as soon as possible".[82] However, in December 2002, the government provided an information note on the subject, stating that "the absence of such an arrangement should not prejudice the enforcement in Macao of awards made in Hong Kong and the Administration considered it unnecessary to have a separate arrangement for reciprocal enforcement of arbitral awards."[83] In 2007, the Mainland and the Macao SAR concluded the Arrangement Concerning Mutual Recognition and Enforcement of Arbitral Awards. In 2010, the government revisited the need and advantages of entering into an arrangement with Macao on reciprocal enforcement of arbitral awards and considered such an arrangement would be

(a) adding certainty to the enforceability of Macao arbitral awards in Hong Kong and vice versa;
(b) establishing a simple mechanism in both jurisdictions on reciprocal enforcement of arbitral awards;
(c) fostering legal co-operation between Hong Kong and Macao in civil and commercial matters; and
(d) enhancing Hong Kong's role as a regional arbitration center for commercial disputes.[84]

Consequently in 2013 the Hong Kong SAR and the Macao SAR signed the Arrangement Concerning Reciprocal Recognition and Enforcement of Arbitral Awards. Finally, the recognition regime of arbitral awards among the three regions has been interconnected. It is notable that those arrangements are still drafted in a parallel bilateral way. As for CICIA, I submit to take a step further to make a comprehensive interregional cooperation arrangement, which should be binding on the Mainland and the two SARs altogether. Compared to ordinary civil and commercial proceedings, one of the main features of cross-border insolvency proceedings is that they are usually operating parallel in the different jurisdictions at the same time. Hence, it will be more efficient for the courts in the different jurisdictions within one country to refer to the uniform rules as formulated in such an arrangement, which will also provide more legal certainty in the process of cooperation and ensure equal protection of the creditors in different regions.

Taiwan in a separate arrangement

The legal cooperation between the Mainland and the two SARs is based on the constitutional arrangement, i.e. the Basic Law,[85] whereas such a legal basis does not exist between the Mainland and Taiwan. It was not until 2009 that the two sides signed the first mutual agreement in matters of legal cooperation (2009 Agreement between Both Sides of the Taiwan Strait on Jointly Fighting against Crimes and Mutual Judicial Assistance, hereinafter, the 2009 Agreement). As explicitly stated in that agreement, civil judgments and arbitral awards can be recognized based on the principle of reciprocity,[86] whereas the Mainland and the two SARs are suggested to take a step further by adopting the principle of comity. Moreover, in practice, as mentioned above (Chapter 2), Taiwan applies parallel rules in dealing with the recognition of civil judgments rendered in different regions. In accordance with Article 74 of the Mainland Act, irrevocable civil rulings or judgments rendered in the Mainland Area shall not be considered the same validity as irrevocable civil rulings or judgments rendered in Taiwan; whereas irrevocable civil ruling or judgment rendered in Hong Kong and Macao, pursuant to Article 42-I of Hong Kong and Macao Act, shall be automatically recognized (Wu, 2011). Although the 2009 Agreement came into effect,[87] it did not really solve the problem. The reasons are two-fold. Firstly, this agreement serves merely as a very general guideline for the cross-strait legal cooperation since its content is general and broad, composed of 24 articles, which covered both criminal and civil cases. In addition, it does not specify the scope of application, i.e. whether or not the insolvency proceeding can be included in the ambit of civil judgments. Secondly, in order to implement the 2009 Agreement, the Supreme People's Court has issued the relevant judicial interpretation with respect to recognition of Taiwan civil judgments.[88] As for Taiwan, recall the protest against ECFA (Chapter 2), which cast doubt on the nature of those cross-strait agreements and what should be the relevant due process in passing them. If they are regarded as treaties, it is stated under the Judicial Yuan Interpretation No. 329 that:

> Within the Constitution, 'treaty' means an international agreement concluded between the R.O.C. and other nations or international organizations whose title may apply to a treaty, convention or an agreement. Its content involves important issues of the Nation or rights and duties of the people and its legality is sustained. Such agreements, which employ the title of 'treaty,' 'convention' or 'agreement' and have ratification clauses, should be sent to the Legislative Yuan for deliberation. Other international agreements, except those authorized by laws or pre-determined by the Legislative Yuan, should also be sent to the Legislative Yuan for deliberation.

Meanwhile, it is stipulated under the Act Governing Relations between the People of the Taiwan Area and the Mainland Area, the agreement document involving the exercise of governmental powers or any matter of political issues, and executed between the Taiwan Area and the Mainland Area shall be submitted to the Executive Yuan for approval and to the Legislative Yuan for record, with a confidential procedure if necessary, where its content does not require any amendment to laws or any new legislation.[89] All those aforementioned cross-strait agreements, including the 2009 Agreement, were passed or intended to be passed in accordance with the Act Governing Relations between People of the Taiwan Area and the Mainland Area, which means, merely through administrative procedure instead of with the consent of parliament. Aware of the problem of procedural legality and also in response to the local turmoil, on 3 April, 2014, the Taiwan government issued the draft of the Regulations on Treatment and Supervision of the Agreements Reached between the

Taiwan Area and the Mainland Area and submitted it to parliament for review. On 6 April, 2014, the President of parliament made the statement that the Cross-strait Trade in Service Agreement would not be discussed in parliament unless the Regulations on Treatment and Supervision of the Agreements Reached between the Taiwan Area and the Mainland Area was passed (Wang, 2014), which remains a draft at the present time. Once passed, the possible influence on the validity of all the cross-strait agreements, including the 2009 Agreement as well as the ECFA, will still need to be observed. Moreover, once passed, the Regulations on Treatment and Supervision of the Agreements Reached between the Taiwan Area and the Mainland Area will serve as the new legal basis for future cross-strait coopera-tion. Although Taiwan is also engaged in economic cooperation with the Mainland, there is still a lack of a mutually accepted legal basis, such as the Basic Law, to ensure the involve-ment of Taiwan in an integrated regional legal cooperation arrangement at this moment. In addition, considering the political reality and the public opinion on the cross-strait relation-ship, cross-strait insolvency cooperation has to be treated in a different manner.

Scope of application

Intra-regional effects only

CICIA established on the basis of a common constitutional foundation shall apply only to intra-regional insolvency proceedings. The center of the debtor's main interests should be located in the Mainland, Hong Kong SAR or Macao SAR. If COMI of the debtor is located in one of the three regions but the debtor operates its establishment outside, CICIA remains applicable for the purposes of recognition of the main proceedings within the three regions.

Definition of insolvency proceedings

The proceedings governed by CICIA should be collective in nature. Any individual action will be precluded because that will result in inefficient realization of the debtor's assets and damage to the creditor's interests as a whole. Hence, the participation in distribution system, which encourages creditors to individually grab the assets under no obligation to share with other creditors and thus decline to file an insolvency petition, should be excluded from the scope of application of CICIA. It is also required under both the EU Regulation (recast) and the Model Law that the insolvency proceedings should be collec-tive proceedings.[90] The difference is the insolvency proceedings are exhaustively listed in Annex A to the EU Regulation (recast).[91] Given the fact that the regions that will enter into CICIA are certain, it is suggested that such an Annex can also be set up to provide greater legal certainty. All kinds of collective proceedings, regardless of whether for the purpose of reorganization or liquidation or interim proceedings should be covered by CICIA. It has been witnessed that the focus of the Regulation has shifted from liquidation and divestment of the debtor's assets[92] to "the rescue of economically viable but distressed businesses and which give a second chance to entrepreneurs".[93] That is also the trend at work in China. In the Mainland, several judicial interpretations have been issued by the Supreme People's Court in matters of reorganization of enterprises, including the Notice of the Supreme People's Court on the Summary of Minutes of the Symposium on the Trial of Cases concerning Reorganization of Listed Companies,[94] Instructive Opinions of the Supreme People's Court on Judicial Safeguards Provided by the People's Court for

Enterprises Mergers and Acquisitions and Reorganization,[95] Opinions of the Supreme People's Court on Equal Protection of Non-state Owned Economy and Promotion of Sound Development of Non-state Owned Economy.[96] All of them consider reorganization as an effective mechanism and encourage enterprises in crisis to make full use of reorganization to restore their business vitality.[97] In Hong Kong, a new statutory company rescue regime was proposed to improve Hong Kong's current corporate insolvency law regime in 2014.[98] In Taiwan, the Draft Debt Clearance Act, which was approved by Judicial Yuan in 2015, added a new chapter of reorganization to the new insolvency law.[99] The collective proceedings should be based on a law relating to insolvency. With respect to this criterion, the EU Regulation (recast) has set up a more restrictive requirement than the Model Law, which requires that proceedings are not qualified as pursuant to laws relating to insolvency unless they are designed exclusively for insolvency situations.[100] Hence, UK schemes of arrangement based on the Companies Act 2006, s 885 are beyond the scope of the recast Regulation. In practice, schemes of arrangement have been utilized to restructure their business in the UK by incorporating choice of law and choice of jurisdiction clauses into the underlying agreement,[101] whereas those companies in fact have no clear links to the UK. As a common law jurisdiction that was deeply influenced by the UK legal system, Hong Kong has also adopted the schemes of arrangement. That kind of restructure strategy also becomes workable in Hong Kong due to the recent decision handed down by the High Court of Hong Kong SAR.[102] Moreover, without a statutory company rescue regime, corporate rescue currently can only be brought about through the procedure of a scheme of arrangement pursuant to the Companies Ordinance.[103] Nowadays, more and more foreign companies doing business in China choose a dual company governance structure (Lee, 2015), which is composed of the onshore operation and the offshore operation. Hong Kong is always chosen as an intermediate place of incorporation in order to connect onshore operations with the offshore operations for more preferential tax rates (Daljit & Susarla, 2011, 2011), which can always be deemed as a sufficient connection with Hong Kong. Although schemes of arrangement indeed address insolvency issues, as told by the case law, its flexibility will make the jurisdiction concerning cross-border insolvency exercised by the Hong Kong Court way too extensive, which in essence contravenes the rule of assessment of COMI. Therefore, once the statutory company rescue regime is built up in Hong Kong, it is suggested to adopt the European approach, which requires that proceedings should be narrowed down to a law designed exclusively for insolvency situations. The collective proceedings should be subject to control or supervision by a court. To properly understand the meaning of "control or supervision by a court", the Guide and Interpretation should be referred to because the EU Regulation (recast) does not provide any specified rules. First of all, a proceeding in which the debtor retains some measure of control over its assets, albeit under court supervision, such as a debtor-in-possession would fulfill the condition.[104] In addition, indirect control or supervision exercised by an actor, such as an insolvency representative, who is subject to control or supervision by the court, can qualify as well.[105] As for the proper time of control or supervision, it recognizes that expedited reorganization proceedings, which need control or supervision by a court at a late stage of the insolvency process, should also be counted in.[106] Last but not least, fully aware of the importance of disclosure of information to the creditors and to preserve the collective nature of the proceedings, CICIA does not allow any confidential proceedings to be recognized and attempts to establish an interregional case register to facilitate exchange of information. In accordance with CICIA, insolvency proceedings should be public.

Exclusion

Personal insolvency

It is suggested to exclude personal insolvency from CICIA. Although a natural person can be declared bankrupt in Hong Kong,[107] Macao[108] and Taiwan,[109] there is no personal insolvency system in the Mainland. The reason was ascribed to the lack of an adequate personal property registered system and a sound social credit environment (Liu, 2011). Instead, as aforementioned, it is the participation in distribution system that takes its place, which cannot be regarded as insolvency proceedings under the proposed regional cross-border insolvency arrangement. As a system related to more fundamental questions about personal exemptions and discharge, it might be quite difficult to persuade the Mainland to accept a cross-border insolvency cooperation system including personal insolvency, which is a system that has not been established there. Moreover, it is also better to start the cooperation with something in common, i.e. corporate insolvency.

Financial institutions

In China, financial institutions are governed by different specialized rules, depending on the types of activities they perform. In the Mainland, in the event that a financial institution, such as a commercial bank, securities company, insurance company, is insolvent, it is the administrative regulations, instead of the EBL, that come into play.[110] In Hong Kong SAR, if a financial institute suffers a serious deterioration in its financial condition, the responsible regulatory authorities, in particular the Monetary Authority, Securities and Futures Commission and Insurance Authority, will initiate a set of supervisory intervention powers to carry out resolutions in accordance with the respective ordinances.[111] In Macao SAR, the Monetary and Foreign Exchange Authority of Macao (AMCM) is responsible for supervision of monetary and financial operations, in particular monitoring the performance of banking and insurance industries and taking relevant rescue measures, in accordance with the specialized rules.[112] The methods of resolution of the Taiwanese financial institutions are scattered in relevant laws and regulations, such as the Insurance Act, the Insurance Deposit Act, the Banking Act, the Financial Institutions Merger Act, the Financial Holding Company Act etc. Financial institutions have not been included in corporate insolvency systems because they relate to vital interests of a large number of individuals that need to be prudentially supervised and protected, which usually requires particularly prompt action. In the context of cross-border insolvency, both the Regulation and the Model Law also exclude financial institutions from their scopes of application.[113] Therefore, it is suggested that financial institutions are also exempted from the scope of application under CICIA.

Recommendation 4 – recognition and reliefs

(1) *An insolvency proceeding commenced in one region, that with respect to the debtor concerned, has the relevant international jurisdiction should be recognized as main or non-main insolvency proceeding and given appropriate effect under the circumstances in every other region.*

(2) *The courts of one region within the territory of which the center of the debtor's main interests is situated shall have jurisdiction to open main insolvency proceedings.*

(3) *The place of the registered office shall be presumed to be the COMI in the absence of proof to the contrary.*

> *It should be possible to rebut this presumption where the debtor's central administration is located in a region other than that of its registered office, and where a comprehensive assessment of all the relevant factors establishes, in a manner that is ascertainable by third parties, that the debtor's actual center of management and supervision and of the management of its interests is located in that other region.*
> *The relevant date at which COMI shall be determined is the date of commencement of the main insolvency proceedings.*

(4) *The courts of another region shall have jurisdiction to open a non-main insolvency proceedings against the debtor if it possesses an establishment within the territory of that other region.*

(5) *Establishment means any place of operations where a debtor carries out a non-transitory economic activity with human means and assets.*

> *The relevant date at which an establishment of the debtor shall be determined is the date of commencement of the non-main insolvency proceedings.*

(6) *Upon recognition of an insolvency proceeding as a main proceeding:*

> (a) *Commencement or continuation of individual actions or individual proceedings concerning the debtor's assets, rights, obligations or liabilities is stayed; but the stay does not affect the right to commence individual actions or proceedings to the extent necessary to preserve a claim against the debtor;*
> (b) *Execution against the debtor's assets is stayed; and*
> (c) *The right to transfer, encumber or otherwise dispose of any assets of the debtor is suspended.*
>
>> *The scope, modification or termination of those aforementioned reliefs is subject to the law of the region where recognition and reliefs are sought. Those aforementioned reliefs do not affect the right to request the opening of an insolvency proceeding in the region where recognition and reliefs are sought.*

(7) *The following interim reliefs may be granted upon request of the insolvency practitioners in the main or non-main proceedings, from the time of filing an application for recognition until the application is decided upon:*

> (a) *Staying execution against the debtor's assets;*
> (b) *Entrusting the administration or realization of all or part of the debtor's assets located in the region to the insolvency practitioner in the main or non-main proceedings, in order to protect and preserve the value of assets*
>
>> *The interim reliefs can be refused to be granted if they would interfere with the administration of a main insolvency proceeding and unless extended, they terminate when the application for recognition is decided upon.*

(8) *Upon recognition of an insolvency proceeding, whether main or non-main, the court may, at the request of the insolvency practitioners in the main or non-main proceedings, grant any appropriate relief that may be available under the laws of this region where recognition and reliefs are sought.*

Comments on recommendation 4

In accordance with the recognition-based approach set up under the overriding objective (Recommendation 2), Recommendation 4 provides the rules of recognition and reliefs mainly by referring to the relevant rules under the Model Law. Jurisdiction only serves as the basis for recognition as main or non-main proceedings, upon recognition of which different reliefs shall be granted accordingly. In the comments, the fundamental principle of recognition and the reasons of choice of reliefs under CICIA will be demonstrated.

Comity as foundation for recognition

Recognition results in the effects of foreign law rendered by a foreign court entering into the sovereignty of the receiving State. Therefore, recognition in essence invokes an evaluation process of whether or not to defer to the laws of a foreign State in any given situation (Schuz, 2015). UNCITRAL acknowledges there are two legal bases for international cooperation in the area of cross-border insolvency: reciprocity and comity.[114] Although one of the key objectives of the Model Law is to establish simplified procedures for recognition of qualifying foreign insolvency proceedings,[115] the evaluation process cannot be waived either on the basis of reciprocity or comity. Reciprocity was specially suggested as a requirement for recognition on more than one occasion in the negotiations that resulted in the Model Law and it was rejected by overwhelming consensus each time (Clift, 2004). Nevertheless, among the 43 jurisdictions enacting the Model Law, there are five of them, which have eventually adopted the reciprocal treatment *de jure* or *de facto* – the British Virgin Islands,[116] Mauritius,[117] Mexico,[118] Romania[119] and South Africa.[120] The doctrine of comity prevails in common law jurisdictions.[121] What is comity? Comity has been described as "the vague and amorphous body of rules and principles which are not legally binding but which are regularly applied in dealings between states and their authorities . . . whose essence lies in mutual respect and accommodation between states and their interests" (Cane & Conaghan, 2008). Comity is also a "complex and elusive" concept (Yamauchi, 2007),[122] which courts have attempted to define for more than a century but have never formed a workable definition (Janis, 2012). A landmark decision was handed down by Judge Gray of the US Supreme Court in *Hilton v Guyot*, who explained comity as follows:

> Comity, in the legal sense, is neither a matter of absolute obligation on the one hand, nor of mere courtesy and good will upon the other. But it is the recognition which one nation allows within its territory to the legislative, executive, or judicial acts of another nation, having due regard both to international duty and convenience and to the rights of its own citizens or of other persons who are under the protection of its laws.[123]

In practice, a court will not hesitate to refuse comity if "according comity is contrary or prejudicial to the interests of the nation called upon to extend its effects".[124] For all those descriptions, comity would not be qualified as a reliable basis for recognition of cross-border insolvency proceedings. According to Paul, however, it is the imprecision and vagueness that has allowed the doctrine of international comity to "mutate over time in ways that respond to different geopolitical circumstances" (Paul, 2008). On the basis of mutual trust, the Regulation provides a simplified mechanism, which allows automatic recognition of opening of insolvency proceedings between Member States in the EU. It also entails that the decision of the first court to open proceedings should be recognized in the other

Member States without those Member States having the power to scrutinize that court's decision.[125] In short, the principle of mutual trust waives the right of the Member States to evaluate whether or not to grant recognition by referring to their internal rules. According to Wessels, both mutual trust and comity have their "shared historic roots in the 17th century Dutch doctrine of 'comitas gentium'" (Wessels, 2005). As indicated by Omar, the principle of mutual trust "has acceptance in the United Kingdom, where it is referred to as the comity principle, although lately the courts have also begun to refer to a doctrine of obligation" (Omar, 2004). It seems that mutual trust within the EU is a strengthened version of comity, which turns the latter from a discrete element into an obligation of respect.

The recognition mechanism under CICIA is built up among the regions where the regional legal order and mutual trust is still under construction and meanwhile some jurisdiction strictly adheres to the principle of reciprocity, such as the Mainland in handling cross-border insolvency cases (see Chapter 3). Considering that the principle of reciprocity, which the Model Law tried to get rid of, could result in a stalemate or retaliatory action concerning recognition and thus goes against the purposes of closer cooperation within a country where integration is ongoing, a balanced solution between mutual trust (strengthened comity) and reciprocity thus needs to be sought on the basis of the flexible nature of comity. Therefore, the recognition mechanism under CICIA sets out jurisdiction as the sole criterion for recognition, as required under the Model Law. According to the doctrine of comity, the judgment concerning the opening of the insolvency proceeding should be recognized based on the respect of one jurisdiction for another (Paul, 2008). Given the fact that comity is a weaker foundation than mutual trust (strengthened comity), a functional dispute settlement mechanism (Recommendation 8) will be introduced into CICIA, which helps to reconcile the conflicts invoked by jurisdiction and safeguard coherent interpretation on crucial provisions, such as COMI. In addition, the functional dispute settlement mechanism is designed in a way that the disputes should be settled down through judicial negotiation and discussion between the Mainland and the SARs on an equal footing, which will contribute to build up mutual respect that is at the core of this idea of comity.

Intentional lack of uniform choice of law rules

CICIA does not provide uniform choice of law rules. From the technical perspective, as addressed by UNCITRAL, it is difficult to find a reconciled solution to uniform choice of law rules due to lack of harmony among diverse local insolvency laws (Clift, 2009). Besides, insolvency systems in different jurisdictions in China are still undergoing development, such as Hong Kong SAR and Taiwan. Accordingly, relevant rules including priority rules, security interests, avoidance of transactions, are still under reform, which makes harmony even more difficult at this moment. In addition, there is a tendency of convergence between harmonization of substantive law and uniform choice of law rules. As remarked by Bridge, "it is a fallacy to believe that uniform substantive law and choice of law are mutually exclusive processes". In accordance with the Basic Law, the SARs are granted legislative power[126] and national laws are not directly applicable to the SARs unless those laws stay outside the limits of the autonomy of the SARs and are listed in the Annex to the Basic Law.[127] Therefore, the interaction of legislation between the Mainland and SARs needs to proceed with due caution. That is why there is no uniform conflict of law rules under the current bilateral legal cooperation arrangement between the Mainland and SARs, in particular in matters of recognition and enforcement of civil and commercial judgments. Without equivalent solid legal foundation for harmony or approximation of laws as in the EU,[128] consensus upon uniform choice of law rules between the Mainland and SARs is necessary, which depends on one region's view on the other regions' law as well as on a number of relevant social, political, financial, and other considerations. Given the fact that the mutual trust between the Mainland and SARs is still under construction, it will probably take a while before such a consensus can be reached.

Minimum reliefs

Without safeguard of uniform choice of law rules, the effects of insolvency proceedings are guaranteed by a list of minimum reliefs pursuant CICIA. The reliefs under the Model Law have been used to a great degree for reference, which are composed of automatic reliefs and discretionary reliefs. Automatic reliefs are mandatory and solely granted upon recognition of the main proceedings alone. Notwithstanding the "automatic" or "mandatory" nature, the automatic reliefs upon recognition of the main proceedings might be subject to certain exceptions, limitations, modifications or termination in accordance with the law of the region where recognition is sought. Discretionary reliefs include provisional reliefs and any appropriate reliefs available upon recognition under the laws of the region where recognition is sought. When deciding whether or not to grant discretionary relief, an issue arises regarding whether the laws can also refer to private international law in that region. As addressed by Fletcher in the context of the Regulation, the law shall only refer to the substantive domestic law of the Member State concerned. Otherwise, it will allow recourse to *renvoi*, which would be inconsistent with "the very objective of harmonization of choice of law rules" under the Regulation (Moss, Fletcher & Isaacs, 2016). Therefore, it is suggested that private international law shall be excluded from the references of the local laws, on the basis of which the discretionary reliefs can be granted so as to prevent the application of *renvoi* and reduce complexity and uncertainty in the course of implementation of CICIA.

Recommendation 5 – public policy

Any region may refuse to recognize insolvency proceedings opened in another region or to enforce a judgment handed down in the context of such proceedings where the effects of such recognition or enforcement would be manifestly contrary to that region's public policy, in particular its fundamental principles or the constitutional rights and liberties of its citizens.

Comments on recommendation 5

Recommendation 5 provides the only negative condition of recognition, which is public policy. The proper degree of discretion on application of public policy will be discussed from both international and domestic perspectives. As a bar to recognition and enforcement of cross-border insolvency proceedings, public policy has been incorporated into both the Regulation and the Model Law. The difference is public policy is interpreted by the CJEU in a very restrictive manner and is expected to be applied in exceptional cases in the EU.[129] Whereas the scope of public policy under the Model Law is considered broader and public policy has been more frequently triggered to refuse to grant reliefs in particular on the basis of its substantive contents in its enacting states (see Chapter 4).

In the EU, the Member States are allowed an area of discretion within the limits imposed by the Treaty. Nevertheless, the CJEU has in fact played the role of supervisor in guiding the Member States to invoke their public policy exception. It has been observed by

Kessedjian that the CJEU no longer hesitates, if it ever did, to look over the shoulder of the Member States and to decide whether a rule that a Member State considers to be mandatory and covered by the public policy exception does indeed qualify to be characterized as such (Kessedjian, 2007). In the case of *Régina v Pierre Bouchereau*, the CJEU held:

> recourse by a national authority to the concept of public policy presupposes, in any event, the existence, in addition to the perturbation of the social order which any infringement of the law involves, of a genuine and sufficiently serious threat to the requirements of public policy affecting one of the fundamental interests of society.[130]

With respect to recognition of civil and commercial cases, the CJEU has repeatedly stressed that:

> Recourse to the clause on public policy in Article 27, point 1, of the Convention can be envisaged only where recognition or enforcement of the judgment delivered in another Contracting State would be at variance to an unacceptable degree with the legal order of the State in which enforcement is sought inasmuch as it infringes a fundamental principle. In order for the prohibition of any review of the foreign judgment as to its substance to be observed, the infringement would have to constitute a manifest breach of a rule of law regarded as essential in the legal order of the State in which enforcement is sought or of a right recognized as being fundamental within that legal order.[131]

It is also indicated in the *Eurofood* case that:

> Considering itself competent to review the limits within which the courts of a Contracting State may have recourse to that concept for the purpose of refusing recognition to a judgment emanating from a court in another Contracting State, the Court of Justice had held, in the context of the Brussels Convention, that recourse to that clause can be envisaged only where recognition or enforcement of the judgment delivered in another Contracting State would be at variance to an unacceptable degree with the legal order of the State in which enforcement is sought inasmuch as it infringes a fundamental principle. The infringement would have to constitute a manifest breach of a rule of law regarded as essential in the legal order of the State in which enforcement is sought or of a right recognized as being fundamental within that legal order.[132]

Although the concept of public policy may vary from one State to another, the continuous efforts of the CJEU have gradually cultivated a consensus that the Member States are very self-restrained in invoking the public policy exception to a very limited extent (Hess/Pfeiffer, 2011). As pointed out by UNICTRAL, there is a dichotomy between the notion of public policy under the domestic law and the notion of public policy as it applies to recognition of the effects of foreign laws. It is emphasized that public policy in the context of international cooperation should be understood more restrictively than domestic public policy.[133] Therefore, a broader understanding and application of public policy to protect local interests is also inconsistent with the genuine intent of the Model Law. Unfortunately, harmonization is "never complete because divergent judicial interpretations create new conflicts" (Fauvarque-Cosson, 2001). The Model Law lacks adjustment mechanism as provided by the CJEU in promoting decisional harmony on coherent interpretation, which results in deviation in practice (Dawson, 2015).

Public policy is an ambiguous and elusive concept. Especially in the Mainland, different terms concerning public policy have been applied, such as fundamental principles of law, state sovereignty and security, socio-public interests, which can probably bring about more problems with respect to proper interpretation. To unify the application of public policy, the Supreme People's Court has taken some measures. For example, Notice on Several Issues Concerning the People's Court's Handling Relevant Affairs to the Foreign or Foreign-Related Arbitration was issued in 1995.[134] It provides that if a lower court decides to refuse to recognize a foreign arbitral award, it should report the case to a corresponding High People's Court for review before the decision is handed down. If the High People's Court accords with the lower court and also declines to recognize the foreign arbitral award, it should report its decision to the Supreme People's Court. Before the Supreme People's Court gives its reply, the refusal decision cannot be handed down.[135] The "Report Mechanism", according to He's case study, which has guided the application of public policy to recognition of foreign arbitral awards, has been conducted in a self-restrained manner (He, 2013). Two merits can be concluded from that mechanism. First of all, it helps to distinguish external from internal public policies expressed in domestic laws. Secondly, it gradually makes clear what constitutes violation of public policies in the context of foreign arbitral awards. Under CICIA, it is suggested to apply a more restrictive interpretation of public policy on a regional level in cross-border insolvency cooperation. Meanwhile, a functional dispute settlement mechanism is to be established (see Recommendation 8) to safeguard harmonious understanding of the provisions, including public policy.

Recommendation 6 – cooperation and communication (single debtor and enterprise groups)

(1) *An insolvency practitioner shall, in the exercise of its functions and subject to the supervision of the court, cooperate and communicate to the maximum extent possible with the courts or insolvency practitioners in other regions.*

(2) *Where insolvency proceedings relate to two or more members of a group of companies, an insolvency practitioner appointed in proceedings concerning a member of the group shall cooperate and communicate with the courts and any insolvency practitioner appointed in proceedings concerning another member of the same group to the maximum extent possible.*

Comments on recommendation 6

Recommendation 6 addresses the issue of cooperation and communication. Considering the legal basis and forms of the current legal cooperation between the Mainland and the SARs, it will be explained why direct court-to-court cooperation and communication is not workable in China's context and proposes a balanced solution.

Legal basis

Considering the significant supervisory role of courts in the insolvency proceedings,[136] cooperation and communication between the courts is regarded as "an essential element"[137] of the coordination of cross-border insolvency proceedings. The problem is whether there is sufficient legal basis to support this kind of cooperation and communication in China.

The Basic Law provides the fundamental legal basis for judicial cooperation between the Mainland and the SARs,[138] which contributes to closer cooperation between the courts within one country. In practice, there is court-to-court cooperation between the Mainland and the SARs, which is stipulated under the bilateral legal cooperation arrangements in civil and commercial matters, including service of judicial documents, taking of evidence and recognition and enforcement of civil and commercial judgments.

Court-to-court cooperation and communication in practice

Service of judicial documents

The Mainland China, Hong Kong SAR and Macao SAR are all Contracting Parties to the Convention on the Service Abroad of Judicial and Extrajudicial Documents in Civil or Commercial Matters (hereinafter, the Hague Service Convention) In accordance with the Hague Service Convention, the main channel to accept the request of service of the documents is through the Central Authority designated by the respective Contracting Parties,[139] who are the Ministry of Justice in the Mainland China, the Chief Secretary for Administration in Hong Kong SAR and the Procuratorate of the Macao Special Administrative Region. Founded on the Basic Law, bilateral arrangements with respect to service of documents in civil and commercial matters were entered into between the Mainland and the two SARs, in which it is stipulated that the service of judicial documents shall be conducted in a court-to-court manner.[140] Requests for service of judicial documents shall be made through the various High People's Courts in the Mainland and the High Court of the Hong Kong SAR or the Court of Final Appeal of Macao SAR. The Supreme People's Court in the Mainland can make direct requests to the High Court of the Hong Kong SAR and the Court of Final Appeal of Macao SAR for service of judicial documents.[141]

Taking of evidence

With respect to the taking of evidence, the situation becomes more complicated. The Mainland, Hong Kong SAR and Macao SAR are all Contracting Parties to the Convention on the Taking of Evidence Abroad in Civil or Commercial Matters (hereinafter the Hague Evidence Convention). Under most circumstances, a judicial authority of a Contracting State will send a letter of request to the Central Authority designated by another Contracting State to obtain evidence.[142] The Central Authorities designated according to the Hague Evidence Convention are the same as under the Hague Service Convention. Between the Mainland and the Macao SAR, requests for taking of evidence shall be conducted in a court-to-court way like that under the bilateral arrangement of service of judicial documents.[143] In practice, it occurred that certain High People's Court in the Mainland sent requests directly to the Hong Kong SAR for assistance in investigation and taking of evidence.[144] Therefore, in 2013, the Supreme People's Court issued a notice in order to instruct the people's courts in the Mainland to properly handle the Hong Kong related judicial assistance in matters of investigation and taking of evidence (Notice of the Supreme People's Court on Further Regulating the Work of People's Courts concerning Hong Kong Related Judicial Assistance in Matters of Investigation and Taking of Evidence, the Notice). It is stipulated under the Notice that before any bilateral arrangement has been made between the Mainland and the Hong Kong SAR, any local people's court may not directly make a request for assistance in investigation and taking of evidence to the Hong Kong SAR or directly accept any request for assistance in investigation and taking of evidence from the Hong Kong SAR. Requests for taking of evidence and investigation of the local people's court shall be submitted level by level to the Supreme People's Court for approval and forwarded through the Hong Kong and Macao Affairs Office of the State Council in the Mainland to the Government of the Hong Kong SAR and vice versa.[145] In December 2016, the Mainland and the Hong Kong SAR entered into the Arrangement on Mutual Taking of Evidence in Civil and Commercial Matters between the Courts of the Mainland and the Hong Kong SAR, which came into effect on 1 March, 2017. The Higher People's Courts are designated as the liaison authorities of the Mainland and their counterpart in Hong Kong SAR is the Administration Wing of the Chief Secretary for Administration's Office of the Hong Kong SAR Government. The parties must make requests for the taking of evidence through their respective designated liaison authorities. In addition, the Supreme People's Court may request the taking of evidence directly through the designated liaison authority of the Hong Kong SAR.[146] Different from the arrangement between the Mainland and the Macao SAR, the arrangement between Mainland and Hong Kong SAR is not direct court-to-court cooperation but through the designated liaison authorities, in particular via the administrative office from the Hong Kong side.

Recognition and enforcement of civil and commercial judgments

An unbalanced situation also exists in the bilateral arrangements with respect to recognition and enforcement of civil and commercial judgments. Under the Mainland and Macao SAR arrangement, the courts of one side can request the other side to verify the genuineness of the judgment.[147] In order to implement the arrangement, the Supreme People's Court and the Court of Final Appeal of Macao shall mutually provide the relevant legal materials. The Supreme People's Court and the Court of Final Appeal of Macao shall mutually circulate the notice on the enforcement of the arrangement every year.[148] That was remarked by Zhang and Smart as "a cross-border cooperative scheme" established under the Mainland and Macao SAR arrangement, which was "not considered appropriate to help to mediate the sharp disparities between common law system in Hong Kong and the Mainland legal system" (Zhang & Smart, 2006).

Courts as supervisors

It suffices to say that the legal foundation provided under the Basic Law can establish direct court-to-court cooperation and communication, such as bilateral judicial assistance in accordance with the Mainland and Macao arrangements. However, it cannot be deemed as a guarantee if either side is not yet ready to cooperate. Considering the absence of court-to-court cooperation and communication pursuant to the Mainland and the Hong Kong arrangements, the willingness of the courts between civil and common law jurisdictions to conduct direct cooperation and communication becomes a key obstacle that needs to be faced. To find a balanced solution between limits on direct cooperation and communication and the courts as an essential element in supervising coordination, it is suggested that the courts under CICIA play the role of supervisors, which monitor cooperation and communication actions conducted by insolvency practitioners. For example, as to be discussed in Recommendation 7, cooperation and communication between insolvency practitioners is designed in the form of cross-border insolvency agreements under CICIA, which shall be approved by the courts.

Recommendation 7 – cross-border insolvency agreements

(1) *In the course of cooperation and communication, insolvency practitioners, who are subject to the jurisdiction of their own courts, can cooperate with each other closely to enter into cross-border insolvency agreements, which shall be approved by the courts.*

(2) *The independence, sovereignty or jurisdiction of the relevant local courts should not be affected by the agreement.*

(3) *The agreement concluded can cover the following basic content:*

    (a) *Allocation of responsibilities between the different courts involved and between insolvency practitioners; including limitations on authority to act without the approval of the other courts or insolvency practitioners;*

    (b) *methods of communication, including language, frequency and means;*

    (c) *sharing of information on claims lodged, the verification and disputes concerning claims;*

    (d) *location, use and disposal of assets;*

    (e) *coordination and harmonization of reorganization plans;*

    (f) *costs and fees;*

    (g) *all other elements that can contribute to efficient coordination of interregional insolvency proceedings.*

        If the courts or the insolvency practitioners after discussion find something useful to add beyond the aforementioned scope, they shall not be limited as long as it is not inconsistent with the local mandatory rules.

(4) *In matters of enterprise groups, the agreement can include:*

    (a) *means of timely communication of any relevant information concerning the group members subject to insolvency proceedings, provided appropriate arrangements are made to protect confidential information;*

    (b) *coordination of the administration and supervision of the affairs of the group members subject to insolvency proceedings;*

    (c) *coordination of the proposal and of reorganization plans;*

    (d) *allocation of powers or responsibilities between insolvency practitioners;*

    (e) *costs and fees;*

    (f) *all other elements that can contribute to efficient coordination of interregional group insolvency proceedings.*

        If the courts or the insolvency practitioners after discussion find something useful to add beyond the aforementioned scope, they shall not be limited as long as it is not inconsistent with the local mandatory rules.

(5) *Complementary cross-border insolvency agreements shall also be allowed to address some issues upon prompt need on an ad hoc basis.*

Comments on recommendation 7

Recommendation 7 provides rules concerning cross-border insolvency agreements. It will examine the inherent features and possible contents of cross-border insolvency agreements under CICIA. It will also explain the incompatibility of a single insolvency practitioner for coordination of group insolvency proceedings in China's context and further discuss the possibility of complementary agreements.

Features of cross-border insolvency agreements

Among various communication and cooperation instruments provided in accordance with the prevailing relevant international insolvency regimes, including the EU Regulation (recast), the UNCITRAL Model Law, the UNCITRAL Practice Guide on Cross-border Insolvency Cooperation, the UNCITRAL Legislative Guide on Insolvency Law: Part III Treatment of Enterprise Groups in Insolvency, the Global Principles and the EU JudgeCo Principles, the cross-border insolvency agreement is the coordinating tool explicitly recommended under all of them.

As an instrument developed from the practice, the outstanding merit of a cross-border insolvency agreement is its flexibility. Ehricke cast doubt on the flexibility of a cross-border insolvency agreement and considered that the agreement entered into in advance might not be able to address the unexpected issues in the course of proceedings or deal with unforeseen events (Ehricke, 2005). To ease the concern about flexibility, it has to be pointed out other significant features of cross-border insolvency agreements. Due to inadequacy of cooperation and communication rules, cross-border insolvency agreements were invented by insolvency practitioners as the alternative solution, which could also generate binding effects. With the development of cooperation and communication in practice, a cross-border insolvency agreement is no longer a pure coordinating instrument but gradually evolves into a medium, which contains a framework of coordination as well as a combination of coordinating instruments and facilitates them to function in an orderly manner. As for the potential disputes arising in the course of insolvency proceedings, joint or coordinated hearings are frequently incorporated into cross-border insolvency agreements as a dispute settlement mechanism.[149] The other feature, as pointed out by Part Three of the Legislative Guide, is that cross-border insolvency agreements "can be regarded as contracts between the signatories or, in case of approval by the court, may obtain the legal status of a court order".[150] Therefore, cross-border insolvency agreements, as contracts in nature, are entered into on the basis of consensus between insolvency practitioners, or sometimes between the courts (Wessels, 2012). Accordingly, a cross-border insolvency agreement should be deemed as a qualified cooperation instrument, which also falls within the ambit of the Basic Law that requires the judicial organs of each region to render assistance to each other on an equal footing.[151]

Contents of the agreements

The scope of the content that is addressed by the cross-border insolvency agreements varies in different legal systems. The contributions of common law countries to the development of cross-border insolvency agreements cannot be underestimated, where high level of discretion can be granted to judges and insolvency practitioners (Taylor, 2007). In the event of potentially conflicting procedural and substantive interests or concerns, courts and insolvency practitioners are allowed to set aside those contents out of the agreement and cooperate to the extent they can reach according to the specific circumstances of individual cases. The scope of the content can expand if there are no ready-made rules for reference. In the AIOC case, it involved insolvency proceedings concerning AIOC Corporation and AIOC Resources AG in the United States and in Switzerland. At that time, the United States had not adopted the Model Law. Switzerland is neither an Enacting State of the Model Law nor a Member State of the EU. In the absence of relevant international insolvency systems, the Chapter 11 Trustee assigned by the US court and the Swiss Bankruptcy

Office appointed by the Swiss court entered into a cross-border insolvency agreement and were committed to taking whatever actions were required in accordance with local legislation "to have any and all claims recognized in both the Chapter 11 Case and the Swiss Proceedings without the need for additional filings by any creditor that has not filed a claim in both proceedings".[152] The scope of the content can also shrink if that is inconsistent with the substantive laws involved. The *Loewen* case in 1999 was such an example.[153] It is said that the Loewen cross-border insolvency agreement has been regarded as a model and "repeated word-for-word in virtually every agreement jointly entered into by U.S. and Canadian courts in the ten years subsequent to its adoption" (Maltese, 2013). The success of the Loewen agreement has been summarized as "it says so little" (Wessels, Markell, Kilborn, 2009). Based on the principle of comity, the Loewen agreement fully acknowledged the independent jurisdiction of the individual courts, i.e. the US court and Canadian court[154] and did not deal with disputable issues such as jurisdiction and applicable law. In addition to court-to-court communication provisions,[155] the Loewen agreement focused on joint recognition of the stay of proceedings and actions as stipulated under the foreign law[156] and the dispute settlement procedure relating to the application of the agreement, including the opening of a joint hearing of both courts.[157] Besides, in accordance with Principle 1 of the Global Principles, nothing incorporated into the cross-border insolvency agreements should (1) interfere with the independence or exercise of jurisdiction of the relevant national courts involved; (2) interfere with the national rules or the ethical principles applicable to an insolvency practitioner; (3) confer substantive rights, to interfere with any function or duty arising out of any applicable law and professional rules or to encroach upon any local law. In the EU, the Regulation has provided systematic rules of jurisdiction, applicable law, recognition and enforcement of cross-border insolvency proceedings. Accordingly, the contents of the cross-border insolvency agreements reached in the EU shall also be reduced to accommodate themselves to the restrictions set under the binding legislation.

In accordance with CICIA, as both SARs are vested with independent judicial power,[158] any forms of cross-border insolvency cooperation, including cross-border insolvency agreements, should not interfere with the independence or exercise of jurisdiction of the relevant local courts involved. In addition, suggestions have been made on the establishment of a balanced regime between a recognition-oriented approach and a jurisdiction-oriented approach. Considering that the uniform choice of law rules might possibly result in interference with local substantial law, it will be incompatible with the restrictions under the current Basic Law,[159] which thus shall be avoided at this moment. With systematic arrangement of recognition, disputes settlement on jurisdiction issues and exclusion of choice of law rules, the contents of cross-border insolvency agreements under CICIA shall not cover the matters that have already been treated or are subject to deliberate omission. Besides, the contents of cross-border insolvency agreements should mainly focus more on procedure, instead of conferring substantive rights to interfere with any function or duty arising from any local law. In addition to this basic content, the specific issues in the course of cooperation and communication are left to the courts or the insolvency practitioners to decide as long as they are not inconsistent with the local mandatory rules. After all, a cross-border insolvency agreement is a flexible tool, whose merits shall be maintained in a flexible way. In the meantime, insolvency proceedings are usually enduring and continuous. Therefore, it is expected that the courts will play the significant supervisory role through the entire process.[160]

Proper means of cooperation and communication for enterprise groups

Cross-border insolvency agreements have been recommended by UNCITRAL as an efficient means to coordinate insolvency proceedings involving enterprise groups,[161] and are
also introduced into the EU Regulation (recast).[162] Meanwhile, there is an instrument parallel to cross-border insolvency agreements in addressing issues concerning enterprise groups,
which is the appointment of a single insolvency practitioner as coordinator to facilitate
administration of multiple insolvency proceedings of the same group in different States as
a whole. That approach has also been jointly suggested by the EU[163] and UNCITRAL.[164]
However, that approach will not be adopted into CICIA.

The main reasons are three-fold. First of all, the appointment of a single coordinator is still
a brand new legislative mechanism, which has not been broadly tested. Whether or not such
coordination can be carried out successfully depends greatly on the level of integration of its
members and its business structure as well as the qualification of that single or the same insolvency practitioner.[165] Secondly, each region has different requirements regarding the qualification of the insolvency practitioners in China. For example, in the Mainland, as aforementioned,
a liquidating committee can also be appointed under the current EBL.[166] In accordance with
judicial interpretation, the members of a liquidating committee can be appointed from the
related government departments, from the social intermediary agencies included in the roster
of administrators, from financial asset management companies as well as from the people's bank
and the financial regulatory institution under relevant laws and administrative regulations.[167]
In practice, the liquidating committee frequently participates in the insolvency proceedings (Li
and Wang, 2010; Zhang and Kuang, 2014),[168] whereas there is no equivalent concept in Hong
Kong SAR and Macao SAR. It could be quite difficult for the two SARs to accept the appointment of a liquidating committee as a proper group coordinator. In addition, considering the
active involvement of governments with extensive administrative powers in the insolvency proceedings of the Mainland, the coordinating ability of lawyers and accountants, who practice
independently as individuals, is in doubt (Li, 2014). Thirdly, among all those instruments,
only cross-border insolvency agreements have been actually applied in Hong Kong SAR alone.
Considering that China is at the very beginning of contemplating cross-border insolvency
cooperation, it is better to start with some familiar cooperation instruments.

A flexible solution with options

Concluding a cross-border insolvency agreement under CICIA cannot contravene the Basic
Law, under which the courts in the SARs are granted independent power and they cannot
be obliged to cooperate in a way they do not feel comfortable with. The independence,
sovereignty or jurisdiction of the relevant national courts should not be affected by the
agreement. The insolvency practitioners are only subject to the jurisdiction of its own court
and can cooperate with each other closely to enter into cross-border insolvency agreements,
which shall be approved by the courts as required in accordance with CICIA. Under the
circumstances that the courts find it necessary to cooperate directly in a court-to-court
manner, the courts can participate in the negotiation process of the agreements accordingly.
Cross-border insolvency agreements are created on an *ad hoc* basis in practice as a prompt
and flexible reaction. Due to the on-going feature of insolvency proceedings, sometimes it
is unlikely to predict the future shape of all conflicts that may emerge and provide legislative
solutions in advance. On-going proceedings shall be accompanied with on-going coordination. According to Wessels, "it is not uncommon, for example, to have agreements addressing general communication and cooperation at the start of insolvency proceedings, followed

by specific agreements on claims procedures at a later point" (Wessels, 2012). Hence under CICIA, complementary cross-border insolvency agreements shall also be allowed to address some issues upon prompt need on an *ad hoc* basis. In case of the conflicts arising from implementation of the cross-border insolvency agreements, the relevant dispute settlement solution is to be found under Recommendation 8.

Recommendation 8 – functional dispute settlement mechanism

(1) *In the course of interregional cross-border insolvency proceedings, a court that seeks explanation of the provisions under CICIA shall report to the Supreme Court of that region, which can request a special meeting to be convened.*

(2) *Explanation given by the special meeting on specific provisions of CICIA serves as proper interpretation on the specific issues arising from the individual case, which deserves due respect of the courts concerned. Upon consensus of the Supreme Courts concerned, the explanation shall have binding effect on that individual case. Upon consensus of all the Supreme Courts, the explanation shall have binding effect on the specific provisions under CICIA.*

(3) *In the course of implementing cross-border insolvency agreements, the courts in the concurrent proceedings can report to the Supreme Court from the respective regions, which can jointly request a special meeting to be convened and refer the disputes arising from cross-border insolvency agreements to the special meeting.*

(4) *In matters of the disputes arising from cross-border insolvency agreements, the opinions or part of the opinions come into binding effect to the extent that all the requesting courts involved agree to accept them, which should be expressly written into the judgments. The opinions are only binding on the individual case referred to the special meeting. If one of the requesting courts disagrees with the opinions or part of the opinions given by the special meeting, those opinions are not binding.*

(5) *Each court of the highest level from the three regions can designate one or two in-house judges to participate in the meeting. After discussion, the participating judges will deliver their joint opinions on the case referred to them.*

(6) *As for Hong Kong, any reference handed down by the special meeting shall not be construed as a direct reference to the courts in Hong Kong SAR except for the disputes concerned or unless the Court of Final Appeal of Hong Kong SAR expressly indicates otherwise.*

Comments on recommendation 8

Given the fact that there is a lack of a legal basis to establish a trans-regional competent court, an embedded dispute settlement mechanism will be introduced into CICIA, which has three main functions – safeguarding harmonious interpretation of CICIA, providing a solution to jurisdiction conflicts and settling down the disputes arising from cross-border insolvency agreements.

Harmonious interpretation

In the course of regional integration, there are plenty obstacles to harmonization or unification of the legal systems, such as different legal terminologies, different legal cultures and different languages etc. According to the experience of the EU, two of them (reluctance about unification and the means of adjustment) have to be in particular addressed in the scenario of regional harmonization, which is supposed to be overcome by the competent judicial authorities.

Reluctance about unification and common awareness

Sometimes judges are reluctant to endorse unification, which is described as the "home-ward trend" (Edlund, 2012). Imagine a judge, who receives law education in their home country, passes the national law exam of their home country, deals with most of the cases in accordance with the national laws of their home country, is requested to adjudicate a case involving cross-border characters. Will they be willing to refer to it or have confidence in applying it correctly? I am afraid at least not at the beginning. In the EU, there was a landmark case of *NV Algemene Transport- en Expeditie Onderneming van Gend & Loos v Netherlands Inland Revenue Administration* (*Van Gend en Loos*), in which the national authority raised a very important question before the CJEU, i.e. whether Article 12 of the EEC Treaty has direct application within the territory of a Member State, in other words, whether nationals of such a state can, on the basis of the article in question, lay claim to individual rights which the court must protect.[169] Both the Advocate-General[170] and the CJEU gave affirmative answers. Further, the CJEU made the following remarks:

> The conclusions to be drawn from this is that the Community constitutes a new legal order of international law for the benefit of which the States have limited their sovereign rights, albeit within limited fields, and the subjects of which comprise not only Member States but also their nationals. Independently of the legislation of Member States, Community Law therefore not only imposes obligations on individuals but is also intended to confer upon them rights which become part of their legal heritage. These rights arise not only where they are expressly granted by the Treaty, but also by reason of obligations which the Treaty imposes in a clearly defined way upon individuals as well as upon the Member States and upon the institutions of the Community.[171]

Public policy is another example. Early in 1974, the CJEU held in the case of *Yvonne van Duyn v Home Office* that the concept of public policy in the context of the Community and where, in particular, it is used as a justification for derogating from a fundamental principle of Community law, must be interpreted strictly, so that its scope cannot be determined unilaterally by each Member State without being subject to control by the institutions of the Community.[172] As for recourse to public policy in matters of recognition of civil and commercial cases, the CJEU has repeatedly stressed that it is not for the Court to define the content of the public policy of a Contracting State; it is nonetheless required to review the limits within which the courts of a Contracting State may have recourse to that concept for the purpose of refusing recognition of a judgment emanating from another Contracting State.[173] The decision of the CJEU explicitly indicated the existence of a EU new legal order on the ground of the Treaties, which not only has effects on governments but also on peoples and on its own institutions. The CJEU clearly put in the mind of national courts that "national legal system no longer forms the central building block for authority within Europe. Rather, legal authority flows from the Treaties with national legal systems having to adapt as sub-units to it" (Chalmers, Davies & Monti, 2010). The CJEU makes continuous efforts[174] to contribute to the common awareness of the EU legal order, which the judges, affiliated with national courts under the national legal systems of Member States, have to be repeatedly reminded of.

Adjustment and constructive interpretation

The other obstacle to harmonization of the legal systems is the means of adjustment. Unlike case law, the legal texts of statutory legislation are fixed and lack dynamism. However, the wording of the legislation could be vague and thus needs further explanation. In addition, in the course of implementation, problems might occur in individual cases, which would result in different understanding of the same rules. Further, it is necessary to revise the content of the legislation with the development of societies and the activities of the Member States. Before the systematic amendment procedure is initiated, which is time-consuming and complicated, constructive interpretation is needed for successful daily operation of the legislation. In the EU, the interpretation task concerning EU Law is undertaken by the CJEU. COMI is such an example. COMI is an influential and inevitable concept in matters of jurisdiction under cross-border insolvency regimes. However, COMI has not been defined under the EC Regulation. Instead, it is designed in the form of a presumption, which is rebuttable. As a fact-intensive criterion, numerous issues will doubtless arise in practice when the individual court has to utilize a terminology at its discretion without a precise definition. The CJEU handed down three important cases that set the tone of COMI in Europe, which are the *Eurofood* case, the *Interedil* case and the *Rastelli* case. From *Eurofood* to *Interedil* and *Rastelli*, the CJEU clearly set up the central administration as the criterion for jurisdiction. It has also streamlined the key conditions for the rebuttal of the presumption, which attaches great importance to a comprehensive assessment of the relevant factors and objective and ascertainable by third parties where the central administration is not located in the state of incorporation. The influence of its contribution has found its way into the proposal with respect to the amendment to the Regulation prepared by the EU Commission as well as the EU Parliament.[175] The key points, such as "central administration", "objective and ascertainable by the third party" and "a comprehensive assessment of all the relevant factors", which directly derived from the judgment rendered by the CJEU, clearly left its track on both legislative proposals. In particular, the relevant opinions in *Interedil* have been mostly referred to and literally codified.[176] All the clarification regarding COMI, which is derived from the case law of the CJEU, has been adopted into the EU Regulation (recast) in the end.[177] It is observed that the CJEU plays a key role in safeguarding the autonomous meaning of COMI.

Lack of a regional court in China and its consequences

In the course of implementing CICIA, China will meet the same problems caused by incoherent interpretation. First of all, although China is one sovereign state, the SARs are vested with independent judicial power, including that of final adjudication in accordance with the Basic Law.[178] Hence, three "supreme courts" equally co-exist under the "one China, two systems" regime. Secondly, although there are regional legislation instruments, i.e. the laws listed in the Annex III to the Basic Law and bilateral arrangements, the Basic Law does not specify the means of constructive interpretation of them but only provides interpretation and amendment mechanisms of the Basic Law itself.[179] It is stipulated under the bilateral arrangement concerning recognition and enforcement of judgments in civil and commercial matters between the Mainland and Hong Kong (the Mainland–Hong Kong Arrangement) that in the event of any problem arising in the course of implementing this Arrangement or a need for amendment of this Arrangement, it shall be resolved through consultations between the Supreme People's Court and the Government of the Hong Kong

SAR.[180] So far, the sole recorded adjustment to the Arrangement only has something to do with procedural issues. For example, due to modification of the provisions in the amended Civil Procedure Law of the Mainland regarding the time limit for application for execution of judgments, the relevant amendment to the Mainland–Hong Kong Arrangement was made in 2008. However, the same adjustment has not been made to the Mainland–Macao Arrangement (Song, 2012). The identical provision can also be found under the bilateral agreement concerning recognition and enforcement of judgments in civil and commercial matters between the Mainland and Macao (the Mainland–Macao Arrangement).[181] Thirdly, although the parties concerned expect that the same judgments can receive the same treatment within a country, the Mainland–Hong Kong Arrangement and the Mainland–Macao Arrangement are different from one another in several aspects, such as the scope of application and the way of determining jurisdiction. Nevertheless, the Mainland, Hong Kong and Macao have not taken any measures to coordinate the differences in the two Arrangements. Moreover, recognition and enforcement of civil and commercial cases at the regional level are handled separately. Accordingly, in the course of implementation, it will be the local courts that interpret the respective arrangements in accordance with their own local rules and legal culture, which gives rise to lack of legal certainty at the regional level.

A solution to jurisdiction conflicts

A crucial jurisdictional concept needs coherent interpretation

As mentioned above, COMI, as a concept determining international jurisdiction in matters of cross-border insolvency proceedings, stirred up conflicts of jurisdiction from time to time in the EU or on a global level. Moreover, the question of where a COMI is located will always be a question of fact (Smart, 1998). As a fact-intensive criterion, it is left to the courts at their discretion to make decision concerning a jurisdictional terminology without a precise definition. In the EU, the role is played by the CJEU, who vigorously applied the fundamental principles as the basis to manage the varying patterns of integration so that the Community structure does not fragment (Weatherill, 1994).[182] In the matters of cross-border insolvency, the principle of mutual trust has also been diligently applied by the CJEU to prevent the distorted understanding of COMI and safeguard the coherent interpretation under the Regulation.[183] As observed by Magnus, the effects of principles for the purpose of unification set by international cooperation instruments, such as the Model Law, can be jeopardized without "a strong central institution" to make interpretation for further uniformity (Magnus, 2012). As pointed out by Dawson, methodological approaches of interpretation are particularly salient in the context of the Model Law's harmonization efforts (Dawson, 2015). A visible example, as previously mentioned, is interpretation concerning time to determine COMI in the American jurisprudence,[184] which deviates tremendously from the relevant provisions, as a pre-insolvency concept, under the EU Regulation (recast)[185] and the Guide and Interpretation of the Model Law (2013).[186] That interpretation directly results in expansion of the scope of factors that can be taken into account to determine COMI so that liquidation activities and administrative functions can be validated as effective factors for the COMI determination. Consequently, more factors can be actually utilized for COMI relocation, which is inconsistent with the genuine purpose of the Model Law. Although CICIA focuses on the recognition issues, the concept of a debtor's COMI is fundamental to the operation of the arrangement. By according more immediate and automatic reliefs to the main proceedings, which is determined by COMI, it becomes crucial to identify where COMI is. Otherwise, the decisive attributes of COMI could be manipulated. In China, there is no equivalent institutional arrangement to support constant harmonization management, like the EU. That means the courts of equal legal supremacy in each region can make competing and conflicting judgments with respect to the interpretation of COMI on the same creditors. The distortion of autonomous meaning as provided under CICIA will put the overriding objective in jeopardy and ultimately impair the function of CICIA itself.

Different interpretation in China

The concepts of real seat and the place of incorporation also coexist in China. In the Mainland, liquidation of a company shall be subject to the jurisdiction of the people's court at the place where the company is domiciled. The domicile of a company refers to the place where the principal office of a company is located. Where the principal office of a company is unclear, the case shall be subject to the jurisdiction of the people's court at the place where the company is registered.[187] Hence, the registered office is a kind of last resort in determining jurisdiction of bankrupt companies. In Hong Kong, the Hong Kong courts can exercise jurisdiction over companies regardless of the place of incorporation. Although a non-Hong Kong company, which has a place of business in Hong Kong, must apply for registration,[188] the Hong Kong courts only exercise the jurisdiction of wind-up over them if the three core requirements are met, which include: (1) There is sufficient connection with Hong Kong. In the context of insolvency there is commonly the presence of assets, but this is not essential; (2) There is a reasonable possibility that the winding-up order would benefit those applying for it; and (3) The court must be able to exercise jurisdiction over one or more persons interested in the distribution of the company's assets.[189] If core requirements (1) and (2) are sufficiently met, the jurisdiction can be established despite the third core requirement not being satisfied.[190] The factors to establish the three core requirements may vary in individual case. For instance, In *Re Pioneer Iron and Steel Group*, the location of the controlling mind and the decision-maker is deemed as a substantial and relevant factor to determine whether or not there is sufficient connection with Hong Kong.[191] Meanwhile, the place of incorporation plays an influential role in Macao. Companies with their registered office in Macao cannot avoid the application of the provisions of Commercial Code of Macao against the third parties by relying on the fact that they do not have their central administration there.[192] Moreover, if the registered office or the central administration is not located in Macao but has long-term business in Macao, it should be bound by the relevant registration law.[193] In Macao, it seems that the ascertainability of the third parties has been attached too much importance, which can result in rebuttal of the fact of central administration.

It is observed that Hong Kong SAR has developed its own jurisdiction criteria in handling cross-border insolvency cases and the Mainland and Macao attaches different emphasis to certain factors relevant to determination of COMI as stipulated under the Regulation. In that case, should China still follow the Model Law approach that does not define COMI on its own but directly refer to the jurisprudence under the EU Regulation? I am afraid the answer is no. Considering its experienced development, it is true that the interpretation of COMI under the Regulation may be relevant under certain circumstances but China also needs to establish its own interpretation system to safeguard its own autonomous meaning of COMI based on its interregional cross-border insolvency cooperation regime. Therefore, it needs to be discussed how to build up a mechanism to safeguard the autonomous meaning on the basis of CICIA.

Dispute settlement concerning cross-border insolvency agreements

Possible solution through arbitration

Cross-border insolvency agreements are utilized as the key mechanism for coordination of insolvency proceedings involving a single debtor as well as enterprise groups under CICIA. Conflicts can arise during the implementation of those agreements, such as the *Nortel Networks* case (Chapter 5). In practice as well as advocated by some scholars, arbitration is recommended as a solution (Gropper, 2012; Kovacs, 2012; Clement, 2014). A key impetus for this proposal is the New York Convention, an influential international instrument, which is effective in over 140 countries and can facilitate the enforcement of arbitral awards and thus efficiently settle related disputes in an efficient and timely manner. Unfortunately, as mentioned previously, the New York Convention does not apply to interregional recognition and enforcement of arbitral awards in China. If arbitral awards are rendered in the Mainland, in Hong Kong and Macao pursuant to the respective local arbitration laws, they will be recognized and enforced in the three regions on different legal bases, which are the Arrangement between the Mainland and the Hong Kong SAR on Reciprocal Recognition and Enforcement of Arbitration Awards and the Arrangement between the Mainland and the Macao SAR on Reciprocal Recognition and Enforcement of Arbitration Awards.[194] According to Tu, many PIL cases may have been settled in the Court of First Instance (CFI) and did not go to the Court of Second Instance (CSI) and the Court of Final Appeal (CFA). One cannot find such cases because court decisions in CFI are not reported in Macao (Tu, 2010). Due to lack of reported cases from Macao's side, I will mainly focus on discussion between the Mainland and Hong Kong. Judge Gao, affiliated with the Supreme People's Court, provided that there were 19 Hong Kong arbitral awards in total, which were accepted for recognition and enforcement by the Mainland courts from 2008 to 2014 (Gao, 2015). According to information released by the Department of Justice of Hong Kong SAR, from 2009 to September 2012, 26 Mainland arbitral awards applied for enforcement and all have been granted enforcement in Hong Kong.[195] However, recognition of the Mainland arbitral awards was not granted without debate. The most disputed issue is public policy.

In the case of *Hebei Import and Export Corporation v Polytek Engineering Co Ltd.*,[196] a Mainland arbitral award was requested by Hebei Import and Export Corporation (Hebei) for enforcement in Hong Kong. Polytek Engineering Co Ltd. (Polytek) failed to set aside the award before the court in the Mainland and sought to resist enforcement in Hong Kong on the ground of lack of notice and inability to present its case in the arbitration proceeding. The decision was made by the Court of Appeal of the Hong Kong SAR unanimously in favor of Polytek and held it would violate the most basic notions of morality and justice of the Hong Kong system if the foreign award in question was to be enforced.[197] Hebei appealed the case to the Court of Final Appeal of the Hong Kong SAR, which overturned the decision of the Court of Appeal of the Hong Kong SAR. The Court of Final Appeal acknowledged that it was considered unacceptable in Hong Kong to conduct the holding of the inspection in the absence of the respondent, but where the defendant proceeded with the arbitration proceeding without raising his objection in a timely manner, he shall be deemed to have waived his right to object.[198] The refusal by a court of supervisory jurisdiction to set aside an award did not debar an unsuccessful applicant from resisting enforcement of the award in the court of enforcement.[199] The position would, however, be different if a party had failed to raise the challenge before the supervisory court. It would then be estopped from raising that point before the court of enforcement.[200] The judgment was handed down before the Arrangements of the Supreme People's Court on the Mutual Enforcement of Arbitral Awards between the Mainland and the Hong Kong SAR was concluded. It demonstrated the pro-enforcement approach adopted by the Court of Final Appeal and at the same time exposed problems in arbitration proceedings in the Mainland. Later in the case of *Gao Haiyan and Another v Keeneye Holdings Ltd and Another* (*Keeneye*),[201] the main concern was whether the mediation-arbitration (med-arb) procedure in the Mainland[202] was compatible with public policy in Hong Kong. In this case the Court of First Instance of the Hong Kong SAR and the Court of Appeal of the Hong Kong SAR had diverse opinions on this issue. There was an arbitral award rendered by a Mainland arbitration institution between Gao Haiyan and Another (Gao) and Keeneye Holdings Ltd. (Keeneye). Keeneye brought a lawsuit against Gao in order to set aside the arbitral award but failed. Gao applied for enforcement of the arbitral award in Hong Kong and Keeneye resisted the enforcement of the Mainland arbitral award on the ground of bias in the process of the Mainland mediation-arbitration. The fact Keeneye relied on was a private dinner in a hotel attended by an arbitrator nominated by Gao and the Secretary General of the Arbitration Institution and a person related to the Keeneye, pushing for a settlement. The Court of First Instance of the Hong Kong SAR stressed that the potential for an appearance of bias arises because of important differences between the mediation and arbitration processes in the Mainland and Hong Kong.[203] The Court of First Instance of the Hong Kong SAR pointed out that

> In particular, what happened at the Shangri-la would give the fair-minded observer a palpable sense of unease. The fair-minded observer would [I (the Judge) believe] be concerned that the underlying message being conveyed to Zeng (affiliate with *Keeneye*) at the dinner with Pan (Secretary General of the Mainland arbitration institution) and Zhou (arbitrator) was that the Tribunal favoured the Applicants. Such underlying message was obviously not spelled out at the dinner. But, against the background of the reservations I have mentioned, there would be more than ample justification for the fair-minded observer's apprehension.[204]

Gao argued that Keeneye must be deemed to have waived any right to raise bias since it had not complained about what happened at the hotel but had instead proceeded with the arbitration. The Court of First Instance of the Hong Kong SAR was unable to accept the suggestion of waiver because the court considered Keeneye was placed in a dilemma. If they were to complain about bias and if the Arbitration Tribunal were actually biased, their complaint would be rejected and they would lose everything.[205] The Court of First Instance of the Hong Kong SAR further held that there was no question of estoppel because the fact that Keeneye accused the Arbitration Panel of bias before the Mainland court does not prevent the Hong Kong court from considering the question of bias from the viewpoint of Hong Kong public policy.[206] The award was set aside on the public policy ground in the first instance. The Court of Appeal of the Hong Kong SAR unanimously overturned the decision of the Court of First Instance of the Hong Kong SAR. First of all, the court believed that a clear case of waiver had been made out. Keeneye attacked Gao's integrity in their supplemental submissions as they have done throughout the arbitral proceedings, but that is not a substitute for a complaint about impropriety or bias, apparent or real, against the Arbitral Tribunal.[207] Moreover, the Arbitral Tribunal and the Xian Court would have been in a much better position to ascertain the facts and to decide whether those facts established a case of actual or apparent bias. Such finding, though not binding, is entitled to serious consideration by our court.[208] As for holding a mediation over dinner in a hotel, a Mainland court is better able to decide whether that is acceptable.[209]

The case of *Keeneye* incurred widespread discussion in academia (Fan, 2011; Georgiou, 2011; Morgan & Man, 2012). Gu and Zhang pointed out that the Court of First Instance of the Hong Kong SAR and Court of Appeal of the Hong Kong SAR have "both gone too far in opposite directions" (Gu & Zhang, 2012). If the opinions of the Court of First Instance prevailed, the Mainland arbitration institutions should have readjusted their public policy to the standard of Hong Kong. Otherwise, the parties concerned could always resist enforcement of Mainland awards before the Hong Kong courts. On the contrary, the Court of Appeal seems to remit everything to the Mainland court. Of course, the points of view of supervisory courts shall receive due respect but the Hong Kong courts are also in the position, as explained by the Court of Final Appeal of the Hong Kong SAR in the *Hebei* case, to examine whether or not there is bias on the basis of its own authority. Influenced by Confucian philosophy of conflict avoidance, mediation is a more acceptable way in arbitration practice of the Mainland. It is reported that around 58% of the Mainland arbitration cases were handled by means of mediation in 2013 (Zhang, 2014). The Chinese way of mediation is characterized as "the most complete integration of mediation and arbitration" (Donahey, 1995). The arbitrators also have a dual role as mediators and the mediation proposal can be raised several times during the course of the proceedings (Fan, 2013). In Hong Kong, if a mediator to the same dispute is appointed to act as arbitrator upon the consent of the parties, the arbitrator must, before resuming the arbitral proceedings, disclose to all other parties as much of that information as the arbitrator considers is material to the arbitral proceedings.[210] As pointed out by Fan, Chinese arbitrator-mediators prefer to meet parties privately and separately, "known as 'caucusing' as long as both parties give their consent" (Fan, 2013). The process lacks transparency. The disagreement between the courts of Hong Kong towards the Mainland mediation-arbitration leaves the interregional arbitration in an uncertain situation. Moreover, the Mainland mediation-arbitration is in need of reform and improvement. Hence, it is difficult to expect arbitration as an appropriate solution to cross-border insolvency before a healthy and reliable local as well as interregional arbitration schemes are built up in China. In addition, learning from the experience of the *Nortel Networks* case, it may not be easy or possible to enter into an agreement to resolve disputes by arbitration in a cross-border insolvency case in the first place.[211]

The alternative solution: joint hearing

Recall the disputes in the *Nortel Networks*: what the parties and the courts looked for is a single jurisdiction with a single constituency to deal with the disputes.[212] In the end, the *Nortel Networks* case was not coordinated via arbitration but by a joint hearing held between the US and Canadian courts simultaneously (Wessels, 2014), which is what the United States and Canada often utilize in the process of cross-border insolvency coordination. Therefore, there are two approaches to resolve inter-group disputes, joint hearing in practice and arbitration for consideration. Although arbitration cannot be the solution to CICIA, arbitration is able to give a final answer to the dispute. The joint hearing is a cooperation and communication mechanism between the courts, which can help to facilitate exchange of information and negotiation. However, the possibility of a competing decision is not removed. In addition, there is a common concern with respect to joint hearing and arbitration, which is the cost involved. Bankruptcy cases deal with insolvent debtors, whose assets are limited. Over the last three decades, it is remarked by Kirgis that the Supreme Court of the United States "recognized only one limitation on arbitrability: cost" (Kirgis, 2009). In the case of *Green Tree Financial Corp.–Alabama and Green Tree Financial Corporation v Larketta Randolph (Green Tree)*,[213] the dispute involved a mobile home financing agreement, which included an arbitration clause. The respondent contended that the arbitration agreement's silence with respect to costs creates a "risk" that she would be required to bear prohibitive arbitration costs, and thus be unable to vindicate her statutory rights in arbitration. Although the plaintiff presented no evidence to prove how expensive the arbitration would be, the Supreme Court acknowledged that a claim of this type might have validity: "It may well be that the existence of large arbitration costs could preclude a litigant such as Randolph from effectively vindicating her federal statutory rights in the arbitral forum."[214] According to a recent survey carried out by White & Case and Queen Mary University, 68% of respondents considered the cost as a deterrent from arbitration, which was placed at the top of the most complained aspects of international arbitration.[215] In 2016, Lord Chief Justice Thomas Cwmgiedd delivered a speech in which he stated, "open justice is a hallmark of democratic society" (Cwmgiedd, 2016). In contrast, confidentiality is often regarded as one of the most valuable characteristics of arbitration (Zlatanska, 2015). In the aforementioned survey, 33% of the surveyed respondents claimed confidentiality as one of the most predominant benefits of arbitration.[216] Confidentiality results in lack of openness, which could "perpetuate public ignorance of continuing hazards, systemic problems, or public needs" (Doré, 2006). Lack of openness also deprives the ability of individuals and lawyers apart from the few who are instructed in arbitrations, to access the law, to understand how it has been interpreted and applied (Cwmgiedd, 2016). Moreover, 64% of the surveyed respondents chose arbitration for the purpose of avoiding specific legal systems/national courts, which was the second most frequently listed valuable characteristics in the survey.[217] Consequently, it reduces the potential for the courts to develop and explain the law and lowers the degree of certainty in the law that comes through the provision of authoritative decisions of the court. In the eye of common law judge, that is "a serious impediment to the growth of the common law" (Cwmgiedd, 2016). Neither can it help to generate harmonized interpretation or provide instructive guidance on an interregional legal cooperation arrangement.

Functional dispute settlement mechanism in China's regional context

To find a balanced approach in China's context, I submit to establish a functional dispute settlement mechanism, which is also built upon interregional court-to-court cooperation and communication. Inspired by the idea of the joint hearing, a special meeting can be organized in order to deal with the all those aforementioned problems and disputes. The functional dispute settlement mechanism shall also fit into the framework of CICIA and be consistent with the Basic Law.

Legal basis

The Basic Law vests independent judicial power upon the SARs and sets the tone that the way of life in the SARs shall remain unchanged at least within 50 years.[218] Therefore, the establishment of a trans-regional court has not been put on the agenda of integration because that arrangement will definitely interfere with the independence of the courts in each region. Instead, the judicial organs are encouraged to render judicial assistance and maintain judicial relations with each other through consultation. Under the Basic Law of Hong Kong SAR, the Hong Kong Special Administrative Region may, through consultation and in accordance with the law, maintain juridical relations with the judicial organs of other parts of the country, and they may render assistance to each other.[219] Under the Basic Law of Macao SAR, the Macao SAR may, through consultations and in accordance with law, maintain judicial relations with the judicial organs of other parts of the country, and they may render assistance to each other.[220] So far, judicial cooperation is conducted in a hybrid manner. All the aforementioned bilateral legal cooperation arrangements were entered into between the Supreme People's Court from the Mainland side and two administrative authorities from the two SARs, i.e. the Department of Justice of Hong Kong SAR and the Secretariat for Administration and Justice of Macao SAR. Moreover, any problem encountered or any amendment needed in the implementation of the arrangements shall be settled by the Supreme People's Court and the governments of the SARs through negotiations.[221] It is noteworthy that under both Mainland–Macao arrangements with respect to mutual recognition and the enforcement of civil and commercial judgments and arbitration awards, the Supreme People's Court and the Court of Final Appeal of Macao are allowed to directly cooperate and communicate with each other for relevant assistance to implement the arrangements.[222] Nevertheless, the equivalent provisions cannot be found in the Mainland–Hong Kong arrangements. The direct cooperation and communication between the courts of the Mainland and Macao is established on the legal basis provided under the Basic Law, which is the same legal basis to establish the Mainland–Hong Kong arrangement. Therefore, in theory the same legal basis will suffice to enable direct cooperation and communication between the courts of the Mainland and Hong Kong, although in reality, as mentioned before, the constitutional conflicts between the Mainland and Hong Kong and the distrust towards the judicial system of the Mainland probably hinder the willingness of Hong Kong to accept direct cooperation and communication between the courts from both sides.

Over 30 years ago, in *Smith Kline & French Laboratories Ltd. v Bloch*, there was a conflict of jurisdiction between the courts in England and the courts in the United States. Lord Denning made the following remarks:

> In the interests of comity, one [court] or other must give way. I wish that we could sit together to discuss it. But as that is not possible, I propose to put the case forward, as we see it here, in the hope that we may come to an agreed solution.[223]

Lord Denning's remarks are instructive. It would be very disappointing that the courts within one country, which have a shared language and culture, cannot cooperate and communicate with each other. Moreover, nowadays due to the development of international business, cooperation and communication becomes an inherent need of cross-border insolvency, in particular, in the case of coordination of insolvency proceedings involving multinational enterprise groups. The courts from different jurisdictions are interrelated by the multiple debtors that belong to one group and they can hardly make a decision "wholly independent of the future actions of the other court" (Westbrook, 2003). For instance, on 11 June, 2015, the CJEU delivered a significant judgment also concerning Nortel Networks.[224] One of the questions referred to the CJEU was whether the courts opening the secondary proceedings have exclusive jurisdiction, or concurrent jurisdiction with the courts opening the main insolvency proceedings, to rule on the determination of the debtor's assets falling within the scope of the effects of those secondary proceedings. The CJEU held that both the courts opening the main proceedings and the courts opening the secondary proceedings have jurisdiction, concurrently, to rule on the determination of the debtor's assets falling within the scope of the effects of the secondary proceedings. That decision will create huge cross-border coordination challenges and accordingly demands the competent courts to jointly work with each other, in particular for fair distribution of the group assets. Considering the current growth of regional economic integration, it is more likely that economic reality will drive the courts in China to accept the appropriate mechanism to coordinate cross-border insolvency proceedings at the regional level, which is to cooperate and communicate with each other.

A special meeting

Given the fact that it is the lack of a legal basis to establish a trans-regional competent court and the need for safeguarding autonomous interpretation of related provisions peculiar to CICIA, which is crucial to its function, as well as a solution to disputes incurred in the course of its implementation, I propose to establish a functional dispute settlement mechanism on the basis of cooperation and communication.

MEETING AS THE PROPER FORM

The functional dispute settlement mechanism is to be established in the form of a meeting. Why should such a meeting be convened? It is inspired by the idea of joint hearing as developed in North America. In 1998, the joint hearing was firstly put in practice in *Re Livent*,[225] in which the joint hearing was allowed by the courts of the United States and Canada via telephone or video-conference (Dargan, 2001). More courts followed this approach either by incorporating the joint hearing provision in the cross-border insolvency protocol or convening a joint hearing in practice.[226] It fits within the rationale of Article 27 of the Model Law. It is also stated under the UNCITRAL Practice Guide on Cross-border Insolvency Cooperation that "joint hearings or conferences have the advantage of enabling the courts to deal with the complex issues of different insolvency proceedings directly and in a timely manner".[227] In accordance with Guideline 10 of the Guidelines Applicable to Court-to-Court Communications in Cross-Border Cases (Court-to-Court Guidelines) a court may conduct a joint hearing with another court. As aforementioned, a trans-regional court is too sensitive to be accepted due to the possibility of violating the Basic Law. Nevertheless, a functional dispute settlement mechanism is needed to facilitate the dialogues between the judges from the three regions in a country, which can also promote regional judicial interaction on the cross-border insolvency issues. The form of meeting conforms with the requirements of the Basic Law, which allows the two SARs to maintain juridical relations with and render assistance to the judicial organs of other parts of the country through consultations.[228] Further, with the development of e-technology, to convene such a meeting does not mean "physical relocation" (Wessels, 2012). Both the Mainland and Hong Kong have adopted e-tech in the process of adjudicating civil and commercial cases. For instance, in the Mainland since use of video-link has been incorporated into the Civil Procedure Law of PRC in 2012, the video-link has been applied by courts in several cases to examine key witnesses living outside the province, where proceedings have been commenced.[229] According to the case law, the courts of Hong Kong also accept e-technology, such as video-conferencing, to be applied to cross-border insolvency cases.[230] Therefore, a meeting is a pragmatic way, which can be facilitated by use of e-technology in China.

PARTICIPANTS

The participants of the meeting are judges of the highest level court from the three regions. So far, as mentioned before, juridical relations between the Mainland and the two SARs are maintained in a judicial and administrative mixed character. Nevertheless, insolvency proceedings are a court-dominant system in in the Mainland and the two SARs, where the courts are the sole authorities that exercise jurisdiction over insolvency proceedings.[231] If CICIA were entered between the Mainland and the two SARs, should the problems encountered in the course of implementation thereof, such as interpretation of COMI, also be solved by way of negotiation between the court and two government institutions? That might not be deemed as appropriate. Slaughter has remarked on a new development in the course of global legal cooperation, i.e. judicial comity, which has four distinct strands (Slaughter, 2003). The first strand she indicated is the ability of the courts to resolve disputes and interpret and apply the law honestly and competently, rather than that of a government.[232] Cross-border insolvency is a matter that should be left to the courts to decide and interference from the government, though more or less inevitable, should be reduced as much as possible. The judges of the highest level court from the three regions, who represent the highest judicial authority in each independent jurisdiction, can better undertake the specialized duties and make trans-regional judicial cooperation more judicialized.

OBJECTIVES OF THE MEETING

One of the most important objectives of the meeting is to provide the opportunity to the judges to exchange points of view on the disputes that are referred to them by the requesting courts. After discussion, they will issue their opinions on specific issues referred to them, which can contain proper interpretation that prevents the autonomous meaning related to the provisions under CICIA from distortion, in particular in matters of jurisdiction, or guiding solutions to certain disputes related to cross-border insolvency agreements. What are the effects of those opinions? It depends on the type of references that the requesting courts seek. In the course of interregional cross-border insolvency proceedings, the courts that seek explanation of the related provisions under CICIA shall report to the Supreme Court of that region, which can request a special meeting to be convened. In accordance with the current regional legal cooperation arrangements, if there is any problem incurred by implementation of the arrangements, the Supreme People's Court and the governments of the SARs are authorized to solve them through joint negotiation.[233] Considering the judicial specialized nature of cross-border insolvency proceedings, it is suggested to grant authority to the Supreme Courts to make a joint explanation. To refrain from interfering with the internal superior judicial authority of the Supreme Courts in the respective region, whether or not to submit such a request is subject to the discretion of the Supreme Courts. Besides, to safeguard the independence of the judicial powers of each region,[234] whether or not the joint explanation handed down by the special meeting can have binding effect on the individual case shall also depend on the joint consensus of the Supreme Courts concerned. Otherwise, it merely serves as proper reference to the individual case. Besides, upon consensus of all the Supreme Courts, the explanation shall have binding effect on the specific provisions under CICIA.

In the course of implementing cross-border insolvency agreements, the courts in the concurrent proceedings can report to the Supreme Court from the respective region, which can jointly request a special meeting to be convened and refer the disputes arising from the cross-border insolvency agreement to the special meeting. In matters of the disputes arising from the cross-border insolvency agreement, the opinions or part of the opinions come into binding effect to the extent that all the requesting courts involved agree to accept them, which should be expressly written into the respective judgment. The effects are merely binding on the individual case. If one of the requesting courts disagrees with the opinions or part of the opinions given by the special meeting, those opinions are not binding. The reference procedure concerning cross-border insolvency agreements is different from the procedure in pursuit of explanation of the related provisions. In the case involving cross-border insolvency agreements disputes, the function of the special meeting is more akin to a joint forum, to which the disputes are submitted for a final decision. Due to the restrictions set up under the Basic Law, it is prohibited to drag the courts concerned into that kind of procedure because it will contravene the rules concerning the power of final adjudication granted by the Basic Law. That is why an extra agreement between the Supreme Courts in the concurrent proceedings is required. It is meant to be designed on a voluntary basis. In addition, the opinions are only binding on the individual case referred to the special meeting, which enables that kind of arrangement not to interfere with the independent judicial power granted to the SARs by the Basic Law.[235] By doing so, it will also make the opinions handed down by the special meeting more acceptable. Both the Mainland and Macao SAR are civil law jurisdictions, where case law does not have general application. As for Hong Kong, it is suggested to include into CICIA that any reference to the special meeting shall not be construed as a direct reference to the courts in Hong Kong SAR except for the disputes concerned or unless the Court of Final Appeal of Hong Kong SAR expressly indicates otherwise.

In addition to resolving the conflicts, the second objective of the meeting is to enable integrated negotiation. As pointed out by Westbrook,

> Judges are not always comfortable with the idea that a court "negotiates" with another court (much less that it negotiates with the parties). Many of the cases in which such negotiation is happening contain no explicit acknowledgement of the negotiation process, but negotiation is in fact an inescapable necessity in modem, cross-border commercial litigation.
>
> (Westbrook, 2003)

The current solution to disputes arising from regional legal cooperation in China is designed in the form of bilateral arrangements,[236] which is through bilateral negotiation. Bilateral negotiation can probably be influenced by the imbalance of political power between the Mainland and SARs, which has been described as "Hong Kong proposes, the Mainland disposes" in the course of implementing CEPA (Puig, 2013). Legal conflicts arising from cross-border insolvency are legal disputes, which should be dragged from bilateral negotiation to open debate in a more adjudicative manner.

The third objective is to promote direct court-to-court communication between the Mainland and the two SARs. Early in 2003, Slaughter indicated that a global community of courts is emerging, which

> is constituted above all by the self-awareness of the national and international judges who play a part. They are coming together in all sorts of ways. Literally, they meet much more frequently in a variety of settings, from seminars to training sessions and judicial organizations. Figuratively, they read and cite each other's opinions, which are

now available in these various meetings, on the Internet, through clerks, and through the medium of international tribunals that draw on domestic case law and then cross-fertilize to other national courts.

(Slaughter, 2003)

Therefore, a more integrated negotiation mechanism built up to include all the three regions in the same platform will help to generate an awareness of a common identity and community, which may gradually increase mutual understanding and achieve consensus between the Mainland and the two SARs.

COSTS

As for the costs incurred, although in disputes arising out of cross-border insolvency proceedings costs shall be covered by the debtor's assets, the functional solution under CICIA in fact will promote court-to-court cooperation and communication and thus will enhance regional judicial cooperation. Considering its possible influence on the public interest, it is also expected to receive some public funding from the support of the governments.

Recommendation 9 – interregional case register

(1) *Each region should be required to publish relevant information on cross-border insolvency cases in a publicly accessible electronic register.*
(2) *Once a cross-border insolvency proceeding is commenced in one region, the court shall immediately inform the communication authority in its own region. The communication authority must publish the information concerning the opening of insolvency proceedings on its e-portal and is also mandatory to inform its counterpart communication authorities concerned in the other regions. Meanwhile, the e-portal of each region should provide interconnection system that links to the registers in other regions.*
(3) *The minimum amount of information is required to be published in the interregional insolvency registers, including:*

   (a) *the date of the opening of insolvency proceedings;*
   (b) *the court opening insolvency proceedings and the case reference number, if any;*
   (c) *the debtor's name, registration number, registered office and current correspondence address;*
   (d) *the name, postal address or e-mail address of the insolvency practitioner, if any, appointed in the proceedings;*
   (e) *the time limit and place for lodging claims, if any, or a reference to the criteria for calculating that time limit.*

   Additional information subject to the local laws shall not be precluded.

(4) *The official language for the relevant information shall be Chinese. The information can also be published in English in Hong Kong SAR or Portuguese in Macao SAR but shall always be accompanied with a Chinese translation.*

Comments on recommendation 9

Recommendation 9 calls for embedding an interregional case register into CICIA. It examines the feasibility of such a register by taking into consideration the current practice in regional legal assistance. It also sets out the basic contents of information that can be disclosed.

Reasons for establishment of an interregional case register

The publicity related to the insolvency proceedings plays a significant role in good functioning of a cross-border insolvency regime. Under the EC Regulation, it is up to the insolvency practitioners to decide whether or not to request publication and registration of the judgment opening insolvency proceedings in another Member State[237] and it is also up to Member States to impose mandatory rules of publication and registration.[238] For a jurisdiction-dominant system, it is of importance that a court is informed about whether the company is already subject to insolvency proceedings in another Member State when it decides the commencement of insolvency proceedings. The lack of information on existing proceedings has resulted in unnecessary concurrent proceedings being launched.[239] According to the EU Commission, there was a public consultation, the results of which illustrated that "the vast majority of respondents (86%) who expressed an opinion agreed that the absence of mandatory publication of the decision opening proceedings was a problem".[240]

In addition, it has been acknowledged under the Regulation and the Model Law that protection of all interested persons is linked to notification requirements.[241] Some of the persons concerned are not aware that insolvency proceedings have been opened, which may have serious consequences on the capacity of the insolvent companies and on the rights of interested or potentially interested persons if they continue to act in good faith in a way that conflicts with the new circumstances, which is thus detrimental to their rights. It is even more so when it comes to creditors. Information concerning publication and registration of the judgment opening insolvency proceedings is necessary for the efficient lodging of claims for creditors in other States. Under both the EC Regulation and the Model Law, notification to foreign creditors is conducted individually under the national rules,[242] which vary as to the form, time and content of notice required to be given in regard to the foreign proceedings. Consequently, there is risk that the information and requirements regarding the lodging of claims given to foreign creditors might not be sufficient. Therefore, the EU Regulation (recast) formulates mandatory rules of publication of relevant information in cross-border insolvency proceedings in publicly accessible electronic registers[243] and requires interconnection of such insolvency registers on the EU level.[244]

Feasibility of an interregional case register

Publicity can be better realized through communication, which is of fundamental importance and helps to remove the uncertainty caused by parallel insolvency proceedings subject to different insolvency legislations. With respect to enterprise groups, cross-border communication can generate a better understanding of the facts and some potential benefits, which may be difficult to be found, due to the complexity of the organization structure and business arrangement of the groups. It can also avoid information distortion, which results from differences in foreign law. Through communication, more reliable responses can be expected from the parties concerned as well as from the courts, which may contribute to a better method of resolution. As aforementioned, the Basic Law provides the legal foundation for interregional legal cooperation.[245] In practice, the legal assistance is not conducted directly between the courts but between the Supreme People's Court and the administrative authorities of the two SARs, in particular, the China Law Unit of the Legal Policy Division of the Department of Justice of Hong Kong and the International Laws Affairs Division of the Law Reform and International Law Bureau of Macao. Those two offices serve as regular institutional communication channels between the courts from each side and each of the institutions has their own online e-portal for information regarding interregional cross-border legal cooperation.[246] Besides, development of judicial information seems to be a top priority to the people's courts.[247] The Supreme People's Court enacted the Provisions on the Issuance of Judicial Documents on the Internet by the People's Courts in 2013.[248] Accordingly since 1 January, 2014 the courts are mandatorily required to publish their judgments on the internet.[249] The Supreme People's Court also established an internet portal as a central public access to judgments of all levels.[250] In February 2016, the Supreme People's Court further issued the Five-Year Plan of the People's Courts on Development of Informatization (2016–2020), in which it is required that the High People's Courts in each province need to promote and update information development, in particular, formulate detailed implementation measures, in the respective jurisdiction (Qin, 2016). In March 2016, a national online case database portal (Faxin) was launched, which aims at providing comprehensive and in-depth information concerning judgments, case analysis and expert opinions. Those institutions can readily be utilized as communication authorities that provide technical assistance for the establishment of an interregional case register. Once a cross-border insolvency proceeding is commenced in one region, the court shall immediately inform the communication authority in its own region. The communication authority must publish the information concerning opening of insolvency proceedings on its e-portal and is also mandatory to inform its counterpart communication authorities concerned in the other regions. Meanwhile, the e-portal of each region should provide an interconnection system that links to the registers in other regions.

Basic contents of information

For CICIA, it is suggested to include the minimum amount of information mandatorily to be published in the interregional insolvency registers, in addition to which additional information subject to the local laws is not precluded. As for what can constitute the basic contents of information to be published, both the Regulation and the Model Law provides some answers. In accordance with National Reports collected in the Heidelberg-Luxembourg-Vienna Report, the following information is considered extremely essential in the course of cross-border insolvency communication: time limits, language requirements, costs and the specific procedures for lodging and proving claims under the *lex fori concursus* (Hess, Oberhammer, Pfeiffer, 2014). The Model Law requires that a reasonable time period for filing claims and the place for filing should be specified.[251] In addition, whether secured creditors need to file their secured claims should also be indicated.[252] The EU Regulation (recast) provides a more comprehensive list of information mandatorily to be published in the insolvency registers.[253] Considering the experiences of international insolvency regimes as well as the character of CICIA, which is a recognition-based system, it is suggested to include the following information into the basic contents required:

(a) the date of the opening of insolvency proceedings;
(b) the court opening insolvency proceedings and the case reference number, if any;
(c) the debtor's name, registration number, registered office and current correspondence address;
(d) the name, postal address or e-mail address of the insolvency practitioner, if any, appointed in the proceedings;
(e) the time limit and place for lodging claims, if any, or a reference to the criteria for calculating that time limit.

With respect to the language of communication, in addition to Chinese, English and Portuguese are both official languages that can be used as an official language by the executive authorities, legislature and judiciary of the respective SAR.[254] For the sake of respecting the ordinary usage of languages in the two SARs, English and Portuguese can be applied but shall always accompanied with a Chinese translation in the course of cooperation and communication, which is the common official language in the three regions, so as to facilitate convenient and efficient communication.

Recommendation 10 – independent intermediaries: separate arrangement for cross-Strait insolvency cooperation (the Mainland and Taiwan)

(1) *The cross-strait insolvency proceedings shall be coordinated by way of appointment of independent intermediaries from both sides.*

(2) *To guarantee the qualification as well as impartiality, the criteria to be appointed as an independent intermediary shall be agreed upon by the both sides. The role and competence of the intermediary can be set out in a protocol or an order of the court.*

(3) *The main duty of the independent intermediaries is to maintain the connection with its counterpart and devise a practical means of conducting cooperation and communication between the courts concerned.*

(4) *Before the appointment of the independent intermediaries, the opinions of the administrators should be consulted especially in matters of the way of conducting communication and coordination. Once appointed, an intermediary should be accountable to the court that appoints him or her and a related protocol can be reached with the approval of the respective courts.*

(5) *The independent intermediaries from the both sides can hold regular meetings either onsite or via e-technological means so that they can keep the courts from both sides informed of possible conflicts or problems in the cross-strait insolvency proceedings.*

(6) *Considering the difference of professional qualification criteria on each side, each side recommends some candidates of independent intermediaries for itself, holding a discussion to select someone both sides can trust and then putting those candidates separately in a closed list so that a consensus can be reached in advance to make sure that the qualifications of the independent intermediaries can be accepted by both sides in the process of coordination.*

(7) *The independent intermediaries should observe the duties in an impartial manner, free from bias, prejudice and any conflicts of interest. If its impartiality is in doubt, the court, after consulting the opinions of the administrators of both sides, can dismiss the independent intermediaries appointed by itself or request the counterpart court to dismiss its independent intermediaries with specific reasons upon the request of the administrators. A new independent intermediary can be selected from the list.*

(8) *The independent intermediaries will be remunerated from the estate of the insolvency proceedings in which the court appointed him or her.*

Comments on recommendation 10

Recommendation 10 builds up a separate arrangement for cross-strait insolvency cooperation through independent intermediaries. The reasons for such an arrangement will be briefly introduced through features of cross-strait cooperation, problems with the right to access and lack of rules on cross-strait cooperation and communication.

Private intermediaries in the process of cross-strait cooperation

Different from direct official contact between the Mainland and the SARs, two non-governmental institutes have been established in order to facilitate cross-strait cooperation and communication. They deal with public affairs and undertake some of the government functions. One is the Association for Relations across the Taiwan Straits (hereinafter the ARATS) from the Mainland side, the other is the Straits Exchange Foundation (hereinafter the SEF) from the Taiwan side. It is stated on the website of SEF that:

> Due to the complex and unique nature of relations across the Taiwan Strait and lack of official contacts between the two sides, the government had been unable to directly exercise public authority in handling issues arising from cross-strait exchanges. Therefore, it had to entrust a *private intermediary body* to exercise public authority over cross-strait matters. In March 1991, the Straits Exchange Foundation (SEF) was established with funds provided by the government and the private sector to serve this function (emphasis added by the author).

As the counterpart to the SEF in the PRC, the ARATS is a non-governmental organization with the similar function set up by the PRC in dealing with the matters with Taiwan, including entering into cross-strait agreements and assisting in cross-strait communication. The two non-governmental intermediaries have engaged in both cross-strait economic cooperation and legal cooperation. For example, the ECFA was signed by the ARATS and the SEF. There are also institutional arrangements under the ECFA. Different from the CEPA, the Joint Steering Committee is replaced with a Cross-Straits Economic Cooperation Committee, which consists of representatives designated by the ARATS and the SEF.[255] The Committee shall be responsible for handling matters relating to the Agreement, including but not limited to:

(1) concluding consultations necessary for the attainment of the objectives of the Agreement;
(2) monitoring and evaluating the implementation of the Agreement;
(3) interpreting the provisions of the Agreement;
(4) notifying important economic and trade information;
(5) settling any dispute over the interpretation, implementation and application of the Agreement in accordance with Article 10 of the Agreement.[256]

To settle disputes in the course of implementing the ECFA, the ARATS and the SEF shall engage in consultations on the establishment of appropriate dispute settlement procedures and expeditiously reach an agreement in order to settle any dispute arising from the interpretation, implementation and application of ECFA.[257] Before any consensus on the dispute settlement mechanism has been reached, any dispute over the interpretation, implementation and application of ECFA shall be resolved through consultations by the ARATS and the SEF or in an appropriate manner by the Cross-Straits Economic Cooperation Committee.[258] In regard to legal cooperation, prior to the 2009 agreement, the SEF, the ARATS and the China Notary Public Association entered into the Agreement on Verification of Application of the Notarized Certificates in 1993, which provided for the two organizations to send copies of notarized certificates involving inheritance, adoption, marriage, birth, death, trust, education, settlement, custody and property rights etc.[259] between the China

Notary Public Association or the local notary public associations and the SEF.[260] If there is any dispute with respect to the implementation of the agreement, it should be resolved via negotiation.[261] It is also provided under the 2009 agreement that any dispute that arises in the process of application of this arrangement shall be settled by way of negotiation between the SEF and the ARATS as soon as possible.[262]

Problems with the right to access

The qualifications of the administrators pose obstacles to cross-strait insolvency cooperation. In accordance with the insolvency laws of the Mainland and Taiwan,[263] lawyers and accountants can be appointed as administrators. Since 2008 Taiwan residents have been allowed to take part in the National Judicial Examination of the PRC.[264] Once they pass the exam, they can apply to practice as lawyer in the Mainland.[265] There are some limitations. If they are appointed as entrusted agents before the court, they can only deal with Taiwan-related marital and inheritance disputes.[266] Otherwise they can only be appointed as consultants in matters of non-litigation cases.[267] In 1999, the Ministry of Finance issued an order, in which it is stated that residents from Taiwan are allowed to sit China's Certified Public Accountant Examination.[268] If they pass the exam, they can apply for the membership with the Chinese Institute of Certified Public Accountants.[269] Once they obtain membership, they can be granted the qualification of accountant after more than two years relevant working experience in an accounting firm in the Mainland.[270] Moreover, Taiwanese accounting firms can apply for provisional license to perform audit-related services[271] and the valid time period of the provisional license has been extended from half a year to one year based on the ECFA.[272] However, Taiwan does not lift the ban on the professional qualification of the lawyers and accountants from the Mainland. It is stated under the Act Governing Relations between the People of the Taiwan Area and Mainland Area that the people from the Mainland cannot take part in the professional examinations unless they have had a household registration in the Taiwan Area.[273] In addition, neither the Mainland nor Taiwan enacted the Model Law. Are the Mainland administrators entitled to have direct access to a court in Taiwan? Probably not. In the aforementioned *Lehman Brothers* case, the joint liquidators appointed by the Hong Kong High Court applied twice with the same Taiwanese court for the recognition of their appointment, one for the appointment as provisional liquidators,[274] one for the appointment as joint liquidators.[275] Considering the unbalanced rules of the professional market entry permit, it is suggested to make simplified proof requirements, especially for Mainland administrators, to apply for recognition before the Taiwanese courts. Furthermore, in order to facilitate direct access to the courts, the common requirements of qualification for insolvency practitioners can be set up, which can be discussed and negotiated between the two sides in advance. Under the conditions set by the common requirements, insolvency practitioners can be provided with procedural standing for participation in the insolvency proceeding in the enacting State.

Lack of rules on cooperation and communication

Considering legal cooperation between the Mainland and Taiwan has just started, as well as the instability of the cross-strait cooperative relationship, it is difficult to expect that a comprehensive cross-strait insolvency framework can be built right now. In particular, consensus on the crucial criteria of recognition and jurisdiction of cross-strait insolvency is unlikely to be reached at present, partly because the local insolvency system is still developing, partly because the legal basis of cross-strait legal cooperation itself is undergoing challenges (i.e. the legality issue of the cross-strait agreements). However, due to the rise of the cross-strait business, there is the need for cross-strait insolvency cooperation and communication, which is not dependent on recognition. In the Yaxin reorganization case, Yaxin Electronics and Yaxin Circuit Board (hereinafter referred to as Suzhou Yaxin) were two enterprises incorporated in Suzhou, the Mainland. Their parent company, Taiwan Yaxin Corporation, was ordered bankrupt by the Taiwan Court. As a result, the cash receivables could not be collected, cash flow failed, and the business plunged into financial difficulties, which dragged Suzhou Yaxin also into insolvency. In 2007, the Taiwan Court opened the reorganization proceeding of the Taiwan Yaxin Corporation upon the application of the banking creditors in Taiwan.[276] On 25 April, 2008, a banking group composed of 15 banks filed a reorganization petition to the local court in the Mainland.[277] The banking creditors from both sides held a meeting and during the meeting the administrators of the parent company gave up the leading administrative authority on its Suzhou subsidiaries (Gu, 2012). From then on, the two reorganization proceedings were operated separately in the two regions. In the end, the reorganization of the parent company failed[278] but the reorganization of the Mainland subsidiaries succeeded (Gu, 2012).

As mentioned before, the 2015 Draft provides some general rules concerning the duty of the domestic and foreign liquidators or administrators to cooperate with each other. The liquidators or administrators appointed in the Taiwan debt-clearance proceedings can request the foreign liquidators or administrators for necessary cooperation and information as well as provide the foreign liquidators or administrators with necessary cooperation and information.[279] However, it has not been specified what kind of assistance and information can be deemed as necessary. From the Mainland side, there is no equivalent provision. In the Yaxin reorganization case, the decision of the administrator of the parent company to give up was very crucial, which later served as one of the reasons that the Taiwan court turned down the reorganization plan because it no longer had any control over the assets located in the Mainland.[280] Moreover, if that give-up decision could be deemed as a protocol, it had not been submitted to the Taiwan court for approval. Therefore, it is better to insert a provision in the cross-strait cooperation between the court and the administrators that the administrators should be required to bear the reporting duties. The courts should encourage liquidators to report periodically, including any practical problems, which have been encountered.[281] Moreover, the case of Yaxin only revealed the tip of the iceberg. Considering the annual cross-strait investment flow between the Mainland and Taiwan, Yaxin will probably not be the last cross-strait enterprise group that needs cross-strait cooperation if it unfortunately goes insolvent. Under that circumstance, exchange of information in cross-strait insolvency cases related to enterprise groups is very important. As stated under the Part III of UNCITRAL Legislative Guide on Insolvency Law, it may promote better understanding of the foreign law in order to lower the possibility of unnecessary conflicts. It also advances the resolution of issues through a negotiated result acceptable to all, encourages the parties concerned to preserve the value that would otherwise be lost through fragmented judicial action, which will especially contribute to the rescue of the group. In addition, communication generates more reliable responses, avoiding the inherent bias and adversarial distortion that may be apparent where parties represent their own particular concerns in their own jurisdictions.

Role of independent intermediaries

Generally speaking, the orderly administration of insolvency cases is governed under the authority of the courts, which is the same case in the both insolvency systems. Nonetheless, it should be taken into account the possible difficulty that the administrators can meet caused by access barriers in the course of cross-strait insolvency cooperation. The Model Law provides the possibility of direct or indirect cooperation between the courts.[282] Against the current economic, political and social background, direct cooperation between the courts is not yet possible in the cross-strait context. Indirect cooperation and communication can be achieved through liquidators or through any person or body appointed to act at the direction of the courts.[283] Moreover, in the Global Principles, an independent intermediary is introduced, as a new professional function to overcome any hurdles in global communication. It is stated in the comment to Principle 23 of the Global Principles that

> Under certain circumstances, the court may wish to refrain from conducting direct communication with another foreign court. . . The court could consider appoint an independent intermediary, whose task is to ensure that an international insolvency case is operated in accordance with these Global Principles and with any specific provisions that are either set out in a protocol or specified in the order made by the court.[284]

It is also stipulated under the EU JudgeCo Principles that courts should consider the appointment of one or more independent intermediaries to ensure that an international insolvency case proceeds in accordance with these EU JudgeCo Principles.[285]

The Mainland and Taiwan have become used to cooperation and communication via non-governmental intermediaries, i.e. the ARATS and the SEF. As private intermediaries entrusted by the governments, they are granted a wide range of power to promote cross-strait cooperation, including entering into cross-strait agreements and handling economic and legal matters concerning the agreements by way of negotiation. (Please refer to Chapter 5, p. 182 for the detailed introduction.) Therefore, it is relatively easier for both sides to accept the role of independent intermediaries in coordinating cross-strait insolvency issues. If there is dispute arising out of cross-strait insolvency, the courts from each side can appoint the independent intermediaries to facilitate communication and cooperation. To guarantee the qualification as well as impartiality, the criteria to be appointed as an independent intermediary shall be agreed upon by the both sides. The relationship between the independent intermediaries and the administrators is also very important. Before the appointment of the independent intermediaries, the opinions of the administrators should be obtained, especially in matters of the way of conducting communication and coordination. The role and competence of the independent intermediary can be set out in a protocol or an order of the court.[286] A model of protocol can also be formulated between both sides in dealing with the role of independent intermediaries in the cross-strait insolvency coordination and the main content of the agreement shall include:

(1) equal treatment towards any administrators; e.g. any notice made by a court should be given to each of the liquidators;
(2) communication methods that can be used and deemed effective;
(3) the way of confirmation of receipt and keeping the exchange of information in store in case of any mistake or misunderstanding;
(4) circumstances that require immediate notice.

The main duty of the independent intermediaries is to maintain the connection with its counterpart and devise a practical means of conducting communication between the courts concerned. The independent intermediaries from both sides can hold regular meetings either onsite or via e-technological means so that they can keep the courts from both sides informed of the possible conflicts or problems in cross-strait insolvency proceedings. An intermediary should be accountable to the court that appoints him or her and will be remunerated from the estate of the insolvency case in which the court appointed him or her.[287] To qualify as an independent intermediary, the independent intermediary should also hold relevant educational background, professional license, experience, as well as any other relevant experience or accomplishments.[288] Considering the difference of professional qualification criteria on each side, a consensus should be reached in advance to make sure that the qualifications of the independent intermediaries can be accepted by both sides in the process of coordination.

There is another requirement, which is crucial to cross-strait insolvency cooperation. The independent intermediaries should observe their duties in an impartial manner, free from bias, prejudice and any conflicts of interest.[289] In particular, if an independent intermediary holds very strong political opinions towards the cross-strait relationship, the independent intermediary and the court from the other side might have doubts of their impartiality, which might lead to failure of cooperation. The possible solution is that each side recommends some candidates for independent intermediaries for itself, holding a discussion to select someone both sides can trust and then putting those candidates separately in a closed list. In the course of cross-strait cooperation and communication, the court, after consulting the insolvency practitioners of both sides,[290] can dismiss the independent intermediary appointed by itself or request the counterpart court to dismiss its independent intermediary with specific reasons upon the request of the administrators. Such a request for dismissal should be given due regard by the counterpart court since it is difficult to proceed with cooperation and communication if the court from the other side no longer trusts the appointed independent intermediary. A new independent intermediary can be selected from the list. Last but not the least, independent intermediaries should be compensated from the estate of the insolvency proceedings in which the court appointed him or her.[291]

Conclusion

In pursuit of a solution to China's interregional cross-border insolvency cooperation, neither the Regulation nor the Model Law can be entirely referred to. Based on comparison between the two regimes, the guiding principle, it is desired to make a balanced arrangement, which tailors the merits of the Regulation and the Model Law into China's context. Accordingly, there are 10 recommendations provided under CICIA, which cover the overriding objective, the form, the scope, recognition and reliefs, public policy, cooperation and communication, cross-border insolvency agreements, the establishment of case registers and cross-strait insolvency cooperation.

Recommendation 1 provides the guiding principle of CICIA. The classic principle of universality meets constant resistance from the principle of territorialism because the latter mirrors the concern of judicial sovereignty of each independent jurisdiction. There is a common solution under the Regulation and the Model Law to the conflicts between universalism and co-existence of parallel proceedings, which is cooperation and communication, which is more neutral to ease the tension caused by competition among jurisdictions, in particular in the case of enterprise groups because it is difficult to identify a "home" for multiple debtors. Therefore, it is suggested to adopt the coordinated approach by attaching emphasis on cooperation and communication for CICIA.

The main purpose of Recommendation 2 is to find a balanced solution between the jurisdiction-based approach under the Regulation and a recognition-based approach under the Model Law by setting out the overriding objective of CICIA. The decision depends on whether or not the equivalent legal basis is available in China's context. To establish a cross-border insolvency system involving compulsory jurisdiction and automatic recognition, like the Regulation, it should rely on strong legal foundations, governed by the principle of mutual trust, flowing from the principle of sincere cooperation under the EU Treaties. In China, a regional legal system is established under the Basic Law. Driven by legal pluralism, problems arise from proper interpretation of the relevant provisions of the Basic Law in the process of judicial intersection between the Mainland and SARs. It is obvious that the principles of sincere cooperation and mutual trust are pretty much at the preliminary stage in China's regional legal system. Accordingly, it is suggested to adopt a recognition-based system for CICIA, which focuses on recognition and reliefs. Meanwhile, a functional dispute settlement mechanism will be tentatively invented to ease the possible tension between recognition and jurisdiction.

There are two objectives of Recommendation 3: to find a proper form for China's inter-regional cross-border insolvency cooperation as well as to what extent the arrangement shall apply. China's complex group composition has impact in the form to be chosen. Even under the circumstances that the international conventions can be implemented in both the Mainland and the two SARs, it is still necessary to make some regional arrangements. As a soft law instrument, the Model Law is a recommendation in essence. However, for a region that is undergoing integration governed by common constitutional arrangements, the degree of certainty achieved in relation to harmonization is expected to be higher. It is suggested to establish a uniform and comprehensive cooperation arrangement for cross-border insolvency so that the courts in the different jurisdictions can refer to the same rules in handling parallel proceedings. Considering the political reality and a lack of sufficient legal basis, cross-strait insolvency cooperation has to be treated in a separate manner. In addition, CICIA shall cover insolvency proceedings that are collective proceedings and the center of the debtor's main interests should be located in the Mainland, Hong Kong SAR or Macao SAR.

Recommendation 4 provides rules concerning recognition and reliefs. In practice, there are two legal bases for international cooperation in the area of cross-border insolvency: reciprocity and comity. The doctrine of comity prevails in common law countries and its inherent imprecision and vagueness makes the doctrine a seemingly unreliable basis for recognition. However, it is its flexible nature that has enabled comity to adapt itself to different geopolitical circumstances. Moreover, both mutual trust and comity have shared historic roots in the 17th century Dutch doctrine of '*comitas gentium*' and mutual trust within the EU can be deemed as a strengthened version of comity, which turns the latter from a discrete element into an obligation of respect. The recognition mechanism under CICIA is built up among the regions where mutual trust is still under construction and meanwhile some jurisdictions strictly adhere to the principle of reciprocity, which the Model Law tried to get rid of. To find a balanced way, comity can serve as a proper foundation for recognition under CICIA, which is softer than mutual trust (strengthened comity) but strong enough to promote cooperation between equals. Without uniform choice of law rules, which have been intentionally excluded from this arrangement, the arrangement provides a list of minimum reliefs to make up for the effects of insolvency proceedings, which are composed of automatic reliefs solely upon recognition of main proceedings and discretionary reliefs. When deciding whether or not to grant discretionary reliefs, the law, on the basis of which the discretionary reliefs can be granted, shall only refer to the substantive domestic law of the region in order to avoid recourse to *renvoi* and reduce complexity and uncertainty. As a bar to recognition and enforcement of cross-border insolvency proceedings, it is suggested to apply a more self-restrained interpretation of public policy under Recommendation 5 on a regional level in cross-border insolvency cooperation than under the domestic law.

Recommendation 6 formulates provisions regarding cooperation and communication under CICIA. The Basic Law provides the fundamental legal basis for judicial cooperation between the Mainland and the SARs, which contributes to closer cooperation between the courts within one country. However, whether or not to conduct direct court-to-court cooperation depends on the willingness of the courts, in particular between civil law and common law jurisdictions. Considering that courts are regarded as an essential element in the process of cooperation, a balanced solution is proposed that the courts play the role of supervisors, who monitor cooperation and communication actions conducted by the insolvency practitioners.

Rules of cross-border insolvency agreements are introduced into CICIA through Recommendation 7. Cross-border insolvency agreements have been recommended by UNCITRAL as an efficient means to coordinate insolvency proceedings involving enterprise groups, which is also introduced into the EU Regulation (recast). It is also the only means that has been actually applied in cross-border insolvency proceedings in Hong Kong alone. Besides, the cross-border insolvency agreement is a flexible tool, whose merits shall be maintained in a flexible way. If the courts or the insolvency practitioners after discussion find something useful to add beyond the aforementioned scope, they shall not be limited as long as it is not inconsistent with the local mandatory rules because not everything that is not explicitly permitted is actually inadmissible. By referring to the experience of the EU and UNCITRAL, cross-border insolvency agreements under CICIA will focus more on procedure matters.

Recommendation 8 develops a functional dispute settlement mechanism under CICIA. Given the fact that there is the lack of a legal basis to establish a trans-regional competent court, an embedded dispute settlement mechanism will be introduced into the regional arrangement, which has three main functions – safeguarding harmonious interpretation of the arrangement, providing a solution to jurisdiction conflicts and settling disputes arising from cross-border insolvency agreements. In the course of regional integration, there are a lot of obstacles to harmonization of the legal systems. Without an equivalent central authority such as the CJEU, which makes interpretation for further uniformity, such a decisive jurisdiction term might be manipulated. In China, each region has its own jurisdiction criteria. That is why China also needs to establish its own interpretation system to safeguard its own autonomous meaning of COMI based on CICIA. In addition, cross-border insolvency agreements are utilized as the key mechanism for coordination of insolvency proceedings involving a single debtor as well as enterprise groups under CICIA. In practice, conflicts arise during the implementation of those agreements, which need to be properly settled. In China's context, such a functional dispute settlement mechanism needs to be built upon interregional court-to-court cooperation and communication. Inspired by the idea of joint hearing, a special meeting can be organized in order to deal with all those aforementioned problems and disputes. First of all, the functional dispute settlement mechanism shall fit into the framework of CICIA, which is consistent with the Basic Law. There is legal basis under the Basic Law that provides direct cooperation and communication between the courts of the Mainland and SARs. Nowadays due to the development of international business, courts from different jurisdictions are inter-related by the multiple debtors that belong to one group and they can hardly make a decision wholly independent of the future actions of the other court for fair distribution of the group assets and prevention of parallel litigations. The functional dispute settlement mechanism is to be established in the form of a special meeting, which is inspired by the idea of a joint hearing. The special meeting has three main objectives. One of the most important objectives of the meeting is to provide the opportunity for judges to exchange points of view on the disputes that are referred to them by the requesting courts. The second objective of the meeting is to enable integrated negotiation. To include all three regions in the same platform can better prevent the influence caused by the imbalance of political power between the Mainland and SARs. The third objective of the mechanism is to encourage direct communication between the judicial authorities from the three regions, which will help to generate an awareness of a common identity and community, which may gradually increase the mutual understanding between the Mainland and the two SARs. The effect of the special meeting depends on the type of references that the requesting courts seek.

The establishment of an interregional case register is proposed under Recommendation 9 because the publicity related to the insolvency proceedings plays a significant role in good functioning of a cross-border insolvency regime. The Basic Law provides the legal foundation for interregional legal cooperation. In practice, there are institutions that can readily be utilized as communication authorities that provide technical assistance for establishment of an interregional case register. Once a cross-border insolvency proceeding is commenced in one region, the court shall immediately inform the communication authority in its own region. The communication authority must publish the information concerning opening of insolvency proceedings on its e-portal and it is also mandatory to inform its counterpart communication authorities concerned in the other regions. Meanwhile, the e-portal of each region should provide an interconnection system that links to the registers in other regions. For CICIA, it is suggested to include the minimum amount of information mandatorily to be published in the interregional insolvency registers, in addition to which additional information subject to the local laws is not precluded.

A separate cross-strait insolvency arrangement is established under Recommendation 10 through independent intermediaries. Given the complex and unique nature of relations across the Taiwan Strait and lack of official contacts between the two sides, two non-governmental institutes have been established in order to facilitate cross-strait cooperation and communication, which have engaged in both cross-strait economic cooperation and legal cooperation. In addition, the rules of the professional market entry permit are unbalanced. Therefore, it is difficult to expect that a comprehensive cross-strait insolvency framework can be built up right now. The way that both sides get used to such a framework is to cooperate and communicate via the non-governmental intermediaries. With respect to cross-border insolvency, in accordance with the Principle 23 of the Global Principles and Principle 17 of the EU JudgeCo Principles, an independent intermediary, a new professional function, is introduced to overcome any hurdles in global communication. By referring to the current means of cooperation, it seems that the gaps between the Mainland and Taiwan will tentatively be filled in via the intermediaries, which is relatively easier for both sides to accept. The main duty of the independent intermediaries is to maintain the connection with its counterpart and devise a practical means of conducting communication between the courts concerned.

Notes

1 Part of the contents in Chapter 5 has been published (Gong, 2014). However, due to the revision of the EU Regulation (recast), the current Chapter 5 is a recast of its published predecessor.
2 Available at: http://www.unesco.org/languages-atlas/index.php (Latest accessed on 25 August, 2017)
3 *Re HIH case* (*McGrath & Ors v Riddell & Ors* (Conjoined Appeals) [2008] UKHL 21), para. 30; *CReditors of Navigator Holdings plc* [2006] UKPC 26; [2007] 1 AC 508, 517 at para. 17; *Singularis Holdings Limited v PricewaterhouseCoopers* [2014] UKPC 36, at 23.
4 US Bankruptcy Code, §362.
5 Ibid., §105.
6 American Law Institute, Transnational Insolvency Project, International Statement of United States Bankruptcy Law, published by Executive Office, American Law Institute, 2003, 73–74.
7 Virgós/Schmit Report (1996), at 19 (c); EC Regulation, recital (22); EU Regulation (recast), recital (65).
8 EU Regulation(recast), recital (41), (42), (45).
9 EU Regulation(recast), recital (48).
10 Guide and Interpretation, para. 231.
11 *Re Daisyteck-ISA Ltd* [2003] BCC 562; [2006] High Court of Justice Birmingham 2006 EWHC 1296 (CH D); see also Pannen, Klaus (ed.), European Insolvency Regulation, De Gruyter Recht, 2007, ft.274; See also EU Commission Explanatory Memorandum, Proposal for a Regulation of the European Parliament and of the Council amending Council Regulation (EC) No 1346/2000 on insolvency proceedings, Strasbourg, 12.12.2012, COM (2012) 744 final, p. 36.
12 Working Group V (insolvency law), UNCITRAL, Facilitating the Cross-border Insolvency of Multinational Enterprise Groups, A /CN.9/WG.V/WP.128, 2015, para. 18.
13 EC Regulation, Article 31.
14 EU Regulation (recast), recital (48); the Model Law, Chapter IV.
15 EU Regulation (recast), Chapter V, Section I; Draft Legislative Provisions on the Cross-border Insolvency of Enterprise Groups Working Group V (insolvency law), Articles 9–18, in: UNCITRAL, Facilitating the Cross-border Insolvency of Multinational Enterprise Groups, A /CN.9/WG.V/WP.128, 2015.
16 American Law Institute and International Insolvency Institute, Transnational insolvency: global principles for cooperation in international insolvency cases: report to the ALI, Philadelphia. PA: Executive Office, The American Law Institute, 2012, (no page number is provided in the online version).
17 Basic Law of HKSAR, Article 95; Basic Law of Macao SAR, Article 93.
18 Permanent Bureau of HCCH, Continuation of the Judgments Projects, Preliminary Document No. 14 of February 2010 for the attention of the Council of April 2010 on General Affairs and Policy of the Conference, Prel. Doc. No. 14, Feb. 2010, para. 5.
19 Permanent Bureau of HCCH, Some Reflections on the Present State of Negotiations on the Judgments Project in the Context of the Future Work Programme of the Conference, Preliminary Document No. 16 of February 2002 for the attention of Commission I (General Affairs and Policy of the Conference) of the XIXth Diplomatic Session, Prel. Doc. No. 16, Apr. 2002, para. 3.
20 Legislative Council Paper No. CB (2)722/01–02(04), 20 December, 2001, para. 18; see also para. 5.46.
21 EU Regulation (recast), recital (42), Article 36.
22 The Model Law, Article 28; Guide and Interpretation, paras. 224–226.
23 C-341/04 *Eurofood IFSC* [2006], para. 40; Case C-444/07, *MG Probud Gdynia sp. z o.o.* [2010] ECR I-00417, para. 28.
24 EC Regulation, recital (22); EU Regulation (recast), recital (65).
25 The Model Law, Article 20(1).
26 C-341/04 *Eurofood IFSC* [2006], para. 40; Case C-444/07, *MG Probud Gdynia sp. z o.o.* [2010] ECR I-00417, para. 28; Case C-116/02, *Erich Gasser GmbH v MISAT Srl.* [2003]

ECR I-14693, para. 72; Case C-159/02, *Gregory Paul Turner v Felix Fareed Ismail Grovit and Others* [2004] ECR I-03565, para. 24.

27 Case C-116/11, *Bank Handlowy w Warszawie SA v Christianapol sp. z o.o.* [2012] (*Bank Handlowy*).

28 Ibid., paras. 17–24.

29 Ibid., para. 73.

30 EU Commission Explanatory Memorandum, Proposal for a Regulation of the European Parliament and of the Council amending Council Regulation (EC) No 1346/2000 on insolvency proceedings, Strasbourg, 12.12.2012, COM (2012) 744 final, p. 5.

31 Case C-116/11, *Bank Handlowy w Warszawie SA v Christianapol sp. z o.o.* [2012], para. 62.

32 Basic Law of HKSAR, Article 158; Basic Law of Macao SAR, Article 143.

33 *Democratic Republic of the Congo and Others v FG Hemisphere Associates LLC* [2011] HKCFA 43; (2011) 14 HKCFAR 95; [2011] 4 HKC 151; FACV7/2010 (8 June 2011).

34 The Basic Law of HKSAR, Article 24.

35 *NG Ka Ling and Another v The Director of Immigration* [1999] HKCFA 72.

36 Ibid., paras. 81, 82.

37 Ibid., paras. 88, 89.

38 Ibid., para. 90.

39 Chief Executive of the HKSAR, Report on seeking the assistance of the Central People's Government in resolving the problems encountered in the implementation of the relevant provisions of the Basic Law, 20 May, 1999, p. 1, available at: www.basiclaw.gov.hk/en/materials/doc/1999_05_20_e.pdf (last accessed on 31 March, 2017).

40 Interpretation by the Standing Committee of the National People's Congress of Articles 22(4) and Article 24(2)(3) of the Basic Law of the HKSAR of the PRC, Adopted at the Tenth Session of the Standing Committee of the National People's Congress on 26 June, 1999, p. 1, available at: www.basiclaw.gov.hk/en/basiclawtext/images/basiclawtext_doc17.pdf (last accessed on 31 March, 2017).

41 *Lau Kong Yung and Others v The Directors of Immigration* [1999] HKCFA.

42 Ibid., para. 74.

43 *Democratic Republic of the Congo and Others v FG Hemisphere Associates LLC* [2011] HKCFA 41; (2011) 14 HKCFAR 95; [2011] 4 HKC 151; FACV5/2010 (8 June, 2011).

44 Ibid., paras. 229, 265.

45 Ibid., paras. 233, 267, 266.

46 Ibid., para. 268.

47 Ibid., para. 234.

48 Ibid., para. 269.

49 Ibid., para. 416.

50 Ibid., para. 417.

51 Ibid., para. 76.

52 *HKSAR v Ma Wai Kwan* [1997] HKLRD 761 (29 July, 1997), para. 774D–E.

53 *Democratic Republic of the Congo and Others v FG Hemisphere Associates LLC* [2011] HKCFA 41; (2011) 14 HKCFAR 95; [2011] 4 HKC 151; FACV5/2010 (8 June, 2011), para. 114.

54 The 2016 annual work report of the Supreme People's Court (in Chinese).

55 [2002] Judicial Interpretation No. 5.

56 Ibid., Article 5.

57 [2006] Judicial Interpretation No. 2, art.4; [2008] Judicial Interpretation No. 9, Article 4.

58 Cap 32 Companies (Winding Up and Miscellaneous Provisions) Ordinance, s 184(2); Civil Procedure Code of Macao SAR, Article 1044.

59 Official Records of the General Assembly, Sixty-Fifth Session, Supplement No. 17 (A/65/17), para. 259; A/CN.9/686 – Report of Working Group V (Insolvency Law) on the work of its thirty-seventh session (Vienna, 9–13 November, 2009), paras. 127–130.

60 A /CN.9/WG.V/WP.117, United Nations Commission on International Trade Law Working Group V (Insolvency Law) Forty-fourth session Vienna, 16–20 December, 2013, at 7–16.

61 Ibid., at 8.

62 Basic Law of HKSAR, Article 153; Basic Law of Macao SAR, Article 138.

63 Basic Law of HKSAR, Article 153; Basic Law of Macao SAR, Article 138.

64 Declarations or Other Notifications pursuant to Article I (3) and Article X (1), available at: www.uncitral.org/uncitral/en/uncitral_texts/arbitration/NYConvention_status.html (last accessed on 31 March, 2017).
65 Please visit: www.cisg.law.pace.edu/cisg/countries/cntries-China.html (last accessed on 31 March, 2017).
66 New York Convention, Article VIII-1.
67 CISG, Article 91(1).
68 CISG, Article 93 (1).
69 Hong Kong SAR and the Mainland China: Arrangement Concerning Mutual Enforcement of Arbitral Awards (1999); Macao SAR and the Mainland China: Arrangement Concerning Mutual Recognition and Enforcement of Arbitral Awards between the Mainland and the Macao Special Administrative Region (2007); Hong Kong SAR and Macao SAR: Arrangement Concerning Reciprocal Recognition and Enforcement of Arbitral Awards Between the Hong Kong Special Administrative Region and the Macao Special Administrative Region (2013).
70 Hong Kong SAR and the Mainland Arrangement, Article 7; Macao SAR and the Mainland Arrangement, Article 7; Hong Kong SAR and Macao SAR Arrangement, Article 7.
71 Guide to Enactment, para. 56.
72 Guide and Interpretation, para. 20.
73 The Treaty of Amsterdam, Article 65.
74 TFEU, Article 67.
75 TFEU, Article 81.
76 Basic Law of HKSAR, Article 95; Basic Law of Macao SAR, Article 93.
77 Such as Council Directive 90/314/EEC of 13 June, 1990 on package travel, package holidays and package tours, Article 7; Directive 97/9/EC of the European Parliament and of the Council of 3 March, 1997 on investor-compensation schemes, recital (8); Directive 2000/35 of the European Parliament and of the Council of 29 June, 2000 on combating late payment in commercial transactions, Article 6(3)(a); Directive 2002/74/EC of the European Parliament and of the Council of 23 September, 2002 amending Council Directive 80/987/EEC on the approximation of the laws of the Member States relating to the protection of employees in the event of the insolvency of their employer; Council Regulation (EC) No 2157/2001 of 8 October, 2001 on the Statute for a European company (SE), Article 63.
78 Motion for a European Parliament Resolution – with recommendations to the Commission on insolvency proceedings in the context of EU company law (2011/2006(INI)) (Wessels & Fletcher, 2012).
79 Basic Law of HKSAR, Article 17; Basic Law of Macao SAR, Article 17.
80 Basic Law of HKSAR, Article 18; Basic Law of Macao SAR, Article 18.
81 Basic Law HKSAR, Article 95; Basic Law Macao SAR, Article 93.
82 Minutes of meeting on 9 November, 1999 of the Bills Committee on the Arbitration (Amendment) Bill, 1999 (LC Paper No. CB (2)2016/99–00).
83 LegCo Panel on Administration of Justice and Legal Services, LC Paper No. CB(2)1129/10–11(01), at 23.
84 Ibid., at 24.
85 Basic Law HKSAR, Article 95; Basic Law Macao SAR, Article 93.
86 2009 Agreement between Both Sides of the Taiwan Strait on Jointly Fighting against Crimes and Mutual Judicial Assistance, Article 10.
87 In accordance with the Article 24 of the 2009 Agreement, the Agreement should come into effect within 60 days after the agreement was signed on 24 April, 2009.
88 [2009] Judicial Interpretation No. 4, Supplementary Provisions on of the Supreme People's Court on the People's Courts' Recognition of Civil Judgments of the Relevant Courts of the Taiwan Region.
89 Act Governing Relations between People of the Taiwan Area and Mainland Area, Article 4–2-III, Article 5-II.
90 EC Regulation, recital (10), Article 1(1); EU Regulation (recast), Article 2(1); the Model Law, Article 2(a), Guide and Interpretation, paras. 69–70.
91 EU Regulation (recast), recital (9), Article 2(4).
92 Virgós/Schmit Report (1996), para. 49(b).

93 EU Regulation (recast), recital (10).
94 [2012] Judicial Interpretation No. 261.
95 [2014] Judicial Interpretation No. 7.
96 [2014] Judicial Interpretation No. 27.
97 [2012] Judicial Interpretation No. 261, Article 1(2); [2014] Judicial Interpretation No. 7, Article 5(16); [2014] Judicial Interpretation No. 27, Article 2(6).
98 Legislative Council Panel on Financial Affairs, Consultation Conclusions on Corporate Insolvency Law Improvement Exercise and Detailed proposals on a new Statutory Corporate Rescue Procedure, CB (1)1536/13–14(01), 7 July, 2014, pp. 3–10 and Annex B.
99 The 2015 Draft, Articles 220–286.
100 EU Regulation (recast), recital (16).
101 *Re Apcoa Parking (UK) Ltd and others* [2014] EWHC 997 (Ch), at 39.
102 *Re LDK Solar Co. Ltd.* [2014] HKCFI 2234.
103 Cap 622, ss. 668–670, 673, 674, 677.
104 Guide and Interpretation, para. 74.
105 Ibid.
106 Guide and Interpretation, paras. 75–76; See also Legislative Guide, Part two, Ch IV, paras. 76–94 and Recommendations 160–168.
107 Cap 6 Bankruptcy Ordinance.
108 CPCM, Articles 1185–1198.
109 Taiwan Consumer Debt Clearance Act.
110 EBL, Article 134; commercial bank: Regulations on the Cancellation of Financial Institutions 2001, Banking Supervision Law of the People's Republic of China (2006 Amendment), Regulation of Deposit Insurance System 2015; securities company: Opinions on the Purchase of Individual Creditor's Rights and Securities Trading Settlement Capital of Clients 2004, Notice of the People's Bank of China, the Ministry of Finance, China Banking Regulatory Commission and China Securities Regulatory Commission on Promulgating the Measures for Implementing the Purchase of Individual Credits and the Securities Trading Settlement Capital of Clients 2005, Notice of the People's Bank of China, Ministry of Finance, and China Securities Regulatory Commission on Relevant Issues concerning the Purchase of Individual Credit's Rights of Securities Companies and the Securities Trading Settlement Capital of Clients 2005; insurance company: Measures for the Administration of Insurance Protection Fund (2008).
111 Cap 155 Banking Ordinance; Cap 571 Securities and Futures Ordinance; Cap 41 Insurance Companies Ordinance. It is noteworthy that the Financial Services and the Treasury Bureau of the Government ("FSTB"), in conjunction with the Hong Kong Monetary Authority ("HKMA"), the Securities and Futures Commission ("SFC") and the Insurance Authority ("IA") (together "the authorities") attempted to implement a legislative reform that is needed to strengthen the options available to the authorities for dealing with a crisis situation in which a systemically important financial institution fails, which is expected to be introduced into a Bill to the Legislative Council by end 2015. See Financial Services and the Treasury Bureau, the Hong Kong Monetary Authority, the Securities and Futures Commission and the Insurance Authority, An Effective Resolution Regime for Financial Institutions in Hong Kong: Consultation Paper, 7 January, 2014; see also Financial Services and the Treasury Bureau, the Hong Kong Monetary Authority, the Securities and Futures Commission and the Insurance Authority, An Effective Resolution Regime for Financial Institutions in Hong Kong (second consultation paper): Conclusions from First Consultation and Further Policy Development, 21 January, 2015, p. 2;.
112 Macao Financial System Act, Decree Law No. 32/93/M (of 5 July, 1993); Macao Deposit Protection Regime, Law No. 9/2012, 9 July, 2012; Solvency Ratio (i.e. Capital Adequacy Ratio), Notice No. 011/2015-AMCM; Macao Insurance Ordinance, Decree-Law No. 27/97/M of 30 June; Legal framework for Private Pension Funds, Decree-Law No. 6/99/M of 8 February; Amendments to the Legal Framework of Private Pension Funds, Law No. 10/2001.
113 EU Regulation (recast), Article 1(2); the Model Law, Article 1(2), Guide and Interpretation paras. 55–57.
114 Guide and Interpretation, paras. 214, 215.

115 Guide and Interpretation, para. 29.
116 Insolvency Act of the BVI, Section 437.
117 Pursuant to Insolvency Act 2009 of Mauritius, Article 4, recognition of foreign insolvency proceedings will only be granted if there is sufficient reciprocity in dealing with insolvencies with jurisdictions that have trading or financial connections with Mauritius.
118 Commercial Insolvency Law of Mexico, Article 280.
119 Romanian Law on Regulating Private International Law Relations in the Field of Insolvency, Article 18(1)(e); Law No. 637 of 7 December 2002 on Regulating Private International Law Relations in the Field of Insolvency.
120 Cross-border Insolvency Act (42/2000) of South Africa, Section 2(2)(b).
121 Guide and Interpretation, para. 7.
122 *Laker Airways Ltd v Sabena, Belgian World Airlines* 731 F2d 909 (DC Cir 1984), 937.
123 *Hilton v Guyot* 159 US 113 (1895), 163–164.
124 *Re Thornhill Global Deposit Fund Ltd*, 245 BR 1, at 16 (Bankr D. Mass. 2000).
125 EU Regulation (recast), recital (65).
126 Basic Law of HKSAR, Article 17; Basic Law of Macao SAR, Article 17.
127 Basic Law of HKSAR, Article 18; Basic Law of Macao SAR, Article 18.
128 TFEU, Article 114.
129 *Eurofood*, para. 67; Hess/Pfeiffer, Interpretation of the Public Policy Exception (IP/C/JURI/IC/2010–076), 2011, p. 30 et seq. and pp. 167–168.
130 Case C-30/77, *Régina v Pierre Bouchereau* [1977] ECR I-01999, at 35.
131 Case C-7/98, *Dieter Krombach v André Bamberski* [2000] ECR I-01935, at 37; Case C-38/98, *Régie nationale des usines Renault SA v Maxicar SpA and Orazio Formento* [2000] ECR I-02973, at 30.
132 *Eurofood*, at 63.
133 Guide and Interpretation, para. 103.
134 [1995] Judicial Interpretation No. 18.
135 [1995] Judicial Interpretation No. 18, Article 2.
136 UNCITRAL Practice Guide on Cooperation, III, para. 148.
137 UNCITRAL Practice Guide on Cooperation, II, para. 4.
138 Basic Law of HKSAR, Article 95; Basic Law of Macao SAR, Article 93.
139 The Hague Service Convention, Article 2.
140 Arrangement for Mutual Service of Judicial Documents in Civil and Commercial Proceedings between the Mainland and Hong Kong Courts, Article 1; Arrangement for Mutual Service of Judicial Documents and Exchange of Evidence in Civil and Commercial Proceedings between the Mainland and the Macao SAR Courts, Article 1.
141 Arrangement for Mutual Service of Judicial Documents in Civil and Commercial Proceedings between the Mainland and Hong Kong Courts, Article 2; Arrangement for Mutual Service of Judicial Documents and Exchange of Evidence in Civil and Commercial Proceedings between the Mainland and the Macao SAR Courts, Article 2.
142 The Hague Evidence Convention, Articles 1, 2.
143 Arrangement for Mutual Service of Judicial Documents and Exchange of Evidence in Civil and Commercial Proceedings between the Mainland and the Macao SAR Courts, Articles 1, 2.
144 Notice of the Supreme People's Court on Further Regulating the Work of People's Courts concerning Hong Kong Related Judicial Assistance in Matters of Investigation and Taking of Evidence, No. 26 [2013] of the Supreme People's Court, para. 2.
145 Ibid., para. 3.
146 Arrangement on Mutual Taking of Evidence in Civil and Commercial Matters between the Courts of the Mainland and the Hong Kong SAR, Article 2.
147 Arrangement between the Mainland and the Macao Special Administrative Region on the Mutual Recognition and Enforcement of Civil and Commercial Judgments, Article 7.
148 Ibid., Article 23.
149 ABTC, Ontario Superior Court of Justice, Toronto, Case No. 31-OR-371448 (16 June, 2000), and the United States Bankruptcy Court for the District of Nevada, Case No. 500-10534 (28 June, 2000) (unofficial version). Everfresh, Ontario Court of Justice, Toronto, Case No. 32-077978 (20 December, 1995), and the United States Bankruptcy

Court for the Southern District of New York, Case No. 95 B 45405 (20 December, 1995). Financial Asset Management, United States Bankruptcy Court for the Southern District of California, Case No. 01-03640-304, and the Supreme Court of British Columbia, Case No. 11-213464/VA.01 (2001). Laidlaw, Ontario Superior Court of Justice, Toronto, Case No. 01-CL-4178 (10 August 2001), and the United States Bankruptcy Court for the Western District of New York, Case No. 01-14099 (20 August, 2001). Livent, United States Bankruptcy Court for the Southern District of New York, Case No. 98-B-48312, and the Ontario Superior Court of Justice, Toronto, Case No. 98-CL-3162 (11 June, 1999). Loewen, United States Bankruptcy Court for the District of Delaware, Case No. 99-1244 (30 June, 1999), and the Ontario Superior Court of Justice, Toronto, Case No. 99-CL-3384 (1 June, 1999). Mosaic, Ontario Court of Justice, Toronto, Court File No. 02-CL-4816 (7 December, 2002), and the United States Bankruptcy Court for the Northern District of Texas, Case No. 02-81440 (8 January, 2003). 360Networks, British Columbia Supreme Court, Vancouver, Case No. L011792 (28 June, 2001), and United States Bankruptcy Court for the Southern District of New York, Case No. 01-13721 (29 August, 2001). Pope & Talbot, Supreme Court of British Columbia, Vancouver, Case No. SO77839, (14 December, 2007), and the United States Bankruptcy Court for the District of Delaware, Case. No. 07-11738. Progressive Moulded, Ontario Superior Court of Justice, Commercial List, Court File No. CV-08-7590-00CL (24 June, 2008), and United States Bankruptcy Court for the District of Delaware, Case No. 08-11253 (14 July, 2008). PSINet, Ontario Superior Court of Justice, Toronto, Case No. 01-CL-4155 (10 July, 2001), and the United States Bankruptcy Court for the Southern District of New York, Case No. 01-13213 (10 July, 2001). Quebecor, Montreal Superior Court, Commercial Division, No. 500-11-032338-085, and the United States Bankruptcy Court for the Southern District of New York, No. 08-10152 (JMP) (2008). Solv-Ex, Alberta Court of Queen's Bench, Case No. 9701-10022 (28 January, 1998), and the United States Bankruptcy Court for the District of New Mexico, Case No. 11-97-14362-MA (28 January, 1998). Systech, Ontario Court of Justice, Toronto, Court File No. 03-CL-4836 (20 January, 2003), and the United States Bankruptcy Court for the Eastern District of North Carolina, Raleigh Division, Case No. 03-00142-5-ATS (30 January, 2003). Nortel Network, *Re Nortel Networks Corp*, 426 BR 84 (Bankr D Del 2010), Exhibit A to the Declaration of John Ray, dated 18 February, 2010.

150 Part III of the Legislative Guide, III, para. 50.
151 Basic Law of HKSRA, Article 95; Basic Law of Macao SAR, Article 92.
152 Cross-Border Liquidation Protocol for AIOC Resources, AG, et al., II-C, available at: www.casselsbrock.com/cb/pdf/AIOC.pdf (last accessed on 31 March, 2017).
153 *Re Loewen Group Inc.*, Case No. 99-1244 (Bankr D Del, 30 June, 1999.
154 Ibid., paras. 6–9.
155 Ibid., paras. 10–12.
156 Ibid., paras. 22–24.
157 Ibid., para. 27.
158 Basic Law of HKSAR, Article 19; Basic Law of Macao SAR, Article 19.
159 Basic Law of HKSAR, Article 18; Basic Law of Macao SAR, Article 18.
160 UNCITRAL Practice Guide on Cooperation, III, para. 148.
161 UNCITRAL Legislative Guide on Insolvency Law Part III, para. 14.
162 EU Regulation (recast), recital (49), Article 56(1).
163 EU Regulation (recast), recital (50), Ch.5 Section II.
164 Working Group V (insolvency law), UNCITRAL, Facilitating the Cross-border Insolvency of Multinational Enterprise Groups, A /CN.9/WG.V/WP.128, 2015, Article 18(1); Legislative Guide Part III, Recommendation 251.
165 Ibid; Legislative Guide Part III, Ch.3, para. 44.
166 EBL, Article 24.
167 Provisions of Designating the Administrator, Article 19.
168 [2007] Hubei Jinzhou Intermediate People's Court Civil Bankruptcy No. 14–5 (in Chinese).
169 Case C-26/62, *NV Algemene Transport- en Expeditie Onderneming van Gend & Loos v Netherlands Inland Revenue Administration* [1963] ECR 1.

170 Opinions of Advocate-General Karl Roemer, delivered on 12 December 1962.
171 Case C-26/62, *NV Algemene Transport- en Expeditie Onderneming van Gend & Loos v Netherlands Inland Revenue Administration* [1963] ECR 1, at II-B.
172 Case C-41/74, *Yvonne van Duyn v Home Office* [1974] ECR I-01337, at 18.
173 Case C-7/98, *Dieter Krombach v André Bamberski* [2000] ECR I-01935, at 23; Case C-38/98, *Régie nationale des usines Renault SA v Maxicar SpA and Orazio Formento* [2000] ECR I-02973, at 28.
174 Case C-9/70, Franz Grad v Finanzamt Traunstein [1970] ECR I-00825; Case C-93/71, *Orsolina Leonesio v Ministero dell'agricoltura e foreste* [1972] ECR II-00287; Case C-41/74, *Yvonne van Duyn v Home Office* [1974] ECR I-01337; Case C-403/98, *Azienda Agricola Monte Arcosu Srl v Regione Autonoma della Sardegna, Organismo Comprensoriale n° 24 della Sardegna and Ente Regionale per l'Assistenza Tecnica in Agricoltura (ERSAT)* [2001] ECR I-00103; Case C-8/81, *Ursula Becker v Finanzamt Münster-Innenstadt* [1982]; Case C-80/86, *Criminal Proceedings against Kolpinghuis Nijmegen BV* [1987] ECR I-03969; Case C-14/83, *Sabine von Colson and Elisabeth Kamann v Land Nordrhein-Westfalen* [1984] ECR I-01891; Case C-152/84 *M. H. Marshall v Southampton and South-West Hampshire Area Health Authority (Teaching)* [1986] ECR I-00723; Case C-105/03, *Criminal Proceedings Against Maria Pupino* [2005] ECR I-05285; Joined Cases C-397/01 to C-403/01, *Bernhard Pfeiffer and Others v Deutsches Rotes Kreuz, Kreisverband Waldshut eV* [2004] ECR I- 08835.
175 European Parliament legislative resolution of 5 February 2014 on the proposal for a regulation of the European Parliament and of the Council amending Council Regulation (EC) No 1346/2000 on insolvency proceedings (COM (2012)0744 – C7-0413/2012–2012/0360(COD)).
176 *Interedil*, para. 59.
177 EU Regulation (recast), recital (30).
178 Basic Law of HKSAR, Article 2; Basic Law of Macao SAR, Article 2.
179 Basic Law of HKSAR, Articles 158, 159; Basic Law of Macao SAR, Articles 143, 144.
180 Arrangement on Reciprocal Recognition and Enforcement of Judgments in Civil and Commercial Matters by the Courts of the Mainland and of the Hong Kong Special Administrative Region Pursuant to Choice of Court Agreements between Parties Concerned, Article 18.
181 Arrangement Concerning Mutual Recognition and Enforcement of Arbitral Awards between the Mainland and the Macao Special Administrative Region, Article 22.
182 See Case C-6/64, *Flaminio Costa v E.N.E.L.* [1964] ECR I-01141, at 585, 594; Case C-22/70, *Commission of the European Communities v Council of the European Communities (ERTA)* [1971] ECR 273; at 263; Case C-165/91, *Simon J. M. van Munster v Rijksdienst voor Pensioenen* [1994] ECR I-04661, para. 32; Case C-41/74, *Yvonne van Duyn v Home Office* [1974] ECR I-01337, para 12; Case C-51/76 *Verbond van Nederlandse Ondernemingen* [1977] ECR 113, para. 23; Case C-148/78, *Criminal Proceedings against Tullio Ratti* [1979] ECR I-01629, paras.20–23. Case C-9/70, Franz Grad v Finanzamt Traunstein [1970] ECR I-00825, para. 5; Case C-105/03, *Criminal Proceedings Against Maria Pupino* [2005] ECR I-05285, para. 43.
183 *Eurofood*, paras. 39–42; *Interedil*, para. 51; *Rastelli*, para. 31.
184 In *Re Fairfield Sentry Ltd.*, 714 F3d (2d Cir. 2013); In *Re Suntech Power Holdings Co., Ltd.*, Case No. 14-10383(SMB), Written Opinion Signed On 17 November, 2014.
185 EU Regulation (recast), recital (31), Article 3(1), para. 2.
186 Guide and Interpretation, paras. 141, 149, 159.
187 Provisions of the Supreme People's Court on Several Issues concerning the Application of the Company Law of the People's Republic of China (II) (2014 Amendment), Judicial Interpretation No. 2 [2014], 20 March, 2014, Article 24(1).
188 Cap 622, s 776.
189 *Yung Kee Holdings* [2012] 6 HKC 246, at 70 and *Re Beauty China Holdings Ltd* [2009] 6 HKC 351, at 23.
190 [2013] HKCFI 324, para. 28.
191 *Re Pioneer Iron and Steel Group* [2013] HKCFI 324, para. 38.
192 Commercial Code of Macao, Article 175-II.

193 Ibid., Article 178-I.
194 Arrangements of the Supreme People's Court on the Mutual Enforcement of Arbitral Awards between the Mainland and the Hong Kong Special Administrative Region (1999), Preamble; Arrangement between the Mainland and the Macao SAR on Reciprocal Recognition and Enforcement of Arbitration Awards (2007), Article 1.
195 Department of Justice of HKSAR, LC Paper No. CB(4)333/12–13(01).
196 *Hebei Import and Export Corporation v Polytek Engineering Co Ltd.* [1999] HKCFA 40; [1999] 1 HKLRD 665; (1999) 2 HKCFAR 111; [1999] 2 HKC 205; FACV10/1998 (9 February, 1999).
197 Ibid., paras. 54, 67.
198 Ibid., para. 75.
199 Ibid., para. 85.
200 Ibid., para. 88.
201 *Gao Haiyan and Another v Keeneye Holdings Ltd and Another* [2011] HKCA 459; [2012] 1 HKLRD 627; [2012] 1 HKC 335; CACV79/2011 (2 December, 2011).
202 Arbitration Law of PRC, Article 51.
203 *Gao Haiyan and Another v Keeneye Holdings Ltd and Another* [2011] HKCFI 240; [2011] 3 HKC 157; HCCT41/2010 (12 April, 2011), para. 73.
204 Ibid., para. 54.
205 Ibid., paras. 85–87.
206 Ibid., paras. 95, 96.
207 Ibid., para. 60.
208 Ibid., para. 64.
209 Ibid., para. 99.
210 Cap 609, ss 32, 33.
211 Motion, *Re Nortel Networks, Inc.* (25 April, 2011), ECF No. 5307; Opposition & Cross-Motion to Compel Arbitration; *Re Nortel Networks, Inc.* (19 May, 2011), ECF No. 5444; Reply, *Re Nortel Networks, Inc.* (2 June, 2011), ECF No. 5571.
212 *Re Nortel Networks Corp*, 426 BR 84 (Bankr D Del 2010), Exhibit A to the Declaration of John Ray, dated 18 February, 2010, para. 16.
213 *Green Tree Financial Corp.- Alabama and Green Tree Financial Corporation v Larketta Randolph*, 531 US 79, 2000.
214 Ibid., at 90.
215 White & Case and Queen Mary University, 2015 International Arbitration Survey: Improvements and Innovations in International Arbitration, 2015, p. 7, available at: www.arbitration.qmul.ac.uk/docs/164761.pdf (last accessed on 31 March, 2017).
216 Ibid.
217 Ibid.
218 Basic Law of HKSAR, Articles 2, 5; Basic Law of Macao SAR, Articles 2, 5.
219 Basic Law of HKSAR, Article 95.
220 Basic Law of Macao SAR, Article 93.
221 Arrangements of the Supreme People's Court on the Mutual Enforcement of Arbitral Awards between the Mainland and the Hong Kong Special Administrative Region, Article 11; Arrangement of the Supreme People's Court between the Mainland and the HKSAR on Reciprocal Recognition and Enforcement of the Decisions of Civil and Commercial Cases under Consensual Jurisdiction, Article 18; Arrangement between the Mainland and the Macau SAR on Reciprocal Recognition and Enforcement of Arbitration Awards, Article 15; Arrangement between the Mainland and the Macao Special Administrative Region on the Mutual Recognition and Enforcement of Civil and Commercial Judgments, Article 22.
222 Arrangement between the Mainland and the Macau SAR on Reciprocal Recognition and Enforcement of Arbitration Awards, Article 14; Arrangement between the Mainland and the Macao Special Administrative Region on the Mutual Recognition and Enforcement of Civil and Commercial Judgments, Article 23.
223 *Smith Kline & French Laboratories Ltd. v Bloch* [1983] 1 WLR 730.
224 Case C-649/13, *Comité d'entreprise de Nortel Networks SA and Others v Cosme Rogeau and Cosme Rogeau v Alan Robert Bloom and Others* [2015].

225 *Re Livent Inc.* between United States Bankruptcy Court for the Southern District of New York (Hon. Arthur Gonzales), Case No. 98-B-48312, and Ontario Superior Court of Justice, Toronto (Mr. Justice J.D. Ground), Case No. 98-CL-3162, (11 June, 1999).

226 *Everfresh*, Ontario Court of Justice, Toronto, Case No. 32-077978 (20 December, 1995), and the United States Bankruptcy Court for the Southern District of New York, Case No. 95 B 45405 (20 December 1995); *Solv-Ex Canada Limited and Solv-Ex Corporation*, Alberta Court of Queen's Bench, Case No. 9701-10022 (28 January, 1998) and the United States Bankruptcy Court for the District of New Mexico, Case No. 11-97-14362-MA (28 January, 1998); *Livent*, United States Bankruptcy Court for the Southern District of New York, Case No. 98-B-48312 and the Ontario Superior Court of Justice, Toronto, Case No. 98-CL-3162 (11 June, 1999); *Loewen*, United States Bankruptcy Court for the District of Delaware, Case No. 99-1244 (30 June, 1999) and the Ontario Superior Court of Justice, Toronto, Case No. 99-CL-3384 (1 June, 1999); *AgriBioTech Canada Inc.*, Ontario Superior Court of Justice, Toronto, Case No. 31-OR-371448 (16 June, 2000), and the United States Bankruptcy Court for the District of Nevada, Case No. 500-10534 (28 June, 2000) (unofficial version); *Greater Beijing First Expressways Limited*, United States Bankruptcy Court for the Southern District of California, Case No. 01-03640-304, and the Supreme Court of British Columbia, Case No. 11-213464/VA.01 (2001); *Financial Asset Management Foundation*, United States Bankruptcy Court for the Southern District of California, Case No. 01-03640-304 and the Supreme Court of British Columbia, Case No. 11-213464/VA.01 (2001); *360Networks*, British Columbia Supreme Court, Vancouver, Case No. L011792 (28 June, 2001) and United States Bankruptcy Court for the Southern District of New York, Case No. 01-13721 (29 August, 2001); *Laidlaw*, Ontario Superior Court of Justice, Toronto, Case No. 01-CL-4178 (10 August, 2001), and the United States Bankruptcy Court for the Western District of New York, Case No. 01-14099 (20 August, 2001); *PSINet*, Ontario Superior Court of Justice, Toronto, Case No. 01-CL-4155 (10 July, 2001) and the United States Bankruptcy Court for the Southern District of New York, Case No. 01-13213 (10 July, 2001); *Mosaic, Ontario Court of Justice*, Toronto, Court File No. 02-CL-4816 (7 December, 2002) and the United States Bankruptcy Court for the Northern District of Texas, Case No. 02-81440 (8 January, 2003); *Systech Retail Systems Corp.*, Ontario Court of Justice, Toronto, Court File No. 03-CL-4836 (20 January, 2003), and the United States Bankruptcy Court for the Eastern District of North Carolina, Raleigh Division, Case No. 03-00142-5-ATS (30 January, 2003); *Quebecor*, Montreal Superior Court, Commercial Division, No. 500-11-032338-085 and the United States Bankruptcy Court for the Southern District of New York, No. 08-10152 (JMP) (2008) (Date collected from Annex I to UNCITRAL Practice Guide on Cross-Border Insolvency Cooperation).

227 UNCITRAL Practice Guide on Cross-border Insolvency Cooperation, para. 154.

228 Basic Law of HKSAR, Article 95; Basic Law of Macao SAR, Article 93.

229 Prel. Doc. No 1 - provisional edition pending completion of the French version), ft. 624.

230 *Re Chow Kam Fai David* [2004] HKCA 111; [2004] 2 HKLRD 260; [2004] 2 HKC 645; CACV295/2003.

231 EBL, Article 3; Hong Kong Companies Ordinance (Cap 32), s 176; Civil Procedure Code of Macao, Article 20.

232 Ibid.

233 Arrangement of the Supreme People's Court between the Mainland and the HKSAR on Reciprocal Recognition and Enforcement of the Decisions of Civil and Commercial Cases under Consensual Jurisdiction, Article 18; Arrangement between the Mainland and the Macao Special Administrative Region on the Mutual Recognition and Enforcement of Civil and Commercial Judgments, Article 22.

234 Basic Law of HKSAR, Article 2; Basic Law of Macao SAR, Article 2.

235 Basic Law of HKSAR, Article 2; Basic Law of Macao SAR, Article 2.

236 Arrangement of the Supreme People's Court between the Mainland and the HKSAR on Reciprocal Recognition and Enforcement of the Decisions of Civil and Commercial Cases under Consensual Jurisdiction, Article 18; Arrangement between the Mainland and the Macao Special Administrative Region on the Mutual Recognition and Enforcement of Civil and Commercial Judgments, Article 22.

237 EC Regulation, Article 21(1).
238 Ibid., Article 21(2).
239 EU Commission Explanatory Memorandum, Proposal for a Regulation of the European Parliament and of the Council amending Council Regulation (EC) No 1346/2000 on insolvency proceedings, Strasbourg, 12.12.2012, COM (2012) 744 final, p. 24–25.
240 Ibid., p. 25.
241 Ibid; Guide and Interpretation, para. 199.
242 EC Regulation, Article 40(2); the Model Law, Article 14(2).
243 EU Regulation (recast), Article 24.
244 Ibid., Article 25.
245 Basic Law, Article 95; Basic Law Macao SAR, Article 93.
246 China Law Unit of the Legal Policy Division of the DoJ of Hong Kong www.doj.gov.hk/eng/about/lpd.html (last accessed on 31 March, 2017).
    International Laws Affairs Division of Law Reform and International Law Bureau of Macao www.dsrjdi.ccrj.gov.mo/en/zzjg_show.asp?#l (last accessed on 31 March, 2017).
247 Supreme People's Court: Five-Year Plan of the People's Courts on Development of Informatization (2013–2017) (in Chinese).
248 Provisions on the Issuance of Judicial Documents on the Internet by the People's Courts [2013] Judicial Interpretation No. 26, hereinafter the 2013 Interpretation.
249 The predecessor of the 2013 interpretation was Provisions on the Issuance of Judicial Documents on the Internet by the People's Courts, [2010] Judicial Interpretation No. 48, which was passed by the Supreme People's Court in 2010. By then, it was stated that the courts may issue judgments on the internet ([2010] Judicial Interpretation No. 48, Article 2). Now it has been replaced by the 2013 Interpretation, which provides that the courts should issue judgments on the internet ([2013] Judicial Interpretation No. 26, Article 4).
250 [2013] Judicial Interpretation No. 26, Article 2.
251 The Model Law, Article 14(3)(a).
252 The Model Law, Article 14(3)(b).
253 EU Regulation(recast), Article 24(2).
254 Basic Law of HKSAR, Article 9; Basic Law of Macao SAR, Article 9.
255 ECFA, Article 11 (1).
256 Ibid., Article 11 (1).
257 Ibid., Article 10 (1).
258 Ibid., Article 10 (2).
259 The 1993 Agreement on Verification of Application of the Notarized Certificates (the 1993 Agreement), Article 10 (2).
260 Ibid., Article 1(1).
261 Ibid., Article 7.
262 The 2009 Agreement, Article 22.
263 EBL, Article 24; the 2015 Draft (Taiwan), Article 31.
264 Measures for the Implementation of National Judicial Examination, Article 24.
265 Administrative Measures for the Practice of Law in the Mainland by Taiwan Residents Holding the National Legal Profession Qualifications, Article 2.
266 Ibid., Article 3.
267 Ibid.
268 [1999] The Ministry of Finance Assistance Order No. 12 (abolished), Article 3; Later it was superseded by [2008] The Ministry of Finance Accounting Order No. 4, Article 3.
269 Ibid., Article 13.
270 Measures on Certification of Accountants, [2005] The Ministry of Finance Order No. 25, Article 4, 23.
271 Notice of the Ministry of Finance on Issuing Provisional Measures on Oversea Accounting Firms Perform Temporary Audit-related Services in the Mainland (2011, Decree No. 4), Article 2.
272 Ibid., Article 7.
273 The Act Governing Relations between People of the Taiwan Area and Mainland Area, Article 22-II.
274 Taipei District Court Trial on Application No. 1037 [2008].

275 Taipei District Court Trial on Application No. 514 [2009].
276 Taipei Shilin District Court Reorganization No. 1 [2007].
277 Suzhou Intermediate Court, Analysis of the Bankruptcy Reorganization in Practice – Study of the Yaxin Case, in: People's Court Daily, 7 May, 2009.
278 Taipei Shilin District Court Reorganization No. 3 [2010].
279 The 2015 Draft, Article 317(1).
280 Taipei Shilin District Court Reorganization No. 3 [2010].
281 Guideline 16.5, European Communication and Cooperation Guidelines for Cross-border Insolvency, Developed under the aegis of the Academic Wing of INSOL Europe, July 2007.
282 The Model Law, Article 25.
283 Ibid., Article 25(1).
284 Global Principles, Comment to Principle 23.
285 EU JudgeCo Principles, Principle 17.
286 Global Principles, Principle 23.4; EU JudgeCo Principles, Principle 17(1).
287 Global Principles, Principle 23.5(iii); EU JudgeCo Principles, Principle 17(2)(iii).
288 Global Principles, Principle 23.5(i); EU JudgeCo Principles, Principle 17(2)(i).
289 Global Principles, Principle 23.5(ii); EU JudgeCo Principles, Principle 17(2)(ii).
290 Global Principles, Principle 23.4; EU JudgeCo Principles, Principle 17(1).
291 Global Principles, Principle 23.5(iv); EU JudgeCo Principles, Principle 17(2)(iv).

Reference list

In English

Balz, M., "The European Union Convention on Insolvency Proceedings", 70 Am Bankr LJ 485, 1996, 531

Bariatti, Stefania, *Cases and Materials on EU Private International Law*, Hart Publishing, 2011, p. 42

Berends, André, "The UNCITRAL Model Law on Cross-border Insolvency: A Comprehensive Overview", 6 Tul. J. Int'l & Comp. L. 320, 1998, pp. 323

Bufford, Samuel L., *United States International Insolvency Law 2008–2009*, Oxford University Press, 2009, pp. 4

Buxbaum, Hannah, "Rethinking International Insolvency: The Neglected Choice-of-Law Rules and Theory", 36 *Stanford Journal of International Law*, 2000, 23

Cane, Peter, and Conaghan, Joanne, *The New Oxford Companion to Law* (online version), Oxford University Press, 2008, www.oxfordreference.com (last accessed on 31 March, 2017)

Chalmers, Damian, Davies, Gareth, Monti, Giorgio, *European Union Law* (2nd ed.), Cambridge University Press, 2010, p. 15

Chan, Cora, "Reconceptualising the Relationship between the Mainland Chinese Legal System and the Hong Kong Legal System", *Asian Journal of Comparative Law*, Vol. 6, issue 1, 2011, p. 3

Clark, Leif M., Goldstein, Karen, "Sacred Cows: How to Care for Secured Creditors' Rights in Cross-Border Bankruptcies", 46 Tex. Int'l L.J. 513, 2011, p. 524

Clement, Zack A., "Position Paper Supporting Greater Use of Arbitration in Connection with Insolvency Matters", 21 April, 2014, www.iiiglobal.org (last accessed on 31 March, 2017)

Clift, Jenny, "The UNCITRAL Model Law on Cross-border Insolvency – A Legislative Framework to Facilitate Coordination and Cooperation in Cross-border Insolvency", 12 Tul. J. Int'l & Comp. L., 2004, 325

Clift, Jenny, "International Insolvency Law: The UNCITRAL Experience with Harmonization and Modernization Techniques", 11 Y.B. Private Int'l L. 405, 2009, p. 424

Clift, Jenny, "Choice of Law and the UNCITRAL Harmonization Process", *Brooklyn Journal of Corporate, Finance & Commercial Law*, Vol. 9, Issue 1, 2014, p. 33

Cwmgiedd, Thomas, "Developing Commercial Law through the Courts: Rebalancing the Relationship between the Courts and Arbitration", The Bailii Lecture 2016, 9 March, 2016, para. 39, available at: www.judiciary.gov.uk/wp-content/uploads/2016/03/lcj-speech-bailli-lecture-20160309.pdf (last accessed on 31 March, 2017)

Daljit, Kaur and Susarla, Kamesh, "Anti-Tax Avoidance Developments in Selected Asian Jurisdictions", *Asia-Pacific Tax Bulletin*, Volume 17, No. 4, 2011, p. 261

Dargan, Sean, "The Emergence of Mechanisms for Cross-Border Insolvencies in Canadian Law", 17 Conn. J. Int 'l L., 122 (2001)

Dawson, Andrew B., "The Problems of Local Methods in Cross-border Insolvencies", 2015, p. 4, available at: http://iiiglobal.org/iii-prize-in-insolvency.html (last visited on 31 March, 2017)

Donahey, "Seeking Harmony: Is the Asian Concept of the Conciliator/arbitrator Applicable in the West", 50. Disp. Res. J.,1995, pp. 74–78

Doré, L. K., "Public courts versus Private Justice: It's Time to Let Some Sun Shine in on Alternative Dispute Resolution", 81 Chi-Kent L. Rev 463, 2006, p. 487

Eco, Umberto, *The Search for the Perfect Language*, Blackwell, Oxford, UK,1995

Edlund, Hans Henrik, *The Concept of Unification and Harmonization, in: Fogt, Morten M. (ed.), Unification and Harmonization of International Commercial Law – Interaction or Deharmonization?*, Wolters Kluwer, 2012, pp. 12, 14

Ehricke, Ulrich, *Die Zusammenarbeit des Insolvenzverwalter bei grenzüberschreitenden Insolvenzen nach der EUInsVo, Wertpapier-mitteilungen; Zeitschrift für Wirtschafts-ung Bankrecht* (WM), 2005, 397

Fan Kun, *The Risks of Apparent Bias When an Arbitrator Act as a Mediator: Remarks on Hong Kong Court's Decision in Gao Haiyan* (in Chinese), 13 China Yearbook of Private International Law, 2011, pp. 535–556

Fan Kun, *Arbitration in China – A Legal and Cultural Analysis*, Oxford University Press, 2013, p. 166

Fauvarque-Cosson, "Benedicte, Comparative Law and Conflict of Laws: Allies or Enemies – New Perspectives on an Old Couple", 49 Am. J. Comp. L. 407, 2001, p. 412

Fletcher, Ian F., *Insolvency in Private International Law. National and International Approaches, Oxford Private International Law Series*, (2nd ed.), Oxford University Press, 2005, 6.01

Georgiou, Phillip, "The Real Risk of Bias in "Chinese Style" Arbitrations" (2011) "Asian Dispute Review" 89

Gong Xinyi, A Middle Way – "Tailoring the Model Law and the Regulation into China's Context", *Norton Journal of Bankruptcy Law and Practice*, October 2014, Vol. 23, Issue 5, Article 9, pp. 691–738 (Westlaw citation: 23 No. 5 JBKRLP-NL Art. 9)

Gropper, Allan L., "The Arbitration of Cross-border Insolvencies", 86 Am. Bankr. L.J., 201, 2012

Gu, Weixia, Zhang, Xianchu, "The Keeneye Case: Rethinking the Content of Public Policy in Cross-Border Arbitration between Hong Kong and Mainland China", 42 Hong Kong L. J. , 2012, 1001, 1014

Guzman, A.T., *How International Law Works: A Rational Choice Theory*, Oxford University Press, 2007, p. 14, 40

He, Qisheng, "Public Policy in Enforcement of Foreign Arbitral Awards in the Supreme People's Court of China", 43 Hong Kong L. J.1037, 2013, p. 1041

Hess/Pfeiffer, *Interpretation of the Public Policy Exception* (IP/C/JURI/IC/2010–076), 2011, p. 30 et seq. & pp. 167–168

Hess, Oberhammer, Pfeiffer, *European Insolvency Law-The Heidelberg-Luxembourg-Vienna Report on the Application of Regulation No. 1346/2000/EC on Insolvency Proceedings* (External Evaluation JUST/2011/JCIV/PR/0049/A4), C.H.Beck.Hart.Nomos, 2014, paras. 944–945

Hsieh, Pasha L., "Facing China: Taiwan's Status as a Separate Customs Territory in the World Trade Organization", 39 *Journal of the World Trade* 6, 2005, p. 1195

Jackson, Thomas H., *The Logic and Limits of Bankruptcy Law*, Beard Books, 2001, p. 5

Janger, Edward J., "Universal Proceduralism", 32 Brook. J. Int'l L. 819, 2007, p. 824

Janger, Edward J., "Virtual Territoriality", 48 Colum. J. Transn'l Law 401, 2010

Janis, Mark W., *International Law* (6th ed.), 2012, Wolters Kluwer, p. 373

Kessedjian, Catherine, "Public Order in European Law", *Erasmus Law Review*, Vol. 01, Issue 01, 2007, pp. 30

Kirgis, Paul F., "Arbitration, Bankruptcy and Public Policy: A Contractarian Analysis", *American Bankruptcy Institute Law Review*, Vol. 17, No. 2, Winter 2009, 503, p. 515

Klamert, Marcus, *The Principle of Loyalty in EU Law, Oxford Studies in European Law*, Graig, Paul, De Búrca, Gráinne (Series editors), Oxford University Press, 2014, p. 1

Kovacs, Robert B, A "Transnational Approach to the Arbitrability of Insolvency Proceedings in International Arbitration", *Norton Journal of Bankruptcy Law and Practice* Sept.–Oct. 2012, pp. 521–635

Larouche, Pierre, Cserne, Péter (eds.), *National Legal Systems and Globalization, New Role, Continuing Relevance*, T.M.C. Asser Press, Spinger, 2013, 12

Lee, Emily, "Comparing Hong Kong and Chinese Insolvency Laws and Their Cross-border Complexities", *The Journal of Comparative Law*, Vol. 9(2) 2015, pp. 259–260

Li Ling, "Corruption in China's Courts", in Randall Peerenboom (ed.), *Judicial Independence in China: Lessons for Global Rule of Law Promotion*, Cambridge University Press, 2010, pp. 201–202

Li Shuguang & Wang Zuofa, "Review of the PRC Bankruptcy Law in 2009", *INSOL International Technical Series* Issue No. 11, March 2010, p. 5

Li Yuwen, *The Judicial System and Reform in Post-Mao China: Stumbling Towards Justice*, Routledge, 2014, pp. 19–20, 199–234

Long Xiaoning, Wang Jun, "Judicial Local Protectionism in China: An empirical study of IP case", 42 *International Review of Law and Economics*, 2015, p. 59

LoPucki, "Cooperation in International Bankruptcy: A Post-Universalist Approach", 84 Cornell L. Rev. 750, 1999

LoPucki, Lynn M., "The Case of Cooperative Territoriality in International Bankruptcy", 98 *Michigan Law Review*, 2000, 2216

LoPucki, Lynn M., "Global and out of Control?" 79 Am. Bankr. L.J. 79, 2005

Lowell, John, "Conflict of Laws as Applied to Assignments for Creditors", 1 Harv. L. Rev. 259, 1888, 264

Magnus, Ulrich, "Harmonization and Unification of Law by the Means of General Principles", in Fogt, Morten M. (ed.), *Unification and Harmonization of International Commercial Law – Interaction or Deharmonization?*, Wolters Kluwer, 2012, p. 171

Maltese, Michele, "Court-to-Court Protocols in Cross-border Bankruptcy Proceedings: Differing Approaches between Civil Law and Common Law Legal Systems", 2013, at 15–16 & ft.48. www.iiiglobal.org/iii-prize-in-insolvency/2013iiiprizeannouncement.html (last accessed on 31 March, 2017)

Mathews, Gordon, Ma Eric Kit-wai, Lui, Tai-lok, *Hong Kong, China: Learning to Belong to a Nation*, Routledge Contemporary China Series, 2008, p. 3

McCormack, Gerard, "Universalism in Insolvency Proceedings and the Common Law", Oxford Journal of Legal Studies, Vol. 32, No. 2, 329, 2012, 347

Morgan, Robert and Man Sin Yeung, "Enforcement of Foreign and Mainland Arbitral Awards in Hong Kong: Med-Arb, Public Policy and Waiver" *Asian Dispute Review* 28, 2012

Moss, Gabriel, "Group Insolvency – Choice of Forum and Law: the European Experience under the Influence of English Pragmatism", 32 *Brooklyn Journal of International Law* 1005, 2007, 1007

Moss, Gabriel, Fletcher, Ian F., Isaacs, Stuart (ed.), *The EC Regulation on Insolvency Proceedings: A Commentary and Annotated Guide* (2nd ed.), Oxford University Press, 2016, paras. 4.04, 5.73

Omar, Paul, *European Insolvency Law*, Ashgate Publishing, 2004, p. 105

Paul, Joel R, "The Transformation of International Comity", 71 *Law and Contemporary Problems*, 2008, pp. 20, 23

Peerenboom, Randall, "Judicial Independence in China: Common Myths and Unfounded Assumptions", in: Randall Peerenboom (ed.), *Judicial Independence in China: Lessons for Global Rule of Law Promotion*, Cambridge University Press, 2010, pp. 81–82

Pottow, John A.E., "A New Role for Secondary Proceedings in International Bankruptcies", 46 Tex. Int'l L.J., 2011, p. 582

Puig, Gonzalo Villalta, "A Quasi-Adjudicative Dispute Settlement Mechanism for CEPA: The Rule of Law in Trade Relations between Mainland China and Hong Kong", *Chinese Journal of International Law*, Vol. 12(2), 2013, p. 306

Ramzy, Austin, "China and Taiwan Hold First Direct Talks Since '49", *New York Times*, 11 February, 2014

Rasmussen, Robert K., A "New Approach to Transnational Insolvencies", 19 *Michigan Journal of International Law*, 1999, 1

Rudbordeh, Amir Adl, "An analysis and hypothesis on forum shopping in insolvency law: From the European Insolvency Regulation to its Recast", p. 51, available at: www.iiiglobal.org/node/1932 (last accessed on 31 March, 2017)

Schroeter, Ulrich G., "The Status of Hong Kong and Macao under the United Nations Convention on Contracts for the International Sales of Goods", 16 *Pace International Law Review*, 2004, p. 311, ft 14, www.schroeter.li/pdf/Schroeter_16_Pace_Intl_L_Rev_2004_307.pdf (Last accessed on 31 March, 2017)

Schuz, Rhona, "The Doctrine of Comity in the Age of Globalization: between International Child Abduction and Cross-border Insolvency", Brook. J. Int'l L. Vol. 40, No. 1, 2015, p. 33

Slaughter, Anne-Marie, "A Global Community of Courts", 44 Harv. Int'l L.J., 2003, pp. 192, 206

Smart, Philip, *Cross-border Insolvency* (2nd ed.), Butterworth, 1998, p. 162

Tai, Benny Y.T., "Chapter 1 of HK's New Constitution", in: Chan Ming K and So Alvin Y (eds.), *Crisis and Transformation in China's Hong Kong*, HK: HK University Press, 2002, pp. 189–219, esp. at 211

Tam, Maria Wai-chu (editor-in-chief), "Basic Law – the Source of Hong Kong's Progress and Development, in: 15 Anniversary Reunification", 2012, pp. 86–87, www.basiclaw.gov.hk/en/publications/book/15anniversary_reunification_ch2_3.pdf (last accessed on 31 March, 2017)

Taylor, Stephen, "The Use of Protocols in Cross Border Insolvency Cases", in: Pannen, Klaus (ed.), *European Insolvency Regulation*, De Gruyter Recht, 2007, p. 682

Trautman, Donald T., et al., "Four Models for International Bankruptcy", 41 Am.J. Comp. Law, 1993, 575–576

Tu Guangjian, "The Conflict of Laws System in Macao", 40 Hong Kong L. J. 85, 2010, p. 86

Tung, Fredrick, "Is International Bankruptcy Possible", 23 Michigan J Intl L 31, 2001, 77

Twining, William, "Normative and Legal Pluralism: A Global Perspective", 20 *Duke Journal of Comparative and International Law* 47, 2010, pp. 488, 489

Van Calster, Geert, *European Private International Law*, Hart Publishing, 2013, p. 25

Wang Wei, "CEPA: A Lawful Free Trade Agreement Under "One Country, Two Customs Territories?", 10 Law & Bus. Rev. Am. 647, 2004, p. 654

Weatherill, Stephen, "Beyond Preemption? Shared Competence and Constitutional Change in the European Community", in D. O'Keeffe and P.M. Twomey (eds.), *Legal Issues of the Maastricht Treaty*, Chancery Law Publishing, 1994, pp. 13–33, 32

Wessels, Bob, *The Comity Principle, Amice, Rutgers-bundel* (Opstellen, op 26 April 2005 aangeboden aan prof. mr. G.R.Rutgers ter gelegenheid van zijn afscheid van de Rijksuniversiteit Groningen), Kluwer, 2005, p. 359

Wessels, Bob, Markell, Bruce A., & Kilborn, Jason J., *International Cooperation in Bankruptcy and Insolvency Matters*, Oxford University Press, 2009, at 43

Wessels, Bob, *International Insolvency Law* (3rd ed.), Vol. X, Deventer: Kluwer, 2012, paras. 10018, 10030, 10195, 10199, 10551, 10855p, 10939, 10334e, 10377–10379

Wessels, Bob, "Cross-border Insolvency Agreements: What Are They and Are They Here to Stay?" in: n: N.E.D. Faber, J.J. van Hees, N.S.G.J. Vermunt, *Overeenkomsten en insolventie, Serie Onderneming en Recht*, deel 72, Kluwer 2012, p. 370

Wessels, Bob, Fletcher, Ian, *Harmonisation of Insolvency Law in Europe*, Preadviezen Nederlandse Vereniging voor Burgerlijk Recht, Kluwer, 2012

Wessels, Bob, "Contracting out of Secondary Insolvency Proceedings: The Main Liquidator's Undertaking in the Meaning of Article 18 in the Proposal to Amend the EU Insolvency Regulation", *Brooklyn Journal of Corporate, Finance & Commercial Law*, Vol. 9, issue 1, 2014, p. 87

Wessels, Bob, "On the Future of European Insolvency Law – INSOL Europe Academic Forum's 5th Edwin Coe Lecture", Parry, Rebecca, *European Insolvency Law: Current Issues and Prospects for Reform*, INSOL Europe, 2014, pp. 135–141

Wessels, Bob, "Nortel Network Joint hearing as a test case for EU JudgeCo Principle 10?", 13 May, 2014, http://bobwessels.nl/2014/05/2014-05-doc8-nortel-network-joint-hearing-as-a-test-case-for-eu-judgeco-principle-10/ (last visited on 31 March, 2017)

Westbrook, Jay L., "A Global Solution to International Default", 98 Mich.L.Rev. (2000), at 2292–2293

Westbrook, Jay L., "International Judicial Negotiation", 38 Tex. Int'l L.J., 2003, p. 567, 569

Westbrook, Jay L., "Chapter 15 at Last", 79 Am. Bankr. L.J.713, 2005, p. 716

Westbrook, Jay L., "Theory and Pragmatism in Global Insolvencies: Choice of Law and Choice of Forum", 65 Am. Bankr. L.J. 457, 1991, p. 460

Woelki, Katharina Boele, *Unifying and Harmonizing Substantive Law and the Role of Conflict of Laws*, Leiden/Boston: Martinus Nijhoff Publishers, 2010, pp. 18–19

Wu, Chien-Huei, "A New Landscape in the WTO: Economic Integration Among China, Taiwan, Hong Kong and Macao", *European Yearbook of International Economic Law*, Vol. 3(2012), pp. 241–242

Wu Wei-Hua, "Does a Fixed Civil Judgment Rendered in Mainland China and Recognized by a Taiwanese Court have any Impact on Taiwan's Legal System? – Analysis of Taiwan Supreme Court Judgments" (96) Tai Shang Tzu No. 2531 (2007) and (97) Tai Shang Tzu No. 2376 (2008), *National Taiwan University Law Review* 6:1, 2011, 35

Yamauchi, Keith D., "Should Reciprocity Be a Part of the UNCITRAL Model Cross-Border Insolvency Law?" in: 16 *International Insolvency Review*, Winter 2007, Issue 3, p. 150

Zhang Haizheng, Kuang Jingting, "Corporate Reorganization Case Analysis under China's New Bankruptcy Law", *International Corporate Rescue*, Vol. 11, issue 3, 2014, p. 177

Zhang Xianchu, Smart, Philip, "Development of Regional Conflict of Laws: On the Arrangement of Mutual Recognition and Enforcement of Judgments in Civil and Commercial Matters between Mainland China and Hong Kong SAR", 36 Hong Kong L. J. 553, 2006, pp. 565, 567

Zlatanska, Elina, "To Publish, or Not to Publish Arbitral Awards: That is the Question . . .", *Arbitration*, Vol. 81, No. 1, 2015, 25–37, p. 26

In Chinese

Chen Yonghui, Shen Shuangwu, "The Supreme People's Court and the Hong Kong SAR Signed Arrangement on Reciprocal Recognition and Enforcement of Judgments in Civil and Commercial Matters by the Courts of the Mainland and of the Hong Kong Special Administrative Region Pursuant to Choice of Court Agreements between Parties Concerned", *People's Court Daily*, 15 July, 2006, p. 1

Gao Xiaoli, "The Development of the Arrangements Made by the Mainland with Hong Kong and Macao for Legal Assistance in Civil an Matters from the Perspective of Mainland People's Courts", *China Law*, Issue 06, 2015, p. 80

Gu Zhihao, "The First Successful Reorganization Case of Unlisted Company after the New EBL Is Implemented: Comments on Reorganization of Yaxin Electronics and Yaxin Circuit Board", *Law Review of Corporate Reorganization & Restructuring*, 2012, pp. 43, 46–57

Jiang Baoguo, "A Comparative Study on the Recognition and Enforcement of Civil and Commercial Judgments Arrangements between the Mainland, Hong Kong and Macao – with special reference to the Practice of Hong Kong", *Legal Forum*, No. 5 (Vol. 22, Ser. No. 113), Sep., 2007, p. 71

Liu Jing, "Credit Deficiency and Legislation Preference: Explanation of Difficulties to Establish China's Personal Insolvency System", *Social Scientist*, Issue 2, 2011, p. 100

Qin Jin, Zhou Qiang "Host a Supreme People's Court Meeting on Specialized Topics: to promote transformation and upgrading of the People's Courts on Development of Informatization", *Legal Daily*, 23 February, 2016, available at: www.legaldaily.com.cn/index_article/content/2016-02/23/content_6495307.htm (last visited on 31 March, 2017)

Song Xixiang, "Reciprocal Recognition and Enforcement of Civil and Commercial Judgments between the Mainland and Macao", *Academic Journal of One Country, Two Systems*, Vol. 4, 2012, p. 93

Wang, Jin-Pyng, Statement of the President of the Parliament on 26 April, 2014, www.cna.com.tw/news/firstnews/201404060077-1.aspx (last accessed on 31 March, 2017)

Zheng Wei, "A Preliminary Discussion on the Mechanism of Interpreting the Basic Law of the Macao SAR", *Academic Journal of "One Country, Two Systems"*, Vol. I, 2009 p. 159

Zhang Wei, "Annual Acceptance of Arbitration Cases Exceeded 100,000 for the First Time", 7 June, *Legal Daily*, 2014, at 6

Summary

The idea of China's Inter-Regional Cross-border Insolvency Arrangement (CICIA) reflects an ongoing trend concerning harmonization of cross-border insolvency law through internal legislation of regional institutions and also best practices set out in soft law, including guidelines and principles contributed by the international organization (UNCITRAL), non-governmental organizations (III, INSOL etc.) and even private parties active in the area of restructuring and insolvency law. That trend is a response to regional integration and globalization, which intensifies interregional and international legal interaction and the need for one jurisdiction to always apply its own law is gradually reduced.

Unfortunately, there are walls erected or being erected across the world, which frustrate such harmonization. Some of them might be physical. Some of them are invisible. One of the obstacles is the diversity of cross-border insolvency laws and the lack of a clear understanding thereof. For instance, throughout the Asian region, there appears to be a great deal of reluctance to follow this trend (Spigelman, 2007). The adoption rates of the Model Law in Asia remain very low; it has only been enacted by Japan (2000), the Republic of Korea (2006), the Philippines (2010) and Singapore (2017). In addition, most of the cross-border insolvency rules applied in Asian jurisdictions are conservative. China is such an example. In the Mainland, there is only one article (Article 5 of the EBL) that provides recognition criteria for foreign cross-border insolvency proceedings, which are subject to a set of public policy exceptions with no clear standards. Hong Kong's current insolvency laws are based loosely on law from England that dates back to 1929. As of 2016, the Hong Kong government is still pondering whether it is appropriate to introduce s 426 of the UK Insolvency Act 1986 into Hong Kong.[1] The current cross-border insolvency rules of Macao (1999) and Taiwan (1935) are dependent on the principle of territoriality. Both rules have the same goal that creates a ring fence of assets in favor of local creditors (Garcia, 2015; Gong, 2013). What is the reason for the common phenomenon of undeveloped cross-border insolvency in Asia? A speech delivered by the Chief Justice of Singapore Chan Sek Keong provided some proper reference. The answer relates to the correlation between the law and the economy. His Justice mentioned that "ring-fencing of assets of foreign companies for the benefit of local creditors has been a feature of the Singapore insolvency regime since 1967" (CHAN, 2011). At that time, Singapore, as a developing economy, was only a recipient of capital and therefore did not experience the problems of cross-border insolvency affecting global companies from those economies that make investments (CHAN, 2011). Accordingly, the need for a well-established cross-border insolvency system was relatively low. The landscape of the Asian economy is undergoing changes. According to the World Investment Report 2017, China is now the second largest investing country in the world.[2] In 2016, FDI out flows from developing Asia rose by 7 per cent to $363 billion, mainly because of surging

FDI out flows from China. "An improved economic outlook in ASEAN and China is likely to lift investor confidence and help boost FDI inflows in 2017 and beyond".[3] At the meantime, Singapore is "the leading outward investing economy in ASEAN",[4] which finally adopted the Model Law in 2017. It is apparent that the current Asian cross-border insolvency systems do not reflect how individual nations have experienced the growth of economies. What then is the possible consequence? Given the fact that assets no longer move in a single direction, insistence on a territorial approach can possibly invite reciprocal treatment by other jurisdictions, which may ultimately affect assets invested abroad. For instance, Hong Kong is now in the process of reforming its corporate insolvency law. In deciding whether or not to introduce the Model Law into its statutory insolvency legislation, the Hong Kong government considered that the attitude of its major trading partners (including the Mainland and Singapore[5]) in this regard should be closely monitored in advance.[6] More importantly, such reciprocal attitude may trigger more concerns about economic cooperation within a country or a possible regional economic community, where there are integrated agreements on trade and commerce (such as CEPA and FTAAP[7]) and assets that can be moved out of the jurisdictions more easily.

Trust issues also constitute one of the obstacles. Some jurisdictions may not have trust relations with those jurisdictions they have to deal with and thus the consideration of the rights and authority of other jurisdictions may vary. As a result, the focus of harmonization is heavily dependent on the level of interaction between the jurisdictions because it requires a proper balance between "retention of forum-state regulatory authority and acknowledgment of the equal authority of other states within their own territory" (Brand, 2005). According to the classic perspective, such harmonization should abide by the principle of universality, which attached importance to the concentration of insolvency proceedings within one forum. That principle above all raises important questions regarding the jurisdictional subpart of private international law. As Beale once remarked, "the power of a sovereign to affect the rights of persons, whether by legislation, by executive decree or by the judgment of a court is called jurisdiction" (Beale, 1923). In order to approach the traditional principle of universality, it entailed that States needed to compromise their sovereign authority for cooperation in cross-border insolvency. That approach was only partly achieved in the EU. Through its decade-long integration process, the EU has evolved into a single community of laws with common values and legal principles shared between its members.[8] As a result, the Member States have delegated part of their "sovereign" function of law-making to the regional institutions. That possibly explains why the Regulation is able to adhere to the principle of universality albeit in a modified manner because it harmonized interregional cross-border insolvency in such a way by removing the need for reference to national rules for the purposes of determining the proper jurisdiction, applicable law or recognition. The implementation of the EU Insolvency Regulation opened the era of the cross-border insolvency. It activated interaction between the uniform Union law and national insolvency law of the Member States as well as interconnection in matters of cross-border insolvency between the Member States. Unfortunately, due to the referendum held in the UK, the UK triggered its retreat negotiation in accordance with Article 50 of the Treaty on the European Union on 29 March, 2017, which in essence weakens mutual trust between the neighbors.

In the more globalized societies of today, insolvency proceedings require cooperation across many different jurisdictions around the world. Nonetheless, without geographic advantages, overlapping time zones, shared culture and shared languages, we no longer live enmeshed in such "thick trust relationships" (Cook, 2005) as the EU legal system used to rely on. Against that background, UNCITRAL set up facilitating recognition of foreign insolvency proceedings as the main line of the Model Law. The most important jurisdictional element, COMI, is utilized under the Model Law merely to determine the degree to which a court must recognize a foreign proceeding, whereas COMI helps determine which Member State takes precedence when proceedings have commenced in multiple jurisdictions within the EU (Story, 2015). Moreover, before the Model Law was drafted, UNCITRAL conducted several consultations with judges, practitioners, interested organizations and governments. One of its key findings was that the crucial function in cross-border insolvency cooperation was performed by the judges and practitioners from various jurisdictions, in which assets of the debtor might be found, especially by entering into cross-border insolvency agreements.[9] That way of cooperation was voluntarily driven by the individual insolvency case itself, which efficiently linked the insolvency proceedings, and its feasibility has been tested in practice worldwide. Instead of a centralized and concentrated method suggested by the classic principle of universality, the Model Law created an interconnected network structure via cooperation and communication between the courts and practitioners. Due to UK's retreat, the potential influence of the EU law on common law system as well as its exemplary role on interregional legal cooperation between the Mainland and Hong Kong is in question. No matter the outcome, the result of Brexit vote has frustrated the trust relationships and sincere cooperation as the EU legal system used to rely on. Moreover, without a common final dispute resolver, legal cooperation between the EU and the UK might encounter similar problems concerning decisional harmony in matters of cross-border insolvency as in China's interregional context. Accordingly, it is essential to look for a coordinating mechanism which both the EU and the UK choose to abide, corresponds to the way the different jurisdictions interact with each other in a flattened globalized world and promotes mutual understanding through direct exchange of information and opinions. In the future, that coordinated approach might help the UK and the EU to establish a new cross-border insolvency cooperation regime through interaction on the basis of mutual respect and it is expected to bring more mutual understanding to the neighbors.

China's interregional cross-border insolvency cooperation involves the interplay between an emerging regional legal order and cross-border insolvency. For a sovereign state that has gone through reunification and closer economic interaction, whether or not the creditors can recover their claims in the event of trans-regional insolvency will become a decisive factor for interregional investment. Besides, it is also necessary to harmonize regional legal conflicts for the purpose of further integration. After comparing the cross-border insolvency systems in the four regions and referring to two leading international insolvency regimes, the Regulation and the Model Law, the book provides 10 recommendations for China's Inter-Regional Cross-border Insolvency Arrangement (CICIA)[10] by tailoring the merits of relevant international experience in China's context in a balanced manner. First of all, CICIA opts for the coordinated approach as its guiding principle (Recommendation 1). In order to smoothly attain the goal of reunification, the Mainland made commitments that it would partly restrict its sovereign authority to guarantee the high degree of autonomy of the SARs, including the legislative power and the independent judicial power.[11] Those commitments have been honored and incorporated into the Basic Law with an effective term for 50 years.[12] To arrange for a centralized cross-border insolvency cooperation structure, as advocated by the principle of universality, it requires the Mainland to further compromise its sovereign authority and the SARs to restrain their high degree of autonomy. That has been unlikely to happen so far. For example, the Mainland and the Hong Kong SAR had difficulty in reaching consensus on rules of jurisdiction when negotiating the bilateral arrangement about reciprocal enforcement of judgments in civil and commercial matters. In order to avoid the deadlock situation, both sides decided to allow the parties concerned to enter into choice of court agreements instead. More importantly, the legal cooperation between the Mainland and the SARs is established by way of granting legal assistance based on consensus via the judicial organs in each region,[13] which serves as a proper legal foundation for the coordinated approach.

It also needs to be taken into account that the principle of universality lays a great deal of emphasis on the matter of jurisdiction. As Westbrook remarked, choice of forum was the "explicit focus of the universalist rule and choice of law was a result of universalism often implicitly assumed" (Westbrook, 1991). For instance, the Regulation adopted *lex fori concursus* as the basic rule of its uniform choice of law system (Moss, Fletcher, Isaacs, 2016). It requires that the law of the Member State, in which its court is competent to open insolvency proceedings, shall determine the conditions for the opening, conduct and closure of insolvency proceedings.[14] Hence, under the Regulation, the outcome of insolvency proceedings essentially depends much more on jurisdiction. In addition, allowing only one single proceeding running worldwide could lead to a "fight over who gets to be the COMI in any given bankruptcy" (Pottow, 2011). That is why the Regulation and the Model Law allow the opening of non-main (territorial/secondary) proceedings, which can make the competition less intensive. However, the main insolvency proceedings are ensured to play the dominant role under the Regulation.[15] Main insolvency proceedings rendered by a competent court of a Member State, once opened, shall be automatically recognized in all other Member States. Such automatic recognition is guaranteed by the principle of mutual trust under the EU Treaties. The problem is the COMI model is a fact-sensitive criterion. It took some time for the CJEU to have the chance to clarify some issues surrounding the use of the COMI concept. However, the manipulability of COMI remains since the facts can be changed (Eidenmüller, 2009) and more importantly, the advantages to become the main proceedings are considerable under the EU regime. That incentivised forum shopping, abusive or not, and resulted in disputes over jurisdiction. Although the recast Regulation provided suspension periods hoping to counter abusive forum shopping,[16] it has been argued by the Commission that these types of measures are not sufficiently effective to achieve the objective of resolving the issues of abusive forum shopping, reasoning that such a measure could be circumvented by skilled professionals and would not improve legal certainty for creditors because it would replace the current uncertainty relating to the determination of COMI by a new uncertainty relating to the time the COMI shifted.[17] It seems that the effects of the suspension periods still need to be tested in the course of implementation even though the measure has been finally introduced into the recast Regulation.

It is acknowledged that mutual trust is essential to a regional legal order. By comparing the development of mutual trust in the EU and in China, it is observed that mutual trust is pretty much at the primary stage in China's regional legal system. To foster the trust relationship, it is better to avoid fighting tooth and nail on jurisdictional issues. Besides, the legal foundation for the establishment of such a compulsory jurisdiction system for cross-border cooperation in insolvency cases as under the Regulation is still under construction. Therefore, CICIA set out for a balanced approach by choosing the recognition-based system as its overriding objective (Recommendation 2). Considering that each jurisdiction has its territorial judicial authority in China, it is suggested to use comity as the foundation for recognition under CICIA (Recommendation 4). That approach results from a balance between mutual trust (strengthened comity) that functions in the EU and reciprocity that actually operates in China and its underlying requirement is the equal respect of the authority of one jurisdiction for another. As for the effects of recognition, they are not governed by the uniform choice of law rules because of the restricted scope of uniform legislation under the Basic Law regime and the difficulty in harmonization of substantive law in reality. Instead, they are guaranteed by a list of minimum reliefs under CICIA by referring to the experience of the Model Law. In accordance with the limits on the exercise of judicial authority connoted by comity, public policy is the only exception to recognition under CICIA, which needs to be interpreted in a self-restrained manner (Recommendation 5).

In compliance with the guiding principle based on the coordinated approach adopted by both the Regulation and the Model Law, cooperation and communication is the cornerstone of CICIA (Recommendation 6). The coordinated approach received global support from academic and practical innovations (such as Global Principles and EU JudgeCo Principles). Above all, the courts and the insolvency practitioner play an indispensable role in the insolvency system. That is also the case in China. In the Mainland, the courts have been granted substantial and procedural power in accordance with the EBL.[18] The EBL also provides for a set of functions of the administrators,[19] which is accompanied with a couple of judicial interpretations concerning appointment and compensations of administrators.[20] Considering that Hong Kong SAR is a common law jurisdiction, the dominant role of the courts is self-explanatory. Insolvency practitioners are most of the time liquidators, whose duties are considered onerous, including the functions to "conduct a thorough investigation into the affairs of a company, winding up its business and distribute the remaining assets between parties who hold an interest in the company" (Hickin, 2012). In Macao SAR, any creditor can bring an insolvency proceeding to court.[21] Once the insolvency proceedings begin, the court immediately appoints a bankruptcy administrator,[22] who will help supervise the debtor both in running his business[23] as well as managing his other assets.[24] Since the local insolvency system relies on the courts and insolvency practitioners to operate smoothly, they are also key actors in the field of cross-border insolvency. One of their most important contributions is the invention of cross-border insolvency agreements (protocol). Faced with the daily necessity of dealing with insolvency cases, the insolvency profession developed the most common means that facilitates cross-border cooperation and communication of multiple insolvency proceedings in different jurisdictions in the absence of widespread adoption of facilitating national or international law.[25] Due to their inherent flexibility, cross-border insolvency agreements gradually shift from a coordination instrument to a medium, which contains a framework of coordination as well as a combination of coordinating instruments and facilitates them to function in an orderly manner. Therefore, cross-border insolvency agreements are recommended as a key mechanism that can be utilized by the courts and insolvency practitioners to coordinate the interregional insolvency proceedings involving a single debtor and enterprise groups under CICIA (Recommendation 7). Cooperation and communication is also possible because each region has the same language, i.e. Chinese, and the technical assistance on exchange of relevant information provided by the responsible authorities is also available on the basis of the Basic Law. Therefore, it is suggested to include the minimum amount of information mandatorily to be published in the interregional insolvency registers under CICIA so as to promote the publicity related to the insolvency proceedings (Recommendation 9).

Furthermore, it is suggested to establish a functional dispute settlement mechanism under CICIA (Recommendation 8). The main focus of CICIA, which is almost identical to the Model Law, lies in two aspects: recognition and coordination. Both Fletcher and Wessels have previously pointed out that the success of the Model Law is not dependent on the number of States that decide to enact the law, but heavily relies on in what manner countries choose to enact it (Fletcher, 2005; Wessels, 2006). As observed, there are indeed a number of deviations from the Model Law in the enacting States, most significantly including diverse interpretation of COMI, proper understanding of public policy and penetration of the reciprocity requirement. As explored and examined in the aforementioned case studies, those deviations pose a great obstacle to the objective of uniformity and predictability as required under the Model Law.[26] They are partly caused by its flexible nature since the States might not adopt the Model Law uniformly.[27] They may also be attributed to a lack of efficient institutional support equivalent to that from the CJEU. In compliance with the Basic Law and the guiding principle of CICIA, a functional dispute settlement mechanism is proposed in the form of a special meeting, which is convened on the basis of interregional court-to-court cooperation and communication. A special meeting can be initiated for two grounds. One relates to explanation of the related provisions under CICIA. The other arises from disputes concerning the cross-border insolvency agreement. The effects of those two kinds of explanation are different. Upon consensus of the Supreme Courts concerned, the explanation given by the special meeting on specific provisions of CICIA shall have binding effect on that individual case. Furthermore, upon consensus of all the Supreme Courts, the explanation shall have binding effect on the specific provisions under CICIA. Under this circumstance, the courts are supervisors for the entire arrangement through cooperation and communication, which achieve harmonious interpretation on the regional level, in particular safeguarding China's own autonomous jurisdiction and resolving jurisdiction conflicts. In the case involving cross-border insolvency agreements disputes, the function of the special meeting is more akin to a joint forum, to which disputes are submitted for a final decision. The opinions are only binding upon the consensus of all the requesting courts involved and only effective on the individual case referred to the special meeting. As remarked by Rabatel and Deparis based on their observation of the appointment of liaison magistrates, "nothing quite compares to a direct exchange, face-to-face, between two people who know each other and meet regularly" (Rabatel & Deparis, 2015). The special meeting is expected to provide the opportunity to judges to exchange points of view and achieve consensus. Thus, it can further help to generate an awareness of a common identity and community, which may gradually increase mutual understanding between the Mainland and the two SARs.

Nonetheless, doubts arise over the feasibility of that functional dispute settlement mechanism. Indeed, there are alternative methods, whereas the mechanism proposed under CICIA is a balanced approach between popular academic recommendation and government preference. Some insolvency scholars give serious consideration to the use of arbitration as a supplement to international insolvency cases (Ehmke & Lewis, 2016; Clement, 2014; Bufford, 2014; Gropper, 2012; Westbrook, 2011). Due to the wide adoption of the New York Convention, enforceability of awards is regarded as arbitration's most valuable characteristic,[28] which is accordingly the "principal attraction for using international arbitration in the context of international insolvency cases" (Bufford, 2014; Kovacs, 2012). However, as aforementioned in Chapter 5, interregional recognition and enforcement of arbitral awards is granted on a different basis in China.[29] According to the Hong Kong International Arbitration Center (HKIAC), the Mainland remains the most frequent users of Hong Kong arbitration service.[30] For instance, there were about 116 (2010), 96 (2011), 93 (2012) and 65 (2013) Mainland-related arbitration cases handled by HKIAC on an annual basis.[31] Nevertheless, from 2008 to 2014, there were only 19 Hong Kong arbitral awards in total, which were accepted for recognition and enforcement by the Mainland courts (Gao, 2015). Those associated amounts are considerably uneven, which indicates that enforceability of interregional arbitral awards in the Mainland may not be very promising. The other important benefit of arbitration is neutrality. As aforementioned in the main text of the dissertation (Chapter 3), it is true that there is government interference, in particular local protectionism, on the insolvency proceedings in the Mainland. Considering the impartiality of the judicial systems, arbitration can be used to avoid the local courts. Nevertheless, the law and legal institutions cannot be independent of or altogether immune from politics (Zhang, 2014). For example, unemployment rates and revenue are the common concern of most governments around the world. Accordingly, under insolvency regimes, some creditors, such as employees and tax authorities, are usually entitled to special priority (Martin, 2005) in addition to the principle of equal treatment of creditors. Under that circumstance, who should have the proper authority to settle disputes arising from the insolvency proceedings without jeopardizing the objectives of national insolvency law? Depending on the nature of the issue, it might be difficult for states to cede that kind of authority to independent arbitrators who are not bound to adhere to any country's bankruptcy laws (Peacock, 2015). In addition, arbitration "is a matter of consent, not coercion".[32] In practice, it is difficult for the parties concerned to reach an agreement to arbitrate since insolvency proceedings are associated with crucial interests.[33]

More importantly, China prefers to resolve sovereignty-related disputes through negotiation and consultation by the parties concerned, rather than submitting them to any third-party settlement procedures. The recent arbitration on the South China Sea issue is such an example, in which the Chinese government refused to participate in the arbitration and claimed that it could legally ignore the pending arbitral award.[34] In matters of interregional legal cooperation, if there is any dispute arising from the current arrangements, as aforementioned in Chapter 5, it should also be settled through negotiation. China's interregional cross-border insolvency arrangement is a part of China's regional legal order. CICIA, however, recommends placing the balance of power in the hands of the judiciary. Although the regional legal order emerged upon reunification, it is not purely sovereignty-related. In essence, it requires a balance between two equally important political considerations, i.e. local prosperity and stability and the sound and sustainable development of regional integration. Nonetheless, the result of a government-led negotiation can probably be influenced by political power, which might not be deemed as impartial and equal and thus might not be acceptable to the public (Puig, 2013). Arbitration is a form of party choice of dispute settlement mechanism. Its party-driven nature requires adaptability of the system and processes in order to meet private needs. For example, confidentiality is one of its outstanding merits. Therefore, arbitrators in the cross-border insolvency context are under no obligation to take into consideration the development of regional legal order. That reduces the potential to give proper interpretation or guidance on CICIA, which can impede its implementation. It is the courts on behalf of each region that have the ultimate authority to decide whether or not to recognize the rights and authority of other jurisdictions, which consequently contributes to the growth and progress of China's regional legal order. Hence, it is more appropriate for the courts to play the key role in performing the correctional function to restore the balance in China's interregional context.

Abiding by the principle of collectivity and seeking an integrated regional legal order, it is intended to establish a uniform and comprehensive interregional cooperation arrangement in China (Recommendation 3). Nonetheless, there is a lack of a binding constitutional foundation on legal cooperation between the Mainland and Taiwan. Therefore, Taiwan is to be put in a separate cooperative mechanism under CICIA (Recommendation 10). Given the experience of the cross-strait cooperation, which is mainly conducted via two non-governmental intermediaries from each side, as well as the significance of communication and cooperation, independent intermediaries are introduced to overcome the hurdles in the course of cross-strait insolvency cooperation. The main duty of independent intermediaries is to maintain the connection with their counterpart, devise a practical means of conducting communication between the courts concerned and keep the courts from the both sides informed of possible conflicts or problems in the course of cross-strait insolvency proceedings.

To conclude, CICIA with its 10 recommendations is merely a modest and elementary attempt to address one of the issues arising out of China's interregional legal cooperation. It tentatively seeks a balance between the desire for law unification and the reality of legal diversity, levels of integration and conflicts of interests, international standards and characteristics unique to China as well as sovereignty and autonomy within a country. Considering the challenges and difficulties encountered, it is fully acknowledged that it must take time to finally achieve a well-accepted solution. Nonetheless, legal cooperation is not for conventions, treaties or agreements. It is for the common welfare of the national economy and its citizens. That is why we have to work on something. For each interregional cooperation and communication and for each dispute properly resolved, the individual courts make a contribution to forming mutual trust and shaping the interregional legal order. Trust is not a given. It has to be built bit by bit.

Notes

1 Bills Committee on the Companies (Winding Up and Miscellaneous Provisions) (Amendment) Bill 2015, Summary of views of submissions and Government's responses, CB (1)481/15–16(04), 25 January 2016, Government's responses No. 60.
2 UNCTAD, World Investment Report 2017: Investment and the Digital Economy, p. xi
3 UNCTAD, World Investment Report 2017: Investment and the Digital Economy, p. 51
4 UNCTAD, World Investment Report 2017: Investment and the Digital Economy, p. 54
5 Trade and Industry Department of Hong Kong SAR, Hong Kong's Principal Trading Partners in 2015, available at: www.tid.gov.hk/english/trade_relations/mainland/trade.html (last accessed on 31 March, 2017).
6 Bills Committee on the Companies (Winding Up and Miscellaneous Provisions) (Amendment) Bill 2015, Summary of views of submissions and Government's responses, CB (1)481/15–16(04), 25 January 2016, Government's responses No. 59.
7 Asia–Pacific Economic Cooperation (APEC) is a regional economic forum established in 1989, which is composed of 21 members. Its recent activity involves discussions on the possible pathways to the Free Trade Area of the Asia-Pacific (FTAAP). In November 2014, APEC Leaders endorsed the "Beijing Roadmap for APEC's Contribution to the Realization of the Free Trade Area of Asia-Pacific (FTAAP)". The roadmap provides for a "Collective Strategic Study on Issues related to the Realization of the FTAAP" to be concluded by the end of 2016.
8 TFEU, Article 2(2), Article 4(2)(j).
9 UNCITRAL/INSOL Colloquium on Cross-Border Insolvency, 17–19 April, 1994, Vienna, A/CN.9/398 – Cross-border insolvency: report on UNCITRAL-INSOL Colloquium on Cross-Border Insolvency, paras. 12–13.
10 Please note that the Summary aims at reinforcing the main line of CICIA. Therefore, in the Summary, the 10 recommendations of CICIA may not be discussed strictly in sequence.
11 Joint Declaration of the Government of the United Kingdom of Great Britain and Northern Ireland and the Government of the People's Republic of China on the Question of Hong Kong, 3(3); Joint Declaration of the Government of the People's Republic of China and the Government of the Portuguese Republic on the question of Macao 2(2).
12 Basic Law of Hong Kong SAR, Article 5; Basic Law of Macao SAR, Article 93.
13 Basic Law of Hong Kong SAR, Article 95; Basic Law of Macao SAR, Article 5.
14 EC Regulation, Recital (23), Article 4; EU Regulation (recast), Recital (66), Article 7.
15 EU Regulation (recast), Recital (48).

16 EU Regulation (recast), Recital (31), Article 3(1).
17 EU Commission, EU Commission Staff Working Document Impact Assessment Accompanying the document – Revision of Regulation (EC) No 1346/2000 on insolvency proceedings, Strasbourg, 12.12.2012, p. 35.
18 Substantial powers mainly include adjudication of the matters affecting the amount and value of the bankruptcy estate, including revocation of preferences and fraudulent transactions (EBL, Articles 31–33), determining the claims of the parties in relation to their entitlement to the ownership of some of the properties in the bankruptcy estate (EBL, Article 58) and approving their application to take back their ownership (EBL, Articles 34–39) and approving the application of set off rights (EBL, Article 40). Procedural powers mainly include the power to accept the case (EBL, Article 10), appoint the administrators (EBL, Article 22), to convene the first creditors' meeting (EBL, Article 62), to approve the asset realization plan and the distribution (EBL, Article 116) and the plan of reorganization (EBL, Article 86), to declare the debtor bankrupt (EBL, Article 107), to terminate the procedure (EBL, Article 108), and to supervise the implementation of the plan of reorganization (EBL, Article 91).
19 EBL, Article 25.
20 Provisions of the Supreme People's Court on Designating the Administrator during the Trial of Enterprise Bankruptcy Cases [2007] Judicial Interpretation No. 8; Provisions of the Supreme People's Court on Determination of the Administrator's Remunerations [2007] Judicial Interpretation No. 9.
21 Macao Civil Procedure Code, Article 1082.
22 Ibid., Article 1049–1(a).
23 Ibid., Article 1050.
24 Ibid., Article 1050–1.
25 UNCITRAL Practice Guide on Cross-Border Insolvency Cooperation, Ch.II, para. 12.
26 The Model Law, Articles 3, 8.
27 Guide and Interpretation, para. 92.
28 White & Case, 2015 International Arbitration Survey: Improvements and Innovations in International Arbitration, p. 5, available at: www.arbitration.qmul.ac.uk/docs/164761.pdf (last accessed on 31 March, 2017).
29 Arrangement between the Mainland and the Hong Kong SAR on Reciprocal Recognition and Enforcement of Arbitration Awards ; Arrangement between the Mainland and the Macao SAR on Reciprocal Recognition and Enforcement of Arbitration Awards.
30 Annual Statistic Report of HKIAC, available at: www.hkiac.org/zh-hans/about-us/statistics (last accessed on 31 March, 2017).
31 Ibid.
32 *Re Nortel Networks, Inc.*, No. 09–10138, 2013 WL 1385271, at 10.
33 Ibid., at 2–5 (Bankr D Del Apr. 3, 2013).
34 Vice Foreign Minister Liu Zhenmin Meets with US Media Delegation to Discuss South China Sea Issue (20 May, 2016); Wang Yi Talks about South China Sea Issue: Facts will Tell and Justice will Prevail (24 May, 2016); Foreign Ministry Spokesperson Hua Chunying's Regular Press Conference on 27 May, 2016; Article by Ambassador Tian Xuejun: China Will Not Fall into the Trap of South China Sea Arbitration; Foreign Ministry Spokesperson Hong Lei's Regular Press Conference on 8 June, 2016, all available at: www.fmprc.gov.cn/wjb/eng_search.jsp (last accessed on 31 March, 2017).

Reference list

Beale, Joseph H., "The Jurisdiction of a Sovereign State", *Harvard Law Review*, Vol. 36, No. 3, 241–262, 1923, p. 241

Brand, Ronald A., "Balancing Sovereignty and Party Autonomy in Private International Law: Regression at the European Court of Justice", *University of Pittsburgh School of Law Working Paper Series*, 2005, p. 9, available at: http://law.bepress.com/pittlwps/art25 (last accessed on 31 March, 2017)

Bufford, Samuel, "International Insolvency Law & International Arbitration – A Preliminary Perspective", 23 *Journal of Bankruptcy Law & Practice*, 670, 2014

Chan Sek Keong, "Cross-border Insolvency Issues Affecting Singapore", 23 SAcLJ, 413, 2011, pp. 415, 419

Clement, Zack A., "Position Paper Supporting Greater Use of Arbitration in Connection with Insolvency Matters", available at: www.iiiglobal.org/sites/default/files/17position_paper_supporting_greater_use_of_arbitration_in_connection_. . . . pdf (last accessed on 31 March, 2017)

Cook, Karen S., Hardin, Russell, Levi, Margaret, *Cooperation without Trust?* Vol. IX, Russell Sage Foundation Series on Trust, p. 196, 2005

Ehmke, David, and Lewis, Alfred, "Navigating Scylla and Charybdis: International Arbitration and National Insolvency", p. 23, available at: www.iiiglobal.org/node/1932 (last accessed on 31 March, 2017)

Eidenmüller, Horst, "Abuse of Law in the Context of European Insolvency Law", 6 ECFLR 1, 2009, p. 5

Fletcher, Ian F., *Insolvency in Private International Law: National and International Approaches*, Oxford University Press, 2005, para. 873

Gao Xiaoli, "The Development of the Arrangements Made by the Mainland with Hong Kong and Macao for Legal Assistance in Civil Matters from the Perspective of Mainland People's Courts", *China Law*, Issue 06, 2015, p. 80

Garcia, Augusto Teixeira, *Macao Insolvency Law and Cross-border Insolvency Issues*, New Zealand Association for Comparative Law: hors série (Wellington) XIX, 2015, p. 341

Gong Xinyi, "To Recognize or Not to Recognize? Comparative Study of Lehman Brothers Cases in the Mainland China and Taiwan", *International Corporate Rescue*, Vol. 10, Issue 4, Chase Cambria Publishing, 2013, p. 242

Gropper, Allan, "The Arbitration of Cross-Border Insolvencies", 86 Am. Bankr. L.J. 201, 2012

Hickin, John, "Role and Status of Liquidators", in: Kwan, Susan, *Company Law in Hong Kong (Insolvency)*, Sweet & Maxwell, 2012, at 2.001

Kovacs, Robert B, A "Transnational Approach to the Arbitrability of Insolvency Proceedings in International Arbitration", *Norton Journal of Bankruptcy Law and Practice* Sept.–Oct. 2012, p. 529

Martin, Nathalie, "The Role of History and Culture in Developing Bankruptcy and Insolvency Systems: The Perils of Legal Transplantation", 28 B.C. Int'l & Comp. L. Rev. 1, 2005, p. 33

Moss, Gabriel, Fletcher, Ian F., Isaacs, Stuart (ed.), *The EU Regulation on Insolvency Proceedings* (3rd ed.), Oxford University Press, 2016, at 4.05

Peacock, Lauren L., "A Tale of Two Courts: The Novel Cross-border Bankruptcy Trial", 23 Am. Bankr. Inst. L. Rev. 543, 2015, p. 567

Pottow, John A.E., "A New Role for Secondary Proceedings in International Bankruptcies", 46 Tex. Int'l L.J., p. 582, 2011

Puig, Gonzalo Villalta, "A Quasi-Adjudicative Dispute Settlement Mechanism for CEPA: The Rule of Law in Trade Relations between Mainland China and Hong Kong", *Chinese Journal of International Law*, Vol. 12(2), p. 306, 2013

Rabatel, Bernard, Deparis, Olivier, "'Liaison Magistrates' Their Role in International Judicial Cooperation and Comparative Law", in: Mads Andenas and Duncan Fairgrieve (eds.), *Courts and Comparative Law*, Oxford University Press, 2015, p. 617

Spigelman, J. J., "International Commercial Litigation: An Asian Perspective", 37 *Hong Kong Law Journal* 859, 2007, p. 859

Story, Sean E., "Cross-border Insolvency: A Comparative Analysis", 32 Ariz. J. Int'l & Comp. L. 431, 2015, p. 455

Wessels, Bob, "Will UNCITRAL Bring Changes to Insolvency Proceedings Outside the USA and Great Britain? It Certainly Will", *International Corporate Rescue*, Vol. 3, issue 4, 2006, p. 200

Westbrook, Jay L., "Theory and Pragmatism in Global Insolvencies: Choice of Law and Choice of Forum", 65 Am. Bankr. L.J. 457, 1991, p. 461

Westbrook, Jay L., "International Arbitration and Multinational Insolvency", 29 Penn St. Int'l. Rev. 635, 2011

Zhang Wenliang, *Recognition and Enforcement of Foreign Judgments in China – Rules, Practice and Strategies*, Kluwer Law International, 2014, p. 324

Annex

List of recommendations to CICIA

Recommendation 1 – guiding principle

Acknowledging the lack of cooperation in matters of cross-border insolvency despite the increasingly closer economic relationship, the guiding principle that embodies the entire arrangement is designed to promote the fair and efficient administration of China's inter-regional cross-border insolvency proceedings in a coordinated manner.

Recommendation 2 – overriding objective

Aware of restrictions set by the constitutional arrangements and the lack of functioning fundamental principles, the overriding objective of the arrangement is to facilitate recognition of interregional cross-border insolvency proceedings.

Recommendation 3 – form and scope

(1) Considering China's complex internal structure and desiring more predictability and more legal certainty at the regional level, an interregional cross-border insolvency arrangement (CICIA) is to be established.
(2) CICIA is binding on the Mainland and the two SARs altogether. In accordance with CICIA, cross-strait insolvency cooperation between the Mainland and Taiwan is subject to a separate arrangement.
(3) CICIA applies only to proceedings where the center of the debtor's main interests is located within the Mainland and the two SARs.
(4) CICIA shall apply to public collective proceedings, including interim proceedings, in accordance with the laws relating to insolvency in which proceedings the assets and affairs of the debtor are under the control or supervision by a court for the purpose of rescue, reorganization or liquidation.
(5) CICIA shall not apply to insolvencies concerning natural persons and financial institutions, which are governed by special insolvency regimes in the three regions.

Recommendation 4 – recognition and reliefs

(1) An insolvency proceeding commenced in one region, that with respect to the debtor concerned, has the relevant international jurisdiction should be recognized as main or non-main insolvency proceeding and given appropriate effect under the circumstances in every other region.

(2) The courts of one region within the territory of which the center of the debtor's main interests is situated shall have jurisdiction to open main insolvency proceedings.

(3) The place of the registered office shall be presumed to be the COMI in the absence of proof to the contrary.

It should be possible to rebut this presumption where the debtor's central administration is located in a region other than that of its registered office, and where a comprehensive assessment of all the relevant factors establishes, in a manner that is ascertainable by third parties, that the debtor's actual center of management and supervision and of the management of its interests is located in that other region.

The relevant date at which COMI shall be determined is the date of commencement of the main insolvency proceedings.

(4) The courts of another region shall have jurisdiction to open a non-main insolvency proceedings against the debtor if it possesses an establishment within the territory of that other region.

(5) Establishment means any place of operations where a debtor carries out a non-transitory economic activity with human means and assets.

The relevant date at which an establishment of the debtor shall be determined is the date of commencement of the non-main insolvency proceedings.

(6) Upon recognition of an insolvency proceeding as a main proceeding:

(a) Commencement or continuation of individual actions or individual proceedings concerning the debtor's assets, rights, obligations or liabilities is stayed; but the stay does not affect the right to commence individual actions or proceedings to the extent necessary to preserve a claim against the debtor;

(b) Execution against the debtor's assets is stayed; and

(c) The right to transfer, encumber or otherwise dispose of any assets of the debtor is suspended.

The scope, modification or termination of those aforementioned reliefs is subject to the law of the region where recognition and relief are sought. Those aforementioned reliefs do not affect the right to request the opening of an insolvency proceeding in the region where recognition and reliefs are sought.

(7) The following interim reliefs may be granted upon request of the insolvency practitioners in the main or non-main proceedings, from the time of filing an application for recognition until the application is decided upon:

(a) Staying execution against the debtor's assets;

(b) Entrusting the administration or realization of all or part of the debtor's assets located in the region to the insolvency practitioners in the main or non-main proceedings, in order to protect and preserve the value of assets.

The interim reliefs can be refused to be granted if they would interfere with the administration of a main insolvency proceeding and, unless extended, they terminate when the application for recognition is decided upon.

(8) Upon recognition of an insolvency proceeding, whether main or non-main, the court may, at the request of the insolvency practitioners in the main or non-main proceedings, grant any appropriate relief that may be available under the laws of this region where recognition and reliefs are sought.

Recommendation 5 – public policy

Any region may refuse to recognize insolvency proceedings opened in another region or to enforce a judgment handed down in the context of such proceedings where the effects of such recognition or enforcement would be manifestly contrary to that region's public policy, in particular its fundamental principles or the constitutional rights and liberties of its citizens.

Recommendation 6 – cooperation and communication (single debtor and enterprise groups)

(1) An insolvency practitioner shall, in the exercise of its functions and subject to the supervision of the court, cooperate and communicate to the maximum extent possible with the courts or insolvency practitioners in other regions.

(2) Where insolvency proceedings relate to two or more members of a group of companies, an insolvency practitioner appointed in proceedings concerning a member of the group shall cooperate and communicate with the courts and any insolvency practitioner appointed in proceedings concerning another member of the same group to the maximum extent possible.

Recommendation 7 – cross-border insolvency agreements

(1) In the course of cooperation and communication, insolvency practitioners, who are subject to the jurisdiction of their own courts, can cooperate with each other closely to enter into cross-border insolvency agreements, which shall be approved by the courts.

(2) The independence, sovereignty or jurisdiction of the relevant local courts should not be affected by the agreement.

(3) The agreement concluded can cover the following basic contents:

(a) Allocation of responsibilities between the different courts involved and between insolvency practitioners; including limitations on authority to act without the approval of the other courts or insolvency practitioners;

(b) methods of communication, including language, frequency and means;

(c) sharing of information on claims lodged, the verification and disputes concerning claims;

(d) location, use and disposal of assets;

(e) coordination and harmonization of reorganization plans;

(f) costs and fees;

(g) all other elements that can contribute to efficient coordination of interregional insolvency proceedings.

   If the courts or the insolvency practitioners after discussion find something useful to add beyond the aforementioned scope, they shall not be limited as long as it is not inconsistent with the local mandatory rules.

(4) In matters of enterprise groups, the agreement can include:

(a) means of timely communication of any relevant information concerning the group members subject to insolvency proceedings, provided appropriate arrangements are made to protect confidential information;

(b) coordination of the administration and supervision of the affairs of the group members subject to insolvency proceedings;

(c) coordination of the proposal and of reorganization plans;

(d) allocation of powers or responsibilities between insolvency practitioners;

(e) costs and fees;

(f) all other elements that can contribute to efficient coordination of interregional group insolvency proceedings.

> If the courts or the insolvency practitioners after discussion find something useful to add beyond the aforementioned scope, they shall not be limited as long as it is not inconsistent with the local mandatory rules.

(5) Complementary cross-border insolvency agreements shall also be allowed to address some issues upon prompt need on an *ad hoc* basis.

Recommendation 8 – functional dispute settlement mechanism

(1) In the course of interregional cross-border insolvency proceedings, a court that seeks explanation of the provisions under CICIA shall report to the Supreme Court of that region, which can request a special meeting to be convened.

(2) Explanation given by the special meeting on specific provisions of CICIA serves as proper interpretation on the specific issues arising from the individual case, which deserves the due respect of the courts concerned. Upon consensus of the Supreme Courts concerned, the explanation shall have binding effect on that individual case. Upon the consensus of all the Supreme Courts, the explanation shall have binding effect on the specific provisions under CICIA.

(3) In the course of implementing cross-border insolvency agreements, the courts in the concurrent proceedings can report to the Supreme Court from the respective regions, which can jointly request a special meeting to be convened and refer the disputes arising from cross-border insolvency agreements to the special meeting.

(4) In matters of the disputes arising from cross-border insolvency agreements, the opinions or part of the opinions come into binding effect to the extent that all the requesting courts involved agree to accept them, which should be expressly written into the judgments. The opinions are only binding on the individual case referred to the special meeting. If one of the requesting courts disagrees with the opinions or part of the opinions given by the special meeting, those opinions are not binding.

(5) Each court of the highest level from the three regions can designate one or two in-house judges to participate in the meeting. After discussion, the participating judges will deliver their joint opinions on the case referred to them.

(6) As for Hong Kong, any reference handed down by the special meeting shall not be construed as a direct reference to the courts in Hong Kong SAR except for the disputes concerned or unless the Court of Final Appeal of Hong Kong SAR expressly indicates otherwise.

Recommendation 9 – interregional case register

(1) Each region should be required to publish relevant information on cross-border insolvency cases in a publicly accessible electronic register.

(2) Once a cross-border insolvency proceeding is commenced in one region, the court shall immediately inform the communication authority in its own region. The communication authority must publish the information concerning the opening of insolvency proceedings on its e-portal and is also mandatory to inform its counterpart

communication authorities concerned in the other regions. Meanwhile, the e-portal of each region should provide an interconnection system that links to the registers in other regions.

(3) The minimum amount of information is required to be published in the interregional insolvency registers, including:

(a) the date of the opening of insolvency proceedings;
(b) the court opening insolvency proceedings and the case reference number, if any;
(c) the debtor's name, registration number, registered office and current correspondence address;
(d) the name, postal address or e-mail address of the insolvency practitioner, if any, appointed in the proceedings;
(e) the time limit and place for lodging claims, if any, or a reference to the criteria for calculating that time limit.

Additional information subject to the local laws shall not be precluded.

(4) The official language for the relevant information shall be Chinese. The information can also be published in English in Hong Kong SAR or Portuguese in Macao SAR but shall always be accompanied with a Chinese translation.

Recommendation 10 – independent intermediaries: separate arrangement for cross-strait insolvency cooperation (the Mainland and Taiwan)

(1) The cross-strait insolvency proceedings shall be coordinated by way of appointment of independent intermediaries from both sides.
(2) To guarantee the qualification as well as impartiality, the criteria to be appointed as an independent intermediary shall be agreed upon by the both sides. The role and competence of the intermediary can be set out in a protocol or an order of the court.
(3) The main duty of the independent intermediaries is to maintain the connection with its counterpart and jointly devise a practical means of conducting cooperation and communication between the courts concerned.
(4) Before the appointment of the independent intermediaries, the opinions of the insolvency practitioners should be sought especially in matters relating to conducting communication and cooperation. Once appointed, an intermediary should be accountable to the court that appoints him or her and a related protocol can be reached with the approval of the respective courts.
(5) The independent intermediaries from the both sides can hold regular meetings either onsite or via e-technological means so that they can keep the courts from the both sides informed of the possible conflicts or problems in the cross-strait insolvency proceedings.
(6) Considering the difference of professional qualification criteria on the each side, each side recommends some candidates for independent intermediaries for itself, holding a discussion to select someone both sides can trust and then putting those candidates separately in a closed list so that a consensus can be reached in advance to make sure that the qualifications of the independent intermediaries can be accepted by both sides in the process of coordination.
(7) The independent intermediaries should observe their duties in an impartial manner, free from bias, prejudice and any conflicts of interest. If its impartiality is in doubt,

the court, after consulting the opinions of the insolvency practitioners of both sides, can dismiss the independent intermediaries appointed by itself or request the counterpart court to dismiss its independent intermediaries with specific reasons upon the request of the independent intermediaries. A new independent intermediary can be selected from the list.

(8) The independent intermediaries will be remunerated from the estate of the insolvency proceedings in which the court appointed him or her.

Index